NORTH CAROLINA'S
FREE PEOPLE OF COLOR
1715–1885

North Carolina's Free People of Color
1715–1885

Warren Eugene Milteer Jr.

Louisiana State University Press
Baton Rouge

Published by Louisiana State University Press
Copyright © 2020 by Louisiana State University Press
All rights reserved
Manufactured in the United States of America
First printing

DESIGNER: Michelle A. Neustrom
TYPEFACE: Livory
PRINTER & BINDER: Sheridan Books, Inc.

LIBRARY OF CONGRESS CATALOGING-IN-PUBLICATION DATA

Names: Milteer, Warren E., Jr., author.
Title: North Carolina's free people of color, 1715–1885 / Warren Eugene Milteer Jr.
Description: Baton Rouge : Louisiana State University Press, [2020] | Includes
  bibliographical references and index.
Identifiers: LCCN 2019047542 (print) | LCCN 2019047543 (ebook) | ISBN 978-0-8071-
  7176-9 (cloth) | ISBN 978-0-8071-7377-0 (pdf) | ISBN 978-0-8071-7378-7 (epub)
Subjects: LCSH: Free African Americans—North Carolina—History. | Racially mixed
  people—North Carolina—History. | North Carolina—Race relations—History.
Classification: LCC E185.93.N6 M58 2020 (print) | LCC E185.93.N6 (ebook) |
  DDC 305.8009756—dc23
LC record available at https://lccn.loc.gov/2019047542
LC ebook record available at https://lccn.loc.gov/2019047543

For my parents

Contents

Illustrations follow page 114.

NORTH CAROLINA'S
FREE PEOPLE OF COLOR
1715–1885

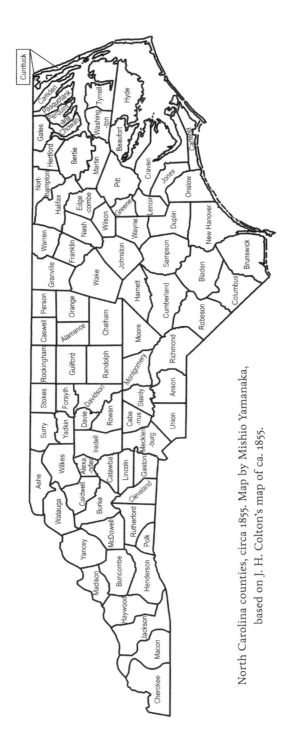

North Carolina counties, circa 1855. Map by Mishio Yamanaka, based on J. H. Colton's map of ca. 1855.

Introduction

In 1902, not long after the publication of a series of now-famed works that included *The Conjure Woman, and Other Conjure Tales* and *The Wife of His Youth and Other Stories of the Color-Line*, Charles Waddell Chesnutt sat down to pen a lesser-known article titled "The Free Colored People of North Carolina" for Hampton Institute's *Southern Workman*. Born to parents who were free persons of color before the Civil War, Chesnutt used his intimate knowledge of the population of his study along with other sources to describe the social position and ancestral origins of the "free colored people." He wrote that "the status of these people, prior to the Civil War, was anomalous but tenable." In describing their origins, Chesnutt mentioned mixtures between "Negroes," "whites," and "Indians." He argued that many free people of color, "perhaps most of them, were as we have seen, persons of mixed blood."[1] A careful search through court records, censuses, vital records, church minutes, wills, deeds, newspapers, pension files, and oral histories confirms a picture of life for free people of color remarkably similar to the one described by Chesnutt more than a century ago.[2]

A Disorderly American South

For over a generation, historians have depicted eighteenth- and nineteenth-century North Carolina and the rest of the American South as regions dominated by strict racial hierarchies. Their versions of the American South usually include three distinct groups: whites, blacks, and Indians encapsulated in a social hierarchy that placed whites over all other groups. Yet the stories of those categorized as "free people of color" reveal a more disorderly American South. In the colonial and early national periods, North Carolinians and their laws privileged the free over the enslaved, regardless of the racial categories ascribed to them. While the degree to which free people of color were the legal superiors of slaves varied across time, this book argues that the legal position of free people of color generally remained closer to that of whites than to that of slaves. Orlando Patterson explained that slaves were the "socially dead" agents of their masters with no legally recognized connection to kin or ancestors.[3] Historians have repeatedly shown that slaves in every society developed strong social bonds, but none of those relations were legally binding. In contrast, North Carolina law always allowed free people of color, like whites, legal personhood and recognized connection to kin. Even during the 1850s and 1860s, when legal limitations were greatest, free people of color retained numerous privileges unavailable to enslaved persons, including the right to own property, access to the courts, the right to keep their wages, and the freedom to leave the state without permission.

Free people of color from the colonial period through Reconstruction faced many social, economic, and legal challenges. Prejudice, poverty, and violence were among their various experiences. Yet these obstacles never condemned them to a position close to slave status. The ability to own real and personal property, seek restitution in the courts, and maintain legally recognized bonds to family distinguished even the poorest free person of color from the most fortunate slaves. At any moment, the circumstances of an enslaved person could change forever with the death of a master, a collection of a debt, or a master's decision to sell an enslaved person away from all things familiar. Many enslaved people never met such changes in circumstance, but the possibility that lingered over them made their position distinct in comparison to free persons.[4]

North Carolinians' attempts to categorize themselves into "races" imbued with specific legal and social privileges, natural attributes, and values always conflicted with their efforts to understand one another in terms of gender, class, reputation, kinship, and occupation. This internal struggle prevented them from agreeing about the proper social relations between those categorized as "white" and those classified as "free people of color." Across time, radical political figures emerged who preached that free people of color and slaves were part of a degraded race naturally beneath all whites. Yet their ideology fully captured the minds of only some people. Following Chief Justice Roger B. Taney's pronouncement in the Dred Scott decision that people of color were not citizens, white politicians in North

Carolina as a whole rejected the opportunity to adopt the radical proslavery point of view and instead continued to argue that free people of color were citizens of the state.[5]

For many North Carolinians, radical proslavery beliefs failed to fulfill their practical needs in certain situations to understand their neighbors outside of a racialized worldview. Unlike their radical counterparts, they could still be advocates for slavery but not use free people of color as scapegoats for societal ills and their bondspeople's agitations. North Carolinians viewed racial categorization as important only in certain contexts. Discrimination based on racial categorization was situational. As a result, for most of the period in which "free people of color" operated as a category, free men of color, who could vote until 1835, had more political rights than white women did. In a society that privileged the wealthy over the poor, propertied free people of color had access to exclusive social networks and, for a short period, additional political privileges such as the right to vote for senators, which neither women nor propertyless white men could access. Skilled free people of color found niches in a labor-short economy and even negotiated with their alleged social superiors. Throughout the period in which slavery existed in North Carolina, free people of color carved out spaces to raise their families, make a living, and sometimes enjoy life's luxuries. They built a variety of social networks with neighbors, free and enslaved, white and of color. Free people of color never made up a segregated racial community of their own, nor did they form a wide alliance with enslaved people. Sometimes the political or social objectives of free people of color and enslaved persons intersected, just as the goals of whites and free people of color overlapped.

In the same environment in which some free people of color thrived, others found conditions troubling and occasionally even threatening. The competition of ideas about the position of free people of color among white North Carolinians created opportunities for certain individuals and problems for others. Of course, many free persons of color experienced both ups and downs. Although they were not enslaved, some free people of color found life in North Carolina difficult. Sporadic violence committed by white vigilantes, discriminatory laws and whites' willingness to enforce those edicts, whites' preferential treatment of other whites, and maybe most importantly, poverty and exploitation had deep effects on free people of color. North Carolina, like so many other parts of British North America and later the United States, was a society filled with great inequalities and individuals willing to exploit, politicize, and exacerbate social disparities. In a place in which people understood their world through hierarchies of race, gender, and wealth, discrimination always coexisted with opportunity and access. Ideologues and politicians with the aid of supporters cultivated coalitions and power by arguing for a society that placed men over women and whites over people of color and justifying the impoverishment of those with the least access to capital. Furthermore, opportunity and access for one group of people commonly came at the expense of others. The contrasting experiences of well-to-do and poor free persons of color follow Seth Rockman's argument that "the early republic's economy opened up new possibilities for some Americans precisely because it closed down opportunities for others."[6]

Radicals were unsuccessful in implementing the most extreme parts of their agenda, such as the mass enslavement or deportation of free persons of color. Yet radical proslavery thought made an indelible mark on North Carolina's social and political order. Slavery's most ardent defenders led an attack that gradually chipped away at the legal status of free people of color. As attempts to curb the influence of the Slave Power grew across the United States, radicals throughout the South, using free people of color largely as scapegoats, intensified their attacks on the privileges and liberties of free persons of color.[7]

From the late eighteenth century, radicals had begun to observe both a national and an international collapse in slavery. The gradual breakdown of slavery in the northern states; the Haitian Revolution, which birthed a republic out of a former slaving colony; the outlawing of slavery in some of Spain's former American colonies; the amelioration and eventual abolition of enslavement in the United Kingdom's vast empire; and the growing anti-slavery movement in the United States demonstrated that southern slavery was under siege and that slavery more broadly was crumbling. These happenings helped to spur a radical reaction, which included attacks on free people of color. Disparaging free people of color was part of a defense of slavery that argued that society should be divided into two parts: one free and white and one composed of enslaved persons of color. According to radicals, this was the natural order. In such a society, there was no room for free people of color. Driven by this ideology, radicals used a politics of fear: fear of a changing social order, fear of collusion between free people of color and slaves, and fear of northern influence on their communities, to win elections and push legislation that adversely affected the status of free people of color. The more radicals attacked free people of color, the more forcefully they could argue that they, not their more moderate counterparts, were the most ardent defenders of slavery and therefore the strongest advocates for what appeared to be the South's increasingly distinctive way of life. Legislation that adversely affected free people of color was a politically cheap way to appease constituencies of slaveholders, fearful whites, and white organized labor without dealing with their society's lack of economic diversity, vast wealth inequality, or inability to convince enslaved people that bondage and its brutalities were their inherent lot.

When North Carolina lawmakers enacted legislation discriminating against free people of color, they were followers, not leaders. Throughout the eighteenth and nineteenth centuries, North Carolina's free people of color lived in a place known for its sluggishness and traditionalism. Commonly known as the "Rip Van Winkle State," North Carolina was cashstrapped, undereducated, economically underdeveloped, and late in its expansion of political rights to all white men. Between 1815 and 1850, onethird of the state's population, including many free people of color, left for better opportunities to the west. Over 30 percent of people born in North Carolina lived in other states by 1850. North Carolina's slowness, however, may have been a benefit to free people of color in certain ways. North Carolina was the last southern state to disfranchise free men of color. Legislators in Raleigh also failed to pass further restrictions on the lives of free people of color that appeared in the law books of other southern states such as limits on real property ownership and requirements to establish relationships with white guardians.[8]

North Carolina's less than dynamic political and social development does not preclude its importance in understanding the position of free people of color in the South. Nearly 12.8 percent or a little more than oneeighth of the free people of color in the slave states lived in North Carolina on the eve of the Civil War. North Carolina consistently had one of the largest populations of free people of color in the South, only trailing Maryland and Virginia through most of the pre–Civil War period. The first federal census in 1790 counted 4,975 "all other free persons" out of a total population of 393,751, which included 100,572 slaves and 288,204 whites (see table 1). By 1860, North Carolina's population of free people of color

TABLE 1. North Carolina Population, 1790–1860

Year	Free People of Color	Slaves	Whites	Total
1790	4,975	100,572	288,204	393,751
1800	7,043	133,296	337,764	478,103
1810	10,266	168,824	376,460	555,500
1820	14,612	205,017	419,200	638,829
1830	19,543	245,601	472,843	737,987
1840	22,732	245,817	484,870	753,419
1850	27,463	288,548	553,028	869,039
1860	30,463	331,059	631,100	992,622

had increased to 30,463 out of a total population of 992,622, which included 331,059 enslaved people and 631,100 whites. The census takers for 1860 classified a slight majority of free people of color, 15,583, as female while counting 14,880 free persons of color as male.[9]

Free people of color lived throughout North Carolina's diverse environments from the Appalachian Mountains to the coastal plain. Most of the state's free people of color, however, resided in North Carolina's eastern and piedmont regions. From the early national period to the eve of the Civil War, the counties with the largest populations of free people of color were all situated in these areas. In 1790, the counties with one hundred or more free people of color included Beaufort, Bertie, Craven, Currituck, Granville, Halifax, Hertford, Nash, Northampton, Orange, Robeson, Sampson, and Wake (see table 2). By 1860, seven coastal and piedmont counties boasted over one thousand free people of color: Craven, Granville, Halifax, Hertford, Pasquotank, Robeson, and Wake (see table 3). Over one-third of North Carolina's free people of color lived in these seven localities. In all of these counties, the populations of free persons of color and enslaved people were higher than the state averages of 3.07 percent and 33.35 percent, respectively, while the white population was below the state average of 63.58 percent.[10] Centered in the agricultural coastal and piedmont regions, free people of color tended to live in counties with large slave populations, but the counties with the highest percentages of enslaved people did not necessarily have large populations of free persons of color. In places such as Pitt County and Jones County in the coastal region, slaves made up more than

TABLE 2. North Carolina Counties with More Than
100 Free Persons of Color in 1790

County	Free Persons of Color
Northampton County	462
Halifax County	443
Bertie County	348
Craven County	337
Granville County	315
Robeson County	277
Hertford County	216
Nash County	188
Wake County	180
Sampson County	140
Beaufort County	129
Currituck County	115
Orange County	101

TABLE 3. North Carolina Counties with More Than
1,000 Free Persons of Color in 1860

County	Free Persons of Color
Halifax County	2,452
Pasquotank County	1,507
Robeson County	1,462
Wake County	1,446
Craven County	1,332
Granville County	1,123
Hertford County	1,112

half of the populations. Yet the percentages of free people of color were below the state average. The localities with the smallest populations of free people of color were confined to the western part of the state. Census data for 1860 shows sixteen counties with fewer than one hundred free people of color, all in the western piedmont and mountains. The counties with the smallest populations of free people of color included Jackson, with 6; Haywood, with 14; and Madison, with 17.[11]

Understanding Racial Categories

It is important to emphasize upfront that "free people of color" operated in society as a category and not as a term that referred to a fixed group of people. North Carolinians may have imagined otherwise, but the evidence in this book demonstrates that "free person of color" was not necessarily a label an individual carried for life. For someone to categorize another individual as a "free person of color" did not mean that the label became an essential part of that individual's being. "Free person of color" was simply a label that signaled an individual was free but not considered "white" in a society dominated by an ideology that called for the acceptance of white categorization as normative. North Carolinians labeled as "free people of color" those *assumed* to be free people of African descent, free people of Native ancestry whom the state did not recognize as politically autonomous, free persons with heritage in the East Indies, and a variety of individuals with mixed ancestry. They sometimes used "free negro," "free mulatto," "free mustee," and "free black" interchangeably with "free person of color," but "free person of color" was the most frequently used term. In addition, this seems to be the term most widely accepted by those who fell into the category. For these reasons, "of color" is the term I use throughout this book.

Twentieth- and twenty-first-century historians have used "negro," "black," and "African American" instead of or in conjunction with "person of color." Yet to embrace their usage is to accept that racial categories are fixed to specific groups of people with specific collective histories. These scholars' usage of categories suggests that terminology can shift, but the people those categories describe are essential, historical groups. The evolution of racial categories, however, is more complex. All of these terms, especially "African American," are loaded with twentieth- and twenty-first-century connotations of African ancestry, which do not necessarily apply to the subjects of this study or their descendants. As this book demonstrates, not all individuals categorized as "free people of color" had African ancestry, and they are not collectively the ancestors of people described today as "blacks" or "African Americans." Large numbers of people who today are the descendants of "free people of color" self-categorize or are classified by others as "white" and "Indian."[12] The story of free people of color may be one of the best examples of racial categories being made and remade in American history. Additionally, some older descendants of free people of color have explained to me that their ancestors understood "black" to be a derogatory term and not one they embraced as a self-descriptor. These assertions are confirmed by the contrasting use of terminology between nineteenth-century radical proslavery propagandists, who frequently used the term "black" in their writings, and other North Carolinians, who commonly used "of color."[13]

I have found evidence that the category "free people of color" included individuals without African ancestry, most notably Native peoples. Scholars of Native American history have uncovered numerous examples of Native people being categorized as "black," "colored," or "mulatto."[14] Ruth Wallis Herndon and Ella Wilcox Sekatu argued that such labeling of Native people was a form of "documentary genocide."[15] I agree that such labels obscure ancestral distinctions. I also think and show, however, that racial categories have never truly acted as accurate indicators of ancestry. Whites in nineteenth-century North Carolina were quite aware that they had branded Native peoples as "colored" and even after such labeling retained memory, or at least a belief, that certain free people of color were Native peoples. With this understanding, I urge scholars to reimagine the genesis of racial categorization for Native peoples. In the United States, as in other parts of the Americas, all Native people did not fall into the "Indian" category. Some Native people lived under the designation "colored," experienced the legal limitations associated with such a designation, lived in communities in which racial categorization was imposed and not self-ascribed, and described themselves as "colored" people while still retaining memories of their indigenous heritage.

Jack D. Forbes's important, but often neglected, *Black Africans and Native Americans* showed that the categorization of a diversity of people including Africans, East Indians, and Native peoples as "black," "colored," and a host of other ambiguous color terms dates to at least the sixteenth century. Even before this point, Europeans used color to describe a diversity of people. Forbes demonstrated that racial categories had their earliest origins in attempts to describe and order human beings.[16] I find that "negro," "colored," and other terms did the same work in eighteenth- and nineteenth-century North Carolina. North Carolinians sought to apply racial categories as descriptors of difference and as tools to organize society. In North Carolina, as in most of the European-colonized world, officials used racial categories in their attempts to define status. Today's racial and ethnic language blurs distinctions among racial categorizations, ancestry, and culture while attempting to ignore the historical baggage of legalized hierarchy making. We discuss whites, European Americans, and Caucasians as one people, blacks or African Americans as another, and we refer to other racialized people in a similar fashion. This book shows, however, that not all people of African descent are "black" or "African American" today, all "white people" are not solely of European ancestry, and all Americans with indigenous heritage are not "Indians." Historians of the United States have rarely taken this reality into serious consideration, but the story of free people of color shows why we should.

In this book, I demonstrate that racial categories are fluid cognitive organizational structures designed to support the human need to classify and organize everything in their world and not indelible markers of ancestry, culture, shared experience, or affiliation. Sociologists Rogers Brubaker, Mara Loveman, and Peter Stamatov have explained, "Race, ethnicity, and nationality exist only in and through our perceptions, interpretations, representations, classifications, categorizations, and identifications. They are not things *in* the world, but perspectives *on* the world—not ontological but epistemological realities."[17] Racial categories become elements within ideologies when people begin to imagine those whom they categorize as members of distinct groups with collective attributes, values, and thoughts. I recognize that many North Carolinians before the Civil War believed that all of humanity could be divided into races with distinct features. Nevertheless, I do not let their assumptions guide my analysis. Instead my work examines the problems and conflicts North Carolinians encountered when trying to categorize their population. The most radical adherents to a racial order attempted to place people into racial categories and then fix those racialized beings within legal and social hierarchies. Yet I reveal how their view of the world regularly conflicted with reality.

By demonstrating that racial categorization was not the dominant form of social hierarchy in North Carolina and instead intersected with other schemes for organizing society, this study challenges the notion that in the United States people employed racial categories in a manner significantly different than in other parts of the globe. The dominant narrative that argued that race was the most important scheme for hierarchy making in mainland British North America and later the United States has led scholars to focus on understanding how the United States was so different from the rest of the world, especially Latin America.[18] This book, however, suggests that at least in North Carolina, Americans used racial categories in ways similar to people in various countries. The findings in this book that show racial categories intersected with gender, wealth, and other forms of hierarchy mesh neatly with scholarship examining the use of racial categories in other regions of the world, including parts of the former British Empire and Latin America.[19]

Furthermore, challenging essential understandings of race permits a closer examination of the role gender played in the lives of free people of color. We oversimplify the life experiences of free people of color when we examine their lives only through a racialized lens. As Kimberlé Crenshaw noted, "when the practices expound identity as woman or person of color as an either/or proposition, they relegate the identity of women of color to a location that resists telling."[20] Moving away from essential understandings of race allows us to appreciate fully the gendered life experiences of free people of color. By recognizing that racial discrimination intersected with patriarchy and gender discrimination, the important differences in the lives of free women of color and free men of color become more evident. While studying the effects of racial discrimination on free people of color, it is easy to overlook that discrimination affected women and men differently. Several scholars have provided us with a better understanding of the experiences of free women of color in different areas of the South.[21] This study advances their work and integrates the experience of free women of color in North Carolina into a larger narrative about free people of color that takes gender into serious consideration when evaluating the various experiences of free people of color in the colonial and early national periods.

Background

Historians have debated the position of free people of color in the South since the beginning of the twentieth century. Among the first books on the topic were John Henderson Russell's *The Free Negro in Virginia, 1619–1865* (1913) and James M. Wright's *The Free Negro in Maryland, 1634–1860* (1921). Russell and Wright laid the groundwork for the debates about free people of color.

Russell argued, "By the middle of the seventeenth century there were negroes who were free from all forms of legal servitude or slavery, but they were not absorbed into the mass of free population. Their color adhered to them in freedom as in servitude, and the indelible marks and characteristics of their race remained unchanged."[22] Wright's assessment was equally bleak but less empathetic. He contended that "free negroes" had "been raised above the slaves and had become entitled to the legal privileges and immunities of freemen under the common law." Wright, however, concluded that "the shifting from one legal category to another left negro persons unaltered with respect to fitness for the station they had thereby attained. It did not make them independent of doles from the larders and ward-robes of the whites; it did not essentially change their occupations, their abodes, or their diversions; it failed to raise their intellects above those of the slaves, with whom they continued to associate and consort."[23]

Over two decades after the publications of Russell's and Wright's studies, John Hope Franklin authored the first book-length study about free people of color in North Carolina. In *The Free Negro in North Carolina, 1790–1860*, Franklin sought to place North Carolina within a larger discussion about free people of color in the slave states. Franklin's study generally followed the organization of the earlier studies but greatly exceeded them in depth of research and variety of source materials. He gave his readers a clear sense of the lived experience of free people of color and showed class and educational diversity, self-determination, and participation within the larger society. Yet, in words similar to those of his predecessors, Franklin concluded, "The effort of North Carolina to discipline the free Negro and to prevent his overturning the established order resulted in the reduction of the free Negro's position to one of quasi-freedom. . . . The same circumscriptions that served to hamper the free Negro in the legal and economic spheres were present as he sought a place in the social life of the State. The walls of restriction that almost completely encircled him cut many of the lines of communication between him and the larger community."[24]

In the 1970s, Ira Berlin produced a study of free people of color in the antebellum South that largely aligned with Franklin's work in its structure and arguments. This important work was the first major region-wide study of free people of color in the South. In *Slaves without Masters: The Free Negro in the Antebellum South*, Berlin, like Franklin, suggested that free people of color experienced a steady decline in their status. He argued that "once free, blacks generally remained at the bottom of the social order, despised by whites, burdened with increasingly oppressive racial proscriptions, and subjected to verbal and physical abuse." Berlin took his contentions a step further, reflecting the conclusions of Russell and Wright, and suggested, "Free Negroes stood outside the direct governance of a master, but in the eyes of many whites their place in society had not been significantly altered. They were slaves without masters." Berlin's work also painted a picture of a southern society highly bifurcated by racial categorization. While noting exceptions in Lower South cities such as Charleston and New Orleans, Berlin contended that "free Negroes and slaves" more generally joined together "to create a united black caste."[25]

Since the publication of Berlin's work, a series of local studies on free people of color have caused historians to rethink older conclusions about their position in the pre–Civil War South. Many of these works describe free people of color who defied legal discrimination and second-tier status to find personal and financial success.[26] In all of these works to various degrees, free people of color were active participants in society. Melvin Patrick Ely's *Israel on the Appomattox*, however, has posed the greatest challenge to earlier generations' interpretations of life for southern free people of color. In Prince Edward County, Virginia, Ely uncovered wide webs of social entanglement among free people of color, whites, and slaves. He argued "many Southern whites felt secure enough to deal fairly and even respectfully with free African Americans partly because slavery still held most blacks firmly in its grip. That paradox helped make room for a drama of free black pride and achievement to unfold in an Old South where ties of culture, faith, affection and economic interest could span the barrier between black and white."[27] In the hierarchical society of Prince Edward County, he discovered justice for free people of color from all-white juries, close personal relationships between whites and persons of color, and regular local disregard for state acts discriminating against free people of color. Since the publication of Ely's study, a small number of scholars have followed his lead.[28] Yet scholars continue to debate the extent to which the experiences of free people of color were more like the "slaves without masters" model or more like those described by Ely.[29]

This book continues the push to reevaluate older conclusions about the lives of free persons of color in the South. The book's first chapter analyzes how North Carolinians determined who was a person of color and explains how they defined and documented free status. This section reveals that the origins of free people of color in North Carolina were much more diverse and complicated than suggested by earlier scholarship. The second chapter explores the intricate intersections between racial categories, gender, and wealth that undergirded the legal and social situations of free persons of color in the colonial period. This book explains how norms developed during the colonial period created precedents for the ways North Carolinians treated and understood the free people of color in their communities. The chapters that follow each look at specific aspects of life for free people of color in late eighteenth- and nineteenth-century North Carolina: the political debates concerning their legal position, their interactions with the justice system, their family lives, their social and economic interactions, and the continued importance of gender and wealth in their life experiences. Together these chapters reveal that even during the most politically contentious moments, free people of color maintained important rights, privileges, and relationships that placed them distinctly beyond the toils of human bondage. The book's final sections highlight the important changes that reshaped life for free people of color during the understudied Civil War and Reconstruction periods.

❧

CHAPTER 1

Making Race, Remembering Freedom

Constructing Racialized Liberty

As George and Joseph Bennett prepared to leave Gates County, North Carolina, to cross into neighboring Virginia, the two young men met with local justices of the peace to obtain freedom papers. These documents would prove their liberty in the event their free status ever came into question. The justices provided each man with a document dated May 14, 1794, that explained that he was "free born" and the son of "an Injun [*sic*] and a free woman." In case someone needed to verify that the papers pertained to the men who possessed them, each freedom document gave a physical description of the holder. George's free papers described him as "about Twenty five years of age . . . about five feet seven Inches high with a scar over his Left . . . Eye" while Joseph's pass stated he was "about Twenty four years of age about five feet nine Inches high with a scar over his Right eye."[1] After receiving the free papers, the Bennetts made their way to Norfolk County, Virginia. What happened to Joseph is unclear, but George eventually left Virginia. He returned to Gates County to reside in the community known by locals as "Indian Town." There, George lived among other descendants of the indigenous Chowan people. When George and Joseph were children, the county clerk had recognized their indigenous heritage and registered them as "Indian" in the court's minute book.[2] The clerk also described them as "Indian" in the 1790s, when they participated in the sale of the last piece of the Chowan reservation.[3] Yet when the census enumerator came through the Indian Town neighborhood in 1810, he classified George Bennett along with the other Chowan descendants as "free colored" persons.[4]

The story of George and Joseph Bennett reveals that a person became a "free person of color" not through something purely biological but through an intellectually complex process of categorization. Therefore, George Bennett could be an "Indian" in one context and "free colored" in another.

Other incidents described in this chapter tell a similar story. "Free person of color" was a sociopolitical construct that denoted free status and categorization as not white. Yet this construct only functioned because North Carolinians supposed that through a series of determinations a person could be categorized as "white," "Indian," "negro," "mulatto," "mustee," or "of color." This is what sociologists Sarah Daynes and Orville Lee aptly described as "belief in race."[5]

People in early North Carolina had to decide individuals' racial categorizations through processes of evaluation, even when they believed racial categories corresponded to biology.[6] They used a series of schema such as skin color, hair texture, behavior, reputation, and features of one's ancestors to construct racial categories and organize individuals within their society into those categories. Their evaluations and decisions produced a situation in which people with a spectrum of physical features and various family histories fell into the same categories. The census taker may have categorized George Bennett as a "colored" person because of his physical appearance or based on his understanding that Bennett had non-European ancestry, or in the vernacular of the early nineteenth century, "negro" or "Indian" blood.

Before the end of the Civil War, freedom was something that had to be proven, and public memory through either individual understandings or documentation was the only way people could establish their freedom. Community members recognized a person as free because they recognized aspects of that person's past that signaled liberty. As in the case of the Bennetts and many others, they were free because their neighbors recalled that their mother was free, a standard designated within the law. Neighbors' memories of their liberation from enslavement supported others' freedom. North Carolinians also used documents to reinforce public memory of freedom.

Making Race

In the eighteenth and nineteenth centuries, North Carolinians spoke of and understood racial categorization or a person's so-called "race" through ancestry. They believed that individuals were free persons of color because of their lineage or "blood."[7] In reality, however, they actually had to rely on schemas to categorize people as "white," "Indian," "colored," "negro," "mulatto," or "mustee." Sociologists have defined schemas as "mental structures in which knowledge is represented."[8] Examples of schemas used to determine racial categorization included skin color, hair texture, behavior, reputation, and memories about an individual's ancestry. North Carolinians believed that through their sight and memory they could successfully categorize a person as white or not white. They agreed that dark skin made someone "colored" while fair skin made someone "white." This is the aspect of so-called "race" that is cultural. Yet because schemas such as dark skin and fair skin are mental representations and not actual things in the world, North Carolinians regularly failed to agree on the border between dark skin and fair skin and therefore sometimes struggled to classify people, inconsistently categorized people, or disagreed about individuals' categorizations.

Legal experts and common people all attempted to define free persons of color by discussing ancestry. In their 1857 opinion for the case *State v. Chavers*, members of the North Carolina Supreme Court declared, "free persons of colour may be then for all we can see, persons coloured by Indian blood, or persons descended from negro ancestors beyond the fourth degree."[9] The state's highest jurists provided North Carolinians with what appeared to be a clear definition of who should be categorized as a free person of color. Other North Carolinians offered similar yet less straightforward definitions. Writing in the 1850s, William D. Valentine, an active member of the Whig Party and attorney in eastern North Carolina, explained, "Free negroes are slaves and their descendants emancipated by Quakers and other benevolent whites once owners of them. The mulatto is the offspring between the white and the negro, or between the Indian and the negro, or between the white and the Indian."[10] Recalling the experiences of his antebellum childhood, O. W. Blacknall wrote that free people of color

> are almost wholly a hybrid race. . . . Of course the proportion of those with blood more or less mixed was very much larger. Indeed, of all the hundreds of free negroes that I have known from childhood, I cannot now recall a dozen black or very dark ones . . . many, if not the larger part, of the free negroes whose freedom dates back further than this century show traits of mind and body that are unmistakably Indian. In many instances, long, coarse, straight black hair and high cheek-bones are joined with complexions whose duskiness disclaims white blood and with features clearly un-African. True, these extreme types are the exception; but the majority shade up to it more or less closely.[11]

All of these definitions reveal a complexity of backgrounds, while project-ing a simplistic view of the world in which people can be separated into pure "races" and hybrid "races." All of these nineteenth-century men be-lieved that race was something observable and quantifiable. Yet racial cat-egorization was a more convoluted process.

People believed that ancestry could be connected to racial categorization largely because the schemas they associated with certain types of ancestry aligned with the assumed ancestry or race of an individual. North Caro-linians could be certain that Sam Bailem was a person of color because his skin was "very black."[12] Even Tom Mitchell's "yellow complexion" unam-biguously fell within their definition of a person of color.[13] Thomas Bows-er's "bushy head" of hair along with his "very dark complexion" supported his categorization as a colored person.[14] J. M. Harris, however, had to know something about William Revills's family background in order to recog-nize him as a person of color because Revills's "nearly white" complex-ion allowed him to "pass as a white boy" potentially.[15] A stranger might have considered Revills to be "white," but the public memory shared among those who knew him best allowed them to classify him as "colored."

The case of William P. Waters, however, reveals that North Carolinians' assumptions about the essential nature of race in their society were flawed. Racial categorization was not something fixed in biology, but something to be determined through a process of evaluation. Generally, these evaluations were unconscious, but in the courtroom the role of schemas in determin-ing racial categorization became clear. In the case of William P. Waters, his neighbors determined that he was a person of color through memories of his ancestors and their physical attributes. In the winter of 1842, William P. Waters and Zilpha Thompson appeared at the Ashe County Superior Court session charged with the crime of fornication and adultery. The couple stood charged with this crime not because one of the parties was married to an-other person or because they failed to participate in a marriage ceremony or post a marriage bond. William and Zilpha landed in the courtroom because someone in their neighborhood believed William was a "man of color" and Zilpha was a "white woman." According to North Carolina law, free people of color and whites could not marry, and any marriage performed on their behalf was void. Yet when the court asked William and Zilpha to answer the charges, William pled innocent and declared that he was not a man of color with "negro or Indian ancestors" but "descended from Portuguese."

In order to decide the validity of the charges against William and Zilpha, the court listened to numerous witnesses recount their memories of William's ancestors. One declared that William's grandmother was "not as black as some negroes," while another witness bemoaned that William's grandparents were "coal black negroes," and yet another stated that William's grandfather was "white." The case ended with a guilty verdict. According to the court, William P. Waters was a "man of color."[16] Waters's community did not classify him as person of color because of something observable or quantifiable but because the public remembered his ancestors to have certain traits. The trial of William P. Waters is just one of many examples that demonstrate that people cognitively constructed racial categories. Some evaluations of racial categorization required trials while others needed only a simple glance. Nevertheless, racial categorization had to be determined through a process of evaluations. Sometimes, this process of evaluation was conscious, while in other instances categorization took place without effort.

Racial categorization was ultimately a product constructed in the minds of people who used "race" as a way to frame their world. These people believed that nature and not their minds divided the human species into "whites," "negroes," "mulattoes," "Indians," "mustees," and "colored people." Yet the failure of individuals to classify the people around them consistently exposes the cognitive origins of racial categories. Various North Carolina court records document the inconsistent use of racial categories. In 1771, the Edenton District court clerk referred to Philip Chavis of Anson County as a "negro," "mulatto," and "mustee" within the same set of documents for a single civil case.[17] In another example, from 1795, a clerk simply referred to a man from Bertie County called "John" as a "mulatto or Indian." In a statement written by his attorney, this same John is labeled "a free man of colour."[18] In theory, Negroes, mulattoes, mustees, and Indians were supposed to be different types of people. Even eighteenth- and nineteenth-century dictionaries provided the public with specific definitions of these racial terms. These examples, however, show that lines between categories in practice were poorly defined and ambiguous.[19]

Nowhere were the issues of inconsistent classification and the construction of racial categories more problematic than in the case of North Carolina's indigenous people. By the early nineteenth century, most of North Carolina's indigenous population east of the Appalachians became subject to shifting categorization, which has led some scholars and lay people alike to believe that Native populations of the region had disappeared. In reality, they were simply recategorized from "Indians" to "colored persons," "mulattoes," or "negroes." From the colonial period into the early national era, whites began a slow process of reclassifying Native peoples from "Indians" into ambiguous others, thereby eliminating the legal distinctions between a diversity of Native peoples and other people classified as persons of color. From their arrival in the Americas, colonists bound Native peoples to certain areas of land just as they associated their neighbors in Europe to certain territories. The earliest maps of North Carolina show territorial boundaries for each Native nation that inhabited a particular area. From this point on, the colonists would associate certain land masses with particular Native people. Colonization itself, however, threatened to destroy the colonizers' system of organizing Native people. Through the seventeenth and eighteenth centuries, the colonizers appropriated thousands of acres of Native land for their own use and thus pushed Native people off the exact lands that these colonists had used to define distinct Native populations. Native peoples no longer fit definitions of "Indian" created during the earliest days of colonization as Native peoples' life ways changed from those observed by the earliest colonists and the lands once controlled by Native people were transferred to the hands of non-Natives.[20] In the eyes of some non-Natives, these Native peoples were no longer "Indians" but simply "colored people."

The historical record provides a few examples of the reclassification of Native peoples from "Indian" to others.[21] The Chowans and Mattamuskeets went through processes that convinced local officials to reclassify them. These processes generally included the dissolution of their reservations in eastern North Carolina and changes in their life ways, including the incorporation of European-colonial methods of farming into traditional agricultural practices. Many other Native peoples in North Carolina likely went through similar processes during the colonial period but have stories that are poorly documented compared to those of the Chowans and Mattamuskeets. In Gates County, Chowans appeared in court minutes and deeds as "Indians" during the 1780s. For example, James, Benjamin, Patience, Sarah, Nancy, Elizabeth, Darkes, and Christian Robbins appear as "Indians" in a 1782 deed.[22] By the first census in 1790, however, these "Indians" had become "free others" and later "free colored persons."[23] Ten years later, the census enumerator classified James, Sarah, and Darkes Robbins as heads of households of "other free persons" in contrast to "white persons."[24] Record keepers categorized the descendants of the Mattamuskeets, who had intermarried with both people of European and people of African descent, in nineteenth-century records as "mulattoes" and "free persons of color."[25]

By understanding racial categories as products of cognitive processes, we can begin to recognize the diverse backgrounds and stories encompassed within these categories. Free persons of color were not a group per se but a complicated mixture of people connected by their neighbors' and often their own perceptions of the world. North Carolinians imagined that those they categorized as free people of color shared common traits that distinguished them from those people classified as white. Yet in their appearances and family backgrounds, they were as diverse as any other imagined community.

Remembering Freedom

North Carolina law stated that an individual's freedom could either be established through birth, as the child of a free mother, or through manumission, a legal process in which an enslaved person became a free person. The legal statutes related to freedom were simple, but the process of establishing free status was much more complex. Freedom was not something a person could simply declare or something that individuals could reveal through their physical appearances. Although many people believed that freedom was connected to appearance, examples too numerous to mention counter those assumptions. North Carolinians associated whiteness with freedom and blackness with slavery in theory, but in real life there were enslaved people with pale skin and blond hair and free people with chocolate brown complexions. A person's liberty, instead, was a function of public memory within local communities. Neighbors believed a person was free because they remembered that that individual had a connection to a free foremother or received his or her liberty through manumission. Memory of freedom could be a function of the understandings of local people, sometimes passed down from generation to generation. Records such as court records or freedom papers also served as important building blocks in the construction of public memories of liberty.

During the nineteenth century, free people of color most commonly supported their claims to freedom through their neighbors' statements, which specified that their maternal ancestors were free women of color. Communities depended on this form of public memory in order to distinguish free people from the enslaved. On June 15, 1832, Nancy Perry swore that "Benjamin Case is a free man of col[or] about the age of twenty two years and that he was born in Currituck County of the state aforesaid and Sally Case of colour was [h]is mother a free woman of col[or]."[26] In a similar case from Northampton County, Jesse Smith, on March 12, 1835, certified that he was "acquainted with Sally Jenkins a free girl of colour" and knew "her mother and father to be free persons of colour."[27] Freedom in these cases was not something visible but something remembered by people in the community.

Throughout North Carolina's history, communities recognized the children of white women as free, regardless of who may have been the fathers of the children. Public memory of a free person of color having a white foremother was the strongest evidence one could have to establish freedom. William Gaston reported from sources who lived during the colonial period that most of the free people of color who were born during that time established their free status through their connections to white maternal ancestors.[28] Public memory of connections to white maternal ancestors continued to play an important role in proving the liberty of free people of color into the national period.

Numerous white people attested to their neighbors' connections to white women in order to support their free status. During July 1799, Sarah Bennett gave a statement to the Wayne County court supporting Isaac Edens's free status. Bennett explained that she was "well acquainted with a woman by the name of Ann Edens and the said Ann Edens was Delivered of a black child who is now Isaac Edens" and declared that "Isaac Edens was Free born as his mother was a White woman."[29] In 1813, the Onslow County court certified the free status of the Hammond family based on their connection to a white maternal ancestor. The court clerk recorded, "Serena Hammond and Asa Hammond late in the possession of John Willy and Mary, Sukey, and Daphne Hammond the three young children of Serena Hammond are all free born, they being the children and grandchildren of Susannah Hammond Dec'd a free white woman."[30] In both of these cases, public memory was essential to establishing the status of individual free persons of color. Isaac Edens could continue to live as a free person because Sarah Bennett remembered his mother was a white woman. In the case of the Hammond family, their white maternal ancestor was dead. Yet the memory of their foremother's status ultimately determined how the Onslow County community treated Susannah Hammond's descendants.

The example of the Bennetts from Gates County at the beginning of this chapter was just one instance of neighbors supporting freedom claims by establishing individuals' connections to a free "Indian" foremother. In 1804, county clerk affirmed that Price Longtom and Jordon Longtom were free persons by stating that their mother Mary "Polly" Longtom was "an Indian woman."[31] Because freedom was a function of memory and not something observable, occasionally some people who were legally free had their liberty challenged by those who attempted to hold them in bondage. Memories of descent from "Indian" foremothers became important to the cases of some North Carolinians who believed they were illegally held in slavery. In 1785, Jenny Ash, "a mulatto woman," petitioned the justices of the Bertie County court for her freedom and that of her children. Jenny asserted that she was the daughter of Nanney Ash, "an Indian and Free born" and that James Gardner was holding both herself and her children in slavery under the threat of sending them out of the state.[32] Although examples exist, statements connecting the lineages of free people of color to "Indian" foremothers are rare. By the nineteenth century, North Carolinians living east of Cherokee country had largely given up trying to draw a distinction between people they believed to be indigenous and other people that they classified as persons of color.[33] Consequently, many declarations of freedom in which the foremothers were Native women likely refer to them as people of color and not specifically "Indian."

During the colonial and early national periods, the term "Indian" was not limited to indigenous Americans. Memories of "Indian" foremothers sometimes pertained to people from Asia and the Indian Ocean region. Some free people of color could trace their ancestry back to these "East Indians," a term used in the British Empire in reference to persons from South Asia. In 1777, Peter Charles came to the Craven County court to declare that he was "an East India Indian and Free Born" and argued that John Edge Tomlinson illegally held him as a slave. After evaluating the claims of Charles and Tomlinson, the court declared "Peter Charles is an East India Indian, and justly Intitled [*sic*] to his Freedom."[34] As a person with origins in the East Indies and therefore a descendant of a woman with the same heritage, the court could certify and document Charles's claim to liberty for posterity. The Dove family, also of Craven County, obtained their freedom by proving their direct maternal line started with an "East Indian" woman. During the 1740s, Mary Dove pursued a case against Leonard Thomas for her freedom and that of her children. She claimed that her grandmother was an "East Indian" woman and free. With the help of William Smith of Craven County and the testimony of Alexander Sands alias "Indian Sawony," the son of an "East Indian" woman, Mary Dove and her children secured their freedom. Many years after this case, Ann Ridgely of Anne Arundel County, Maryland, dictated a history of the Dove family in order to support the suit of William Dowrey, a grandson of Mary Dove, who remained in slavery into the 1790s. Ridgely's deposition explained that "the Grand Mother of Mary Dove was a yellow woman and had long black hair, but this deponent doth not know whether she was reputed to be an East Indian or a Madagascarian, but she has understood that she was called in the family Malaga Moll, her name being Mary."[35] Malaga Moll was probably one of an unknown number of people with ties to the Indian Ocean region who landed in the British Colonies during the colonial period. From the late seventeenth century into the eighteenth century, people from the Indian subcontinent became important parts of the developing British Empire. Many of them became servants in British households or sailors on transoceanic voyages.[36]

The very limited discussion of people from the East Indies in the historical record makes it impossible to determine the extent of their role in the growth of the free population of color. The existing sources do not provide enough information to estimate the number of East Indians present in Britain's mainland North American colonies. The East Indian ancestors of free people of color are likely invisible for many of the same reasons that obscure Native peoples' connections to the free population of color. If denoted in the records, they were often categorized as "East Indians," "East Indy Indians," "East India Indians," or simply "Indians." "Indian" of course was a term used to categorize indigenous Americans as well as Asians. As explained earlier, colonial officials, and later state officials often lumped people once described as "Indian" with other persons of color into simple, ambiguous categories. In some instances, the British categorized people with ties to the East Indies as "blacks."[37] Some people of East Indian descent, like the Dove family, possibly had Native, African, or European ancestors. Colonial officials may have described these people, like others of mixed heritage, with ambiguous terms such as "mulatto" or "negro."

Public memory and its preservation through legal documents upheld North Carolina's manumission process, an important avenue to freedom for persons of color. Records pertaining to manumissions reveal that former slaves became free through multiple avenues. During the colonial period, North Carolina law made manumission a very difficult process and required freed people to leave the colony after receiving their liberty. With the outbreak of the American Revolution, however, lawmakers liberalized the manumission laws by removing the requirement of expulsion from North Carolina. Yet, during both the colonial and national periods, the law required an enslaved person to perform some type of "meritorious service" in order to gain liberty. The law never defined "meritorious service," leaving local courts and the legislature with great flexibility in deciding which candidates for freedom would receive their liberty and which would remain enslaved. Therefore, former slaves received their liberty underneath the label "meritorious service" for a variety of reasons, including service to their masters or the community, self-purchase or purchase by a friend or family member, or through the ideologically driven desires of their masters.[38]

Some enslaved people were both lucky and ingenious enough to save money and purchase their liberty. Through self-purchase, they moved from categorization as enslaved to classification as free people of color. In 1812, Augustus Cabarrus petitioned the Chowan County court seeking to emancipate his enslaved man Jim Williams. Cabarrus explained to the court that Williams was "an orderly, well behaved fellow, that he has paid your petitioner his full value, and for his meritorious services." After considering Cabarrus's request, the court granted his petition. Following Williams's liberation, Cabarrus and two others posted a bond certifying that Williams would not become a charge to the county.[39] Molly Horniblow, also of Chowan County, gained her liberty through a similar arrangement. Hannah Pritchet, the sister of Horniblow's mistress, purchased Horniblow at her sister's estate sale. After purchasing her, Pritchet petitioned the court and secured Horniblow's freedom. In exchange for securing her liberty, Pritchet required Horniblow to pay back the cost of her purchase.[40] Enslaved people whose masters allowed them to purchase their freedom were fortunate. The earnings of slaves legally belonged to their masters, and the law did not require masters to share any wages with slaves. Slaves who purchased their liberty usually had to be very industrious and skilled in order to raise the necessary funds. Enslaved people also had to have the appropriate social skills to build strong trusting relationships with their masters. They had to persuade their masters that they deserved privileges beyond the limitations imposed on them by a slave system that implied that enslaved people existed for the sole benefit of their masters.

Free people helped their family members move from enslaved status to free status by purchasing their relatives and then petitioning for their liberty. In 1774, Samuel Drury of Bertie County, "a free negro," completed the process of freeing his daughter Milly. Before petitioning the county court for Milly's liberty, Drury purchased his daughter from her former master. With his daughter in his possession and the aid of an attorney, the court gave Drury permission to "free and manumit his said Daughter."[41] Prior to seeking permission from the Pasquotank County court to manumit his family, Thomas Sylvester, "a free man of colour," had purchased his wife Joan and children from Jeremiah Symons. In 1797, he petitioned the court for their freedom. In response to the request, the court ordered that Joan and her children Abba, Nancy, Jerry, and Annaritta "be manumitted & set free."[42]

Although the vast majority of enslaved people owned by their white relatives remained in bondage, some white people sought to manumit their enslaved family members. In 1798, Ann G. Daly petitioned the Craven County court on behalf of her deceased brother John Daly. She explained to the court that she was in possession of "a certain female mullattoe [sic] slave named Mary about the age of twenty years" and that "Mary has always been reputed to be the child of the said John Daly decd, and in that light treated & regarded by the said John in his life time." She testified that her brother stated repeatedly his desire to free Mary. On these grounds, Ann petitioned for Mary's liberty, and the court granted her application.[43] Other free people of color likely received their liberty through the same means. These cases are often difficult to document, however, because most applications by white family members rarely stated the relationship between the emancipated person and the former master or mistress.

Local courts defined "meritorious service" widely and permitted the liberation of persons of color for performing an assortment of acts. In his 1791 petition, Samuel Street of Craven County explained that he was "the owner of a negro woman slave called Delia aged about forty" and wished to free her because she "acted as a faithful & attentive nurse to his oldest son & that from her breast his infancy was supported."[44] Sometime during February 1797, twelve Perquimans County petitioners asked their county court to liberate Phillis for her service as "a Midwife and Doctress." After considering the petition, the court approved Phillis's emancipation.[45] Frank, "a mulatto man," received his freedom from John Hogg in 1818 because he was "honest, industrious, sober and well disposed" and most importantly a "good carpenter."[46] Some manumission requests were less specific and defined meritorious in more ambiguous terms. On May 27, 1791, the Orange County court permitted Anne Hooper to liberate "John, her negro slave," because he had "had faithfully and Honestly served his late master Wm. Hooper Esq. Dec'd and also his present mistress."[47] At the Brunswick County court, on July 11, 1792, James Walker received approval to manumit "Minerva a female mulatto slave" after county officials concluded that the enslaved woman had performed "sufficiently meritorious" service."[48]

Magistrates allowed masters to liberate the enslaved under the auspices that the labor of those people contributed to their masters' educations. Africa Parker received his freedom from the Orange County court in 1799 after his master, William Cain, convincingly argued that Parker endowed him with valuable skills. Cain explained in his manumission petition that Parker "taught and instructed your Petitioner, and one of his other slaves, in the art and mystery of Malting, Brewing, and distilling grain, whereby your Petitioner hopes to derive great profit and gain."[49] Thomas Jordan of Pasquotank County presented a similar contention about his enslaved man Luke in order to persuade the court that his slave fulfilled the law's meritorious service requirement. In his 1799 petition, Jordan stated that Luke "for many years was hired out" and that "the monies arising" helped pay for his education.[50]

Government officials accepted not only service to masters but also service to the local community, state, or country as forms of "meritorious service." Following the American Revolution, at least a few slaves received their freedom for their service during the war. In 1784, legislators passed a bill manumitting Edward "Ned" Griffin, a Revolutionary War veteran and former slave of William Kitchen of Edgecombe County. During the Revolution, Griffin served as a substitute in the American army. Eight years later, an enslaved man Jack also obtained his liberty based on his Revolutionary War service. Jack's former master recalled that Jack single-handedly captured the crew of a British privateer, and in the process, released his master and others held as prisoners by the enemy. In a slightly different case, George Merrick of New Hanover County asked that legislators to grant freedom to his slaves Richard, Dolly, and Nathan. In his 1791 petition, Merrick explained to the assembly that during the American Revolution, Richard and Dolly prevented many of Merrick's slaves from deserting to the British. Taking this explanation into account, the General Assembly passed a bill to free Merrick's three bondspeople.[51]

Ideological reasons drove some masters to seek their slaves' liberations. The legislature and magistrates generally denied such attempts to manumit and cited the requirement of "meritorious service." The "meritorious service" requirement that appeared in the Revolutionary-era law was partially a reaction to people's attempts to free large numbers of enslaved people based solely on their opposition to slavery. Yet, on rare occasions, some individuals succeeded in obtaining freedom for enslaved people on ideological grounds. In 1787, Thomas Newby asked the Perquimans County court for permission to liberate "a negro girl named Nacy." He described Nacy as "Verry Trusty" and explained that he hoped to employ her as a "hired servant." Newby sought to emancipate Nacy because he was "clearly convinced . . . that it is wrong for me to hold her as a slave."[52] On June 7, 1799, Samuel Jackson petitioned the Pasquotank County court for permission to "Liberate and set free his Negro Man Ichabud." Jackson explained that Ichabud had "Distinguished himself a faithful servant" and performed "meritorious services." Nevertheless, he also admitted that "Humanity & Gratitude" motivated him to seek Ichabud's freedom.[53]

Meritorious service was a requisite according to law. Government officials, however, occasionally accepted a strikingly fair appearance as justification for liberation. Such appeals argued that people with "white" appearances should not be held as slaves. Stephen L. Ferrand asked the Craven County court to liberate his enslaved woman Caroline on the grounds that she "hath conducted herself with a propriety and decency" and "that she has been brought up in virtuous habits [and] is scarcely distinguishable from a white person in complexion." The county court granted Ferrand's request, and Caroline was liberated under the name "Caroline Lane."[54] Other petitions and wills used similar language to request the freedom of slaves with light complexions. The petitions did not always succeed, but some slaveholders hoped that the physical features of their slaves might sway the sympathies of officials. The light complexions of some slaves were problematic for the slave system on several fronts. In theory, people were supposed to be able to assume who was white and who was not. Yet the process of categorizing people was about more than appearances. The laws of North Carolina and several other states provided legal whiteness to people of mixed ancestry with limited numbers of distant forebears categorized as people of color. (Under the American system of slavery, however, any person born to a slave mother, no matter how many white ancestors he or she had, remained a slave.) Therefore, theoretically there were enslaved people who, if emancipated, could go directly from being enslaved to being white persons.

A variety of motivations drove the reclassification of people from enslaved to free. Yet maybe the most important part of the manumission process was the recording of the emancipations of former slaves in the county court records and state law books. A declaration of freedom required evidence in the form of public memory. Documents along with individuals' recollections supported the continued freedom of manumitted persons and their descendants. Manumitted persons held dual positions in public memory as once enslaved persons and free people. Manumission documents in the form of deeds, wills, and other certified statements helped prevent any blurring of public memory. In a society in which slavery existed, freedom could not be assumed but had to be supported through public recollection. Whether people of color asserted freedom through birth or through manumission, public memories of their status undergirded their claims to liberty. Like racial categorization, freedom status was not something obvious but something that people had to determine.

The role of cognitive processes and memory in the categorization of individuals as free people of color is largely missing from the historical literature. Scholars have approached the topic of free people of color as an examination of a subset of a defined "African American," "black," or "negro" group without considering how the category was imagined or applied. Mentions of people of color, mulattoes, Negroes, mustees, and Indians throughout the rest of this book should be read as reflections of how particular North Carolinians understood their world in the eighteenth and nineteenth centuries. Many of the people whose neighbors classified them as people of color may have self-categorized differently. Furthermore, this chapter demonstrates that North Carolinians often could not agree how to categorize one another. Sometimes individuals found applying racial categories difficult and had to use multiple terms from their racial lexicon to describe a single person.

✠

CHAPTER 2

Colonial Liberties, Colonial Constraints

Defining Freedom in Early North Carolina

When William Chavis of Granville County died sometime in the 1770s, he left an estate of hundreds of acres of land, eleven enslaved women, men, and children, livestock, and numerous trinkets. Chavis was a literate man who owned books and an inkstand. During his life, he operated his own inn or tavern, was politically active, and regularly appeared in the county courts to conduct business. As he was one of the most affluent people in his part of North Carolina, people in Granville County continued to remember Chavis's name and legacy at least until the 1890s. In many ways, his life was a model of not only how Britain's American colonial scheme paid off for the British crown and aristocracy, but also how slavery and the appropriation of Native lands could make common men into masters of their own small worlds. William Chavis was the master of his household, a master over men and women, yet he was categorized in his community as a "Negro."[1]

Chavis's categorization as a "Negro" exposed him to discriminatory taxation and probably subjected him to the sneers of white people who equated his racial categorization with inferiority. Yet Chavis was still among the fortunate in colonial America. Living in a society that assessed human value based on intersecting hierarchies of legal status (slave or free, head of household or dependent), national origin, sex, religious affiliation, reputation, family connection, and skin color, Chavis was far from the bottom of the social order.[2] As a free man and head of household with wealth and respectability, he enjoyed an overall social position above that of most people of color in the colony, and because of the pronounced importance of gender discrimination, legal status, and wealth disparity in the shape of society, Chavis, even as a "Negro," had more political privileges, rights, and power than every woman and girl and every servant or slave, regardless of racial categorization.

In colonial North Carolina, free status protected persons of color like William Chavis from the almost unlimited power masters wielded over slaves and firmly placed all free people of color in a legal position above slaves. Social customs and the law created critical distinctions in the life experiences of free persons of color based on sex, servitude status, and personal wealth. The "white" versus "colored" racial dichotomy used in theory to divide masters from slaves and the colonizers from the colonized indeed promoted and produced inequality. Yet the colonists' belief in race and a hierarchy of racial categories could only partially dictate the outcomes for those deemed persons of color. As Anne McClintock argued, "no social category exists in privileged isolation; each comes into being in social relations to other categories, if in uneven and contradictory ways."[3] Racial categorization did not overshadow but instead intersected with gender and wealth. Colonial North Carolina lawmakers had not concluded that racial categories were society's most valuable hierarchical concepts. Among the general public were those who were less than fully convinced that categorization as a Negro, mulatto, mustee, or Indian denoted a caste-like second-class status for free persons of color that overrode all other highly valued forms of hierarchy.[4]

Racial Categorization, Gender, and Class in the Law

Generally, colonial laws that pertained to any particular classification of free people of color used some combination of racial categorizations, sex, and class, sometimes in conjunction with age, in order to provide North Carolinians with a guideline for appropriate social behavior and to construct social boundaries. During the colonial period, only one law equally applied to all persons of color regardless of freedom status, gender, or wealth. North Carolina's political elites concerned themselves primarily with providing the master class with the legal tools to extract work from and control the lives of slaves and servants. As a result, with few exceptions, most of the laws that mentioned racial categories primarily affected slaves and servants of color, especially women and girls. Free men of color who were heads of households or property holders were immune from the legal code's harshest effects. They held a legal status only slightly below that of free white men of the same class and maintained privileges unavailable to women of all classes and servants of any racial classification.

Racial distinctions did not become an important part of North Carolina's legal code until 1715. By 1715, North Carolina was behind colonies such as Virginia, which had begun to encode racial distinctions in its laws during the second half of the seventeenth century.[5] "An Act Concerning Servants and Slaves" helped bring North Carolina in line with the laws of other colonies. The new act sought to control the behavior of servants and slaves and to discourage sexual and familial relations between whites and people of color. In regard to persons of color, "Negro, Mulatto, or Indyan" slaves, not free people of color, were the law's primary targets. Most sections of the act treated servants equally, regardless of their racial categorization.

Several sections of the act, however, had significant impacts on the lives of a certain segment of the free population of color, the poor. These sections sought to control sexual and familial interactions between whites and persons of color and outlined ways to punish whites who blurred informal distinctions between the European colonizers and slaveholders and people of color. Section XIV targeted "White women whether Bond or Free" who had "a Bastard child by a Negro, Mulatto or Indyan" and required those women to pay a six-pound fine or to be sold by the parish into two years of servitude. Most importantly, Section XV dictated that the children born to these women become bound servants until they reached the age of thirty-one. While being born to a white mother provided many among the early generations of free people of color with legal status as free, the forced servitude connected to their foremothers' illicit behavior prevented them from enjoying all of freedom's possibilities. They had trouble accessing certain social and political privileges such as personal property ownership, which was inaccessible to servants. As a result, these free persons of color were unable to accumulate wealth at the beginning of their adult lives. Sections XVI and XVII constrained the ability of white women to legitimize their relationship with men of color and prevent the bastardization of their children by strongly discouraging intermarriage. Section XVI penalized white men and women who married "any Negro, Mulatto or Indyan Man or Woman" with a fine of fifty pounds. The following section mandated the same fine for any person that might marry such couples.[6]

Following the lead of colonies such as Virginia and Maryland, the North Carolina General Assembly passed one of the few colonial laws directed at free people of color outside of the servant class in 1723.[7] "An Act for an additional tax on all free Negroes, Mulattoes, Mustees, and such Persons, Male and Female, as now are, or hereafter shall be, intermarried with any such Persons, resident in this Government" targeted what the assembly described as "great Numbers of Free Negroes, Mulattoes, and other persons of mixt Blood, that have lately removed themselves into this Government." This law imposed a tax on "free Negroes, Mulattoes, and other Persons of that kind, being mixed Blood, including the Third Generation . . . both Male and Female, who are of the age of Twelve years and upwards." In cases of free men of color, the act also punished their white spouses by deeming them tithable.[8] The law had no direct effect on the tax status of white men or men of color, as people who fell under both categories had been tithable before 1723. In seeking to discourage marriage between whites and free people of color as well as to dissuade the settlement of free persons of color in North Carolina, however, the General Assembly had changed the tax status of all free women of color, white women married to people of color, and free children of color twelve years old and over. Before this point, the only women and children who were taxable were slaves, and the masters of those slaves were responsible for paying the tax. This law imposed a true burden on families with a husband or wife who was a free person of color, especially for poorer families that were unable to pay the tithe.

Reinforcing their alleged commitment to curb the growth of free people of color in the colony, the General Assembly also placed greater restrictions on a particular category of free persons of color, the recently emancipated. In 1715, the General Assembly had prohibited emancipated persons from remaining in North Carolina more than six months after receiving their liberty. Yet, according to the 1723 act, recently freed persons had tried to defeat the law by removing temporarily from North Carolina and then returning after briefly living in another jurisdiction. In order to close this loophole in the law, lawmakers now required that all freed persons who illegally reentered North Carolina be sold into seven years of additional service.[9] This provision, unlike the sections dealing with taxes, focused on a particular class of free persons of color and likely only had a very limited effect on free people of color as a whole. Even emancipated persons could avoid the consequences of this law by moving to jurisdictions where the people were unaware of their past enslavement. North Carolina was a particularly apt place for such deception because of the rapid westward movement that took place in the colony in the 1700s and the constant influx of new settlers into the province. Furthermore, colonial officials in newly settled areas, where the local economy needed laborers and artisans, were unlikely to press any new settlers about their previous status if they could somehow contribute to the community.[10]

During the 1740s, the General Assembly continued to use a set of laws that largely affected only certain segments of the free population of color. The legislature passed reiterations and amended versions of the laws of the 1710s and 1720s. The General Assembly of 1741 reissued the laws concerning intermarriage between whites and persons of color and those concerned with white women who bore children who were people of color. In the same year, the governing body amended the laws dealing with emancipated persons. The new legislation required meritorious service for all emancipations. Additionally, the law redefined the penalty for all freed persons who attempted to return to North Carolina after their required removal from sale into seven years of service to reenslavement. In 1749, legislators adjusted the tax penalty imposed on free people of color. The old law applied the tax to all persons of color up to the third generation from the original African or Indian ancestor. The new act extended the tax to "all Negroes, Mulattoes, Mustees Male or Female, and all Persons of Mixt Blood, to the Fourth Generation."[11]

In 1754, North Carolina lawmakers went against decades of precedent by creating the broadest piece of racially discriminatory legislation in the colony's history. That year, the General Assembly enacted the first law to privilege clearly and without exception all whites over all people of color regardless of freedom status, class, gender, or age. A portion of the law entitled "An Act, for Establishing the Supreme Courts of Justice, Oyer and Terminer, and General Gaol Delivery of North Carolina" declared "that all Negroes and Mulattoes, bond or free, to the Third Generation, and Indian Servants and Slaves, shall be deemed and taken to be incapable in Law to be Witnesses, in any Cause whatsoever, except against each other."[12] From this point on, no person of color could provide testimony against any white person even in cases where a free person of color was a plaintiff against a white defendant. For the first time, white North Carolinians, even those who in every other way were the inferiors of wealthier, better educated, and more highly respected free persons of color were in North Carolina courtrooms the legal superiors of all people of color, bond or free. For over a century after the passage of this law, both persons of color as well as whites concerned with maintaining order and protecting the potency of the law would have to develop creative strategies to overcome the inherent white supremacy imbedded in the North Carolina court system.[13]

The 1754 law did not set a new precedent for colonial legislators. North Carolina lawmakers reverted to a more traditional approach to discriminatory legislation during the 1760s. Legislation passed in 1760 included implications for free people of color but only for a certain segment of the population. That year, the General Assembly changed the terms of service for apprentices from their thirty-first birthdays to their twenty-first or eighteenth birthdays depending on their racial categorization and sex. The law now required all boys to serve their masters until they were twenty-one. The law also obligated courts to bind "every Female" apprentice to "some Suitable Employment 'til her age of eighteen years." Without a clearly stated purpose or reason, this law also required that "every such Female Child being a Mulatto or Mustee" shall serve "until she shall attain the Age of Twenty one Years."[14] The only logic that can be extracted from this law is that legislators believed that mulatto and mustee girls had less of a right to their freedom than white girls. The wording of this law undoubtedly confused many court magistrates when deciding how to apply the law to the larger mass of girls of color. The law does not specifically mention other categories of girls of color except mulattoes and mustees. Furthermore, the law fails to define a "mulatto" or "mustee" or to explain how to delineate between categories of persons of color.

The majority of the colonial-era laws focused heavily on particular classes of free people of color. Intersectionality was important in determining who would be most impacted by discriminatory legislation.[15] The law did not treat women the same as men or the poor the same as the wealthy. Even when lawmakers imbedded racial distinctions in the legal code, other overlapping forms of distinction usually helped to dictate the law's impact. The laws passed by the General Assembly during the colonial period, however, set a precedent for a larger body of discriminatory laws that would appear in the late eighteenth and nineteenth centuries to curb the rights and privileges of free persons of color during the national period.

The Lives of Servants and Apprentices

The lives of free people of color who worked as servants and apprentices varied significantly from the experiences of their unbound counterparts.

The authority masters had over servants and apprentices limited the possibilities for all bound servants, especially women. Masters had almost unlimited rights to the bodies and labor of their servants, and across the colony, they generally sought to take full advantage of these entitlements. The apprenticeship law of 1760 granted apprentices more legal protections than in the past; nonetheless, they had to depend on a political apparatus that was inherently biased to the master class to protect their rights. Servants and apprentices, regardless of racial categorization, had the right to complain to local courts about abuses by masters. In this arrangement, protecting oneself from the abuse of masters was difficult but not impossible.

The historical record suggests that free people of color became part of North Carolina's system of bound servitude largely through legal actions against their mothers. Free persons of color generally did not enter the system of servitude through contractually arranged indentured servitude as was the case with many European immigrants who paid their passage to the colonies through this method. Across North Carolina, courts bound free children of color to masters as punishment for their mothers having children out of wedlock. The laws punishing women and children for bastardy were part of a long English and later British-colonial tradition of regulating the sexuality of the poor and protecting the labor interests of masters who would be responsible for providing housing and provisions for pregnant servant women, whether or not they could work. Even the children who may have been the products of rape or the children of their mothers' masters were forced into servitude. Like neighboring Virginia, North Carolina treated the sexual acts that produced bastard children as consensual regardless of whether mothers actually consented to the acts that led to their children's births.[16]

Generations of children of color found themselves circumscribed by North Carolina's system of servitude largely as the result of their white female ancestors' perceived sexual indiscretions. The laws of servitude prevented servant women, many of whom were in their reproductive primes, from marrying while obligated to their masters' service. As a result, children born to servant white women were bastards, and because North Carolina law required the "mulatto" children born to servant women to be bound out, from birth children known to have fathers who were free people of color automatically joined the servant class.

Delany Bright was one of the children of color who fell into the colony's system of servitude because of the circumstances of her birth and North Carolina lawmakers' desire to control poor servant women and their illegitimate children. On July 10, 1746, Pasquotank County justices bound the two-year-old Delany, whom they described as a "Mallatto Girl" and daughter of "Lydia Bright a white weoman [sic] that was killed by a Tree that fell upon her," to James Burnham. Burnham agreed to provide Delany with "Sufficient Meat Drink Washing Lodging and Apparel fitting for Mallatoes."[17] This agreement between the justices of the court and Burnham demonstrates that North Carolina law provided both local magistrates and masters with broad powers in the lives of young servants of color. By requiring "Meat Drink Washing Lodging and Apparel fitting for Mallatoes," the justices provided Burnham with legal protection if he decided to treat Delany as less than the typical white servant. The apprenticeship agreement gave Delany the opportunity to survive but did not guarantee that she would have the tools to move beyond the servant status of her youth.

The combined pressures of gender, racial, and wealth discrimination sometimes left free families of color in servitude for multiple generations. On May 26, 1733, Ann Burk, a white servant woman from Chowan County, gave birth to a "mulatto" daughter, Judah Burk. Less than two years after her daughter's birth, Ann agreed to bind Judah to Charles and Abigail Jordan. The January 31, 1735, agreement required Judah to "obey" her masters "in all lawfull [sic] services and commands whatsoever fit to employ her about untill [sic] she shall come to the full age and maturity of thirty and one years old." The contract also prohibited Judah from contracting "matrimony with any person" during her period of service.[18] Judah did not marry but failed to engage in the celibacy implied by the marriage ban. As a result, Judah Burk's children fell into North Carolina's system of servitude because their mother was still a servant during her reproductive prime. Judah's inability to contract marriage during her service along with the laws binding out bastard children subjected her children to the same conditions of limited freedom that she had experienced from an early age. From the 1750s into the early 1770s, Judah gave birth to several illegitimate children, whom the Chowan County court bound as apprentices. Even into the nineteenth century, Judah's descendants continued to serve as apprentices to various whites in the area.[19] The experiences of Ann, Judah, and their descendants support historian Karin Zipf's argument that "apprenticeship was an institution employed by the white patriarchal elite as a measure of social control." Stripped of their parental rights, Ann and Judah lost access to their children's labor and "consequently lacked the opportunities of independence enjoyed by white men" who benefited from the work of these women's children.[20] As a result, the Burk family became stuck in successional generations of bound servitude.[21]

Masters' treatment of their servants' indentures as inheritable property cast servants and apprentices firmly below other free persons of color in colonial North Carolina. In his 1753 will, Edmund Chancey of Pasquotank County bequeathed his "servants" Jack Spanyard Boe and Spanyoll Boe until the expiration of their indentures along with livestock and other property to his son Daniel. He also devised Bob Boe, Frank Boe, and Rachel Boe along with her two children, all "servants," through the periods of their indentures, to his daughter Rachel.[22] On May 25, 1741, the sheriff of Edgecombe County liquidated the estate of Thomas Haynes. Among the items sold to the highest bidders were "The service of David Hull a free Negro Boy till he is 21" and "The service of Esther Hull a free Negro Girl till she is 18."[23] In these cases, masters treated their servants' contracts as property that could be transferred without the consent of the parties involved in the indenture agreements. The multigenerational transfer of indentures reveals that some masters viewed the labor of their servants as their property even after death. At first glance, the situations of the servants of such masters appear to be very similar to those of enslaved people, whose labor also could be inherited and transferred. The language in both Chancey's will and Haynes's inventory, however, clarifies that whoever gained the services of the Boes and Hulls had a legal right to their labor only until adulthood. Masters transferred enslaved people's bodies and labor with lifetime rights.

Colonial understandings of appropriate gender roles largely dictated the types of training that masters provided to their young servants. Regardless of apprentices' racial categorizations, masters only trained girls in certain tasks while boys learned skills viewed by both their masters and local officials as appropriate for men. The tasks given to Amiah Sanderlin and Pen Pugh were typical of those assigned by the courts to most girls. In 1756, Elizabeth Lockhart of Bertie County promised to train "Amiah Sanderlin Daughter of Ann Sanderlin a Free Mullattoe Woman" in "the art and Mistery of household Business."[24] During 1765, Bertie County officials bound Pen Pugh, a "mulatoe" girl, to John Pearson to learn spinning.[25] Boys had the opportunity to learn a wider range of trades. In April 1763, the Chowan County court bound four of Rachael Read's "mulatto" sons, Masheck and Shadrack to learn the cooper's trade and Reuben and Jacob to become cordwainers.[26] Other boys learned trades such as farming, carpentry, and blacksmithing.[27] Through the energies and prerogatives of both the local government and the master class, the apprenticeship system served as an important apparatus for the production of a gendered labor force.

Although North Carolina's legal code required servants to submit to their masters in most instances, the law still permitted indentured servants and apprentices to make claims against their masters for excessive abuses. Local courts were willing to hear and sometimes protect the servants of overbearing masters. The courts heard complaints from servants who contended their masters held them beyond the agreed-upon terms of service.[28] In October 1745, Sarah Overton alias Boe, "a servant mallatto wench," asked the Pasquotank County court to grant her liberty from Edmund Chancey after being held beyond the agreed period of service. In order for her to prove her case, the court allowed Overton to locate a Bible that would provide the court proof of her age. Overton apparently produced evidence of her age, and the court ordered Chancey to give her freedom along with freedom dues.[29] Fifteen years after Overton's case, Bob Boe, her son, made a similar complaint to the Pasquotank County court and argued that his master held him "unlawfully & illegally restrained [him] of his liberty."[30] The court found in his favor.[31] Local officials also handled complaints about cruelties. At the November 1756 session of Craven County court, James Dove, "a negro servant," complained to the court on "behalf of himself and Nelly, Sue, Sarah, Moll, and William Dove" of "misusage" by their master, William Smith. The court directed Smith to appear before the court to answer the complaint.[32]

The mothers of servant children were often the most adamant defenders of their children's liberty. Although these women held little influence within the society, they found ways to use the power attached to their free status to protect their children through the local courts. In March 1761, the mother of "Simon a free Negro Boy" with the assistance of a Mr. Herritage complained to the Beaufort County court about the actions of her son's master. She and Herritage declared that Thomas Jasper had "given out in speaches [sic]" that he would "take and carry away" Simon and "sell him for a slave."[33] Following a 1757 Onslow County court decision, Ann Martin, "a free molato woman," regained custody of her two children after making a complaint before the court. The court ruled that John Humphrey, the man who held Martin's children, had no right to them as his servants because he obtained an indenture on the children through "deceit."[34]

Servants sometimes resorted to absconding from their masters rather than taking their complaints to the courts. The courts were a particularly unsatisfactory option for servants who felt in immediate danger or did not trust local officials, many of whom were the peers of their masters. Running away was not necessarily a solution, especially if their masters recaptured them. Nevertheless, the courts still provided runaway servants with due process after their recapture. John Nead alias Ned John, "an Indian man servant," and Solomon Poker, "an Indian servant," fled their masters and lived on the run until their masters had them captured. Later, the two servant men appeared at the September 1730 term of Carteret County court, where justices required them to serve their masters for an additional three years as punishment for running away. In 1750, Violet, a "free negro" from Craven County, ran away from her master and avoided capture for eleven days. Once Violet's master retrieved her, he brought her into the county court. The justices required Violet to return to her master and serve him for an additional twenty-two days.[35] The cases of these runaways suggest that the courts had little sympathy for servants who tried to better their circumstances by leaving their masters without permission. The courts viewed running away as a legal violation and sought to remedy such conduct by forcing servants to fulfill their periods of service.

The power masters had over the lives of servants of color, sometimes for successive generations, limited servants' life choices. Colonial legislators' preoccupation with policing the sexuality of women and girls caused servant women and girls additional hardships. Although lawmakers designed the law in favor of masters over servants, servants of color still had opportunities to express grievances, and more importantly, they had service agreements that provided them with very basic protections. Whatever influence others' beliefs about racial categorizations had on the lives of these servants, those opinions, under law and in practice, could not translate into the legal chattel position of slaves.

The Lives of All Other Free Persons

Much like the free persons described in T. H. Breen's and Stephen Innes's work on Virginia's Eastern Shore during the seventeenth century, free people of color in colonial North Carolina who were neither servants nor apprentices "made personal decisions, and planned for the future in the belief that they could in fact shape their physical and social environments."[36] The acts of their neighbors determined how their second-class racial categorization influenced their lives. The law made slight distinctions between the privileges of free persons based on racial categorization. However, only neighbors' and officials' desires to enforce that law made legal discrimination a burden. Therefore, racial categorization, even among those people of color that shared a common free status, did not produce a uniform experience. Life outcomes of free persons of color varied according to their wealth, gender, work, and reputation. Some people of color became more affluent than most of their white neighbors, while other persons of color could barely afford life's basic necessities. Both the laws and societal norms that produced gender distinctions created a wedge between the lives of free men and women of color and particularly limited women's opportunities in the political and economic realms. Work and reputation operated side by side in a society that valued free people based on their contribution to the local community's day-to-day operations and their adherence to societal norms. Whites who believed themselves superior in some ways to persons of color could also respect their neighbors of color who helped them kill their hogs and plow their fields. Circumstances forced them to value the only blacksmith who provided the community with all of its nails and tools and just happened to be categorized as a person of color.

Economic success distanced a few masters who were free persons of color and major landholders from the mass of people in their localities. Mentioned at the beginning of this chapter, William Chavis lived a life that drastically contrasted with that of both most people of color and most colonists in general. Through land grants, inheritance from his father, and other unknown means, Chavis acquired over a thousand acres of land. He was also one of the largest slaveholders in his Granville County community. According to tax records from 1758, Chavis's six slaves made him the largest slaveholder in his tax district that year. Three years later, only one person in the Fishing Creek District of Granville County owned more slaves than Chavis.[37] Chavis exploited a system that placed capital acquisition over white racial domination, and he profited through careful decision making and successful negotiation within the colonial power structure.[38]

Between the most accomplished free people of color, such as William Chavis, and the poorest free persons of color was a class of yeomen. These yeomen owned small collections of personal property and possibly dozens of acres of arable land, but were the masters of no one beyond their dependent family members. Peter George of Craven County was one of these yeomen. At his death in 1763, George owned 250 acres of land, five head of hogs, carpenter's and shoemaker's tools, and several other items, which he distributed among his two sisters and a brother in his will.[39] The families of Thomas Archer, Gabriel Manley, James Nickens, Joseph Hall, and William Weaver, all described as "mulattoes" in a 1751 Bertie County tax list, also fell into North Carolina's yeomanry of color.[40] The heads of these families owned from one hundred to several hundred acres of land.

These small landholders not only were successful in providing for themselves but also demonstrated to their community that their work was imperative to that community's survival and development. Members of these families were skilled tradesmen, such as Gabriel Manley, a cooper who made barrels for his community. They also provided labor for public projects. In 1754, when Bertie County officials called for the construction of a road from Alexander Cotton's ferry to Deep Creek, the court recruited William Weaver, Thomas Archer, and Archer's two sons, John and Hancock, along with several of their white neighbors to construct the thoroughfare.[41]

Below the free persons of color who were members of the master class and yeomen were the poor free people of color whose lives contrasted drastically from those of propertied persons and were only a step up from those bound in servitude. The major difference between the poor free people of color and servants was the law obligated the latter to serve a master and follow that master's guidance while the poor had more personal liberty. Nevertheless, the poor did not always have the resources to exercise or protect their freedom of choice. As a person who was free but poor, "Negro Toney" of Pasquotank County struggled to maintain the little semblance of liberty in his possession. In 1748, Toney landed in court after James Cleeves complained that Toney had borrowed his canoe and not returned it. Toney explained to the court that he "happened to loose" the vessel, and in response, the court ordered him to pay Cleeves a fine of three barrels of corn. Toney was too poor to pay this fine, but the court was determined that its judgment would be fulfilled. The court sent Bennett Morgan, the constable, to confiscate from Toney several pigs, an iron pot, pot hook, a pot lid, run-let, lye tub, and two turkeys, which Toney later described as "all the things [he] . . . had in the world."[42]

The court's decision could have ruined Toney. Toney was free, but without his few worldly possessions, he likely would have struggled for the most basic necessities. Not long after the confiscation of his property, Toney's luck seemed to turn when the canoe resurfaced in "good order as when borrowed." Toney attempted to restore the canoe to Cleeves, but he refused to accept the vessel. In a petition to the court, Toney requested that the constable return his property, which Morgan had yet to sell, and that the court require Cleeves to accept the canoe. Toney also offered to "pay the corn" owed if his property was returned to him.[43] The court granted Toney's request and ordered that the court evaluate the canoe for dam-age.[44] Toney's dilemma demonstrates the significance of freedom in his life while highlighting the difficulties poverty imposed on him. As a free per-son, Toney had the right to challenge Cleeves's claim against him and to petition the court to protest what he viewed as an injustice. Yet poverty placed Toney in constant fiscal jeopardy.

Poverty always had the potential to threaten freedom's potency, but gender norms and laws that defined women and girls as permanent depen-dents stood as a threat to the lives of women across the wealth spectrum and racial hierarchy.[45] For women of color in propertied families, the deaths of husbands led to the dispersion of family property. Frances Chavis, the wife of William Chavis of Granville County, was forced to purchase many of her husband's personal items at public auction after his death.[46] At the 1760 sale of Joseph Hall of Bertie County, Margaret Hall was unable to pur-chase any of her husband's personal effects.[47] Regardless of class, women with underage children, if married, could lose direct influence over their children at the deaths of their husbands. According to the law, the chil-dren of unmarried women automatically fell under the jurisdiction of local courts, and courts used their legal power to remove children from their mothers' households and place them under the care of masters. Such was the case of several nonservant single women in Beaufort County. At the June 1758 term of court, local officials ordered Rachel Blango, Sarah Blango the younger, Dinah Blango, Bett Moore, Mary Moore, and Keziah Moore, all described by the clerk as "Negroe" women, to appear before the court so that their children could be bound out to "masters."[48]

Wealth disparities, the gender hierarchy, and racial categorization had important impacts on the daily lives of free persons of color. Yet the personal relationships whites built with their free neighbors of color along with those whites' determination to see their associates of color treated as neighbors and not as second-class subjects also performed an equally pertinent role in the actual lived experiences of free people of color. The battle against the additional tax burden imposed on free men of color with dependents highlights some whites' desire to protect their free neighbors of color and the resources those neighbors contributed to their communities. In 1762, several inhabitants of Granville, Edgecombe, and Northampton Counties petitioned the General Assembly for a repeal of the 1723 law taxing the wives and daughters of free men of color. Noting the intrinsic value of their neighbors of color to their localities, they argued that "many Inhabitants of the sd. Counties who are Free Negroes & Mulattoes and Persons of Propbity [*sic*] & good Demeanor and cheerfully contribute towards the Discharge of every public Duty injoined [*sic*] them by Law." They further commented that "but by reason of being obliged by sd. Act of Assembly to pay Levies on their Wives and Daughters as therein mentioned and greatly Impoverished and many of them rendered unable to support themselves and Families with common Necessaries of Life."[49]

The extra tax liability on free families of color extracted financial resources that they could have used to invest in more land, purchase more supplies, and feed more hungry mouths.[50] The petitioners recognized that the law negatively affected their neighbors of color. They may have considered that their neighbors' poverty could ultimately become their own burden. The financial status of individual families was the collective concern of all people in a particular community. The potential detriment of the 1723 law was not the individual problem of an imagined racial community of people of color on the society's periphery but an attack on friends and neighbors. The line of argumentation presented by the mostly white group of petitioners in 1762 failed to persuade lawmakers to amend the colony's statutes. The petitioners' complaint, however, reveals the importance of personal beliefs in shaping the potency attached to racial categories.

In 1771, residents of Granville County again sought the repeal of the discriminatory aspects of North Carolina's tax code. Unlike the previous generation of petitioners, these men used the rhetoric of the Enlightenment to argue their case versus opposing the 1723 law on the grounds of its impracticability. Seventy-five petitioners, both white and of color, stated that "by the act of assembly concerning Tythables it is among other things enacted that all free negroes & mulato women and all wives of free negroes & mulatoes are Declared Tythables & chargable for Defraying the Public County & Parish Leveys of this province which Your Petitioners Humbly conceive is highly Derogatory of the Rights of Freeborn Subjects." Classifying free people of color as "Freeborn Subjects" suggests that the petitioners recognized that British laws and British rights protected all freeborn colonists regardless of racial categorization. They asked the General Assembly to remedy this miscarriage of privilege by passing an act "exempting such free negroe & mulatoe women and all wives other then slaves of free negroes & mulatoes from being Listed as Tythables & from paying any Public County or Parish Leveys."[51]

The General Assembly failed to respond to this petition as it had in 1762. The body's failure to act highlighted a disjuncture between the political goals of North Carolina lawmakers and the principles and needs of people at the local level. In most situations, local people determined the treatment of both whites and persons of color. They used an equation that took respectability, usefulness, wealth, and gender into consideration when making decisions about how to interact with their neighbors and how to regulate those interactions. The kind of discrimination supported by the law of 1723 challenged their ability to shape their own social order and made racial categorization more than simply a method to uphold slavery but also a burden on their society.

Colonial government mandates weakened the impact of white people's affinity for their neighbors of color. Nevertheless, face-to-face interactions regulated by local people rather than discriminatory laws shaped the daily routines of most free people of color. The courtroom was one place where the opinions of local whites about their free neighbors of color counted most. In the courtroom, all-white juries could and did rule on behalf of their free neighbors of color, sometimes against their white neighbors. In 1739, the General Court charged Joseph Bass, a "mulat[t]o," along with Cambridge, "a slave," with breaking into and stealing from the house of Hugh Allen of Chowan County, a white man. At the November term of court, Allen presented evidence against Bass and Cambridge but failed to persuade the court of their guilt.[52] In a 1758 case, Gabriel Manley, a free person of color, sued Barnaby Goodwin, a white "planter," for ten pounds after Goodwin allegedly assaulted Manley. After several witnesses, all white men, testified in the case, the Bertie County court issued a verdict in favor of Manley.[53] In these courtrooms, jurors used an evaluative process that privileged evidence, reputation, and argument over assumptions about a person's racial categorization. These colonial courts and the white men who administered them sought to uphold the public peace over a strict racial hierarchy.[54]

The essential roles that wealth, gender norms, work, and community dependence played in determining the life outcomes of free persons of color reveal that racial categorization was an important but not the dominant form of social hierarchy in colonial North Carolina. Free status placed persons of color in circumstances that contrasted with the legal limitations imposed on servants and the non-personhood given to slaves. In limited numbers, free persons of color not only had more liberty to make life choices than servants and slaves but dictated orders to such persons.

Scholars have overstated the importance of racial hierarchy in the lives of colonial North Carolinians. In his history of North Carolina, William S. Powell contended that in the colonial period, "Blacks, both slave, and free, were considered to be a separate social group."[55] Ira Berlin argued that in the eighteenth-century Chesapeake, which included North Carolina, "tobacco planters collapsed all black people, free and slave, into one subaltern class, in which color—not nationality, skill, or religion—defined all."[56] In reality, other forms of hierarchy such as gender and wealth sometimes overrode a rigid racial order. North Carolina law, like the laws of many other colonies, erratically interjected racial categorization into the lives of North Carolinians. It failed to place racial categorization solidly above distinctions between free persons and enslaved persons or even beyond the legal differences between servants and slaves.

Through the early national period, wealth, sex, respectability, and other forms of hierarchy would continue to coincide with racial categorization and prevent the implementation of a perfectly rigid racial order in North Carolina. During the American Revolution, whites and free people of color joined together to protest the rule of King George III and the British Parliament. Whatever value they gave to imagined racial differences, both whites and persons of color submerged those beliefs as they fought together in the same regiments as neighbors and allies on the battlefields of Trenton, Charleston, Eutaw Springs, and Guilford Courthouse. When North Carolinians wrote their first state constitution in 1776, they developed qualifications for voting that took account of wealth, gender, and free status. Yet they left out qualifications based on racial categorization.[57]

⚜

CHAPTER 3

Debating Freedom

The Radical War against Free People of Color

During the 1858–59 General Assembly session, Lotte W. Humphrey of Onslow County introduced a proposal titled "A Bill Concerning Free Persons of Color." Although the bill's title was somewhat ambiguous, the bill's contents made the objectives of its supporters clear. Sections 2 through 5 explained the variety of ways localities could remove or enslave a free person of color. Section 8 stated: "That two years shall be allowed, from and after the passage of this act, to all free persons of color who now are in this State, to remove out of the same; and all those who shall be found here after that time, without the permission of the General Assembly, shall be arrested and sold as provided in this act." In order to further his agenda, Humphrey also introduced "A Bill to Permit Free Persons of African Descent to Select Their Own Masters and Become Slaves." Humphrey and his radical supporters hoped to purge North Carolina of approximately thirty thousand of its inhabitants or at least enslave them. Their bills were among the most far-reaching pieces of legislation to ever come before the North Carolina legislature, and Humphrey and his supporters knew it.

After Humphrey's presentation of the bills and the bills' assignment to the Senate Judiciary Committee, a newspaper reported that the colonel "had a doubt that some of its provisions might conflict with the constitution."[1] Yet the radical proslavery proposal caused fierce debate and confusion among North Carolinians. Some North Carolinians were not the least bit concerned with the bills' possible constitutional conflict. Viewing the issues proposed in the bill as black and white, James A. Patton of Asheville wrote to Dr. J. S. T. Baird asking him to support the bills. He explained, "The continued inroads of free negroes from the surrounding counties & states has brought so many upon us that they cannot longer be borne. The two states of society are entirely incompatible. They cannot exist together." He con-

49

cluded that "the one state must yield to the other. Either all must be free or all slave. I am not for one in favor of a Quixotic emancipation. All my convictions of right and of social & political welfare are in favor of African Slavery."[2] Hearing of the plan and likely knowing men who shared Patton's convictions, Haywood Day, a free man of color, did not wait to find out the result of Humphrey's proposals. Day packed his bags, left his family behind, and migrated to Ohio.[3]

If taken at face value, Humphrey's bills and the words of James A. Patton and others like him suggest that North Carolinians had grown to despise free people of color. They appear to have reached the point of trying to bend the state constitution in order to remove free persons of color from society or at least take away their liberty so that racial categorization would be consistent with freedom status. However, this was the viewpoint of the most radical proponents of slavery. When Humphrey's bills reached the Senate Judiciary Committee, the committee chair and his members removed them from further consideration. "After mature, diligent, and earnest deliberation," the chairman and his committee concluded that the second bill's "enactment into a statute would be in violation of the organic law of North Carolina" and recommended that the legislature reject the bill.[4] Even upon the dawn of the Civil War, all North Carolinians had not completely turned their backs on their free neighbors of color or more importantly for some, the constitution that protected those free people of color.

Historians have characterized the time between the Revolution and the Civil War as an era of growing hatred toward free people of color and have argued that by the late antebellum period whites had come to a consensus that free people of color had no place in their society. Whites wanted either to enslave them or to remove them from their midst. Scholars have cited the barrage of laws targeting the liberties of free people of color as a reflection of white southerners' general attitude toward them.[5] Laws passed by the legislature, however, reflect only the position of the side that won the debate in the state capitol, not a consensus or even a major shift in public opinion. Radical proslavery ideologues and lawmakers ultimately failed to remove free people of color from their society. Their failure is a clear reflection of their opponents' success in protecting at least some of the rights of free people of color. Free people of color and their white allies offered strong opposition to legislative prohibitions and successfully held back a total denigration of the rights of free people of color.

Since the eighteenth century, North Carolina's free people of color had adapted to life within a society dependent on slavery and displayed, at best, a limited desire to risk their own freedom to secure the liberty of slaves. Free people of color, however, increasingly became the targets of proslavery ideologues seeking to defend slavery in a nation growing increasingly intolerant of the grip slavery's proponents held on the government. Free people of color represented a major problem for the essentialist thinking of North Carolina's radical proslavery men. The existence of free people of color, in many ways, prevented the creation of a society in which social hierarchy could truly be demarcated solely by racial categorization. This problem, as expressed by people like James A. Patton, appears to be part of the reason the most radical proslavery advocates focused their attention on attempts to limit or even take away the liberty of free persons of color. They were willing to attack the idea of freedom in a mad attempt to align racial categories directly with freedom status. These politicians and ideologues sought to make North Carolina a truly black and white world in which black slavery and white freedom were a reality. Yet they ultimately failed because protecting freedom more generally was of greater importance to North Carolinians than successfully removing the exceptions—free people of color—that prevented a seamless fusion between racial categories and freedom status.

Radical proslavery attacks on the rights of free people of color were part of a larger proslavery political offensive. As Michael F. Holt has argued, southern politicians during the nineteenth century, especially following the U.S. war with Mexico, had become engaged in an increasing radical politics that required politicians to demonstrate with growing intensity their willingness to defend slavery from a variety of threats, both real and imagined. Southern politicians consumed themselves with one-upping their political opponents by proving their ability and readiness to protect slavery.[6] Assaults on the rights of free people of color were a way for politicians to ascertain proslavery credentials. By taking away the rights of free people of color, politicians in North Carolina and other parts of the country could point to their success in curbing the tide against slavery. These politicians framed acts that curtailed the rights of free people of color as ways to prevent free persons of color from influencing the slave population and causing disturbances among them. Yet free people of color were largely pawns in a game of reactive politics.

For radical proslavery men, free people of color, who had little to no impact on their power, were a safe target for direct attack. Slavery's advocates strengthened existing beliefs that free people of color were not equal to whites and linked their inequality with the condition of slaves by stressing the importance of racial categorization over free status.[7] They tried to convince the majority of whites that categorization as "persons of color" created a bond between free people of color and slaves that threatened the freedom of all white people. Their narrative suggested that free people of color and slaves together would ultimately conspire to overthrow the white power structure in the United States, just as free persons of color and enslaved people shattered French authority in Saint Domingue during the Haitian Revolution.

The most radical proslavery ideologues saw all nonslaveholders, including whites, as potential allies to the hundreds of thousands of people held in bondage but understood that the political situation of the time prevented them from controlling all threats to slavery. Attacking nonslaveholding white men in order to protect slavery would have confounded the proslavery agenda and highlighted the exclusivity of slaveholding. In order to solve this conundrum, radical proslavery ideologues sought to convince the majority of whites, who had no direct financial interests in human bondage, that slavery was something they should protect and that the inferior status of people of color helped to uphold their own superior social position.[8]

The growing influence of radical proslavery ideology tainted a society that generally accepted the presence of free people of color. Whites' numerical dominance and collective power within the political and economic systems commonly induced free people of color to cooperate with whites. A number of whites viewed free people of color as their neighbors, business partners, in some cases family members, and most importantly as fellow citizens. Some slaveholders saw free people of color, especially those who owned slaves, as potential allies if slave rebellion ever broke out. Unconvinced by the narrative provided by extremist proslavery ideologues, some whites worked with free people of color to fight radical legislation and maintain the status quo. Through the Civil War period, they provided an effective opposition to the most insidious attacks on the liberties of free people of color. Nevertheless, proslavery radicals' incendiary language and ideas, which they spread through the newspapers and imposed through the law, produced fear and promoted abuse. Although the state's majority curbed the influence of this radical fringe, their aggressive campaign in defense of slavery and for the furthering of white people's social and political ascendancy had real consequences for free people of color. Free people of color had to decide whether to remain in their home state and hope that they along with their white allies could keep the radicals at bay or leave North Carolina. They had to consider what might happen if the radicals were victorious.

The Debate during the Early National Period

North Carolina's proslavery radicals began to push an agenda against free people of color from the nation's founding. Through the early national period, they proposed a variety of legislation that would curb the rights and liberties of the state's free persons of color. The lack of a full-fledged radical proslavery movement along with legislative unwillingness to accept many radical propositions kept the extremists at bay. During the end of the eighteenth-century, radicals pushed only two pieces of legislation through the General Assembly that directly targeted free people of color. Liberal ideas that led to the easing of the state's manumission law influenced the society to a greater degree as numerous former slaves left bondage for freedom. The legislature passed more bills providing liberty to enslaved people than bills curbing the rights of free people of color. By the 1810s, however, proslavery radicals began to gain more influence in the legislature. The 1810s and 1820s reared a different breed of politics. By this period, some radicals had identified free people of color as key targets of the proslavery agenda. They sought to bring North Carolina in line with many of its southern neighbors who had imposed tougher restrictions on free people of color. The defenders of the status quo, however, prevented the radicals from enacting the most detrimental aspects of their agenda. The attempted slave rebellions led by Gabriel in Virginia during 1800 and Denmark Vesey in South Carolina in 1822 failed to provide them with legislative victories. At the end of the 1820s, free persons of color could own property, keep guns, and buy and sell liquor. Most importantly, free men of color still could vote, something that separated North Carolina from the majority of slaveholding states.

Events that took place during the American Revolution set the boundaries for many of the most important debates of the national period. When

North Carolinians adopted their state constitution in 1776, they did not use racial categories to discriminate against free people of color. Instead the constitution made certain guarantees to "freemen," including the right to vote if they paid their taxes, met the twelve-month residency requirement, and were at least twenty-one years old.[9] The constitution, therefore, provided free men of color with the franchise. Over the next six decades, those who supported the broad enfranchisement of men would have to fight to protect the rights of free men of color to the vote. Radical proslavery advocates who argued for a highly stratified society in which racial categorization was the most important determinant of rights struggled to accept that free men of color, some of whom were former slaves, could be their political equals. Well into the nineteenth century, they repeatedly attempted to reorganize the political hierarchy and disfranchise free men of color. Beyond the liberal wording of the state constitution, free people of color, their white allies, and enslaved people seeking liberty won another important concession from North Carolina lawmakers during the Revolutionary period. In 1779, the General Assembly passed an act to protect free people of color and slaves from kidnappers. The law provided that anyone who kidnapped "any free negro or free negroes, or persons of mixed blood" with the "intention to sell or dispose" would face the death penalty.[10]

During the 1780s, proslavery legislators were able to push through important limitations on the rights of free people of color by linking them to potentially insubordinate slaves. The 1787 "act to prevent thefts and robberies by slaves, free negroes and mulattoes" stated "that slaves and free negroes are encouraged to rob or steal from the inhabitants all kinds of produce" and implied that they sold the goods to "masters of trading vessels." This law prohibited masters of vessels from entertaining "slaves and free negroes." In a section of the act which appears to have little to do with the original problem that lawmakers allegedly sought to address, the legislature barred "free negroes and mulattoes" from "entertaining" slaves in their homes at night or during the Sabbath and required a fine for any person found guilty of this crime. The law further stated that any free person of color who could not pay the fine could be hired out to someone willing to pay the penalty. The act's final section required "any free negro or mulatto" interested in intermarrying with "any slave" to obtain permission from the enslaved partner's master. A "free negro or mulatto" who failed to follow the act could face a fine of ten pounds payable to the master. Those unable to pay the fine could become the servants of their enslaved partners' masters for the "term of one year."[11] The extent to which county officials used this act to control free people of color is unclear. The role of this law as a model for future legislations, however, is apparent. This law opened the door for more radical legislation in the next century. An emerging generation of lawmakers now had a precedent to point to when seeking to attack free people of color in the defense of slavery. If lawmakers in 1787 could force free people of color into servitude as punishment for their dealings with slaves, the new generation could do the same for other crimes.

The Haitian Revolution and an assortment of other slave rebellions in the Caribbean and South America were likely the catalysts for the successful passage of additional restrictions on the rights of free people of color in the 1790s. In 1795, the General Assembly sought to impose "certain restrictions of free persons of colour who may hereafter come into the state" in addition to curbing the import of slaves by migrants from "the West-India or Bahama Islands, or the French, Dutch or Spanish settlements on the southern coast of America." Lawmakers required free people of color coming into the state to post bonds of two hundred pounds with local sheriffs as promises of "good behavior." Clearly focused on the potential of rebellion in North Carolina, the 1795 law also called on counties to "make presentment of all such free persons of colour as conduct themselves so as to become dangerous to the peace and good order of the state and county." Additionally, the act required "that when any number of negroes, or other slaves, or free people of colour, shall collect together in arms, and be going about the country, committing thefts and alarming the inhabitants of any county, it shall be the duty of the commanding officer of such county, or Captain . . . to call out a sufficient number to suppress such depredations or insurrections."[12]

The radicals would not have another major legislative victory for nearly two decades after the Haitian Revolution scare. Even the stir caused by Gabriel's failed slave rebellion in Virginia at the turn of the century could not thrust the radicals to victory. Their proposals, however, would create the ideological foundation for likeminded people in the future. In 1804, Durant Hatch, a senator from Jones County, presented "a bill to prevent free negroes and persons of colour from voting for members of the legislature."[13] Durant's bill failed to gain enough support for passage. At the 1809 session, the House of Commons considered a similar bill. This bill, however, specifically targeted emancipated persons and called for the prevention of "slaves, hereafter to be set free by the County Courts" to vote for members of the General Assembly, U.S. Congress, vice president, or president. This bill secured enough support in the House for passage but failed to gain traction in the Senate.[14] These attempts to prevent free men of color from voting reveal an early foundation for the disfranchisement movement in North Carolina.

The record of success for the allies of free people of color was mixed in comparison to the radicals' record. In 1801, the allies of free people of color successfully pushed through the legislature a law defending children of color held as apprentices. To protect apprenticed children from being moved out of their home counties and limit the possibility of their masters selling them as slaves in other jurisdictions, the legislature required masters to post bonds with the county courts in the amount of 250 pounds with the promise that they would not "remove" the children from their home counties.[15] Lawmakers who supported the rights of free people of color were not so successful when they attempted to move a "bill to enable free persons of colour to establish their demands for work and labour done." After the presentation of the bill at the 1809 session of the House of Commons, lawmakers rejected the bill. The bill was likely proposed in reaction to the complaints of free people of color. In 1807, Cato Sabo, "a man of color" and doctor from Wayne County, had petitioned the General Assembly asking for the power to prove his accounts in court.[16] With the failure of the bill, free people of color in business continued to have problems collecting their debts from white customers for years to come. In 1821, Ephraim Hammonds petitioned the legislature "for himself and the other colored inhabitants of the town of Fayetteville" and asked that the body provide them with the ability to testify against their white debtors. His petition failed to move out of committee.[17]

With the outbreak of the War of 1812, the radicals within the General Assembly seized an opportunity to insert their agenda into the law. Up to the War of 1812, free men of color had most of the rights and responsibilities of adult male citizens. Like white men, they could vote for members of the lower house and could also vote for members of the upper house if they met the property qualifications. Free men of color also served in the militias as they had since the colonial era. Like whites, free people of color in many jurisdictions were also protected from the testimony of enslaved people, whom many jurists believed could not be trusted because of the unusual influence masters had over their slaves. A slave could provide important testimony, which could help to determine a trial's outcome, but some North Carolinians recognized that slave masters ultimately decided how their slaves testified in court. Masters' threats of violence could shape slave testimony.

At the outbreak of the War of 1812, militia units around the state mustered both free men of color and white men in the defense against the oncoming British invasion. Regiments from counties with large free populations of color such as Halifax, Hertford, Robeson, and Granville all had free people of color attached to their local units.[18] The General Assembly, however, acted to cancel the enlistments of free people of color as armed militiamen. During the first year of the war, the state legislature passed a law prohibiting militia officers from enlisting "any free Negro or Mulatto" unless recruited as a musician.[19]

The historical record provides little insight into the legislature's motive for passing the law. Free men of color who enlisted in the fight to protect their country, a nation many of their forebears had fought to create just a generation and half before, must have been shocked by the legislature's actions. How could the legislature remove men from action at the same time the nation was mounting a defense against stronger and better equipped British forces? How could a white militiaman be worthier of service than one of color? The legislature's answers to these questions are not explained in the surviving historical record, but their reasoning might have revolved around some political motivation to diminish the equality between white men and men of color. Free people of color could not serve beside white men as equals because some legislators believed they were not equals.

By 1814, the political tide had turned and the radical proslavery agenda was in jeopardy in regard to the militia. While the United States was still at war with Great Britain, Jacob W. Leonard of Brunswick County introduced a bill to repeal the 1812 enlistment restriction on free people of color. The bill received approval in the House and the Senate and became part of a larger militia reform law. Leonard's efforts did not lead up to a return of the prewar status quo. Ultimately, those who supported the enlistment of free people of color had to compromise with the more radical elements within the General Assembly. A compromise law repealed the 1812 act and replaced exclusion with discrimination. Free people of color could serve in the militia but only in segregated columns, separate from white troops.[20]

During the state's attempt to clarify the language of its laws, the developing campaign to mark free people of color as clearly unequal to whites made inroads. Since the colonial era, the law prevented persons of color, both free and enslaved, from testifying against whites in court. Yet the law did not specify whether slaves could testify against free people of color. A Revolutionary War–era law establishing courts in the new state of North Carolina declared that "all Negroes, Indians, Mulattoes, and all Persons of mixed Blood, descended from Negro and Indian Ancestors, to the fourth generation inclusive . . . whether Bond or free, shall be deemed and taken to be incapable in Law to be Witnesses in any Case whatsoever, except against each other."[21] Courts interpreted this law to mean people of color could not testify against whites. However, there was no consensus among jurists as to whether slaves could testify against free people of color. Some courts discriminated between free people of color and slaves and prevented slaves from testifying in the cases of all free persons. Other courts drew no distinctions among the various categories of people of color. The 1821 General Assembly sought to clarify this law's purpose and prevent courts from drawing distinctions between enslaved people and free persons of color. The legislators passed a law declaring that all people of color "whether the person or persons whose evidence is offered, be bond or free, shall be admissible and the witness competent, subject nevertheless to be excluded upon any other grounds of incompetency which may exist."[22]

The 1821 law that made slaves competent witnesses against free people of color was a direct challenge to the long-established position of free people of color as members of a distinct middling category. Legislators lowered the legal status of free people of color by making them equals with slaves in the courtroom. This action blurred the distinction between freedom and enslavement and placed racial categorization above freedom status. Categorization as "colored" was gradually becoming more of a problem for free people of color living in a society that some white men proclaimed was designed and created only for them. Nevertheless, legislators had a long way to go if they intended to make slaves out of free persons of color. Through the 1820s, free people of color maintained numerous privileges, including the right to vote and the right to petition the legislature.

Beyond the halls of the General Assembly, debates over the proper position of free people of color took place at the local level. The submission of legislative petitions by individual citizens served as a key method used by the many sides of the debate over the positions of free people of color in North Carolina. Petitioners both white and of color expressed their opinions about the status of free people of color. Petitions served as a means for members of the public to express their grievances and allowed legislators to receive feedback from their constituents.

Local discussions concerning the status of free people of color in society promoted coalition building between free persons of color and their white allies. These coalitions sought to challenge the developing political campaign against free people of color. The 1821 law allowing slaves to testify against free people of color became the target of several Hertford County citizens. In 1822, fifty-two free men of color petitioned the legislature in protest of the new act. They challenged the contention that slaves were their legal equals and asked the legislature "whether their situation even before the Revolution was not preferable to the one in which their dearest rights are so slight a tenure as the favour of slaves and the will & caprice of their vindictive masters for it cannot escape the notice of your Honorable Body that persons of this description are bound to a blind obedience, and know no Law, but the will of their masters." To strengthen their argument, they also highlighted the participation of several of their number in the American Revolution. The legislature's effort to conflate the status of free people of color with that of slaves appalled these citizens of Hertford County. The petitioners, as free people, valued the distinct separation between their own status and that of slaves. Slaves had an opposing position to free persons of color in a society that traditionally drew a stark line of separation between the rights of the free and limited personhood of slaves. Free people of color fought in the American Revolution in order to progress further up the ladder of freedom, not to fall below the status they had during the colonial days.

An even larger number of white men from Hertford County joined their neighbors of color in protest, submitting their own petition. Among this group of eighty-four white men were many slaveholders. Yet they seemed to have feared the empowering of corrupt slave masters and argued that the new law would produce "the most serious mischief."[23] The General Assembly ultimately ignored these calls to repeal the 1821 law. This joint protest, however, demonstrates that opinions about the proper position of free people of color in society were spread across the spectrums of racial classification and wealth status.

Free people of color resisted attempts to downgrade their position in society, but they were not alone. At least a few whites understood that attacks on the rights on free people of color threatened the political and social system at large. Some free people of color had received their liberty because of their former masters' determination that they deserved the same privileges as free men. This law challenged the right of those former masters to pass on full civil rights to the newly freed people. More importantly, discrimination against free people of color conflicted with many well-to-do whites' sense of respectability and honor. The white men who supported their neighbors' attempts to fight injustice believed that free people of color could fit their ideal of respectability and industry. In the eyes of these men, free people of color were dependable, sober, hardworking citizens, and valued neighbors. Many well-respected whites knew that the same could not be said about a scattering of their white neighbors who violated the values associated with industry, Christianity, and decency. The socially inept carried the scorn of their neighbors and the fear of their often-abused slaves. Yet the new law enhanced their power while demoting more respectable and valuable community members who just happened to be persons of color.

Between 1826 and 1827 radical legislators tested their colleagues' willingness to fall in line with their neighbors in Virginia and South Carolina. These legislators presented a comprehensive act that would force free people of color to register with local governments, prohibit the immigration of free persons of color from other states, and permit counties to control further the lives and labor of poor free people of color. As of 1826, North Carolina trailed behind its neighbors in creating a discriminatory legal environment for free people of color. In 1793, Virginia lawmakers had passed legislation that required "free negroes and mulattoes" to register with their counties and penalized people who employed "free negroes and mulattoes" without certificates. They also enacted a statute forbidding the migration of "free negroes and mulattoes" into the state. South Carolinians crafted and enacted an immigration ban in 1820.[24]

North Carolina's radical lawmakers faced stiff opposition to their proposals. In early 1826, their bill fell to defeat in the state legislature. Not until the early part of the following year could radical legislators claim a partial victory. After purging the registration requirement from the bill, lawmakers in the House ushered a much weaker bill through, and the Senate approved the changes. The new law banned the immigration of "any free negro or mulatto" into North Carolina. Those who failed to abide by the new law could face stiff penalties including a $500 fine or hiring out. The legislation also criminalized the importation of free people of color by other people. In addition, the new law allowed counties to hire out "any free negro or mulatto . . . who is able to labor, shall be found spending his or her time in idleness or dissipation, or who has no regular or honest employment or occupation." The children of such persons could also be bound out.[25]

Although the 1827 statute placed a new burden upon free people of color, it also included specific protections for the persons it might affect. The act required masters and mistresses to provide "any free negro or mulatto" who "maybe held to service under this act" clothing and food, "treat him or her with humanity," and teach that person a trade or employment. Masters or mistresses who failed to abide by the law could be prosecuted. Furthermore, the law granted jury trials to free persons of color accused of illegally immigrating or idling. Local officials could not simply round up free people of color and put them to work or remove them from the county without going through the tedious and often slow process of moving them through the court system.[26]

The 1820s ended with a defeat for radical proslavery advocates in the General Assembly. On November 28, 1829, the Senate Judiciary Committee received a resolution requesting consideration for the passage of a law "to constitute three Justices of the Peace in any county in the state as a competent tribunal to try free negroes and mulattoes for all offences against the state, other than Capital, without the intervention of a jury."[27] Upon receipt of the request, however, the Judiciary Committee ruled that "such a provision of the Law would be unconstitutional" and removed the proposal from further consideration.[28] Unlike neighboring Virginia, proslavery radicals never successfully pushed a bill stripping free people of color of their right to trial by jury through the North Carolina legislature.[29] In Virginia, proslavery radicals used the Nat Turner rebellion to pass legislation stripping away the rights of free people of color by connecting the liberties of free people of color to the exposed weaknesses in the state's management of enslaved people. The reaction to the Turner rebellion within the North Carolina General Assembly was less extreme.

A portion of society believed that all whites should be the legal and social superiors of all other people, free or enslaved, but their belief did not go uncontested. Free people of color and their friends suggested that the

Constitution gave them grounds to protest injustices. By using the right to petition the government, free people of color established that they were citizens with constitutionally protected rights. Some North Carolinians tried and succeeded in making them second-class citizens, but nonetheless free people of color were citizens.

The Debate in the Antebellum Era

By the 1820s, the radicals and their allies within the General Assembly had successfully chipped away at a few of the liberties of free people of color, but radicals had failed to curb some of their most fundamental rights and privileges. By the end of the decade, free men of color continued to vote in significant numbers. They retained the right to own all types of property, including real estate and slaves, and maintained all of their constitutionally guaranteed rights, including the right to bear arms. The politics of the 1830s, however, altered the trajectory, and free people of color would face unprecedented challenges to their rights as citizens. Yet free people of color, their attorneys, and their supporters sought ways to overcome the tide of injustice sweeping across the South. They fought the new status quo in which white people, no matter their class or reputation, would be presumed both socially and legally the betters of all free persons of color. Some of the restrictions placed upon free people of color by the legislature during the early 1830s did not specifically target the rights of free people of color. Instead, they sought to limit the influence of all free persons, whether white or of color, on enslaved people. As historian William W. Freehling explained, "Slaveholders admitted they feared white no less than black dissent."[30]

To enhance the social divides among free people of color, whites, and slaves, lawmakers passed an "act more effectually to prevent intermarriages between free negroes or free persons of colour and white persons and slaves, and for other purposes." This law, passed during the 1830–31 winter session of the General Assembly, strengthened the colonial law that discouraged marriage between whites and persons of color. The act declared a marriage between "any free negro or free person of colour to a white person" unlawful, and all marriages contracted after the law's passage were "null and void." Before the passage of this law, free people of color and whites could still marry, but the threat of fines or social custom strongly discouraged such unions. Like the colonial law, this legislation threatened any minister or magistrate conducting such marriages with fines and imprisonment at the "discretion of the court." The final section of the act declared unlawful "any free negro or free person of colour to intermarry or cohabit and live together as man and wife with any slave." Any "free negro or person of colour" found guilty of breaking this law could face a fine and imprisonment or "whipping not to exceed thirty-nine lashes."[31] This part of the law gave slave masters more control over who interacted with their slaves. Before the passage of this law, a slave master could do little to prohibit a slave from engaging in a relationship with a free person, and even less to keep the free person physically away from an enslaved spouse or lover outside of the bounds of the master's land. After the law's passage, the threat of fines, whippings, and jail time undoubtedly pushed at least a few free persons, both white and of color, to reassess or better conceal their interactions with slaves.

In November of 1830, Governor John Owen provided cover to proslavery radicals by calling attention to an "incendiary publication" circulating in the southern states. He argued that the publication was an attempt to "sow sedition among our slaves." He went on to claim that "some of the free persons of colour in the State, have permitted themselves to be used as agents, for the distribution of seditious publications."[32] The "incendiary publication" that the governor alluded to was David Walker's *Appeal to the Coloured Citizens of the World*. David Walker, a free person of color originally from North Carolina, highlighted the injustices of slavery and the hypocrisy within the American political system.[33] Many slaves and free people of color knew the social and political system was not designed in their favor, but Walker reiterated these beliefs for the public and confirmed masters' suspicions that people of color were not content with their lot.

Discussion of Walker's statement against injustice and slavery permitted proslavery radicals to build coalitions with more moderate proslavery politicians in order to push through their agenda. By passing tough legislation, proslavery politicians of both sorts could report to their constituents that they had defended slavery from outside attacks. Lawmakers took advantage of the moment and passed an act that required fines, imprisonment, or whippings for free people of color convicted of teaching slaves to read or write or providing them with reading materials. Whites faced the same punishments as free people of color except for whipping.[34] The inclusion of potentially harsher punishment for free people of color versus whites convicted of educating slaves played more into the proslavery ideology and scapegoating than serving as a reaction to a real threat.

Radical proslavery lawmakers transformed the most everyday interactions into sites of possible slave conspiracy. A law prohibiting free persons from gaming with slaves targeted free people of color and whites who might potentially threaten slave masters' property rights through their interactions with slaves. Like the literacy law, free people of color potentially faced worse punishment than their white counterparts found guilty of the same crime. All free persons could face fines and imprisonment, but only a "free negro, mulatto or person of mixed blood" could receive whipping as punishment.[35] The threat of extra-aggressive punishment for free people of color reflects some lawmakers' belief in white superiority. In theory, this law protected the property rights of masters and sought to prevent slaves from gambling away their masters' property, which included any property or money held by slaves. The state did not recognize the property ownership of enslaved people although many masters allowed slaves to keep personal property.

During the 1830–31 session, proslavery radicals also pushed two acts through the legislature tightening restrictions on the movements of free persons of color. The new legislation constricted the movements of free people of color who were North Carolina residents but traveled outside of the state. The new law specified that "any free negro or person of colour" who left the state and was "absent for the space of ninety days or more" could not return to North Carolina.[36] Free persons of color who traveled for business such as merchants and sailors now faced problems returning home if they left for more than ninety days. Most free people of color did not travel out of the state for such long periods, but the passage of this law created another limitation on free people of color that further distinguished their status from that of whites.

The second of the restrictive laws sought to prevent nonresident free people of color from interacting with persons of color inside the state. The law sought to thwart communication between free persons of color working on incoming ships and resident slaves and free people of color. It imposed a serious fine of $500 on ship captains who allowed free people of color aboard their ships to communicate by writing or spoken words with resident people of color. This act prescribed harsh punishment for any free person of color or enslaved person engaging in the prohibited conversations. A free person of color found guilty of this crime would face "thirty nine lashes on his or her bare back." The legislation also required free persons of color to remain on board their ships for at least thirty days while docked. Those brought on shore before thirty days while their ships were anchored were to be placed in jail at their own expense until their ship left. If a free person of color remained in North Carolina after the ship departed, that person could also face up to thirty-nine lashes.[37]

Both laws directly affecting free people of color were indeed tied to legislators' attempts to use free people of color as scapegoats for the spread of antislavery sentiments in the nation. Members of the General Assembly certainly knew that free people of color were not the sole agents of the country's developing antislavery movement. They may have tried to convince themselves or at least some members of the general public that free people of color were a menace to society, but facts on the ground rarely supported this position. Lawmakers' attacks on free people of color from outside the state were parts of a developing radical proslavery tactic that tried to play on white southerners' fear and dislike of outsiders and outside influence in their local politics.[38]

At the 1830–31 General Assembly session, lawmakers not only targeted free people of color directly but also attempted to clamp down on the growth of their population. During the session, they modified the manumission regulations to make emancipations more difficult by requiring $1,000 bond per person emancipated. Additionally, lawmakers attempted to prevent recently emancipated people from remaining in the state by demanding their removal from North Carolina upon their emancipation.[39] The political and social environment pushed lawmakers to make emancipations more difficult but the idea of restricting manumissions was not new. North Carolina had restricted manumissions in the colonial period. Neighboring state Virginia had required the removal of former slaves upon manumission in 1806.[40] Years before the passage of the 1830–31 restrictions on emancipation, radical lawmakers had attempted to prohibit manumissions. At the 1828–29 General Assembly session, James Graham of Rutherford County had proposed a "bill to prevent the emancipation of slaves" before the House of Commons.[41]

Through many of their acts, members of the 1830–31 General Assembly characterized free people of color as potential vagrants and leaders of slave rebellion. Yet individuals within the legislative body understood that at least some free persons of color did not fit this negative portrayal. In December of 1830, the legislature passed a bill to make an exception to the 1827 law preventing free people of color from moving into North Carolina, a law which this same legislature would reinforce with the previously mentioned acts regarding the entrance of free people of color into the state. At the town of Milton, fifty-nine white men from Caswell County signed a petition asking the legislature to allow Thomas Day, a free person of color and local cabinetmaker, to bring his wife, Aquilla Wilson Day, into North Carolina from neighboring Halifax County, Virginia. The General Assembly responded favorably to this request and passed a special bill allowing Aquilla Day to reside in North Carolina.[42]

Thomas Day's reputation and position undoubtedly swayed his supporters and the General Assembly to act in his favor. Day was a regionally renowned master craftsman and came from a slave-owning family. In a note attached to the petition, Romulus M. Saunders, Milton native and former speaker of the state house, wrote, "I have known Thomas Day . . . for several years past and I am free to say that I consider him a free man of color of very fair character—an excellent mechanic, industrious, honest and sober in his habits—and in the event of any disturbance amongst the Blacks, I should rely with confidence upon a disclosure from him as he is the owner of slaves as well as of real estate."[43]

According to his supporters, Day's reputation and financial success were grounds to exempt Aquilla Day from the law. By passing the bill in favor of the Days, legislators publicly admitted that their own prescriptions could be unjust in at least certain special cases, such as those of well-to-do free people of color. Members of the legislature cast a wide net of suspicion upon all free persons of color. Yet they conceded that the interests of free people of color in the antislavery cause varied among individuals. Legislators knew that the sentiments of all free people of color could not easily fall into one simple set of beliefs. However, they did not recognize that as the General Assembly continued to target free people of color with further restrictions, oppression slowly pushed free people of color into circumstances that bred common cause with antislavery advocates. Slavery was always an affliction for the enslaved person seeking freedom, but slowly efforts to secure slavery were beginning to affect all Americans, especially the South's free people of color.

Legislative attacks on free people of color advanced into the 1831–32 session of the General Assembly as radical proslavery ideologues continued to link free people of color to abolitionism and slave rebellion. The *Tarborough Free Press* reported, "An incendiary paper, 'The Liberator,' is circulated openly among the free blacks of this city; and if you will search, it is very probable you will find it among the slaves of your county."[44] Other newspapers reprinted the article in an attempt to further fan the hysteria. The birth of William Lloyd Garrison's *Liberator*, an abolitionist weekly, on the first day of 1831 and the rebellion of Nat Turner in Virginia later that year motivated the General Assembly to respond through legislative action. Among the laws passed during the 1831–32 session was "An act pointing out the mode whereby the militia of this State shall hereafter be called into service in cases of insurrection or invasion, and outlawed runaway negroes."[45] Legislators passed this law as an assurance that if a slave insurrection occurred like the one led by Turner in neighboring Virginia, North Carolina would be prepared to quell it swiftly. Lawmakers included free people of color in the language of the law alongside slaves as possible agents of insurrection although most of them, apprentices being the exception, had no bondage to rebel against. A few free people of color had slaves who indeed may have risen against them and slaughtered them in their beds as Turner and his accomplices did to members of the slaveholding class of Southampton County.

Fear of a conspiracy between slaves and free people of color created the environment for the General Assembly also to pass "an act for the better regulation of the conduct of negroes, slaves and free persons of color." This law placed severe restrictions on slaves whose masters allowed them to move about freely. The act also declared that "it shall not be lawful under any pretence for any free negro, slave or free person of color to preach or exhort in public, or in any manner to officiate as a preacher or teacher in any prayer meeting or other association for worship where slaves of different families are collected together."[46] This law, like previous acts, implied that free people of color were among the primary agents of rebellion. According to the radical proslavery ideology of the 1830s, free people of color were more likely than whites to promote rebellion among the slaves.

During the 1831–32 session, lawmakers not only wanted to limit the interactions of free people of color with slaves but convinced themselves that some free persons of color should have a legal condition very similar to enslavement. "An act to provide for the collection of fines imposed upon free negroes or free persons of colour" allowed sheriffs to hire out free people of color found guilty of crimes but could not afford to pay their assessed fines. The poorest of free people of color were now subject to peonage in which a person would pay the fine on the convict's behalf, and in exchange, the law required the convict to serve that person for up to five years. The new act instructed that the rules that applied to apprenticeships would guide the relationship between masters and their convict servants.[47] The law did not push free people of color into slavery, as most would find ways to pay their fines; however, poor free people of color could now end up in a situation only one step above it.

The Nat Turner rebellion created an important opportunity for radicals to push through legislation to tamp down on the liberties of free people of color. The fears stoked by the rebellion, however, did not provide radicals with cover to implement all of their ideas. Representative Joseph Robertson presented a bill "to prevent slaves and free persons of color from commanding boats on [the] Roanonke river" before the legislature. Following the reading of the bill, the House "postponed" the bill indefinitely, virtually ending its prospects of passage.[48] A petition introduced by Senator Richard D. Spaight on behalf of some of his New Bern constituents failed to gain traction in the 1831–32 session. The petitioners sought to convince the General Assembly that "free negroes" should not have the right to vote. They used a convoluted argument about the origins of the state constitution to suggest that "free negroes" should not have the franchise but also cited the Nat Turner rebellion to support their point. Their memorial stated, "A very large portion of our population are slaves, and recent occurrences must deeply impress on your Honorable Body the vital necessity of keeping them in a state of discipline and subordination." The petitioners continued, "Your memorialists believe they hazard nothing in saying that permitting free negroes to vote at elections contributes to excite & cherish the spirit of discontent and disorder among the slaves."[49] The petition highlighted the way proslavery radicals used the Nat Turner rebellion as an opportunity to attack free people of color and further linked the liberties of free people of color with the agitation of the enslaved population. Most of the rationale presented in the petition had nothing to with the Turner rebellion directly. The rebellion simply became another justification for lawmakers to support the radical proslavery agenda. If lawmakers were not convinced by the argument that people of color were inherently unequal, a point repeated throughout the petition, the Turner rebellion could push them toward the petitioners' cause. Although the ideas expressed in this petition failed to move the General Assembly, they would appear again in future debates concerning free people of color and the franchise.

The laws of the early 1830s did not escape public scrutiny after their passage, and some whites were unsupportive of the legislature's most recent actions. North Carolinians of this era like those of the previous decades expressed their displeasure in the form of petitions. In 1831, 114 residents of Wilmington, the state's most important port, petitioned the legislature to amend the quarantine act of 1830, which required free people of color to remain on board ships docked at North Carolina ports for at least thirty days. The petitioners argued, "This act, which is ostensibly an act for the regulation of the ingress of free persons of colour into the State—To effect which object it compels vessels having such persons of colour on board to ride at quarantine for thirty days previously to a prohibition of entry & which your petitioners think more injurious to the commercial and mercantile interests of our Town than the polluting intercourse of the blacks possibly could be to its political safety." These petitioners were more concerned with economic stability and profits than with imagined threats from free people of color. The Senate finance committee took up the Wilmington residents' grievances, but concluded that a final decision was outside of their power to determine.[50]

The Quakers, as adamant supporters of the rights of free people of color, expressed their disgust with legislators and condemned them for interfering with the teaching of God's word. In November 1834, the Society of Friends meeting at New Garden in Guilford County petitioned for the repeal of several laws passed earlier in the decade. They asked the General Assembly to rescind the law banning the literary instruction of slaves and the act prohibiting people of color, bond or free, from public preaching and exhorting. The Quakers explained: "We consider these laws unrighteous, offensive to God and contrary to the spirit and principles of the Christian Religion; and your Memorialists believe, if not repealed, will increase the difficulties and danger they were intended to prevent." The Quakers' warning seems to suggest that divine providence could come in the form of slave rebellion. They argued that God would seek retribution upon those who prevented others from reading and preaching his word. The society explained that the legislators had the choice to be on the side of either good or evil. They ended their petition with the following: "And may you be influenced by that wisdom which is from above, which is profitable to direct, and which, the Apostle says, 'is first pure, then peaceable, gentle and easy to be entreated, full of mercy and good fruits.' That you may be enabled to enact righteous laws, the operation and execution of which may be a terror to evil-doers, an encouragement to those that do well, and to the praise of God."[51] These words of inspiration fell on deaf ears in the General Assembly. The legislators ultimately failed to respond to the request of the Society of Friends, yet the Quakers' prediction would come true. Slaves, free people of color, and their allies would rise against oppression in the bloodiest carnage nineteenth-century Americans would ever see.

Around the same time that the Quakers submitted their objections, some North Carolinians, especially those in the western counties, began a serious conversation about amending the state constitution. Since the establishment of North Carolina as a colony, the eastern counties had dominated internal politics and by the 1830s were over-represented in the General Assembly. The east continued to dominate state politics because representation was apportioned equally among the counties instead of by population. In 1835, North Carolinians voted by a close margin to hold a convention to amend the constitution in order to remedy this problem and take up other issues of constitutional concern. The suffrage of free men of color was one of the issues brought up at the constitutional convention.[52]

Members of the constitutional convention generally divided themselves between two positions, allowing free men of color to retain the vote or taking away their ballot. By 1835, North Carolina was the only state in the South that still allowed free people of color to vote. Tennessee had disfranchised free people of color one year earlier. North Carolina's neighbors to the north and south, Virginia and South Carolina, had long prohibited free people of color from voting. Some members of the convention thought that North Carolina should follow the example of its fellow southern states. James W. Bryan of Carteret County told the convention, "I have ever entertained the opinion that they had no right to vote, and must confess, that I have heard no argument that convinces me of the incorrectness of that opinion. North Carolina is the only Southern State in the Union that has permitted them to enjoy this privilege; and I venture to assert, that the welfare and prosperity of those States that have excluded them, have been very materially advanced, by denying to them the elective franchise." Appealing to subscribers of white supremacy, he continued, "As I previously remarked, this is a nation of white people—its offices, honors, dignities and privileges, are alone open to, and to be enjoyed by, white people. I am for no amalgamation of colors."[53] Politicians like Bryan sought to align racial categorization with political status. He promoted a society in which all people of color, regardless of freedom status, would be a legal underclass below all whites.[54]

Nathaniel Macon of Warren County offered an account of the role of people of color in North Carolina that largely ignored historical reality in order to support the cause of disfranchisement. Macon presented the blatantly false argument that "free negroes" under British rule were not "subjects" but "denizens." He further contended, "They have been employed to fight, but were never made citizens—they made no part of the political family."[55] This statement ignored the role of free people of color in organized protests against British rule and decades of voting since independence.

Jesse Speight of Greene County declared that "free negroes are not recognized in the Constitution, and are not therefore entitled to vote."[56] Speight was one of the most radical opponents of free people of color in the 1820s and 1830s. In 1825, he presented a bill before the General Assembly "to prevent emancipating societies in the State."[57] He sponsored the 1827 bill prohibiting the migration of free persons of color into the state.[58] Speight openly spoke out against free people of color because he knew they did not support him politically. After the constitutional convention, Speight suggested, "Deduct the free negro votes, and it was no contest at all. It is known that nearly all of them voted against me."[59] Speight's opposition to the voting rights for free men of color was not simply about white supremacy but also about his own ability to maintain power.

Several generations of voting by free men of color convinced others that they should retain the right to vote. Supporters pointed to acts of citizenship, such as the payment of taxes, which suggested free men of color should continue to vote like other citizens. Weldon Edwards of Warren County asked the convention, "An article in the Bill of Rights says, 'that the people of this State ought not to be taxed or made subject to the payment of any impost or duty, without the consent of themselves or their Representatives in General Assembly, freely given.' If this article bears upon our colored freemen equality with the whites, it would appear wrong, while we continue to tax them, to deny them a vote for members of Assembly. . . . Ought they not to be represented in the Legislature also?"[60] Comments made by other members of the convention are like those of either the proslavery radicals or Edwards. Most delegates either thought that the founders designed the franchise and government in general for the sole benefit of white men or that the founders did not intend to privilege white men over free persons of color because they never provided a limitation on voting based on racial categorization.

The status quo lost the debate at the convention, and the delegates voted to disenfranchise free men of color by a narrow margin of 66 to 61. The final amendment read, "No free Negro, free mulatto, or free person of mixed blood descended from negro ancestors to the fourth generation inclusive (though one ancestor of each generation may have been a white person) shall vote for members of the Senate or House of Commons."[61] North Carolinians supported amending the state Constitution by only 27,550 to 21,694.[62] The vote totals demonstrate that North Carolina struggled to define the proper place for free persons of color in society. Even though the South as a region had generally turned against allowing free people of color to live as political equals to whites, some North Carolinians still resisted changes that made no sense to them. These North Carolinians understood that neither the national constitution nor their state constitution explicitly discriminated against free people of color. Those who voted to continue the status quo interpreted the words of the founders literally. They understood that in many ways free people of color were no different from themselves. Whites and free people of color alike fought for American independence, built the economy of the state, and through their taxes supported their local governments' operations.

After the passage of the disfranchisement amendment, those opposed to the actions of the convention expressed concern about the shift that forcefully placed more importance on racial categorization than on wealth and respectability. The *Fayetteville Observer* reported, "There is, so far as we can learn, a general feeling of regret in this community at the total disfranchisement of the free coloured people. There are a few, some eight or ten, of that class, in Fayetteville, who have every qualification of intelligence, respectability, usefulness, and property, to entitle them, fairly, to the exercise of this high privilege."[63] Yet those who supported the disenfranchisement of free people of color set an important new precedent. Now that free people of color could no longer vote, a larger question lingered on the state: Are free people of color citizens at all? Many members of the convention argued that free people of color were not citizens and therefore had no guarantee to the rights of citizenship. The question of citizenship would shape the debate over the position of free people of color into the Civil War era.[64]

Although lawmakers had successfully stripped free people of color of some of their most important rights, proslavery radicals continued their diatribes against them and convinced their colleagues to enact further restrictions. By the 1840s, radical proslavery propagandists and politicians had successfully attached free people of color to the abolitionist cause. In January 1841, the legislature passed a law requiring a license for "any free Negro, Mulatto, or free Person of Colour, [who] shall wear or carry about his or her person, or keep in his or her house, any Shot gun, Musket, Rifle, Pistol, Sword, Dagger or Bowie knife." According to the new legislation, any of these persons carrying the named weapons without license was guilty of a misdemeanor.[65] Lawmakers designed this legislation under the assumption that free people of color were not citizens of the state or nation. Americans during this time generally interpreted broadly the Bill of Rights' guarantee to bear arms. Now the legislature had passed a law that appeared to supersede the national Constitution by challenging one of its principal amendments. Yes, the law still allowed free people of color to bear arms, but now the extension of that privilege was in the hands of local courts instead of the individuals wanting to exercise the right to own weapons.

The legislature's action to restrict free people of color's access to weapons was at least partially in direct response to petitions submitted to the General Assembly over the previous decade, which tied free people of color to potentially rebellious slaves. In 1835, a group of thirty-nine white men from Craven County petitioned the legislature to require free people of color to obtain licenses to carry guns and ammunition. This group cited the possibility that the free persons of color might "distribute guns and ammunition among the slaves for [the] purpose of rebellion and insurrection." The General Assembly apparently made note of this concern but took no direct action at the time.[66] However, the attitude of lawmakers had changed by the 1840s when fifty white citizens of Halifax County requested that the assembly "prohibit Free Negroes and molatoes from carrying or using fire arms under any circumstance what ever."[67] The assembly did not follow this extreme prescription to the growing concern but instead chose to follow

the model supplied by the petitioners of 1835. Members of the General Assembly were likely more comfortable with the plan of the 1835 petitioners
because it still allowed them to privilege favored free people of color in
their communities and also did not challenge the Constitution in the same
way as a complete ban. Legislators could argue that free people of color still
fundamentally had the right to bear arms, but now they simply needed to
apply for a license in the interests of the common good. Compared to free
people of color in states such as Maryland and Virginia, where people of
that status lost their right to bear arms, free people of color in North Carolina still enjoyed relative legal flexibility.[68]

Continuing to use the rationale that free people of color were a menace
to society, in 1845, the legislature gave whites control over the production
of spirits. A group of thirty-six white men from Robeson County had petitioned the legislature in 1840 requesting that the General Assembly take
away the right of the "free colored population" to sell spirits.[69] The request
made no headway until 1845, when a law banning free people of color from
selling liquor passed. The new act granted a monopoly to white liquor producers.[70] Among the interests lobbying for the law was Sion Alford, who
appears in the 1850 census as a Gin Maker.[71] The court records of most counties demonstrate that drunkenness was common among all segments of the
North Carolina population, so the legislature's actions were not a serious
attempt to curtail alcohol abuse. Furthermore, the law did not keep free
people of color from consuming liquor; they simply could no longer sell it.

Beyond using the law to place restrictions on free people of color, the
General Assembly also worked to buttress social divisions between whites
and persons of color. In 1839, legislators passed a bill establishing common
schools for white children. Recognizing that it would be unfair to tax free
people of color for the support of these schools or hoping to prevent free
people of color from arguing that they had a right to attend these schools,
the legislature passed a law to relieve free people of color from any taxation
used to support the common schools in 1843. In 1845, the General Assembly
amended the 1830 law that prohibited marriages between various combination of whites, free people of color, and slaves. The legislature passed a
new act allowing free people of color to marry slaves with the consent of
the slaves' masters.

These laws furthered the importance of racial categories in North Carolina society. The common schools amendment defined public schools as

institutions established for the advantage of white children. Free people of color had no claim to these schools if the legislature did not require them to support public education through their tax dollars. This amendment helped lawmakers to avoid the taxation without representation arguments presented by the proponents of free people of color during the debates of 1835. The marriage law amendment similarly solidified divisions based on racial categorization by allowing free people of color and slaves to marry while prohibiting all marriages between whites and persons of color, even if both parties were legally free.

During the 1850s, the legislature continued to use the law as a tool to curb the liberties of free people of color. Driven by arguments that free people of color might help slaves obtain ardent spirits, the 1859 legislature strengthened the 1845 restriction on the sale of spirits. For fourteen years, the law had forbidden free people of color from selling liquor; now the legislature prohibited anyone from selling liquor to free persons of color. The law stated, "That no person shall sell, or deliver to, or buy for, or be instrumental, either directly or indirectly, in procuring for any free person of color . . . any spirituous liquors, or liquor of which alcohol is an ingredient."[72] This law failed to stop free people of color from obtaining alcoholic beverages, simply forcing the trade underground. The argument for this law was probably the least sound of all the laws passed discriminating against free people of color. In 1850, a large contingent of white men from Washington County argued for the ban in order "to prevent the sale of spirituous liquors to slaves." They claimed that "free negroes" had become the "tools" of slaves trying to obtain spirits. The supporters of the liquor ban never contended that free people of color had become the tools of white liquor dealers, the only people who could legally sell liquor in the state at this time, nor did they acknowledge that whites had equal if not more access to slaves and were therefore the most likely parties to dispense spirits to enslaved people.[73]

As with much of the General Assembly's agenda targeting free people of color, the liquor ban was not a reflection of consensus among North Carolinians but simply a victory for one side of a larger debate. In 1852, when the legislature had considered a bill similar to the one that eventually passed in 1859, fifty-five white men in Hertford County requested an exemption from the ban for their county. The petitioners gave no reasoning for their request, but the size of Hertford County's free population of color probably influenced their proposal.[74] By 1860, approximately one thousand free people of color resided in Hertford County, giving the county one of the largest free populations of color in the state. In the county, slaves and free people of color collectively outnumbered whites by a sizable margin.[75] Liquor distributors only could sell their merchandise to a minority of the county's residents even without the ban, so implementation of the law would further diminish the number of potential buyers. Distributors of ardent spirits in other parts of the state saw this potential problem become a reality after 1859. The 1859 liquor ban especially burdened sellers in the east, where persons of color often made up majorities. In these cases, restrictions on the rights of free people of color were not just bad for them, but bad for business in general.

Members of the General Assembly advocated for some of the most radical ideas concerning free people of color during the 1850s. Yet the proslavery radicals should not be viewed as complete victors in the legislative battles over the place of free persons of color in North Carolina. The radicals won many important victories with real consequences for free people of color. The most ardent defenders of slavery, however, failed more times than they won. During the 1850s, the General Assembly rejected much of the radical agenda concerning free people of color. A host of bills presented at the 1850–51 General Assembly session met defeat. William H. Tripp, a Beaufort County Whig, proposed a bill "to prevent free persons of color from owning or carrying fire arms" before the House. His fellow Beaufort County Whig representative Jesse Stubbs presented a petition calling for an act to tax "colored mechanics" and a levy on "free negroes" to support their removal to Liberia. Neither idea became law during the session. C. H. Wiley of Guilford County asked the House's Committee on Negro Slavery to look into "the expediency and cost of transporting the free negro population" to Vermont.[76] Wiley's proposition may have appeared moderate in comparison to calls to remove free people of color to Liberia, but it too failed to gain traction. Even at the session of 1858–59, the radicals failed to execute their full agenda. As noted at the beginning of the chapter, Lotte W. Humphrey's attempt to legislate the enslavement of free people of color, arguably the most radical proposal of the period, died in committee. A petition from fifty-eight residents of Humphrey's district called for the removal of "free negroes" and described them as "a growing evil." The petition did not help Humphrey's cause. The fact that nearly 10 percent of the signatories carried the Humphrey surname highlighted the intertwined relationship between

Humphrey's cause and the alleged voice of the Onslow County citizens.[77]

Although collectively less moderate than their predecessors, lawmakers of the 1850s did not legislate solely against the interests of free people of color. On a few occasions the legislature made special laws in favor of free people of color. Like previous legislatures, members of the General Assembly granted the manumission of several slaves and then allowed those people to continue to reside in North Carolina without prosecution. During the 1856–57 legislative session, lawmakers also voted to allow a small group of free people of color from Virginia to settle temporarily in Northampton County. Neighbors of the families of Anthony Copeland, Joshua Small, and Warren Boon, all free persons of color, asked the legislature to permit their immigrant neighbors to remain in the county. The petitioners stated that members of these families were "industrious, honest and law abiding people." They showed particular discomfort in losing the skills of Anthony Copeland from the neighborhood as he was "a Brick Mason by trade and a great convenience to the neighborhood." The legislature granted the petitioners' request over a counter petition from another group of Northampton County citizens who argued that the migrants from Virginia were "no better than the generality of that class of people."[78] The Northampton County immigration debate reveals that in the late 1850s North Carolinians still had not come to consensus on the proper place of free people of color in their society. Even with all the laws passed against the rights of free persons of color, some North Carolinians continued to support the presence of free people of color in the state. For every person who feared that free people of color might aid potentially rebellious slaves, there was another person directly benefiting from the skills, business, and neighborly support of a free person of color.

Consequences of the Debate

While lawmakers succeeded in seriously diminishing the legal entitlements of free people of color during the antebellum era, many of their acts continued to be debated in public forums several years after passage. County officials often chose to enforce many of the antebellum-era laws selectively. The immigration law and the law banning marriage or cohabitation between free people of color and slaves were among the laws most selectively and irregularly enforced by local officials. Free people of color sometimes fought those discriminatory laws that officials chose to enforce. Several cases involving free people of color accused of breaking these laws appeared in front of the North Carolina Supreme Court. Lawyers and defendants came up with several crafty explanations and appeals to try to circumvent or directly challenge discriminatory legislation.

The immigration ban of 1827 and the strengthened version of the law issued four years later may have been the most irregularly enforced of the laws targeting free people of color. Since the colonial era, people of all backgrounds living on the lines with Virginia and South Carolina regularly crossed their borders to conduct business, visit family, start new lives, and find marriage partners. The previously mentioned cases of Thomas Day and Aquilla Wilson Day and the immigrants to Northampton County are just a few examples of free people of color moving across the state border. Unlike these individuals, most free people of color who traveled across the border to settle in North Carolina never requested permission from state officials. Movement across the border apparently was so commonplace that county officials generally ignored it, and even selective enforcement does not appear to have become widespread until the 1840s and 1850s. In 1844, the Gates County court attempted to institute a mass round-up of illegal immigrants from Virginia. The court introduced before a grand jury the cases of at least fifteen free people of color that illegally entered the state. Gates County officials seemingly were not serious about removing these persons as many of them still lived in the county six years later during the enumeration of the 1850 census.[79]

Irregular enforcement and prosecution also curbed the influence of the 1830–31 law banning marriage or cohabitation between free people of color and slaves. Similar to the cases of enforcement of the immigration law, local officials usually prosecuted this law through random round-ups. At the spring 1844 term of Caswell County court, officials decided for the first and only time to round up free people of color to prosecute them for living as man and wife with slaves. The court called in twelve men and women to face charges under the law.[80] The court action evidently had some purpose outside a desire to enforce the law. Maybe the justices of the peace wanted to send a signal to free people of color and slaves in an attempt to prevent further relationships from developing. Perhaps these court orders responded to outcries from the public over the general lack of enforcement of the law. Officials most likely only became concerned with the marital activities of slaves and free people of color when neighbors of the couples or masters of the enslaved partners expressed concern.

For some politicians, the place of free people of color was settled, but many free people of color, even into the late 1850s, still believed that they were citizens with rights that white men had to respect. They were unwilling to comply with the increasingly unreasonable and politically motivated demands of the Slave Power. North Carolina's free people of color led the most important opposition to the antebellum actions of the legislature. Using the courts as their tool, free people of color and their attorneys mounted well-argued attacks against the laws, often citing conflicts with the federal Constitution.

Free people of color used one of the legal rights that they still retained, the right to trial by jury, to show that the public debates over their rights remained unsettled. In 1837, the North Carolina Supreme Court heard the case of Charles Oxendine, a free person of color, charged almost two years earlier with assault and battery. At the fall 1835 term of court in Robeson County, justices ordered Oxendine to appear in court to face charges for allegedly assaulting another free man of color, Alfred Lowry. The sheriff could not locate Oxendine, and even a year later, he was nowhere to be found. During the spring of 1837, Oxendine turned up to face justice. Presented to a jury of white men, Oxendine pled guilty, and the court required him to pay the significant fine of $15. Oxendine explained to the court that he was unable to pay the substantial fine, so the court offered an alternative punishment. Based on Oxendine's categorization as a "free negro," the court decided to implement the 1831 act allowing sheriffs to hire out free persons of color unable to pay their fines. Oxendine and his lawyers decided not to accept this punishment and appealed to the state Supreme Court on the grounds that "the Act of Assembly of 1831 authorizing the hiring of free persons of color to pay the fines imposed on them is unconstitutional and void." The court granted Oxendine's appeal and the local court passed the case to the state's most esteemed jurors. In a somewhat convoluted decision written by Justice William Gaston, the state Supreme Court ruled that because Oxendine pled guilty instead of being found guilty, the county court "erred" and could not apply the law of 1831 to Oxendine's case. Thus, the court avoided ruling on the law's constitutionality, but another case would force the court to make a decision.[81]

Less than a year after Oxendine appeared in front of the high court,

William Manuel, another free man of color, continued the fight against the 1831 law. At the spring 1838 term of Superior Court in Sampson County, a jury found Manuel guilty of assaulting John Wadkins and ordered the defendant to pay a $20 fine. Like Oxendine, Manuel was unable to pay the hefty penalty. The Sampson County court followed the Robeson County precedent and ordered the sheriff to hire out Manuel. Manuel's lawyers took up the argument of the Oxendine team and sought a reversal of Manuel's sentence based on the unconstitutionality of the 1831 act. In front of the state Supreme Court, Manuel's lawyers argued that hiring out free people of color to pay their fines constituted cruel and unusual punishment and violated the laws protecting insolvent debtors from imprisonment for debts. The state offered the court the counterargument that free people of color were not citizens and that therefore the laws about cruel and unusual punishment and insolvent debtors did not apply to them. In its decision, the Supreme Court disregarded the arguments of the state, which made its case based on the recent decision to disenfranchise free people of color and the contention that free people of color had no part in the foundation of the state government during the Revolution. The court offered the most obvious counterargument and listed all of the numerous other inhabitants of the state, including women, minors, and landless men, who in some form also fit the prosecution's definition of noncitizens. This clarification could be celebrated as a small victory for free people of color, but the overall decision was not so favorable.

In a decision written by Justice William Gaston, the Supreme Court ruled that the law of 1831 was constitutional and allowed the sheriff of Sampson County to hire out Manuel. Free people of color indeed could be hired out for failure to pay fines, and the court records of many counties demonstrate that a few, but nowhere near a majority, of convicted free people of color became the victims of this decision. The Manuel case, however, was just the beginning of resistance by free people of color. While the defense's arguments in the Manuel case failed, free people of color persisted in the battle against discrimination, and for the next two decades, the Supreme Court would continue to hear their voices.[82]

Using a constitutional justification, free people of color and their attorneys challenged the law requiring free people of color to obtain licenses to carry weapons in the Supreme Court. In 1844, the Supreme Court heard the case of Elijah Newsom, a free person of color from Cumberland County.

In the summer of 1843, the Cumberland County court formally charged Newsom with carrying a shotgun without obtaining a license to carry the gun within the last year. In April of the following year, Newsom finally appeared in court where a jury found him guilty. Newsom and his defense appealed the decision to the Superior Court, which concurred with the original guilty decision. Unwilling to accept this judgment, the Newsom team asked the Supreme Court to consider the case. In front of the Supreme Court, Newsom's defense argued that the law of 1841 requiring free people of color to acquire licenses to carry weapons was unconstitutional because it conflicted with the Second Amendment of the U.S. Constitution and North Carolina's Bill of Rights.

In an opinion written by Justice Frederick Nash, the court responded to this line of argumentation by stating: "The constitution of the United States was ordained & established by the people of the United States for their own government & not for that of the different States—the limitations of power contained in it & expressed in general term are necessarily confined to the General government & not for that of the different states." The court further denied that the weapons law conflicted with the state Bill of Rights. The Supreme Court also decided to use this opportunity to further clarify the position of free people of color in North Carolina. The court ruled: "We must therefore regard it as a principle settled by the highest authority, the organic Law of the country, that the free people of colour are not to be considered as citizens, in the largest sense of the term, or if they are, they occupy such a position in society as justifies the Legislature in adopting a course of policy in its acts peculiar to them."[83] Basing its decision on this logic, the court found in favor of the state. Free people of color could no longer call upon the federal Constitution in order to protect themselves from the tyranny of the state. The Newsom decision affirmed the position of free people of color as a legal middling group in the state, who were free, yet subjected to handicaps which free whites could avoid. For the next two decades, free people of color would have to deal with the implications of this decision. Throughout the period, local courts frequently prosecuted free people of color for carrying weapons without licenses. Yet free people of color continued to resist.

After the Newsom decision, free people of color and their attorneys changed their tactics. The Supreme Court heard several cases in which free people of color challenged guilty verdicts on the grounds that they were not free people of color at all or that their amount of Indian or Negro "blood" did not meet the required amount in order to classify them as people of mixed blood or free persons of color. Couples challenged verdicts based on the law forbidding marriage between free people of color and whites on these grounds but failed to win their cases.[84] Several individuals defended themselves from prosecution for violating the weapons law of 1841 by claiming they did not fit the legal definition of a free person of color. These claims were generally difficult to prove, especially if a defendant's community had recognized him and his family as free persons of color for generations. Prosecutors usually found some older person who would attest to one of the ancestors of the accused being a "coal black negro."[85]

Attempts to change the legal status of free people of color through the high court usually failed. However, the case *State v. Chavers* was an important exception to this trend. In the spring of 1857, a jury in Brunswick County found William Chavers guilty of carrying a weapon without a license. Chavers and his defense appealed this decision to the Supreme Court on the grounds that the prosecution was unable to prove definitively that William Chavers was indeed a "free negro." Chavers did not contend that he had no "negro" ancestors but instead argued that he did not fit the definition of a "negro," which required that a person descend from "negro ancestors to the fourth generation." The defense asserted "to the fourth generation means that the propositus [person involved] must be five steps or descents removed from a black ancestor, whether attended with purification of blood or not, for being a penal statute, it must be construed strictly." The Chavers team's explanation did not intend to challenge definitions of whiteness and proclaim that Chavers was white, but that a "free negro" had a specific ancestral requirement that Chavers did not meet. The Supreme Court rejected this argument, but entertained another idea based on Chavers's categorization as a "free person of color" in his indictment.

The defense argued that the law clearly defined who counted as a "free negro" under the law but failed to specify who could be counted as a "free person of color." Because of this failure to define "free person of color," the defense contended that it would be impossible for a jury to determine whether Chavers was a free person of color and whether the law applied to him. In a decision written by Justice William H. Battle, the Supreme Court ruled that the lower court's judgment against Chavers could not be sustained on these grounds. Without a clear definition of free person of color "a person who is not a free negro" could potentially fit within parameters of the act. In order to correct the problem for future cases, the court offered a definition of free persons of color—"may be then for all we can see, persons coloured by Indian blood, or persons descended from negro ancestors beyond the fourth degree."[86] The Chavers case was a significant ruling for the defendant, but more importantly, the case displayed the illogic and intellectual limitations encoded in some of the state's discriminatory legislation. Over the generations, lawmakers had failed to develop a consistent racial vocabulary to use in discriminatory legislation. Sometimes they referred to "free persons of color" while in other cases they used "negro," "mulatto," "mustee," "Indian," or other supposedly more specific terms, none of which they clearly and consistently defined. Their inconsistent vocabulary created problems for local officials, who had to execute laws without clear guidelines to help them determine who fell into certain categories. As discussed in chapter 1, even when lawmakers created definitions for racial categories, those definitions did not match up with the processes people in day-to-day life used to categorize their neighbors.

Arguably one of the biggest blows to the radical proslavery agenda came from the Supreme Court in the 1859 case *State v. Lawrence Davis*. In this case, lawyers for the defendant asked the court to consider the right of a "free negro" to self-defense. Before the case reached the Supreme Court, a Craven County jury had convicted Davis of assaulting Edward Hewitt, a white man, and fined him $10. After hearing the case on appeal, the Supreme Court overturned Davis's conviction. In the opinion written by Justice Richmond Pearson, the court declared, "the natural right of self-protection is not inconsistent with that feeling of submission to white men which his [the free negro's] lowly condition imposes and public policy requires should be exacted." In reference to Hewitt's actions upon Davis, Pearson further exclaimed, "An officer of the town having a notice to serve on the defendant, without any authority whatever, arrests him and attempts to tie him! Is not this gross oppression? For what purpose was he to be tied? What degree of cruelty might not the def[endan]t reasonably apprehend after he should be entirely in the power of one who had set upon him in so high handed and lawless a manner? Was he to submit tamely? Was he not excusable in resorting to the natural right of self defense?"[87]

In *State v. Lawrence Davis*, the court failed to challenge white supremacy directly and did not argue for equality between free people of color and white people. Justice Pearson evidently did not believe whites and people of color were equal.[88] Yet the court left room for free people of color to protect themselves from physical violence by white people who believed they had the right to dominate free people of color. Most notably, the case provides important insight into the way the state Supreme Court viewed the significance of the Dred Scott decision. In 1857, the U.S. Supreme Court ruled against Dred Scott, whose freedom suit had climbed from the lower courts until reaching the high court's docket. In the court's majority opinion, Chief Justice Roger B. Taney contended that "negroes of the African race" historically were "so far inferior that they had no rights which the white man was bound to respect."[89] The North Carolina Supreme Court did not agree with Taney's opinion. Although the North Carolina high court did not cite the Dred Scott decision, Justice Pearson's words suggest that North Carolina law required white men to respect the rights of free people of color within certain limits, including the right of free persons of color to defend themselves.

The cases presented to the North Carolina Supreme Court demonstrate that even on the eve of the Civil War, radical proslavery ideologues had failed to build full consensus over the social position of free people of color. Some lawyers and judges argued and ruled in support of discrimination. Other jurists, not necessarily the friends of free persons of color, understood the shortcomings in the discriminatory legislation, and in the Chavers case, recognized when these gaps in the law jeopardized the freedoms of the greater populace. These cases also reflect the willingness of free people of color to defend their own position in society. With the passage of every discriminatory law, their legal position slightly diminished. Yet these cases demonstrate that free people of color recognized themselves as free subjects and not slaves without masters. Slaves had no legal right to marriage to protect, no cruel or unusual punishment that the law could protect them from, and no citizenship to defend.

From the early national period to the last days before the outbreak of the Civil War, North Carolinians argued over the place of free people of color in their society. Since colonial times, free people of color had maintained a position higher than that of enslaved people. At the beginning of the national period, free men of color enjoyed a privilege, the right of suffrage, that no white woman or white minor enjoyed in North Carolina. In 1835, a constitutional convention denied free men of color the vote by a slight majority. The 1835 constitutional amendment preventing free men of color from voting was both race-based and gendered. The amendment's acts were equally intersectional in their effect. Free men of color lost their right to vote. Yet free women of color had never had such a right. The amendment should not be viewed simply as racial discrimination. The law also created important gendered ramifications.

The legislature passed a series of bills in the name of curbing the complicity of free persons of color with potentially rebellious slaves but failed to execute the most extreme parts of the radical proslavery agenda. Lawmakers could not adequately respond to questions about the sanctity of their actions, and at times, even agreed to make special provisions for free people of color. In reality, lawmakers were not at war with free people of color, who barely made up 10 percent of the state's population of color at any particular time and who composed an even smaller percentage of the state's general population. Free people of color served as the scapegoats of the radical proslavery ideologues and as the antithesis of the argument that the promises of life, liberty, and the pursuit of happiness did not belong to persons of color. Proslavery advocates could not defend slavery from abolitionists' attacks if they accepted that some persons of color acted as their equals in courts and voting booths. They could not effectively argue for white supremacy and simultaneously court free men of color for votes. In the minds of the enemies of abolition, North Carolina could not save the peculiar institution and protect the liberty of free people of color, many of whom were the children of slaves or had been slaves themselves.

CHAPTER 4

Community and Conflict

Free People of Color in Society

The diaries of William D. Valentine of eastern North Carolina reflect the conflicting viewpoints of white North Carolinians about the free people of color in their midst. In his writings, Valentine railed against the continued presence of free people of color in his community and called for their removal to Africa. He claimed free people of color were largely a menace to society. Yet, like so many other white North Carolinians, Valentine relied upon, sometimes became indebted to, and occasionally praised individual free people of color. Vely Bizzell, a free woman of color, washed and mended Valentine's clothes at the rate of $1 per month. In 1854, Valentine owed the survival of his home to Nat Turner, a free man of color. During the morning of November 17, Valentine and his guests found the kitchen roof on fire. Hearing the alarm, Turner came to Valentine's house and then proceeded to climb to the kitchen roof, where he received buckets of water from a series of people below. With the help of Turner and others, Valentine's kitchen sustained little damage. After the event, Valentine described Turner's aid as "good service, grateful service."[1] Even though Valentine's politics sometimes belittled free people of color collectively, in daily life he realized how valuable his free neighbors of color were to his own existence and community stability.

Valentine's cognitive dilemma about the place of free people of color in society reflected a much broader problem for North Carolinians. Free people of color, whites, and slaves lived as neighbors, prayed in the same churches, worked on the same land, sometimes socialized together, and occasionally shared bonds of kinship. Yet white North Carolinians grappled with the exact position free people of color should hold in their society. Some whites judged their neighbors of color like they appraised the values of other white people. They appreciated and supported their free neighbors

86

of color who met their personal standards for appropriate industry and behavior. Other whites subscribed to an ideology that suggested people of color were inherently inferior to themselves. Some hoped to see free people of color purged from society. If lawmakers failed to remove them from society, these whites at least hoped to keep free people of color in complete subordination. As the evidence in this book has demonstrated, however, there was a deviation between the law and the social reality. Another segment of the white population appeared to have maintained a flexible and inconsistent viewpoint. These people, including William D. Valentine, believed that free people of color to varying degrees were their inferiors but failed to treat them as complete outsiders. They could despise free people of color collectively and simultaneously praise and befriend individual free people of color who met their standards for decorum and propriety. They viewed their favored free neighbors of color as exceptional while arguing that free people of color as whole were substandard. These whites spoke of the world in a black-white duality but acted and lived in a reality that was much more complex.

White people's inconsistent and sometimes malleable viewpoints created complicated and often unpredictable experiences for free people of color. In several respects, free people of color were highly integrated in North Carolina localities. They lived near or with white people, had regular conversation with their white neighbors, and built economic relationships with them. Nonetheless, segregation based on racial categorization crept into some public institutions. On occasion, vigilantes harassed free people of color, and the most vicious individuals attacked them and destroyed their property. Free people of color generally could expect congenial relations with their white neighbors but remained cautious of troublemakers.

Community

Instances of neighborliness and amiability among free people of color and their white neighbors appear more regularly in the historical record than examples of whites oppressing free people of color. Like their colonial predecessors, national-era free people of color and whites lived in the same communities, shared civic responsibilities, and socialized collectively. At the local level, free people of color and whites regularly interacted in relationships of mutual dependence.

From the beginning of North Carolina's postcolonial existence, free people of color and whites cooperated as neighbors and allies. The outbreak of the American Revolution united free persons of color and whites under the independence cause. Free people of color joined their white neighbors to take loyalty oaths to the state government. Jethro Trumbell, a free man of color, along with several of his white Bertie County neighbors, declared an oath of allegiance to North Carolina. They promised to defend the state against King George III. Lewis Anderson along with Edward, Hardy, Benjamin, and Nathan Bass, all free persons of color, followed other Granville County citizens in swearing to a similar pledge. Some men took the allegiance oath quite literally and enlisted with the Continental Army or served in local militia units. In other cases, community leaders drafted men to fight for the rebel cause. Free people of color and whites mustered and fought together and ultimately won American independence through a joint effort.[2]

Following the American Revolution, free people of color and whites continued to serve together for the common defense. At the beginning of the War of 1812, free men of color enlisted along with white men in local units. Two men named John Scott along with Halvin Ash, James Ash, Solomon Locklear, Samuel Locklear, Arthur Manly, and Hansel Hathcock, all free men of color, were members of Halifax County regiments. Members of the Granville County units who were people of color included Lemuel Tyler, Thomas Evans, William Evans, Jeremiah Anderson, Moses Pettiford, and Zachariah Mitchell. Moses Pettiford served as fourth sergeant in his regiment, ranking seventh in a company of seventy-eight men.[3]

While the second war against Britain was in progress, the state legislature prevented free men of color from enlisting as soldiers and only permitted them to serve as musicians in militias. Free men of color continued to muster along with whites in this capacity through the Civil War. In 1821, William Boon was the fifer and David Rooks was the drummer in Captain William Lee's Gates County militia company. During the 1830s, Isham Locklear of Robeson County served as the musician in Captain McNeill's militia company.[4] These musicians' participation in the militias was a continuing symbol of the interconnection between whites and free people of color in North Carolina communities. Although the state legislature severed a broader level of camaraderie between free men of color and white men during the War of 1812 by prohibiting free men of color from serving as the equals of white militiamen, the presence of free men of color as musicians continued to symbolize the mutual duty of all free men to serve their common localities.

Sometimes communities reflected on and celebrated the intertwined histories of free people of color and whites and publicly displayed continued tolerance for social interactions across racial boundaries. In 1858, citizens of Fayetteville celebrated the sixty-fifth anniversary of the Fayetteville Independent Light Infantry, a post-Revolutionary militia unit. The commemoration included target firing, a dinner at "Farmers' Hall," and reciting of the ode "The Grave of Hammond." The celebrated Hammond in the grave was the infantry's former musician Isaac Hammonds, a free man of color and Revolutionary War veteran. Even on the eve of the Civil War, North Carolinians still could gather to celebrate the accomplishments of their communities without excluding the contributions of persons of color.

As in the colonial period, free men of color and white men shared duties in county public works projects up to the Civil War. Road work was the most common task. In 1816, the Northampton County court ordered hands from the households of Stephen Walden, Kinchen Roberts, John Walden, Anthony Roberts, and Elijah Roberts, all free men of color, along with their white neighbors to work the road from Frederick Stanton's to Nathaniel Stevenson's.[5] At an 1842 session of Robeson County court, officials required Jeremiah Revels and John Revels, free men of color, and ten white men to work the road between "the Whiteville Road and Elizabeth Road."[6] Road work by law was a shared duty of free men, regardless of racial categorization. Only the wealthiest members of a community could exempt themselves by sending substitutes.

Polling places were communal spaces where free men of color and white men shared civic responsibility until a state constitutional convention disfranchised free men of color in 1835. The scant surviving evidence does not reveal how free men of color voted but demonstrates that they participated in the franchise in several localities across the state. In 1819, Micajah Reid was the only free person of color to cast a vote in the Gates County election for a member of the U.S. House of Representatives. In 1835, during the last election in which free people of color in Orange County participated, 24 percent of the voters at Lee's Store were free men of color. Voting records for the counties with the largest free populations of color are not among the surviving county records, but free men of color undoubtedly turned out in large numbers in these counties. One of the delegates at the 1835 constitutional convention claimed that Halifax County, which consistently had one of the largest free populations of color during the 1800s, had two to three hundred voting free men of color.[7]

Beyond elections, free people of color and whites sometimes came together to advocate for other issues of wide community interests. They used petitions to express their grievances to both local and state officials. In 1802, David Poan, Henry Smith, Shaderick Jacobs, John Chavis, James Jacobs, William Chavis, and Samuel Jacobs, all free men of color, joined dozens of their white Bladen County neighbors to oppose the employment of county laborers on a construction project to expand the Waccamaw Stream. The designers of the project planned to use the expansion for boats and wafts. The petitioners explained to the county justices that they were willing to continue working the county's roads, which they saw as their "Duty." Yet they adamantly opposed helping to expand the waterway and believed the venture would "not be profitable to us or the public."[8] In this case, these men, white and of color, saw the construction project as outside of their communal interests. They gathered together as Bladen County citizens and members of the laboring class to protest what they saw as an overreach by local administrators.

During the 1830s, the Fayetteville Temperance Society included members, both white and of color, who worked together to curb alcohol use in their community. Leading free people of color in Cumberland County, including Solomon Nash and George W. Ragland, were active in the organization. The group appointed these men to police the conduct of "coloured members of the society." Temperance supporters met at various churches in the area to discuss how to bring an end to alcohol use around the world. At an 1834 meeting, the body passed a resolution stating: "That the respectable moderate drinker is the greatest obstacle which prevents the success of the Temperance enterprize [sic]."[9] The example of the temperance society reveals how common beliefs brought people together in antebellum North Carolina. The temperance cause united some whites and people of color while undoubtedly bringing them into conflict with whites and persons of color who hoped to maintain access to alcoholic beverages.

Free people of color and whites even as convicts, criminals, and runaways came together for their common interests. In 1803, Jacob Hammonds, "a mulatto man," along with Littleberry Wilson and Jesse Robinson, both white men, escaped together from a Fayetteville jail where

Hammonds and Robinson awaited trial for horse stealing and Wilson for murder.[10] On the night of November 30, 1821, Meredith Chavis, "a free mulattoe, about six feet high, slender made, freckled face, quick spoken, a shoemaker by trade" whom the court had recently had whipped, fled from the Orange County jail with Archibald Brown, a white man who was "about forty years of age, five feet nine or ten inches high, tolerably square built, fair complexion, with some pimples of bumps on his face indicative of the habit of intoxication."[11]

Community events such as estate sales brought free people of color and whites into regular contact and show the concurrent interests of community members. On December 22, 1837, the personal property of Nathan Bass of Granville County, a free man of color, came up for sale after his death. Bass's administrator offered an assortment of tools, livestock, and perishable goods. Several local free people of color attended the sale, including William Pettiford, Warner Bass, Arthur Taborn, Lewis Pettiford, Polly Bass, Polly Evans, and Morris Evans. William Pettiford purchased the most valuable lot at the sale, five barrels of corn. Several white men also attended the sale, including D. T. Paschall, John Jenkins, William D. Allen, Edward Speed, William Dickerson, and Benjamin Knight. After the death of Henry Bow of Pasquotank County, a free man of color, Bow's administrator sold an assortment of property from a sorrel horse to kitchen furniture. Bow's wife, Polly Bow, and relative Tully Bow purchased several of the items at the 1845 sale. Wilson Brothers, Moses Overman, and Isaiah Simpson, all white men, purchased livestock.[12]

Churches in pre–Civil War North Carolina were important sites of interaction among people of different racial classifications and classes. Records for churches across the state reveal the presence of free people of color among congregations with white and enslaved members. Free people of color subscribed to a diversity of beliefs and were members of various Christian denominations, including the Baptist, Catholic, Methodist, Episcopalian, Moravian, and Presbyterian churches.[13] On April 18, 1824, Louisa Lewis and Mary Jane Hamilton, "coloured children," became members of the Christ Church of New Bern after their baptisms.[14] The minister of the Sacred Heart Cathedral Catholic Diocese of Raleigh traveled the state to baptize people including Thomas, "a colored and freed child three months old the son of Miles Howard & Matilda" of Halifax County in 1842.[15] In 1855, Pleasant Spencer, "coloured member" of Oxford Presbyterian Church in Granville County, received a letter from his congregation allowing him to transfer his membership to the Presbyterian Church in Raleigh.[16]

Cushing Biggs Hassell, a white Martin County Baptist minister, maintained relationships at various levels with free people of color in his community, especially those connected to his church. In his diary, he noted the deaths of several people, both of color and white, in the area. On June 29, 1849, Hassell recorded, "Old Dicey Cotanch a coloured woman died last night."[17] As a minister, Hassell initiated all people received into his congregation, including Nancy Hyman, a free woman of color, whom he baptized in the Roanoke River on August 11, 1850. The next Friday, Hassell along with two white women visited the homes of free people of color who attended his church. The group first visited the home of Malichi Keese to see Malichi's wife, Penny, who recently had joined the congregation. Following the stay with Penny Keese, they stopped to see Elizabeth Hyman and her daughter-in-law, Nancy, who just the weekend before had joined the church. Hassell described the visit with the Hymans as "a pleasant interview" in which he enjoyed "hearing the experiences of these new members."[18]

A few free men of color ministered in religious establishments and preached to audiences that included both whites and persons of color. John Chavis, a Presbyterian minister, was one of the most influential. During the beginning of his career in the early 1800s, Chavis traveled widely in both North Carolina and Virginia preaching the word, converting souls, and taking notes on the state of religious activity in different localities. By the 1830s, proslavery advocates began to target ministers like Chavis, arguing that free people of color who preached to slaves were likely agents of agitation among the enslaved population. Chavis and other preachers like him may have been progressive in their beliefs about delivering a Christian message to all people regardless of racial categorization, but he was no political radical. In his report, Chavis vehemently stated that "it is truly a matter of thankfulness to black people, that they were brought to this country; for I believe thousands of them will have reason to rejoice for it in the ages of eternity."[19] This position undoubtedly made slave masters comfortable and therefore allowed Chavis to complete his work for whites and persons of color alike.

After North Carolina lawmakers prohibited free people of color from preaching, some white people still sought out the expertise and talents of their most skilled ministers of color. In 1840, thirty-one supporters of William B. Hammons of Buncombe County, including three pastors, asked the legislature to exempt him from the law prohibiting free people of color from exhorting and preaching in public. They declared that "William B. Hammons who we believe if he was tolerated to speak in Publick [*sic*] would be a means of doing much good we think his gifts and graces will well justify him to speak in Publick [*sic*]." In an attempt to appeal to the sensibilities of a largely proslavery assembly concerned with the potential influence of free people of color over slaves, the petitioners noted that Hammons "keeps company with no negroes all his association is with white people and no person that knows him doubts his sincerity as a religious carracter [*sic*]."[20] The Buncombe County petition demonstrates that Hammons's supporters recognized him as an insider in their community and not someone living on society's margins. Hammons's supporters not only viewed him as a respectable person but also as a valuable asset to their community. White neighbors defended Hammons's right to preach because they were primarily concerned with filling their preaching position with someone who could best fulfill their spiritual needs. In this situation, lawmakers had imposed qualifications based on racial categorization that challenged the independence of religious institutions.

When North Carolina lawmakers established public schools in 1839, they explicitly prohibited free people of color from attending these schools. This decision, however, did not determine how free people of color or whites could be educated in private settings. There are also examples of free people of color and whites sharing educational opportunities before the passage of the 1839 law. At the beginning of the nineteenth century, the minister John Chavis operated a school in Raleigh for both white children and children of color. At Chavis's school, white children received their lessons during the day, and children of color obtained their instruction during the evening. In an advertisement for his school, Chavis promised parents that they "may rely upon the strictest attention being paid, not only to their Education but to their Morals."[21] Whites also played an important role in the education of free people of color, both as instructors and supporters. During the 1810s in Hertford County, the guardians of the mixed-ancestry children of Noah Cotton, a white man, paid a white tutor to educate the Cotton children. In 1839, Harriet Peck, a white Quaker educator, operated an evening school for free people of color in Guilford County. Peck recalled that free people of color sacrificed greatly to attend her school. She stated that "the anxiety manifested by the poor creatures to learn is indeed great, quite a number of them walk several miles. . . . Two boys of a family of Burnses who live two miles distant, came [to school], one of them with no outside jacket and not even a vest, the other not much more comfortably clad." Peck's school not only educated children but instructed entire families. She explained that "there is one man who attends regularly with his family of 5 children, Thomas Smothers."[22] In the 1850s, Mahala Buffaloe, a free woman of color from Wake County, paid Isabella Hinton Harris, a white woman, to educate her daughter.[23]

In different areas of North Carolina, at least some whites believed that neighborly responsibility included caring for less fortunate free people of color. Well into the late antebellum period, wardens of the poor in several counties accepted responsibility for poor and disabled free people of color along with significant numbers of whites and sometimes abandoned slaves. Granville County officials provided various sorts of support to disadvantaged free people of color. In 1829, the wardens paid George Pettiford, a free man of color, for Jeston Bass's care and Lewis Pettiford, a free man of color, for maintaining Mourning Taborn. Later that year, the wardens remunerated Lewis Pettiford for Mourning Taborn's burial.[24] On May 18, 1835, one of the wardens instructed John Mallory, superintendent of the poorhouse, to pick up "Allen Chavis a free man of color" who lay "unwell" and was "unable to provide the means of support" and "bring him to the poor house and administer to his comfort & relief in every way his situation may require."[25] Orange County's wardens sustained free people of color in multiple ways, including paying for their regular support and burials in addition to providing them with housing at the county poorhouse. On November 26, 1844, the wardens agreed to reimburse Dixon Corn for the burial of Kizzy Jeffries, a free woman of color. A September 6, 1847 list of inhabitants included Charles Whitmore and Littleton Jeffries, both free men of color, among thirty-eight residents of the poorhouse.[26]

In many instances, whites assisted their free neighbors of color who sought to leave the state for other parts of the country. Sometimes, they crafted letters of support on behalf of free people of color. Writing from Fayetteville on April 22, 1854, John H. Cook and A. A. McKethan explained to Governor David S. Reid that "Henry Evans a free man of color his wife & children are about to migrate to Ohio & desire to make arrangements which will permit himself & family to pass by public conveyance from the

Southern States without interruption. He is accompanied by his brother & brother in law." Cook and McKethan requested the governor provide Evans with something that could "facilitate their easy passage."[27] Bryan W. Herring made a similar gesture toward "Daniel Simmons a coloured man" when he wrote to the governor on April 28, 1855. In his letter from Mount Olive in Wayne County, Herring indicated that Simmons "is anxious to leave the state and wishes to have your certificates and the seal of the state affixed to them."[28] In both the cases of Evans and Simmons, the governors provided the migrants with the requested documents. Some whites gave financial assistance to free persons of color. Sally Pettiford, a free woman of color who once lived in Guilford County, recalled "that her said husband died in the county of G[u]ilford in the said state of North Carolina on or about the 26th day of December 1859, and the Denomination of Quakers made up money after the death of her said husband and sent her & her family to the said Gallia County, Ohio."[29]

Familiarity between free people of color and whites often developed during their childhoods. The experiences of John E. Patterson, a free person of color, and Andrew Johnson, a white person and seventeenth president of the United States, reflect the situations of countless North Carolinians, both white and of color, in the years before the Civil War. Patterson recalled that Johnson and he were "well acquainted & play mates & neighbours" during their childhoods in Raleigh. As boys growing up in the early nineteenth century, Patterson and Johnson went between their mothers' homes and yards where they played "marbles & other amusements of youthful enjoyment."[30] They matured in a world in which people frequently understood community as their family, friends, and neighbors, regardless of racial categorization or status.

Nothing more clearly demonstrates white people's acceptance of free people of color as part of their communities than the many efforts individual whites made to secure and protect the free status of their neighbors of color. Free people of color, especially before traveling outside of their home counties, often went to court to obtain free papers, which they could carry on their person to prove their free status. In support of their applications and to verify their claims to freedom, free people of color sought testimony from their neighbors, generally whites who had known them for a long time. In 1831, Sarah Turner, a free woman of color, had her white neighbor, Sarah Jackson, swear a statement of her status. Affirming her intimate knowledge of Turner's condition, Jackson told a Pasquotank County justice of the peace that she knew Turner's "mother to be a free woman & that the said Sall was born in her kitchen in her presence."[31] In the case of Mary, a free person of color, Nancy Wilson wrote to the justice of the peace: "Please . . . give Mary her free papers I know her to be free for I raised her for I took her from A white woman her mother."[32] The multigenerational associations of whites and free people of color offered further support for the applications of free people of color. William Gregory of Pasquotank County wrote of Sarah and Courtney Spellman: "I have no doubt but they are [free born]. Their grandmother was a free woman & lived on my father's land—and to the best of my knowledge, I have never known a Spellman that was a slave."[33] The statements given by these white supporters demonstrate that free people of color and whites had intimate knowledge of one another's lives. People could not produce such levels of familiarity in a truly bifurcated society.

Conflict

The same social conditions that made free people of color integral to their localities also promoted several forms of backlash from whites who wanted a different society. The fact that free people of color enjoyed many opportunities and privileges including some level of communal acceptance drove certain white people to harass them and work toward their subjugation. Many of these whites envisioned a society in which white people always received preference over people of color or never had to compete against them. Some imagined a drastically different society from their own in which whites and people of color were segregated physically in all aspects of life. The most radical of them hoped for the complete removal of people of color from North Carolina and from the country. They believed that the United States was a nation founded by white men and made for white men. Although the whites who took extreme actions against free people of color were in the minority, their activities created fear and sometimes serious problems for free persons of color and their supporters.

White town leaders across the state created numerous obstacles for free people of color without completely denigrating them to the status of the enslaved. Throughout the early national period, town leaders issued numerous edicts that curbed many basic freedoms for free people of color living in their communities. Town leaders in places such as Hillsborough and Tarboro imposed curfews on "free negroes." Fayetteville leaders passed an ordinance requiring free persons of color to register with town officials. In Hillsborough, leaders went further and required "free negroes" to post bonds for good behavior. The town's leadership also promoted a white monopoly on peddling in the town by imposing a hefty $1 per day tax on vendors of color.[34]

The extent to which white leaders enforced any of these ordinances is unclear. Yet their existence suggests that local leaders sought to politicize the position of free people of color in their communities and potentially if not actually curb the self-determination of free people of color. On occasion, New Bern patrollers used their authority to harass free people of color. In 1827, patrollers arrested Bob Hazle, "a free negro," after finding him on the street at ten o'clock at night. A local newspaper reported that Hazle, upon encountering the patrol, told the officers that he "was as free a man as any body—that he had a right to travel when and where he pleased." Yet the patrol brought him into the police office. After a guilty verdict for "disorderly conduct," officials forced Hazle to post a bond for good behavior.[35]

During times of localized unrest, often the result of alleged or reported slave rebellions, local white powerbrokers allowed the lower-class whites to harass free people of color. After the enslaved man, Nat Turner, led a fatal rebellion against the white elites of Southampton County, Virginia, a community that lay on the eastern half of the North Carolina–Virginia border, some whites incited disorder in their communities under the guise of protecting these communities from copycat actions. Harriet Jacobs, an enslaved woman and granddaughter of a free woman of color, Molly Horniblow, explained that the period that immediately followed the 1831 Turner rebellion was "a grand opportunity for the low whites, who had no negroes of their own to scourge." In the town of Edenton and the rest of Chowan County, Jacobs revealed, "Colored people and slaves who lived in remote parts of town suffered in an especial manner. In some cases the searchers scattered powder and shot among their clothes, and then sent other parties to find them, and bring them forward as proof that they were plotting insurrection. Every where men, women, and children were whipped till the blood stood in puddles at their feet. . . . The dwellings of the colored people, unless they happened to be protected by some influential white person . . . were robbed of clothing and every thing else the marauders thought worth carrying away."

Before the patrol arrived at the house of Molly Horniblow, Jacobs prepared her grandmother's home for inspection although they were one of the families who could depend on white elites' protection. When the rabble entered Jacobs's grandmother's house, "They snatched at every thing within their reach. Every box, trunk, closet, and corner underwent a thorough examination. A box in one of the drawers containing some silver change was eagerly pounced upon." Jacobs recalled the jealous reaction of the poor whites upon discovering the high quality of some of Horniblow's personal possessions. After days of searching, "at last the white citizens found that their own property was not safe from the lawless rabble they had summoned to protect them. They rallied the drunken swarm, drove them back into the country, and set a guard over the town." Following weeks of unrest, "nothing at all was proved against the colored people, bond or free. The wrath of the slaveholders was somewhat appeased by the capture of Nat Turner. The imprisoned were released. The slaves were sent to their masters, and the free were permitted to return to their ravaged homes."[36]

White vigilante action against free people of color and enslaved people was not limited to Chowan County after the Turner insurrection. On August 31, 1831, Solon Borland of Murfreesboro wrote to his brother Rocius Borland in Raleigh, "Five negroes have been apprehended and commited [*sic*] to jail since you left here—two of them in this place—Mrs. Roberts' Jack & Weston's Isaac one from the upper part of the county a free man named London Gee a Baptist preacher—two from Northampton—one belonging to Henry Deberry & the other named Sam Brantley a Baptist preacher."[37] *Niles' Weekly Register* reported, "Every free negro at Raleigh had been arrested and examined—and some were ordered to leave the city, because they could not give a good account of their mode of subsistence: but it has not yet been stated, we think, that any *free negro*, either in Virginia or North Carolina, has been found guilty of a participation in the outrages contemplated or committed. This, surely, is much to the credit of this class of persons."[38]

Violence and terrorism were important tools for those whites who sought white domination of every aspect of social life. In 1818, white vigilantes Abner Knight, John Somerel, and William Day forcibly entered the Halifax County home of Uriah Dempsey, a "mulatto man," in search of stolen wheat. After allegedly finding evidence of the stolen wheat in Dempsey's home, the three men proceeded to assault the free man of color by whipping him.[39] In 1842, a white terrorist group, self-described as the "Raleigh Regulators," destroyed a log schoolhouse attended by children of color. In response, Judge Thomas Ruffin declared that he hoped "we shall be able to get some of them before our Sup[erio]r. Court and that the Judges will there teach them that this is a land of law yet, and that when they set themselves up superior to the law, it is a usurpation not to be endured or tolerated in the old North State however well it may flourish in the meridian of Mississippi and some other Western States."[40]

Lynching would become much more prevalent in North Carolina after the Civil War and Reconstruction. Nevertheless, some white terrorists used this tactic before that time to incite fear among free people of color. In the same year of the burning of the school in Raleigh, vigilantes attacked Allen Jones, a free man of color and one of the parents of the Raleigh schoolchildren. On October 22, 1842, the *Raleigh Microcosm* reported, "Allen Jones, a free negro of this city, was violently forced from his house a few nights ago, and so severely *lynched* by a mob, that for a while it was thought he would not recover." The newspaper suggested that most people in Raleigh strongly detested this act and claimed, "This outrage has been promptly rebuked by our citizens, who held a large public meeting on the 18th, and adopted resolutions condemning in strong and just terms this violation of the peace and order of the city by the mob, and requesting the city authorities to offer a suitable reward for the apprehension and conviction of the persons engaged in it; and also to employ counsel for their prosecution."[41] In a less sympathetic, yet forceful manner, the *Raleigh Register* denounced the attack on Jones. The newspaper described Jones as "somewhat obnoxious" but determined, "Now, with regard to *Allen Jones,* he may be a bad man, and, for argument's sake, we will admit that he is a great rascal, but that fact affords no plea of justification or excuse in the world, for the outrage which has been perpetrated. If a man's house—his castle, as the law defines it—is to be forced open at midnight, the locks broken, and he taken out and butchered, to gratify the vindictive feelings of any set of individuals, it is worse than idle to talk about the security which the law gives—for its boasted supremacy is but a farce, and the Courts of Justice, ridiculous mockery." Most concerned with the restoration of order, the paper concluded, "For, if a high-handed outrage, like this, is permitted to pass without a vigorous effort to discover the perpetrators, no man can tell what will be the next step, or who will be the next victim. The fact that the individual, who has been mal-treated, belongs to a degraded *caste*, so far from relaxing the efforts of all concerned, should rather stimulate them; for as it is the proudest boast of our Republican country, that no one is so *high* that the law cannot reach him, so ought it to be, that no one is so *humble or low*, as to be beneath its protection."[42] The attack on Allen Jones was an offense against the community because it was an action against the peace and order in the town. The action made Raleigh and its citizens look bad, not superior.[43]

Along with violence, some whites unleashed what John P. Green described as "petty persecutions and insults" upon their free neighbors of color. In 1850s New Bern, John's mother Temperance Durden Green dealt with such problems from her most "crude" white neighbors. In one incident, a jealous neighbor tarred Temperance's prized rooster and mutilated his bill. Temperance also faced harassment from white patrolmen "who were constantly visiting residence sections of the colored people, in quest of firearms, and 'war munitions.'" Her son described these patrollers as "respecters of no persons of color." Upon "unceremoniously" entering the house, they would "rummage the drawers of the side-board and bureau."[44]

Some whites preferred free people of color leave the country versus subjugating them within the nation. From the late 1810s, organizations across the United States including in North Carolina worked to transport free people of color out of the country to places such as Liberia and Haiti. These organizations sought public and private support to pay for the removal of free people of color and soon-to-be emancipated persons. They hoped that by removing these populations, the nation could truly become a utopia for white people. The American Colonization Society was the best-organized and most vocal of the associations seeking the removal of free people of color. In 1826, the national society sent a request for support to the North Carolina General Assembly. The organization sought assistance for sending free people of color to the "Colony at Liberia." Mechanics groups that appeared in North Carolina and other parts of the country by the middle of the nineteenth century also promoted the removal of free people of color. Their motives, however, were more practical than purely ideological. They sought to eradicate free people of color from the United States in order to eliminate them as economic competitors. In an 1850 announcement, a mechanics group in Beaufort County explained their position: "The Mechanics of Washington and its vicinity view with alarming apprehension the increasing introduction of negro labor in competition with their own, thereby tending to deprive them of their only means of support earned by the sweat of the brow, and also to degrade them to the level of co-laborers with base born negroes and slaves." In reaction to this perceived problem, the organization called for legislators to pass "an act providing for the taxation of free negroes for the purpose of raising a fund to colonize them in Africa."[45] The efforts to remove free people of color from North Carolina received some support from the public and organizers successfully resettled a small number of free people of color.[46]

Kidnappers were a serious problem for free people of color. These abductors were not so much interested in creating a new social order as they were in manipulating the existing social order for their benefit. As the values of slaves continued to increase up to the Civil War, criminals found overly tempting the prospect of making a small fortune by stealing a free person of color and selling that person for a profit. Kidnappings of free people of color occurred with some regularity across the country, including in North Carolina.[47] In 1848, Governor William Alexander Graham received a letter from George W. Crawford of Washington, Texas, informing him of the case of a "free mullatto boy." Crawford explained that William Delk of North Carolina had transported the boy, "John Nelson son of Hannah Nelson . . . a white woman," to Texas and sold him as a slave.[48]

The white neighbors of free people of color often abhorred the abduction of their community members and posted ads in newspapers requesting the return of their neighbors and friends. An advertisement in the December 15, 1801, edition of the *Raleigh Register* reported the kidnapping of Lettice Burnett, "a free girl of colour, about twelve or thirteen Years of Age," from Wayne County. The announcement promised that "whoever shall give information on the said free Girl, so that she may be restored to her friends, on giving Notice to Levin Watkins, Esq. of Duplin County, will be well rewarded for their Trouble."[49] Distraught by the kidnapping of a young free girl of color, Catherine Free of Craven County, a white woman, issued a similar notice in several March 1820 issues of the *Hillsborough Recorder*. Free reported, "On the evening of Saturday the 19th instant, the house of the subscriber on Swift Creek was entered during her absence by John Bryan and a free mulatto girl named Dicey Moore, the daughter of Lydia Moore, was forcibly taken and carried away in a chair by the said Bryan. It is believed that he has a forged bill of sale for the girl, purporting to have been executed by her mother." Free did not promise a reward for Dicey Moore's return, but offered a plea: "The editors of southern papers are requested to give the foregoing ad insertion in their respective papers, as possibly it may save from a state of slavery this girl, who has an unquestionable right to her freedom."[50] Free, Moore, and their associates had to depend on the will of white southerners to respect the status of a free girl of color. Although Moore's freedom was the object most in jeopardy, any person who located Moore and refused to notify Free of her whereabouts not only respected criminality over the right to liberty of a free person but additionally challenged white southerners' abilities to maintain their social order.[51]

Segregation in early national North Carolina was not nearly as pervasive as it would become in the post–Civil War period and was largely absent from everyday life. Yet segregation existed within certain public spaces, and many elite organizations excluded free people of color from their ranks. In reaction to whites excluding them from their organizations, free people of color in some instances established their own institutions. In Craven County, free men of color created a fraternal organization that met at St. John's Lodge. The organization's leadership included James Y. Green and Richard Hazle, two of New Bern's most accomplished citizens. Their organization was a branch of the larger network of successful free people of color created in New Bern. John P. Green, the son of John R. Green, a member of this social network, explained, "There was not amongst us any of that, squeamishness with respect to the varying shades of color; all that was required of a person knocking at the door of our social circle for admittance, was—fitness; my dear father who was one of the leaders of the colored society, in the old town, always stoutly maintained that, persons seeking association with others should be congenial and meritorious."[52]

Excluded from the primary leadership positions within churches, some free people of color sought to establish their own places of worship. In the 1850s, free people of color organized Pleasant Plains Baptist Church in Hertford County and New Hope Baptist Church in Gates County. In these churches, unlike in most mixed congregations, free people of color had significant control. Nonetheless, the law that prevented them from preaching kept free people of color out of the pulpits of these churches. The first pastor of Pleasant Plains, Thomas Hoggard, was a white man. The protocol of the Chowan Baptist Association, to which both churches belonged, also kept free people of color from representing their congregations at the association's meetings. At annual meetings of the Chowan Baptist Association, white men represented all churches, including Pleasant Plains and New Hope.[53]

Scattered instances of abuse by whites against free people of color were better than a consistent system of oppression. Nevertheless, some free people of color feared that white elites would allow irregular oppression to transform into systemic subjugation. In a letter dated October 27, 1825, Gustavus A. Johnson, a free man of color from Edenton, frustrated by the growing influence of radical proslavery ideas and their effects on all persons of color, contemplated a move to Africa. He explained, "I have some thought of Leaving the Land of America and going to the distant shores of Africa. . . . There I and my offspring are promised the pure and vital air of Freedom." Viewing Africa as a beacon of liberty, Johnson continued, "it is there that the finger of scorn will be hurried away & it is there and there alone that my infant children will loose the degraded and fearfull [*sic*] spirit of slavery" and concluded, "this and this only Raises my spirit to see the shores off Africa."[54] Johnson remained in North Carolina but was concerned about his future prospects in a state growing increasingly radical in its support of human bondage.

The power structure that supported slavery equally troubled the Roberts family of Northampton County and forced them to consider the consequences of remaining in a state in which some whites sought to trample their liberties. On February 15, 1830, James Roberts, a free man of color originally from Northampton County who had relocated to Indiana, expressed his concerns to his kinsman Willis Roberts, who contemplated returning to North Carolina. James Roberts affirmed "that where there is slavery it is not a good place for us to live, for they [white people] are the most of them very disagreeable and think themselves A Bove free people of coller. We are all ways in danger of thear doing us ingre [injury] by sum way or other." Directly addressing Willis's plan to return to North Carolina, he insisted, "We are now A way from them and I think it the Best fore me when I am out of such a country [North Carolina] to stay A way . . . to think that you ar[e] A going to take youre small children to that place and cant tel[l] how sun [soon] you may Be taken A way from them and they may come under the hands of sum cruel slave holder and you noe that if they can git a colered child they will use them as bad a gine as they will one of their own slaves." Pleading with Willis, James Roberts continued, "I would not this night if I had children take them to such a place and thare to stay fore the Best five

farms in 3 miles Round whare we come frome [Northampton County] fore
I think that I should Be going to do sum thing to bringe them to see trobble
and not enjoy thear selves as a free man but be in [a] plac[e] whar they ar
not able to speak for thear rits."[55]

Unable to exercise the rights enjoyed by whites, many free people of
color still decided to stay in North Carolina. Others, however, saw removal
from their native state as the only way to realize all of life's opportunities,
including those privileges held only by whites at home. Frustrated by his
declining rights in North Carolina, Louis Sheridan left Bladen County with
his family and slaves for Liberia in the late 1830s. Future U.S. senator Hiram
Revels left North Carolina for Indiana to obtain higher education. Brothers
John E. Patterson and Henry I. Patterson abandoned their businesses in
Fayetteville and Raleigh for the more tolerant political environs of Oberlin,
Ohio. Enjoying the opportunities available in Oberlin that their home state
denied them, the Patterson family produced the first woman of color to
earn a bachelor's degree, Mary Jane Patterson. Many of those free people of
color who left North Carolina became some of the most ardent supporters
of the antislavery movement. David Walker left Wilmington at an early age
to become one of the nation's most effective spokesmen against slavery.
John Anthony Copeland, a native of Raleigh, and Lewis Sheridan Leary, formerly of Fayetteville, accompanied John Brown to Harpers Ferry and died
in the attempt to capture the federal arsenal and start a region-wide slave
rebellion in 1859.[56]

Whites' harassment, attacks, and hostility failed to drive away or fully
subjugate the state's free population of color. Yet their actions caused many
free people of color to live with caution and adapt to being around people
who could quickly turn against them. These actions forced free people of
color to realize that although most of their white neighbors abhorred violence against them, those same neighbors were unwilling to fight for a society that provided them with equal protection. They recognized that their
neighbors' racialized defense of slavery and willingness to accept white
domination of political power went directly against their interests. Whites
lived beside free people of color, treated them as neighbors, worked alongside them, and at the same time created an environment for hatred to
flourish. The white neighbors of free people of color allowed politicians to
use them as political pawns, permitted white church leaders to place them
in inferior positions within the church family, and allowed the patrols and

vigilantes to violate their property and persons. Nevertheless, these same neighbors valued relative peace and order over attempts to assert a clear-cut racial hierarchy. These white people preferred certain benefits free people of color brought to society, especially in their roles as workers and consumers.

Commerce

The importance of free people of color to so many local economies helps to explain why the most radical calls for action against them generally failed. Pleas to colonize free people of color outside of the United States floundered in North Carolina for exactly the reason some white mechanics wanted them gone: free people of color were vital to local economies.[57] As skilled laborers and low wage workers, free people of color provided North Carolina with labor that could not be replaced easily. Through the Civil War, white North Carolinians depended on free people of color to construct their buildings, work their farms, and fish their waters. The economy bound together free people of color, whites, and slaves in networks of commerce that powered the movement of people, goods, and services in their localities, state, and nation.

Free craftsmen of color often played an indispensable role in their local economies. Thomas Sheridan, a free man of color and Bladen County carpenter, established himself as an important craftsman in his neighborhood. Sheridan helped to construct Bladen County's Brown Marsh Presbyterian Church. His business acumen undoubtedly contributed to the reputation that allowed him to work on such a project. Sheridan was both highly skilled and literate. As a careful craftsman and businessman, he drew up his own contracts before beginning construction projects. On February 26, 1826, Sheridan wrote out an agreement with Alexander McDowell. In the contract, he promised to weatherboard a kitchen "in a good workman like manner" and to find his own accommodation during the project's duration. At the completion of the kitchen, Sheridan wrote that McDowell would pay him $14.50 "in cash."[58]

Ingenuity and hard work made Thomas Day, a free man of color, one of the most successful cabinetmakers in North Carolina. Day had established himself in Milton by the late 1820s, and by the 1830s, his work had the attention of many of North Carolina's most influential whites. Day's shop, which employed craftsmen, both white and of color, produced furnishings for the homes of Caswell County elites. The Day operation also obtained major contracts from the University of North Carolina, former North Carolina governor David Settle Reid of Rockingham County, and the Milton Presbyterian Church, of which Day and his wife, Aquilla Wilson Day, were members. Day and his employees produced everything from coffins to fine staircases, making Day one of the most important craftsmen in the region.[59]

Free people of color in North Carolina had enemies across the state, but they failed to convince the friends of free people of color, who often benefited greatly from their work, that a purely white society could offer a better alternative to artisans like James Boon. James Boon of Franklin County, a free man of color and carpenter, worked in several North Carolina counties and in each built a strong record and good reputation. Throughout his career, white men wrote letters of recommendation highlighting Boon's value to the communities in which he worked. In 1842, Richard H. Mosley of Halifax County wrote Jesse Faulcon that Boon "is an orderly and well behaved man, and attentive to his business. His work is executed better and with more taste than any persons within my knowledge in this section of country."[60] The next year, Nathan W. Edwards, also of Halifax County, proclaimed that Boon was "an honest straight forward hard working man, in short he is in my opinion a gentleman."[61]

The barber's trade allowed some free men of color to become economically successful and well-respected. Joseph Hostler was one of the most accomplished of this number. Born a slave, Hostler gained his freedom while working as a barber and continued with his craft for decades after securing his liberty. In 1824, Hostler advertised the opening of a new barbershop in Fayetteville "on Hay-street, immediately opposite the Mansion Hotel."[62] By 1833, he had expanded his business to include the sale of high-end grooming products "received from New York."[63] The free man of color Elias B. Revels ran an equally prosperous barbering operation in Lincolnton. During 1837, he advertised himself as a "Barber, Hair Dresser and Perfumer." In his announcement, Revels explained, "He has met with encouragement and success wherever he has followed the business, but it is the natural propensity of all men to make all they can; he therefore, throws himself on the public spirit of the citizens of Lincoln County to render unto him whatever he is deserving of." Confident of his skill, he continued, "Try me gentlemen, and if I fail to please either in shaving or trimming, then say the subscriber has no skill in his business. But again, if I succeed to your fancy, then give me a liberal encouragement. The more I am encouraged the greater will be my exertions to serve you."[64]

The records of the county poorhouses show the multiple ways free people of color contributed to their local economies. County authorities trusted free persons of color to keep these public spaces in working order. During the 1840s, the Perquimans County wardens of the poor regularly depended on free people of color to fulfill their needs and those of the destitute. On several occasions, the wardens paid Penny Norfleet and Clarissa Overton for working as nurses at the poorhouse. They also compensated Overton for delivering meals from the county seat to the poorhouse. Free men of color completed building repairs sponsored by the county's wardens of the poor. In 1843, Isaac Douglas received pay for repairs made on a stall.[65] Three years later, William Douglas made repairs to brickwork and laid "one hearth" on behalf of the wardens of the poor.[66] In the same period, Craven County's wardens paid skilled free men of color for their contributions to the operation of the local welfare system. On July 13, 1841, James Y. Green, a carpenter, accepted payment for kitchen repairs, which included shingling 750 feet of roof, installing a sill, and "patching weatherboarding."[67] The wardens also paid him for installing gutters, shingling, and repairing a mantelpiece for a house. On at least two occasions in 1844, the New Bern blacksmith Richard Hazle provided the poorhouse with metal wares. One order included door hinges and nails. In a second order, Hazle provided W. S. Blackledge, special warden, with staples, plates, and ketches.[68]

Beyond the poorhouses, the state and municipalities depended on skilled free people of color to keep their other public buildings in working order. During the 1830s and 1840s, the state paid Henry I. Patterson, a free man of color, for masonry work on the governor's mansion in Raleigh.[69] At the May 1842 session of court, Chowan County administrators ordered the sheriff to pay $300 to Rigdon M. Green, a free person of color, "as part of his contract for repairs of the Court House."[70] In May 1847, the Wake County court paid William Chavis, a free man of color, for maintaining the pump in front of the county courthouse.[71] During the June 1856 session, Person County officials ordered the sheriff to pay Barnett Bass, a free person of color, $20.50 for "painting the railings [a]round the court house."[72]

Many skilled free people of color contributed to the North Carolina economy by working in the culinary arts. Free women of color, especially in the coastal region, made and sold cakes for a living. During the 1830s,

Caty Webber was a highly reputed cake woman in New Bern.[73] In 1846, the Gates County court gave Amelia Sawyer permission to peddle "oysters and cakes."[74] By 1850, Edward Cochran, a free man of color, had established himself as a butcher in Wilmington.[75] Several issues of the *Raleigh Register* for 1847 included the advertisement for a "NEW ESTABLISHMENT" operated by the confectioner Oscar F. Alston, a free man of color. In his announcement, Alston informed "the Citizens of Raleigh and its vicinity . . . that he has opened a general assortment of Confectionaries . . . and he hopes by prompt attention to business, to merit a part of their patronage."[76]

Free women of color were essential to the production and maintenance of clothing for their communities. The most skilled of these women worked as seamstresses. The 1860 census for Anson County names Victoria Robinson along with Delany and Sarah Conrad as seamstresses in Wadesboro.[77] Other free women of color made a hard living as washerwomen. According to the 1860 census, Susan and Mariah Valentine of Salisbury supplemented their family incomes by washing and ironing. The same enumeration lists Susan and Lucy Evans along with their neighbors Maria and Susan Tann as washerwomen in Warren County. A few free women of color also made livings as spinners. Rebecca Mills of Halifax County contributed to her family's income through this type of work.[78]

Beyond the realm of artisans, certain industries, most notably shipping and fishing, depended on the labor of free persons of color. Free people of color partially and sometimes fully composed crews that headed in and out of North Carolina ports. Except for the captain, every crew member on the schooner *Sally Ann* docked in Beaufort and bound for Haiti was a free person of color. In 1826, John Savastan of Beaufort, Benjamin Gray and Doxy Lee of Currituck County, Thomas Scott and James Hathway of Pasquotank County, and George Elshone, originally from Jamaica and a British citizen, all free people of color, manned the schooner, which successful transported a shipload of emigrants to the Caribbean.[79]

In the eastern part of the state, including Chowan, Hertford, Bertie, Washington, Tyrrell, and Carteret Counties, free women and men of color held irreplaceable positions in the fishing business. In an 1849 report on North Carolina's fishing industry, Lemuel Sawyer, Esq. wrote of the fisheries: "A large gang of hands is required to work them, generally 30 or 40 hands, besides the scores of women, principally negroes, to clean the fish."[80] Whites, slaves, and free people of color worked as hands at the Mount Gallant fishery on the Chowan River in Hertford County. During the 1830s, John Bizzell, Simon Bizzell, Jacob Smith, Joe Archer, Drew Smith, Tom Weaver, and Henry Chavis, all free men of color, were among the hands at the fishery. These men harvested thousands of shad and herring from the river to be exported through the Dismal Swamp Canal to ports such as Norfolk and from there to other parts of the country. Locals also purchased some of the fish processed at Mount Gallant.[81]

By the 1840s, people who could work in the fisheries were in high demand, and free people of color with experience in the field found work. In Gates and Hertford Counties, locals regularly held what was referred to as the "fishing court," where fishermen from around the region came to hire hands for their fishing operations.[82] In 1849, John A. Anderson attended a fishing court in Hertford County to procure workers for the Chesson and Armstead firm out of Washington County. After bargaining with potential laborers at the fishing court, Anderson successfully collected a team of workers, all "mulatto" hands, to send to Chesson and Armstead via the next available ship. Anderson's assembly included four free women of color and thirteen men, some of whom were hired slaves and some free men of color. Writing to Chesson and Armstead, Anderson informed them of the difficulty he had in finding women who could work as fish cutters. The women Anderson found not only had forced him to pay them a wage but also required him to guarantee that they would receive part of the catch. He explained, "The women I could not get on better terms and had to grant them the privaledge [sic] of putting up a Barrell of offal fish each." Besides guaranteeing the women fish in addition to their salaries, Anderson also warned that "I am yet afraid I shall loose Sally Butler. . . . I learn much larger prices have been offered her . . . and perhaps for a different use than what you want her for."[83] Anderson's statements suggest that few people involved in the fishing industry would have supported the removal of free people of color to Africa. While white fishermen in North Carolina would not have welcomed the direct competition of fishing operations owned by free people of color, they needed experienced workers, regardless of racial categorization or status, to keep their operations in production.[84]

During the antebellum period, North Carolina was the top producer of naval stores in the United States, and free people of color tapped into the economic explosion tied to the industry. The nationwide demand for other products derived from trees such as shingles and lumber also provided opportunities for North Carolina's free people of color. In the pine woods of Columbus County, free men of color such as W. H. Mitchell and Owen Moore operated turpentine farms. Young men in their teens and twenties living in Bladen County found working in the naval stores industry as an effective way to support themselves and their families. Armlin, Salter, and Silvester Blanks along with Fred and Andrew Lacewell were among the free men of color collecting resin in Bladen County's woods in 1860. The resin they collected and refined became an extensive range of products, including rubber, soap, lubricants, and lamp fuel. Charles Jones and Allen Reid of Gates County, free men of color, labored in the Great Dismal Swamp in northeastern North Carolina, where gangs of slaves and free people of color transformed cypress trees into shingles.[85]

Free people of color helped to power many of North Carolina's smaller economic engines, including the construction and operation of the railroads. Rail transportation remained minimal in North Carolina, as in much of the rest of the South, until the 1840s and 1850s. Once North Carolina's leaders finally agreed on the importance of the railroads and sought to invest in them, North Carolinians of various backgrounds began to claim a stake in the transportation boom. Sometime before May 1839, Joseph Rowland, a free man of color, moved from Virginia to Granville County to work as a railroad contractor.[86] For most of the 1840s, Shadrack Manly, a "free negro," served as a train fireman. Manly's work eventually led to his death when he fell under the wheel of a moving locomotive in 1849.[87]

In western North Carolina, free people of color participated in the mining industry. During the nineteenth century, North Carolina was a leading producer of gold and iron. The 1850 census lists Jefferson Abbot, Michael Jones, Abner Hedgepath, and Edward Howell as miners living in McDowell County. Shadrack Williams, James Locklayer, and William Davis appear in the same enumeration as miners in Montgomery County. These men were likely working in the gold mines. By this time, several companies had established themselves in North Carolina to take advantage of the state's important yet limited mineral resources.[88]

Localities across the state depended on free men of color to engage in the back-breaking work of well digging. On May 14, 1857, Washington Holt, a free man of color in Caswell County, advertised his services as a well digger in the local paper. In his advertisement, Holt explained that he had "considerable experience in this branch of business, and flatters himself that he can give the amplest satisfaction." He also promised, "The best references can be given as to character, skill in my profession and application to business."[89] In a time in which many people depended on well water for basic survival, the services of Holt and others like him were essential to the daily functions of their communities.

Free people of color played a particularly critical role in North Carolina's agricultural economy. They participated at every level of agricultural production from laborers to planters. Most of these agricultural workers labored on other people's farms as hired hands. Robert A. Jones, a white planter in Halifax County, employed several free men of color to complete short-term work on his farm. On December 14, 1819, Jones paid King James, a free man of color, $10 for work on his barn. In fall 1821, Jones employed Buck and Dolphin Francis, Thoroughgood Dempsey, Arthur Manly, Billy Taylor along with Dempsey, James, Hartwell, and Littleberry Haithcock, all whom Jones described as "Mulatto Labourers," to labor on his farm and mill. All their assignments were short-term, and none of the men worked for Jones more than two weeks. Although Jones gave the men temporary positions in 1821, this was not the only time he depended on them. Three years later, Jones reemployed James Haithcock to labor on a monthly basis at the Wyche Plantation in Halifax County.[90]

Beyond working as laborers on other people's property, free people of color in almost every community with a significant presence of free persons of color could be found working their own farming operations. Most of these agricultural ventures were small-scale farms with no slave laborers. Some farmers worked rented land while others grew crops and raised livestock on their own property. In 1860, Amy James, a washerwoman, operated a small hog farm on one acre of land in Bertie County. During the same year, James's neighbor Nancy Wiggins, who was also a washerwoman, raised pigs and kept bee hives on a smaller parcel of land. Both women were tenant farmers. The Jeffries and Corn families of Alamance County owned and cultivated several hundred acres of farm land on the eve of the Civil War. Ned Corn produced 75 pounds of butter and grew 6,000 pounds of tobacco and 30 bushels of potatoes on 100 acres of improved land. Andrew Jeffries's farm on 150 acres of improved land reaped 3,600 pounds of tobacco and 100 pounds of butter. Dixon, Richardson, and E. G. Corn along with Jesse Jeffries produced similar crops and farm goods on improved tracts that ranged from 60 to 200 acres.[91]

Free people of color worked an assortment of less commonplace trades among the population. At least a few free people of color partially supported themselves and contributed to the state's economy by working in the slaving business. During the turn of the century, Willis Edge, John Edge, Willowby Sammons, and Evan Perkins, all "free mulattoes," worked as slave catchers in Camden County.[92] Some of those free people of color who were lucky enough to own real property set up milling operations on their land. Curtis Snelling maintained a grist mill and sawmill on Mine Creek in Wake County during the 1820s. Up to 1834, Jesse Weaver of Hertford County operated a grist mill on his land. From this mill, Weaver produced ground corn, which he sold to his neighbors.[93] By the 1850s, free people of color had an active role in North Carolina's infant manufacturing sector. Gabe Thompson, a "free negro," worked as an iron melter at the Dixon, Davidson, and Company foundry in Alamance County. At the factory, Thompson helped produce castings for mills, ploughs, wagons, and machines.[94] Limited economic opportunities for women pushed some free persons of color into prostitution. Bettie Sexton and Lavinia Bains, both free women of color, were among the ladies working in late-antebellum Raleigh's sex trade.[95]

Free people of color played particularly important roles in North Carolina's economy as workers and producers. Nevertheless, they also served North Carolina's economic needs as consumers of goods and services. White merchants, tradesmen, and other producers depended on free people of color to buy their goods and services. The daily social interactions of Thomas O'Dwyer, an Irish-born doctor who resided in Murfreesboro during the 1820s, reveal the significance of mutual dependence in the lives of free people of color and whites. Free people of color were among O'Dwyer's many patients who sought relief for various ailments. Jacob Boon, a free man of color, was one of his most frequently visited patients during July 1825. Almost every other day, O'Dwyer set off to visit Boon and offered the ailing man prescriptions. During these visits, he remained at Boon's residence to socialize. Some patients required less attention and simply sought out O'Dwyer for medicine. Tryal Williamson, a free man of color, "called" on the doctor to provide a prescription for his wife and himself. O'Dwyer's interactions with free people of color were not limited to doctor-patient relationships. He frequently hired out his slaves, Bob and Peter, to Peggy Weaver, a free woman of color. O'Dwyer lent money to free people of color, including his one-time patient Tryal Williamson, who paid his note in installments. Beyond his business relationships, O'Dwyer also took notice of free people of color simply as his neighbors. During the spring of 1825, O'Dwyer recorded the deaths of two of his free neighbors of color. On April 9, he wrote "Heard Nathan Boon, mul[att]o, about 45 yrs old, died yesterday. He has labored under Rheum[atis]m for some yrs & was taken with convuls[ive] fits." Later that month, he noted the death of a free woman of color: "Heard Nancy Tann a mul[att]o girl, about 18 yrs old died this afternoon— she was sister to Harrison."[96] In O'Dwyer's experience, free people of color were patients, associates, and neighbors.

During the mid-1850s, Newsome J. Pittman, a white doctor in Tarboro, sustained his business partly by treating free people of color from the surrounding area. Eliza Archer, a free woman of color suffering from uterine issues, maintained an account with Dr. Pittman. The doctor met with Polly Jones several times for similar ailments and sold her remedies for these problems. He also performed a tooth extraction on Jones. Joseph Price paid Pittman $1 to lance an abscess from his eye. For the same price, the doctor removed an abscess from Kiddy Archer's finger. He completed similar services for his white patients.[97] In every sense, Pittman was a community doctor who worked among all segments of the local population, white and of color, free and enslaved.

Wayne County merchants Barnes and Bardin maintained accounts with free people of color and whites in their locality. From the 1830s into the 1840s, free people of color came to the merchants' Black Creek store to purchase a variety of goods. In 1839, Reuben Pettiford visited the store on at least three occasions to purchase rum. During April and May of 1841, Elvy Hagans bought sugar, brandy, snuff, homespun cloth, calico, cakes, and shoes. Washington Reid acquired buttons from Barnes and Bardin in 1842. The following year, he returned to the store for shoes and cotton yarn. Micajah Artis's account for the same timeframe included purchases of wine, molasses, fish hooks, a powder keg, and a cheap processed animal product called "bony meat."[98] The commerce at the Black Creek store helped keep Barnes and Bardin in business while at the same it supported the proliferation of manufactured goods across the country.

Through at least part of the 1840s and 1850s, John N. Benners, a white Craven County farmer and slaveholder, built business relationships with numerous free men of color in his community. They worked for him and obtained merchandise on barter and for cash. On several occasions in 1848,

Benners sold Jesse Mitchell pork and meal. In order to pay for these goods, Mitchell worked for Benners with the exception of one instance, in which he settled part of his debts with a half bushel of pears and melons. In the same year, Joseph Hoover maintained an account with Benners. His account showed the purchase of an assortment of goods that included meal, corn, bacon, tobacco, and pork. Unlike Mitchell, who bartered for purchases, Hoover paid off his account in cash. In 1853, Joseph Banton labored for Benners and paid cash in order to settle his account, which included the rental of a canoe and purchases of meal, corn, molasses, tobacco, pork, and a pair of shoes.[99]

The post-Revolutionary debate over the proper position of free people of color in North Carolina developed largely because free persons of color were so highly integrated in society. Proslavery advocates' case against free people of color would have been less provocative had persons of color truly lived on the periphery of society. The opponents of free persons of color, whether proslavery or white supremacist, worked so hard to depict free people of color as unfit precisely because some free people of color were well-connected, lettered, mobile, influential, and prosperous. The friends of free people of color constructed their rebuttals to these arguments from similar evidence that showed free persons of color were essential to the social and economic well-being of local communities throughout the state.

At the local level, even those whites who believed that persons of color were their inferiors could not easily choose the persecution of free people of color over the maintenance of the general order because free people of color were so ingrained in the larger society. The public debate about the position of free people of color in society revealed the contempt some white North Carolinians had for free people of color. A minority of whites despised free people of color so strongly that they were willing to pay for their permanent removal from the state.[100] While some of their neighbors argued for removal, other white people continued to depend on their free neighbors of color in business and for socialization. Whites repeatedly failed to defend publicly the rights of free people of color to political power yet continued to believe free people of color had rights to property and most importantly their basic liberty.

Charles Waddell Chesnutt was the son of Andrew Jackson Chesnutt and Ann Maria Sampson Chesnutt, free people of color from Cumberland County. Among his canon of works, Chesnutt authored an essay entitled "The Free Colored People of North Carolina," published in 1902. *Courtesy of the Cleveland Public Library Digital Gallery.*

John Anthony Copeland was born free in Raleigh. He relocated with his family to Ohio before joining John Brown at Harpers Ferry, Virginia, in 1859. *Courtesy of the Library of Congress.*

Thomas Day's shop, located in Milton, provided North Carolinians and Virginians with fine furniture and woodworking. The shop's success made Day one of the most respected artisans in North Carolina. Through his business acumen, Day obtained enough wealth to own real property and slaves and to educate his children. *Photograph by the author.*

In *Fact Stranger Than Fiction*, John P. Green recounted his childhood as a free person of color living in antebellum New Bern. Green reflected on the rich social world of free people of color in his community and how harassment from "crude" white neighbors pushed the most successful families to leave North Carolina in search of better prospects in the North. *Courtesy of the Cleveland Public Library Digital Gallery.*

Lewis Sheridan Leary was the son of the prosperous harness maker Matthew N. Leary of Fayetteville. As a young adult, Leary left North Carolina and relocated to Ohio, where he became involved in the antislavery movement. His activism eventually led him to join John Brown at Harpers Ferry, Virginia, where he died during the failed attack on the federal arsenal. *Courtesy of the Oberlin College Archives.*

THOMAS LOWERY.

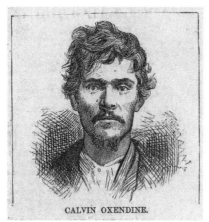

CALVIN OXENDINE.

HENDERSON·OXENDINE.

Thomas Lowry, Calvin Oxendine, and Henderson Oxendine were members of the band led by Henry Berry Lowry that battled conservatives and rebel sympathizers in Robeson County during the late 1860s and early 1870s. From *Harper's Weekly*, March 30, 1872.

Enoch Manuel and Nancy Ann Manuel were the great-grandchildren of Ephraim Manuel of Sampson County. Ephraim Manuel died around 1804, leaving 198 acres as part of his estate. Enoch Manuel is pictured at left with his wife, Sarah Hardin Manuel. Nancy Ann Manuel Bledsoe is pictured at right with her husband, William J. Bledsoe. From George E. Butler, *The Croatan Indians of Sampson County* (Durham, NC: Seeman Printery, 1916), 48, 50.

Mary Jane Patterson was the daughter of Henry I. and Emmaline Patterson of Raleigh. Her father, a skilled bricklayer and plasterer, purchased and emancipated her mother in 1838. The Pattersons later relocated to Ohio, where Mary Jane attended Oberlin College. Mary Jane was the first woman of color in the United States to earn a bachelor's degree. *Courtesy of the Oberlin College Archives.*

George Washington Paul was born in Alamance County during the Civil War. His mother, Kitty Paul, was raised in a household of people with different legal and social positions. Kitty Paul was a free person of color. Kitty's mother, Mary Paul, was a white woman. *From the author's collection.*

Hiram Revels was born free in Fayetteville in 1827. He spent much of his childhood in North Carolina before relocating to the Midwest. After the Civil War, Revels became the first person of color to serve in the U.S. Senate, representing Mississippi. *Courtesy of the Library of Congress.*

Parker D. Robbins, a descendant of the indigenous Chowan people of northeastern North Carolina, served in the U.S. Army during the Civil War and represented Bertie County in the North Carolina General Assembly during Reconstruction. *Courtesy of the State Archives of North Carolina.*

James Grant Reid and Rhobenia Rooks Reid were descendants of the freeborn, interrelated Rooks, Reid, and Burke families of Gates County. James Grant Reid was likely present at the house of his father, Asbury Reid, when federal troops visited in 1864. After the Civil War, Asbury Reid became a leading political organizer in Gates County. *Courtesy of the State Archives of North Carolina.*

Willis Weaver and Sally Jones Weaver were part of the intertwined network of free families of color in Hertford County during the eighteenth and nineteenth centuries. The Weavers were heavily intermixed with other families with deep roots in Hertford County, including the Nickens, Archer, Manley, Hall, and Shoecraft families. *Courtesy of the State Archives of North Carolina.*

CHAPTER 5

Freedom and Family

Relations with the Free and Enslaved

During the 1840s and 1850s, the Lilly boys grew up in a family that crisscrossed the boundaries of racial categories and freedom status. Although Wilson, Raynor, Lee, Benjamin, and Caleb Lilly fell under that category "free persons of color," no one in their immediate family shared the same classification. Their father, Cromwell Felton, was an enslaved "yellow man." Polly Lilly, a white woman, was their mother. Cromwell, Polly, and their children "lived together right along." The boys also grew up around their mother's family members: Polly's parents, brothers, and, sisters. Polly's brother Caleb Lilly recalled being present at the birth of his nephew Raynor. When Polly's father, Nathan Lilly, died, he left Polly the land that she and her children resided on in Perquimans County.[1] In the childhood world of the Lilly boys, people sometimes defined family through kinship, not imagined racial differences or shared sociopolitical status.

The family situations of free people of color regularly disrupted the boundaries that racial categories were supposed to create. Free persons of color had their own understandings about their personal identities and where they fit within the broader social milieu. They placed different values on the importance of freedom status and racial categorization. A percentage of free people of color were emancipated slaves or their descendants and, as a result, shared close familial and social bonds with slaves. Some had enslaved spouses and children, and if their ancestral backgrounds were similar, may have seen no intrinsic difference between themselves and some slaves. Another segment descended from Native people, white women, or others who had been free for so long that they did not share close bonds with slaves. Many of these people lived in what were called "colonies" or neighborhoods primarily composed of free people of color. They practiced endogamous marriage, usually based on class or kinship, including cousin marriage or marriage within a small network of interrelated families. Free people of color in these neighborhoods rejected slaves as acceptable spouses and only occasionally received outsiders into their networks. A few free people of color identified more closely with whites and other free people of color who did the same. These individuals had children with white people and encouraged their children to associate only with whites or children of color with white parents. In the eyes of these people, there were substantial differences among free people of color.[2]

Family Relations among Free People of Color

The legal recognition of unions between free persons of color pushed many individuals to build connections with those who shared the same racial categorization and freedom status. Marriages between free persons of color were the most socially acceptable unions. By discouraging marriages between persons of color and whites, North Carolina law implicitly encouraged marriage between free men and women of color. By the 1830s, state law prohibited marriage between whites and persons of color. During most of the period between British colonization and the Civil War, free people of color and slaves could join in marriage-like unions, but no marriage involving a slave was legally binding, because slaves, as legal nonpersons, could not make contracts.[3]

The historical record reveals that many of the earliest free families of color in North Carolina evolved into complex social networks. Free families of color composed of free men and women of color appear in the tax records of the colonial era. Surviving records for counties such as Bertie and Granville give examples of these family arrangements and reveal widespread endogamy among the earliest free families of color in North Carolina.[4] The behavior of these early families parallels the kinship structure of white colonists who migrated into North Carolina during the eighteenth century. Regardless of racial categorization, close bonds among families played a pertinent role in the development of social life.[5]

One of the largest and oldest kinship networks in North Carolina originated among the free people of color in Granville County. In Granville County, the colonial tax records give the names of some of the earliest free families of color to settle in the area. Most of these families settled around the developing town of Oxford and the Fishing Creek District. Among these were the Chavis, Bass, Anderson, Tyler, Mitchell, Pettiford, Evans, Goings, Hawley, and Harris families. By the late eighteenth century, these families and a few others such as the Days and Taborns had begun to build an extensive network of kinship. The 1785 will of Lewis Anderson reveals that his daughters had married into the Taborn, Bass, and Tyler families. The estate records of Lewis Anderson's son Lewis Anderson show an even more extensive kinship reach with his daughters having married into the Mitchell, Bass, and Goings families. Many of the marriages of the Andersons into these other families likely resulted from the alliances of previous generations. For example, a close relationship existed between the younger Lewis Anderson and Edward Bass, since Bass named Anderson the co-executor of his estate. At some point before Lewis Anderson's death, his daughter Rhoda Anderson married Darling Bass, the son of Edward Bass.[6]

Late eighteenth- and nineteenth-century marriage records further expose the interconnections between the earliest free families of color in Granville County. Of the thirty-one male members of the Bass family with recorded marriages in Granville County before the end of the Civil War, seventeen marriages are between Bass men and one of the early settler families. For the Pettiford men, the percentage is slightly less, with eleven of twenty-seven marriages being contained within these families. The ratio of marriages among the old settler families is fairly similar for the other families. These numbers do not include men who married descendants of the old settler families with surnames other than those previously mentioned. Further genealogical research would likely reveal that many of the names that appear to be those of outsiders may actually have been the names of descendants of the settler families that married outside of the network in one generation and returned to the core network in the next. These numbers also exclude men who married free women of color from the closely related families in surrounding counties in both North Carolina and Virginia. The kinship networks of the Granville County settler families often extended into areas such as Wake and Warren Counties in North Carolina along with Mecklenburg County, Virginia, which is confirmed by records from those localities.[7]

Extensive kinship networks among free people of color connected families in other parts of North Carolina. In Bertie County, and later in the area of the county that became part of Hertford County, the Archer, Manley, Hall, Nickens, Weaver, and Shoecraft families built an extensive kinship network that had actually begun before these families' arrival in North Carolina during the 1740s and 1750s. Interactions among the Nickens, Weaver, and Shoecraft families appear in the records of early eighteenth-century Lancaster County, Virginia. The members of these families along with the other families of color lived in the Tidewater Region of Virginia before moving to North Carolina. Records from Norfolk and Princess Anne Counties in Virginia along with documents from Hertford County show that these families maintained an extensive kinship network from at least the 1730s through the Civil War. Free people of color in Hertford County commonly intermarried with people descended from these early settler families. Occasionally descendants from the Virginia enclave traveled into North Carolina to marry into the Hertford County enclave and vice versa. Relations among descendants of the early settlers in the old Bertie County still exist to the present day.[8]

By the Civil War, expansive kinship networks of free people of color had popped up across North Carolina. Kinship networks stretching through Robeson, Cumberland, and Richmond Counties and into some parts of South Carolina included members of the Locklear, Lowry, Hunt, Jacobs, Chavis, and many other families. In the piedmont counties of Alamance, Orange, and Caswell the Jeffries, Whitmore, Corn, Haithcock, and Guy families were strongly connected through intermarriage. Other counties had similar situations, and in many cases, kinship networks extended well past county and often state boundaries.[9]

In some instances, individuals inside kinship networks went beyond simply marrying into families with close ties and decided to marry cousins. Cousin marriage was particularly common within kinship networks that had remained close for multiple generations. The records for Halifax County show an extensive pattern of cousin marriage among members of the Richardson family. Between 1824 and the beginning of the Civil War, county marriage records show fourteen unions between Richardson brides and Richardson grooms. The Jeffries family of Orange County exhibited a similar pattern. Between 1809 and 1841 fourteen members of the Jeffries clan formed seven cousin marriages.[10] Further genealogical research would likely show that the cousin-marriage patterns of the Richardsons and Jeffrieses were more extensive than the marriages between cousins with the same surname.

Up to this point, this chapter has demonstrated that many free people of color, especially those families that settled earliest in North Carolina, developed close and often interwoven kinship networks. The historical record provides little insight into the motivations of the free people of color that developed these kinship networks. The information that is available about these people does not precisely explain their motives for building strong alliances or reinforcing alliances among their own kin by marrying cousins.

From a historical perspective, strong kinship networks were not uncommon among people in the United States and other parts of the world. Many white elites in the American South married into similarly bound kinship networks and occasionally married their own kin. Elites across the world have intermarried for generations to maintain wealth and status. The idea of maintaining bloodlines has also been part of many elite ideologies. The circumstances of pre–Civil War North Carolina suggest that free people of color had many of the same goals as their more elite contemporaries. Land ownership was particularly common among the families that descended from North Carolina's earliest settlers. Close kinship networks allowed free people of color to pool and maintain economic resources.[11]

Ancestry also may have played an important part in the marriage choices of some free people of color. The neighbors of all the kinship networks mentioned in this section categorized these people as "mulattoes" up to the Reconstruction era. The individuals in these kinship networks had various heritages, but what would have been most important during the era of slavery was that their ancestors had been born free and that they kept a familial distance between themselves and slaves. They could demonstrate to whites and to each other they were untainted by a legacy of slavery and had no personal connection to the slaves who perhaps held a grudge against the prevailing system. When political agitators attempted to ignite fear and prejudice against people of color, both slave and free, these families could show that they were different from the majority of those whom society categorized as "colored."

Marriage between free people of color also guaranteed the succession of property. Many free people of color owned significant amounts of property, including land, livestock, and in some cases slaves. Only free people could legally convey and inherit property. A free person of color who married a slave could not guarantee support to that enslaved spouse and could not pass on any property to their children if the enslaved spouse was a woman, since slave status descended from the mother to the children. A free man hoping to give property to his enslaved family could only do this by finding a way to emancipate his family. A free woman married to an enslaved man could pass on her wealth to her family more easily because her children were free if she was born free or emancipated before the birth of her children. Yet even in this case, the slave husband could not legally inherit anything his wife wanted to leave him. If his wife left him something, he would have to depend on the children to execute her wishes and his master to allow his relationship with his children to continue. These complications could be avoided, however, if both partners in a relationship were free born.

The desires of cautious slaveholders also played a role in strengthening the bonds among free people of color by preventing slaves from joining their ranks. George W. Hilliard, who was born free in Halifax County during the 1840s, explained that the "free born people and the mixed bloods . . . were colonized down there [in North Carolina], the Waldens, Byrds, Jones, Locklayer[s], Hilliards, some of the Sho[e]crafts, the Roberts, Berts, Revels, and several others all lived down there in a sort of colony, they were not allowed to mix up with the slaves down there."[12] John H. Jackson of Wilmington, who was born a slave in 1851, recalled, "We had a lot of these malatto negroes round here, they was called 'Shuffer Tonies,' they was free issues and part Indian. The leader of 'em was James Sampson." He further explained that "We child'en was told to play in our own yard and not have nothin' to do with free issue chil'en or the common chil'ren 'cross the street, white or colored, because they was'nt fitten to 'sociate with us."[13]

Free people of color created close-knit networks among themselves. Many members of the white slaveholding class, who hoped to keep free persons of color from interacting with their slaves, helped reinforce those bonds. The 1830 law outlawing marriages between free people of color and slaves confirms the statements of Hilliard and Jackson. Indeed, some slaveholders were wary that free people of color might influence their bondspeople. The lives of free people of color represented an alternative to slavery. James Sampson was not "fitten" to associate with the slaves of Jackson's master because he represented something the master hoped his young slaves would never desire—freedom, personal success, and prestige. James Sampson was one of the wealthiest free men of color in North Carolina at the brink of the Civil War—a position Jackson's master never wanted for his young slaves.[14]

Family Relations among Free People of Color and Slaves

Family bonds connected people across the boundary between slavery and freedom. From the colonial period into the Civil War era, many families across the state had both free and enslaved members. These mixed families developed when some members of families gained their freedom through emancipation while others remained in bondage. Although free to move away from the places of their enslavement, some emancipated persons could not fathom leaving the areas in which their loved ones and friends still remained in bondage. In other instances, freeborn people intermarried with enslaved people. Some of these freeborn people had fathers born in slavery or parents with slave families and saw no difference beyond their freedom status between themselves and the enslaved population. Others worked beside enslaved people and established close bonds with people they saw as their peers.

Freeborn people of color built relationships with slaves and traversed socially imposed boundaries meant to separate and distinguish the free from the enslaved. Rachel Overton, a "mollatto" woman, was the servant of Aron Jackson of Pasquotank County during the 1750s. While in service to Jackson, Rachel established a family with a "Negro Husband," who presumably was a slave. By 1755, Rachel and her husband had three children, Daniel, Samuel, and Perthenia, who by law also became the servants of Aron Jackson. Fifteen years later, Rachel appears to have gained her freedom from indentured servitude but was still too poor to support a family. That same year, the local court bound her son Lemuel Overton to Charles Blount for eight years. The historical record does not clarify whether Lemuel Overton shared the same father as Rachel's other children.[15]

In the next generation, Lemuel Overton made a choice similar to that of his mother and took up with an enslaved woman named Rose, who was the property of John Mullen of Pasquotank County. While Rose was still the slave of Mullen, she gave birth to the couple's first son, John. Unlike the situation of his mother, Lemuel Overton's relationship had produced a child who was enslaved. By 1795, Lemuel had saved up enough money to purchase his wife and young son from Mullen. When Lemuel and Rose had another son, Burdock, by law he was the slave of his father. Three years after purchasing Rose and their first son, Lemuel Overton petitioned the state legislature with the support of seven white men from his community, including John Mullen, for the freedom of his wife and children. The legislature granted Overton's request, which gave him the liberty to manumit his family. Lemuel was one of the more fortunate free people of color who were able to see their families out of bondage.[16]

The Johnson family's experience illustrates that social divisions could complicate the relations between ex-slaves and those who remained in bondage. Around 1791, Gustavus Adolphus Johnson was born to an enslaved woman. His father was likely his white master, Charles Johnson of Chowan County, a U.S. Congressman. When Gustavus was four years old, Charles Johnson petitioned the General Assembly for Gustavus's freedom. Never mentioning any form of meritorious service performed by a boy so young, the elder Johnson explained to the General Assembly that he held "a certain boy of colour of about four years of age as a slave, being born as such by the Laws of the Country, by the name of Gustavus Adolphus Johnson, and that the white Blood do far prevail that it is almost impossible for any person to discern that he is of mix'd blood." He continued, "Therefore he your petitioner conceives that from principals [sic] both of policy and Humanity, that the said boy . . . should be freed & Liberated, and that you will pass a Law for that purpose and he will ever pray."[17] Without questions about meritorious service, the young Johnson was emancipated by an act of the General Assembly. Unlike many emancipated people, this child benefited from being tied to one of the most influential men in North Carolina.

Although born a slave, Gustavus Adolphus Johnson would live out the rest of his life as a free man, but not a typical free man. In 1802, Charles Johnson died dividing his estate between his legitimate children and Gustavus. The elder Johnson left Gustavus $2,500 for his education and support, an enslaved woman named Lettice and her children, and one-third of the remaining estate not devised to other heirs. From this point on, Gustavus would have relationships with slaves untypical of most formerly enslaved people: he was a slave master. As Gustavus grew into an adult, he continued to hold slaves, and at his death an enslaved woman, Barbara, and her children as well as an old woman named Lucy were part of the estate left to his heirs.[18]

Further complicating the picture of Gustavus Johnson's relations with slaves are the origins of his family. In his early adulthood, Gustavus purchased "a certain yellow girl named Betty" from James R. Bent. This young enslaved woman became Gustavus's wife. While still legally the slave of her husband, Betty gave birth to three children, Mary, Ann, and Charles. In 1822, nine years after purchasing Betty, Gustavus arranged for and secured the emancipation of his wife and three children. Gustavus and Betty remained married for another twenty years before Gustavus's death in the winter of 1842–43.[19]

Many free people of color were never able to purchase and liberate their families and instead had to adjust to the circumstances they inherited through their familial association with bondspeople. This was the case for Polly Mitchell of Chatham County, who was a freeborn woman. Polly's daughter Emma recalled years after emancipation that "my mammy wuz a Free Issue an' my pappy belonged ter de Bells in Chatham County. Pappy wuz named Edmund Bell, mammy wuz named Polly Mitchel. . . . When my mammy married pappy she moved ter de Bell's plantation so we chilluns, longs wid her, wuz lak de udder slaves."[20] Although Polly Mitchell and her children were born free, Polly apparently did not have the resources to purchase and liberate her enslaved husband and allow him to enjoy the same status. The connection between Polly and Edmund caused Polly to choose to stay near her husband and expose her children to plantation life. The children of this couple would have experienced freedom much differently than the children of Gustavus A. Johnson or Lemuel Overton. Although the Mitchell-Bell children were free, they were not privileged. Emma may have been too young to know that the possibilities for her and for the slave children she grew up around were different. Although Emma was born poor, she was not a slave. Her mother's free status provided the Mitchell-Bell family the opportunity to stay united. Polly Mitchell could bring her children to live with her husband precisely because she was free and unrestrained by the demands of a master. Edmund Bell and the other bondspeople on the Bell plantation were attached to the plantation by force.

All of the examples in this section demonstrate the complexity and variety of relationships between free people of color and enslaved people and reveal that building and maintaining families across the divide between freedom and slavery was difficult. Couples used ingenuity and supportive relationships with their neighbors to provide for their families and raise their children to the highest standard that their circumstances could provide. The struggle of these mixed-status couples also helps to explain why so many free people of color rejected these relationships across the boundary between freedom and slavery. As examples in this section show, some free people of color saved up enough money to buy their family members; however, most free people of color never had this chance. Purchasing family members required not just hard-earned money but also the cooperation of spouses' masters, which was something free people of color could not depend on.

Family Relations among Free People of Color and Whites

From the colonial period into the twentieth century, North Carolina law discouraged relationships between men and women of different racial categorizations. Free people of color and whites, however, found ways around the law, and in many cases their neighbors ignored their illicit behavior.[21] The North Carolina legislature did not outright ban marriage between whites and persons of color until 1830, although the law had strongly discouraged such relationships through a series of fines since the colonial period. Once marriage between people of color and whites was prohibited, couples continued to live together in legally adulterous situations, not dissuaded by legislators' politically motivated prohibitions. The preponderance of people of mixed ancestry among the free population of color suggests that these relationships played a significant role in the development of free families of color in North Carolina. Many free people of color grew up with white parents, grandparents, aunts, uncles, cousins, and half-siblings. Racial categories could not delineate the difference between social insiders and outsiders for these youngsters. Society categorized people as "colored" or "white," but racial classifications did not necessarily define the way people saw themselves in relation to others. Racial boundaries could be less important than the bonds of family that so many North Carolinians depended on to survive in a mostly rural, agricultural economy.

The historical record makes it difficult to determine whether relationships between free men of color and white women or between free women of color and white men were more common. Both types of relationships appear in the stories free people of color and their descendants told about their families and the court records that document their histories. Marriage records provide little insight into the question of which relationship was more common since few of these couples went to the courts for marriage bonds or licenses. White men often obscured their relationships with free people of color and slaves in official records such as wills and deeds. The names of children and partners appear in these documents but without qualifying descriptors such as "son," "daughter," or "wife." Many couples also maintained separate official residences, making their relationships invisible in census records. Prosecutions for fornication and adultery or bastardy mention free men of color and white women much more regularly than free women of color and white men, but their predominance is probably more of a sign of white male immunity from prosecution than a lack of relationships between white men and women of color. William D. Valentine of Hertford County complained about the preponderance of white men living in adultery with women of color, not the opposite case, in his community, but the courts charged only two couples with fornication and adultery in his home county.[22]

Christian Wiggins, a free woman of color, and Noah Cotton, a white man, were one of the many couples engaging in sexual and familial relations across the racial divide. Not much is known about the daily interactions between these two people, but several important features of the relationship are clear. At the time of Noah Cotton's death in 1815, some people in Hertford County referred to Christian Wiggins as "Christian Cotton." Although Christian and Noah never married, references to Christian as "Christian Cotton" suggest that her neighbors viewed Christian as the common-law wife of Noah Cotton and not simply his mistress. The surviving evidence does not suggest that Noah Cotton was engaged in any other relationship at the time of his death besides the one he maintained with Christian. During their relationship, Noah and Christian had at least nine children. Before his death, Noah left his plantation and all his possessions to Christian and their children. Like many white men of his era, Noah Cotton did not declare his relationship to Christian and their children in the text of his original will. In the codicil to that will, however, Noah described his children as his "sons" and "daughters." In their adult lives, all the surviving children were called by their father's surname, Cotton.[23]

As a well-connected member of his community, Noah Cotton made important arrangements to insure the care of Christian and their children. Noah's friend and local attorney John Vann was the executor of Noah's estate. Vann arranged for the care of the children by securing their room and board and paying a private teacher to instruct them. Noah's estate records suggest that Christian Wiggins died immediately after Noah Cotton, leaving their children orphans, so Vann was forced to split Noah's and Christian's minor children up among different households. Solomon and Phereby Keen, both free people of color, brought Ricks and John Cotton, two of the couple's sons, into their home. Lucinda Cotton, a daughter of the couple, moved between the homes of James Weaver and David Weaver, who both were free men of color. The children had several white aunts and uncles, but John Vann must have believed it was best to place these children with people of their same status. Vann raised money to support the children by selling the perishable items from Noah's estate, renting out Noah's plantation, and leasing out Harry and Lucy, two enslaved people owned by the estate.[24]

Many of Hertford County's early records were destroyed by fires, making it impossible to know if Noah and Christian's children received all the benefits of their father's wealth. However, surviving records demonstrate that both people of color and whites had a considerable amount of respect for the Cotton children and the relationship of their parents. In 1825, James Copeland, one of Hertford County's representatives in the General Assembly, submitted a bill to legitimize Wiley, Ricks, Micajah, and John Wiggins and officially change their last names to Cotton. Legislators regularly proposed legal actions to legitimize children born out of wedlock, but a request to legitimize a white man's children by a woman of color was an anomaly. The bill to legitimize the Wiggins-Cotton children was defeated in the General Assembly, but its proposal reveals the differing reactions white North Carolinians had to relationships across racial boundaries.[25] Local officials were willing to ignore relationships that violated the law, but there was little political will among lawmakers to give those relationships sanction. Politicians could purport to believe that relationships between whites and people of color should not be a part of their society by failing to officially recognize the children of mixed unions, while at the same time, support white male dominance over the bodies of people of color by ignoring their sexual liaisons and relieving them from prosecution.

In Nash County, Jacob Ing, a white man and local postmaster, played an instrumental role in the lives of his children whom he had with Esther Jones, a free woman of color. During the 1820s and 1830s, Jacob and Esther had at least eight children: William C., Celia, Mary, Elizabeth, Sarah, John C., Matthew, and Lucinda Jones. During their childhoods, both parents helped to raise and maintain the Jones children. In order to secure his guardianship over at least one of his children, Jacob applied to the court to have William apprenticed to him. Upon their maturity, Jacob continued to back his children by providing them with legal support. When his daughters decided to marry, he posted bonds along with their future spouses to ensure the marriages would take place. On December 13, 1844, Ing provided Nash County officials with an endorsement for the union of his daughter Elizabeth with Jesse Boon.[26] In 1856, Jacob supplied the same daughter, who by this time lived in Halifax County, with a document certifying her status as a free woman of color. In his statement, Jacob explained, "I am acquainted with said Elizabeth Boon and have been from her Infancy. She was born March 28th 1824 at my House and lived as one of the family until grown." Certifying Boon's free status, Ing continued: "I further saith that the said Elizabeth's Mother was one Esther Jones (who is now dead)—I was acquainted with the said Esther about Forty years, and during that time she was always reputed to be a free woman of colour."[27] Even upon his death, Ing continued to provide for his children. In his will, he left all of his property to his surviving children and the children of his deceased daughter Lucinda.[28]

In Cumberland County, Ann Chesnutt, a woman whom one observer described as "very bright yellow," and Waddle Cade, a white man, lived together in a partnership for many years. Waddle successfully cared for his children during his lifetime. Census records reveal that Waddle was almost forty years older than Ann, who was born in the 1810s. Maybe this age differential made the relationship beneficial to both parties as Waddle had lived long enough to build a small fortune and could easily provide for a family and Ann was young enough to take care of the daily needs of an aged man. The census suggests that Ann and Waddle did not live together during the early stages of their relationship or that the couple kept separate official residences. Those white men who had enough money to maintain residences for themselves and their partners often kept two homes. These men appear to have been presenting a façade of respectability and legality. An unmarried couple living in the same house could be prosecuted for committing fornication and adultery, but if that same couple officially maintained separate residences, neighbors would not have to admit that a crime was taking place nearby.[29]

Despite separate homes, the couple spent enough time together to produce six children, the first born around 1831. Soon after the birth of Ann's and Waddle's first two children, George Washington Chesnutt and Andrew Jackson Chesnutt, Waddle planned for their future financial security. He

transferred to the boys a tract of land in Fayetteville. This transaction protected the boys from any further threats from the legitimate heirs of Waddle's estate. Andrew Jackson Chesnutt continued to own this tract of land
until his death, when he passed it on to the next generation.[30]

Like couples composed of free women of color and white men, many
free men of color and white women developed long-lasting relationships.
From the colonial era into the last years before the Civil War, free men of
color and white women could be found cohabitating in almost any community with a significant free population of color. Unlike most pairings
between free women of color with white men, these couples sometimes
faced legal challenges. The courts forced these couples to appear in court on
charges of fornication and adultery. In some cases, the men were charged
with bastardy. Even with the law against them, however, these couples
sometimes found that their neighbors were willing to turn a blind eye to
the illegality of their living arrangements.

A visitor to Hertford County during the mid-1800s would have found
many pairings between free men of color and white women. From at least
the 1840s up to their deaths, Henry Best, a free man of color and carpenter, and Elizabeth Baker, a white woman, lived as man and wife, although
their union had no legal sanction. The couple maintained a household and
raised four children. David Boon, a free man of color and blacksmith, and
Louvenia Britt, a white woman, also lived together in the county during
the 1840s. After the birth of their son, Richard Britt, local officials brought
David into court on charges of bastardy. The court required him to post a
bond and pay child support to Louvenia. Tracking down David to pay child
support was not a problem for Louvenia for the couple continued to live together after the birth of Richard. In 1848, the justices of the peace required
David to appear in court again on charges of fornication and adultery. At
the court appearance, the jury found David guilty and fined him $5. In most
cases, fines did not discourage couples from living together. Many couples
simply paid the fines and moved on with their lives. After David's court
appearances, the couple removed from Hertford County and resettled in
Northampton County, where they resided up to the Civil War.[31]

Richard Dempsey, a free man of color, and Morning Lane, a white
woman, of Perquimans County also sought to overcome legal limitations in
order to stay together and care for their family. Early in their relationship,
the couple faced trouble from county officials who sought to prosecute

them for cohabiting without being married. Following the county's attempt to try them, Richard and Morning continued to support one another and their family. During their time together, the couple had at least four children: Patsey, Marsha, Ephraim, and Abscilla. Richard and Morning's children used both the Dempsey and Lane surnames, which was a common practice for children born out of wedlock during the period. Although their children were not his direct heirs under the law, Richard, at his death in 1849, left all his property to Patsey, Marsha, Ephraim, and Abscilla and referred to each as "my daughter" or "my son."[32]

While not the norm, familial relationships between free persons of color and white people were regular occurrences in North Carolina. Although the law attempted to dissuade people from engaging in these relationships, many couples disregarded the rules, and many more North Carolinians silently ignored the illegality of their neighbors' decisions. The cases in which local justices charged free people of color and whites with fornication and adultery reveal that members of local power structures at times defended their laws, but their purposes are less clear. Local government officials targeted free men of color and white women more often than white men and free women of color, even in situations where the number of white men and free women of color commiting the crime was likely greater.

Local officials viewed sex between a white man and any woman as a private act as long as that sex did not violate the claim of another white man over that woman. Free men of color, however, did not enjoy this right to privacy. Local officials could more easily object to the sexual activities of free men of color because their surveillance did not interfere with their dedication to members of their white social circles; it did not challenge the power attached to white manhood. Bringing free men of color into court for their relationships with white women likely had some political incentive for local powerbrokers as well. Whites who despised free people of color in general and felt threatened by any advancement made by them likely enjoyed the spectacle of seeing one of their neighbors of color put in "his place."

Although some white people disliked free persons of color and reacted to the pandering of politicians, other whites viewed free people of color as faithful spouses, determined providers, and responsible parents. Some free people of color and white people realized that difference in racial categorization did not determine one's fitness to be a potential partner. The laws to prevent marriages between people of color and whites were political statements intended to make white families superior to all other families and to provide those families with the benefits of legitimacy. As with most political statements, there are always people within the society who disagreed with the reigning political agenda; this was the case of mixed couples of the eighteenth and nineteenth centuries. Although some white men attempted to use the law and their political voices to convince the public that they were indeed superior, a number of white women understood that many of them simply were not the social and financial equals of the most successful free men of color. Some free men of color were more financially secure and better able to provide for a family than some of their white counterparts. Many free men of color in relationships with white women were tradesmen such as blacksmiths and carpenters. For similar reasons, many free women of color may have found white men to be attractive mates. Economic status could trump racial categorization in these cases. In a society that commonly denied women the chance to make their own livelihoods, a man's ability to provide for a wife and children was imperative to almost any woman pursuing a stable family life.[33]

Physical appearance in conjunction with many free people of color's kinship connections to whites may have played an important role in the choices made by mixed-status couples. This seems to have been the case with the Hussey family of Montgomery County. The children of John and Eleanor Hussey had many generations of white ancestors including their mother. Whites in Montgomery County could not agree whether the Hussey children were "white" or "colored," often classifying them both ways. The Hussey children, however, seem to have associated most closely with whites. All the Hussey children married into local white families. The ownership of slaves by one son in the family further suggests that although some people placed the Husseys in the colored category, they did not associate themselves with most persons of color.[34]

Relationships between free persons of color and whites highlight the limits some individuals placed on the importance of racial categories as a tool to divide their society. The value that members of society placed on racial categories indeed could cause trouble for those categorized as free people of color, but that categorization did not serve as a strict guideline for social behavior or the way free people of color defined social insiders and outsiders. For some free people of color and whites, in certain contexts, categories such as mother and father or son and daughter were more significant than labels such as colored and white.

Single-Parent Families

Most of this chapter has focused on two-parent families; however, many free children of color never lived with both parents. Many children grew up solely under the care of a mother or father. Other children left both parents at an early age to serve as apprentices. These various experiences greatly affected free children of color's views about their place in society. Some children lived with single parents who had strong ties to other free people of color, and these children related closely to members of their mothers' or fathers' social circles. In many cases, free children of color grew up primarily outside of the influence of free people of color. Some of these children were born to white parents and experienced life inside social circles composed primarily of white people. In other cases, free children of color lived with white masters, as their apprentices and servants, and may have had little exposure to other people of color. Children in these situations may have been treated like members of an extended family and may have had access to white social networks. Of course, the historical record also demonstrates that many free people of color lived harsh lives under the dominions of their masters. They likely did not relate much to their masters, and in many cases, may have rejected their masters and other people of those masters' station.

Most children raised in single-parent households lived with their mothers. Many of these children probably associated with their mothers' relatives and friends and developed their self-understanding in reaction to those relations. Eliza Cummings, a free woman of color from Robeson County, raised several children by herself during the middle of the nineteenth century. David Strickland, a free man of color more than a decade her junior, was the father to at least some of Eliza's children. David paid child support but never married Eliza. In another example, Kitty Paul of Alamance County, a free person of color, grew up in a slightly different single-parent household. Kitty's mother was Mary Paul, a white woman, who had children by various men, both white and of color. By the time Kitty was a young girl, she was the only of her mother's children still in their household classified as a free person of color. As an adult, Kitty followed in the footsteps of her mother by becoming the mother of several illegitimate children.[35]

The courts sometimes removed free children of color from the care of single mothers and bound them out to serve as apprentices to masters, both white and of color. Some bound children continued to live in the households of their mothers after the courts issued their apprenticeships, while others lived with their court-appointed masters. Mary Ann Cooper, "a free mulatto girl," lived with her white mistress, Jane Mulder of Davie County, from 1824 until 1836. After living with Mulder, Mary Ann moved into the home of Clement Whittemore, a white man, who allegedly abused his apprentice. In 1841, Pasquotank County justices bound out nine of Nancy Hiter's children to Miles Sawyer, a white farmer in the county. As late as 1850, some of Nancy's children still lived without their mother as a part of Sawyer's household.[36]

Living outside of a family composed of a father and mother shaped the lives of free children of color in a variety of ways. These situations likely presented many free children of color with complex questions about their place in the social order. Many free children of color discovered different answers to queries about their relationship to those who surrounded them. Some chose to associate with other free people of color of similar background as adults, while others decided to abandon the social circles that society suggested that they should join. Again, racial categories, and a sense of groupness, were not congruent.

This chapter has explored the diversity of family situations free people of color experienced up to the Civil War. Their various family experiences contributed to the great diversity of primary social networks used by free people of color in their daily lives. Some free people of color identified with particular free families of color and limited their main social interactions to those circles of interrelated people. Other free people of color did not draw such solid lines but still tended to interact with people of similar economic status whether they were free people of color or whites. In many cases, free people of color did not belong to strong networks of other free people of color because they were outside of the kinship networks of these families.

The diversity of social experiences among free people of color demonstrates that people of color whether free or enslaved used a variety of criteria often excluding racial categorization to discern social insiders from outsiders. Family connections, "mother," "father," "son," and "daughter," sometimes had greater value than "colored," "negro," or "white." North Carolina law sought to discourage unions that brought family values into conflict with ideologies of racial inequality. Yet some North Carolinians chose love and family over division and discrimination.

⚜

CHAPTER 6

Liberty Intersected

Race, Gender, and Wealth

On January 30, 1856, Jane Milton, a free woman of color, submitted a divorce petition to the Guilford County Superior Court requesting a legal separation from her husband, Elisha Milton. With the assistance of George C. Mendenhall, a white attorney, she explained that not long after their marriage, Elisha "commenced abusing her and treating her very badly and within two years after their marriage he whipped her and his shameful abuse increased as he became more intemperate." Sometimes, Jane revealed, "he would run off a few months & return leaving her destitute of the means of support & when at home he provided but little & often nothing at all not even Bread for herself & children." In order to counter her husband's behavior, Jane worked and scraped up enough "to obtain the means of a very poor & scanty living for herself & children & supported them & most of the time also supported him." Even with her efforts, "from idleness and increased habits of intemperance he seemed to grow worse." Elisha ramped up his abuse, and "he seldom passed a week that he did not with his fist or stick beat & cruelly treat" Jane. "After she had worked hard & raised her three oldest children who were Boys to be able to do work to any advantage," Jane explained, Elisha had her sons bound out until age twenty-one "to get the money, which he spent in drinking."

After hiring out their sons, Elisha heightened his abusive behavior against his wife and "often threatened her life and by personal abuse & beating many times rendered her for days unable to work." Jane recalled that "about the month of April 1855, he fell upon her with a walking stick on which he had a large Buckhorn handle or head and abused her by beating over the head & legs & shoulders . . . and made her head bleed very much from the bruises on one side & the blood streamed from her nose and a bruise on her leg so severe & painful as to render her unable to walk for near a month." This final event gave Jane cause to leave Elisha and file for divorce. In addition, Jane noted that Elisha had taken their daughter and gone to live in adultery with Catherine Jones, "a free woman of color."

At the spring 1858 term, the Guilford County court issued a divorce decree based on the fact that Elisha Milton had committed adultery and declared Jane a "feme sole."[1] After this point, Jane was no longer directly at the mercy of Elisha. Yet Elisha's earlier actions along with her position as a poor woman prevented Jane from fully reassembling her life. The 1860 census shows Jane living in the house of a white family without her children.[2] The apprenticeships on her children were still active, leaving her unable to benefit from their work and create a stable family situation. As Elisha's actions reveal, Jane first as a married woman and later as a single woman did not have indisputable custody over her children. As in the colonial period, women, both white and of color, lacked explicit legal guardianship over their children in the national era. Under North Carolina law, children living with their divorced mothers were orphans. Many single and widowed women maintained control over their offspring. Yet only by the consent of local authorities did these women have parental authority. The state's completely male-dominated county courts ultimately determined whether single or widowed women had the right to have guardianship over their children.[3]

This case and many of those that appear in this chapter demonstrate that even in the national period, freedom status, gender, wealth, and other categorical structures continued to intersect with racial categorization. From the American Revolution to the Civil War, North Carolinians would argue and fight over the legal status of free people of color in the courthouses, on the streets, in the newspapers, and in the chambers of the state capitol, and during these debates, radical proslavery forces succeeded in chipping away at the legal privileges of free people of color. Nevertheless, those modifications in the law failed to diminish the importance of gender, wealth, age, or work for free people of color in their everyday lives. In some instances, discriminatory laws pressed North Carolinians to draw clearer distinctions between the privileged and the poor. At the height of radical proslavery power in the South, there were still well-to-do free persons of color who owned enslaved people, kept large homes, and sent their children to college, acts that neither poor whites nor poor free people of color could perform. During the national period, in many instances, North

Carolinians positioned men above women within the law and in society regardless of racial categorization.

The Underprivileged

Many of Jane Milton's challenges were common among North Carolina's underprivileged free people of color. Poor men, women, and children faced the greatest threats to their physical liberty and their abilities to determine their destinies and those of their families. Struggling free people of color, especially women and children, continued to deal with laws that promoted the mastery of the rich over the poor and upheld the influence of elites who sought to extract as much as possible from bound laborers. Across the state, county officials seized the children of poor women in order to bind them as apprentices. By the late antebellum period, the courts had the right to bind out children of poor households headed by men, and on some occasions, exercised it. Laws allowing the hiring out of insolvent convicted and unemployed free people of color targeted the poor and largely through corruption helped establish a convict labor system constructed on the backs of the less fortunate. Inestimable numbers of poor free people of color became entrapped by the opportunism of their more prosperous neighbors. Nevertheless, although recourse for exploitations could be difficult to obtain, they had the right to be heard by the courts, challenge their abusers, and seek redress.

North Carolina's apprenticeship records provide the greatest amount of information about the state's underprivileged free people of color. The records strongly suggest that at some point almost every municipality in the state attempted to impose apprenticeship on poor people of color. John Hope Franklin began a discussion about the system that has become a debate among historians questioning whether apprenticeship was exploitative or beneficial for free people of color.[4] Evidence from around the state suggests that apprenticeships gently opened opportunity's door for some free people of color while giving the most exploitative masters the chance to overwork and abuse their workers. Those who administered the system undeniably challenged the ability of many parents to gain from the labor of their children.

The apprenticeship system of the early national period operated in ways very similar to its late-colonial-period antecedent. The courts maintained the right to bind orphans, who were defined as children with no parents or children of unwed or widowed mothers, to local masters.[5] Justices could bind out children of color until age twenty-one, white boys until the same age, and white girls until their eighteenth birthdays. The law also continued to require masters to teach their apprentices how to read and write. In 1796, the Bertie County court bound "Joe Wiggins a molatto [*sic*] boy" and "Treaser Wiggins a molatto [*sic*] girl" to Blake Raby with assurance that both children would work for Raby until age twenty-one and that the master would instruct each in a trade and teach them to "read, write & cypher."[6] At the August session of Sampson County court during the same year, officials bound out Charlotte, Olive, and John, "the children of Hannah Williams a free mullatto [*sic*]" until their twenty-first birthdays. The court required their masters to provide each child with "1 years schooling."[7]

As in the colonial period, however, some localities issued apprenticeship agreements that did not always follow the guidance of the law. Some of the agreements worked in favor of free children of color by allowing shorter apprentice terms. On April 10, 1810, the Onslow County court issued apprentice indentures to William Cox for two free boys of color, Charles and Ezekiel Chance, and one girl of color, Nancy Chance. Under the law, the court should have bound all three Chance children until their twenty-first birthdays. Yet the bond for Nancy Chance only required her to work as an apprentice until age eighteen, the same term of service required of white girls.[8] The Rockingham County court bound free children of color under the same arrangement. In 1786, the justices coordinated the apprenticeships of four of Fanny Clark's "molatto" children. They bound her daughters Matt, Sal, and Lindy until their eighteenth birthdays and Fanny's son Ben until he reached twenty-one years of age.[9] Other agreements worked against free children of color permitting masters to ignore certain legal requirements. In 1817, William Fields, a Chatham County court chairman, bound free children of color Morris and Visey Evans to James O'Kelly and obligated O'Kelly to instruct the Evanses in the "mystery of farming." Yet someone with a pen struck out the requirement of literacy education for Morris and Visey on the preprinted bond.[10]

Gender discrimination in trade assignments persisted into the national period.[11] County courts continued to limit girls to jobs typically viewed as women's work. Nineteenth-century North Carolinians, like their colonial counterparts, assigned domestic chores to women and girls. Apprentice agreements for boys show that masters offered young men a much wider range of options. On November 29, 1804, the Currituck County court bound four "molatto" children of the Gordon family. The court apprenticed Bets Gordon and Sarah Gordon's daughter Keziah "to learn a woman's employment." In contrast, the master of Nancy Gordon's son James promised to teach him "the farming business" while the court agreed that Sarah Gordon's son Peter would learn to be a "mariner."[12] The binding of children at the March 1814 term of Beaufort County court further emphasizes how county officials discriminated between boys and girls when making trade assignments. During the session, the court bound out twenty-six free children of color. The justices assigned all the girls in this group to two trades and the boys to five trades. The masters of Patsey July Blount Blango, Winny M. Blango, Lucy Moore, Dinah Blango, Mary Tetterton, Nelly Tetterton, and Nancy Tetterton consented to teach them the business of a "spinstress" while Phebe Blango's master agreed that he would instruct her in the business of a "housekeeper." The court ordered John Keys bound to become a wheelwright. Officials apprenticed Benjamin Moore to learn the business of a turner. The masters of Willie Moore Blango, Churchill Conner, and Herman Blango agreed to teach them to be shoemakers. If they completed their assignments, blacksmithing would be the future trades of Anthony Moore, Stephen Moore, Jesse Tetterton, and James Brumfield. The cooper's trade was the assignment of the remaining boys bound out that term.[13] Discrimination in assignments, with few exceptions, guaranteed young women less pay than their male counterparts throughout their lifetimes and reinforced the position of women as dependents.

Abuse of children was a problem from the colonial period that continued to linger in the apprenticeship system into the period of North Carolina statehood. Young adults from around the state complained that their masters held them beyond their terms of service. In 1781, Molly Chavers complained to the Wake County court that Abram and George Martin by "force and threats" had kept her in "hard" servitude although she was born of free parentage and had a right to her freedom. The court agreed with her claim and set her at liberty.[14] Following the Chavers case, "Dempsey Hayes a Man of Yellow Complection" complained to the Wake County court that Robert Hayes had kept him beyond the legally required term of service. On March 7, 1793, the court issued an opinion in Dempsey Hayes's favor.[15]

Other apprentices, their parents, or friends complained about masters' mistreatments. In 1816, the Carteret County justices learned of the alleged abuse of "an orphan boy of colour named Ridden." They ordered the sheriff to deliver Ridden's master, George Gillikin, along with Enoch Gillikin and Elijah Arthur, witnesses, to the next court session to explain the situation.[16] In July 1847, the Moore County court rescinded the apprenticeship of Elias Phillips, "a free Boy of colour," to William Curtis after receiving a report of "cruelty inflicted on the said Boy." After removing the boy from Curtis's custody, the court drew up a new apprentice agreement with Robert H. Phillips, who promised to teach Elias Phillips the "trade and art of farming."[17]

Mistreated apprentices and those who simply detested the idea of being under their masters' control attempted to take their lives into their own hands by running away. In August 1794, Labon Taborn, "a free mulatto," found himself housed in the Orange County jail as a runaway. When Taborn appeared before the county court, he revealed that the Granville County court had bound him to David Bradford, who treated him "ill." Furthermore, Bradford had left Granville County for Rowan County. The record for Taborn's case does not explain whether Bradford had simply abandoned Taborn or attempted to remove him to Rowan County.[18] During the same year, Governor Richard Dobbs Spaight advertised for the return of a "mulatto lad" named James Bateman. His announcement stated Bateman was "about 14 or 15 years old, stout made. Has a large face, very dark, much the appearance of an Indian." Governor Spaight offered a forty-shillings reward for Bateman's return to his New Bern–area plantation.[19]

Some masters went beyond simply abusing apprentices within their own homes and attempted to obscure the freedom of their apprentices and sell them as slaves. "Ruth Tillett a free Born coloured woman" started her life in Currituck County and at an early age her mother, "a Free Woman named Ann Tillett," left her under the supervision of Timothy Mead of the same county. After Ann Tillett's death, Mead sold Ruth Tillett to a man named Blackstock, who in turn sold her to "Barny Coff of Newbern." In New Bern, one master after another sold Tillett upon learning "of her story." While illegally enslaved by John Bishop, Ruth Tillett escaped and returned to her "native country." Bishop hunted down Tillett and sold her to Zachariah Jordan, who promised to pay the purchase price once he received confirmation of Tillett's enslaved status. Ultimately, Bishop would be Tillett's last master. In 1783, at age forty, Ruth Tillett petitioned for her freedom, and the Pasquotank County court supported her claim to liberty.[20] Tillett's case highlights that poverty was a threat to the liberty of some underprivileged free people of color. Eventually, complaints of abuse led to legal reform at the state level. In 1801, legislators revised the state's apprentice laws and required masters to post a bond and give a promise that they would not remove apprentices from their home counties.[21]

Abuse was not the only difficulty free people of color faced under the apprenticeship system. The limited control women had over their children was a problem inherent to the system courts used to bind youngsters. The courts, by taking children from their mothers, hindered poor families of color from moving up the economic ladder. Temperance Chavers understood the limited power she had over her children. In 1810, she explained to the Brunswick County court that she had "raised two Boys Billy and Elick from their births to the present time with much difficulty, trouble & expense." Temperance Chavers continued that her investment in her children had just begun to pay off as the boys had recently reached the age in which they could plow and do other services to help support the family. Recognizing that the court would ultimately decide the fate of her children, she recommended that the children be bound to General Smith "to raise them properly and have them taught useful trades."[22] Children who could potentially help their mothers move out of poverty through their labor instead worked for their well-to-do neighbors, who further secured themselves through the cheap labor of their apprentices. Poor women like Temperance Chavers could only hope that their children, once free from their apprenticeships, could use the skills learned before gaining their independence to support them later in life.

Apprenticeship not only deprived poor mothers of their children's labor and earnings but also custody of their children. Once a master arranged for a child's apprenticeship, the master had sole guardianship over the child and could control a mother's physical contact with her offspring. Rachel Sampson only gained access to her son Edmond after his master explicitly gave her permission to keep him at her home. On February 29, 1840, Edmond's master, Timothy Hunter of Elizabeth City, wrote out a permission slip granting Sampson "the priviledge [sic] of keeping her son Edmond . . . and enjoying or receiving the benefit of his services until such time as I may see fit to call for him and take him home."[23] Hunter's wishes ultimately dictated the level of intimacy that Sampson could cultivate with her son during his childhood. At any moment, the law allowed Hunter to come to Sampson's house, collect Edmond, and do with him what he saw fit.

Some women of color fought back against apprenticeships that hindered their economic progress and threatened to disrupt their families, by petitioning the local courts. In 1824, Zilly Hagans, a free woman of color, along with eleven of her white neighbors petitioned the Wayne County court to prevent the binding of her children. She explained that her "Ennemys [sic]" had spread rumors that the Hagans children were "run[n]ing about in the neighbourhood" in search of food and were likely "to suffer." Zilly Hagans, backed by her supporters, denounced the rumors and pled with the court "not to take my children from me that is able to work and leave me with a parsell [sic] of small children not able to help themselves."[24]

Although free women of color regularly failed to fend off attempts to seize their children, occasionally they could successfully navigate the legal system and disrupt attempts to break up their families. At the June 1817 term of the Chowan County court, John Blount and William Bains complained about a group of "free negroes and mulattoes in their neighborhood, who were often disorderly and troublesome." Additionally, they claimed that the children of these people "had no masters and were likely to be reared in a manner not to their credit, nor for the good of society." In consideration of these allegations, Blount and Bains requested that "some of them might be obliged to give security for their good behavior, and that their children should be bound to proper masters." After they filed their complaint, the state charged thirty free people of color, including members of the James, Reuben, Mustapha, Overton, Dempsey, Mack, Burke, Gaskins, Vickery, and Pea families, with being "Disturbers of the Peace, Sabbath Breakers, Idlers, and common Nuisances to all the good citizens of the state." Unlike many free persons of color in their position, most of these people "except two or three" fended off the charges and preserved the standing of their families.[25] Although Blount and Bains sought to subjugate these families and force them into dependent relationships with the state and the potential masters of their children, these free people of color as individuals with legal standing had the opportunity to fight and win their cases.

On some occasions, women sought to retain control of their children through extralegal means. These women seized their children from their children's masters and left the area. On March 22, 1845, Joseph Arey placed an ad for the return of Mary Ann Bowen, "an indented bright mulatto girl about 15 years old, slender made, with straight black hair," whose mother, Polly Bowen, "took her away." Arey believed Polly Bowen escaped with her daughter to the "neighborhood of Goodwin Bowen, a free man of color in Bladen County."[26] J. J. Gilchrist issued an advertisement for the restoration of his apprentice "Henderson Smith, a bright Mulatto Boy about 14 years old." The January 9, 1857, announcement explained that Henderson's mother, Eliza Smith, took the boy without his master's consent, and Gilchrist thought that the mother and child probably left Fayetteville for Guilford County or Forsyth County.[27]

While some poor women chose to contest the binding of their children, others had no choice but to submit. Trapped in the apprenticeship system for generations, they were too poor to pursue other options. Generations of entanglement in the apprenticeship system defined the families' existence in the community. This was the case for the descendants of Elizabeth White, a free woman of color. By the beginning of the 1800s, Elizabeth White had arrived in Onslow County from Pitt County. Once she had settled in the area, Elizabeth White gave birth to several illegitimate children, whom the county court took up and bound out to masters. One of these children was Oma White, who upon her maturity saw her own children apprenticed out by the court. No later than 1860, Oma had begun to consider leaving North Carolina to settle in a free state. In a petition to the local court, Oma stated that she was the mother of thirteen children and was also a grandmother. She hoped to bring her children and grandchildren with her upon her exodus but realized that some of her grandchildren had to remain in Onslow County to finish out their apprenticeships. Oma explained that she desired to provide the court with a statement of her freedom in order to protect the liberty of the grandchildren left in servitude after her departure.[28] Unable to free her grandchildren from the obligations imposed on them by the courts because of their poverty, Oma White understood how poverty and the apprenticeship laws restricted her life choices.

Marriage could not protect and actually could limit the opportunities for poor women who sought to make decisions on behalf of their children without interference from men. In February 1815, Lydia Pettiford, a free woman of color, came before the Wake County court to seek a remedy to the condition of her children. Lydia explained to the court that before her marriage to Lewis Pettiford, a free man of color and her current husband, she had had two sons, Thomas and Ned. After their mother's marriage, the two boys continued to live with their grandfather Reuben Bass. Thomas and Ned, however, eventually came to live with their mother and step-father after Lewis Pettiford persuaded his father-in-law to turn over the boys to him. Lydia believed that her husband would support her sons but later determined that her sons were "not provided for in such manner as the law directs." Furthermore, she explained that her husband hired out Thomas and Ned against her wishes. Reuben Bass accompanied his daughter to court and affirmed that his grandsons were "likely to suffer in not being provided for."[29]

Lydia Pettiford's dilemma highlights the continued importance of hier-archies beyond racial categorization in the day-to-day lives of free people of color in national-period North Carolina. When Lydia gave birth to her sons, she as a single woman did not have indisputable custody over her chil-dren. As in the colonial period, women, both white and of color, lacked ex-plicit legal guardianship over their children in the national era. Many single and widowed women maintained control over their offspring. Yet their power was supported only by the consent of local authorities. The state's completely male-dominated county courts ultimately determined whether single or widowed women had the right to have guardianship over their children. As they saw fit, courts could grant, take away, and reassign the guardianship of so-called "baseborn" or "orphan children." Lydia's marriage to Lewis Pettiford and her status as his dependent further denigrated her position and created additional challenges to her ability to control her chil-dren's destinies. By bringing her father into the case, Lydia demonstrated her political savvy while at the same time she capitulated to the reality that Reuben Bass's complaint on her behalf may have been her best chance to realize her desires. She would have a difficult time challenging her husband alone, but through her father's voice, she might shift the patriarchal as-sumptions of the court in her favor.

State laws affecting the poor generally targeted women and children. A change in state law during the 1820s, however, permitted local officials to challenge the parental rights of poor free men of color. In 1827, along with passing reforms prohibiting masters from removing free children of color out of their home counties, lawmakers in Raleigh also expanded the number of families of color who could have children taken away and bound out. The new law permitted courts to bind out "the children of free negroes and mulattoes, where the parent, with whom such children may live, does or shall not habitually employ his or her time in some honest industrious occupation."[30] For the first time in North Carolina history, the courts could bind out legitimate children who had living fathers. The 1827 General Assembly never defined "habitually employ" or "honest industrious occupation," leaving the courts leeway to apprentice children from a wide variety of poor families. A glance over the surviving court records reveals that some localities took advantage of this law, but not to the extent of rounding up the children of all poor fathers of color. Representing the Nash County court, Thomas W. Taylor notified Willy Locus, a free man of color, that the court planned to bind out his children Evelina, William, and Rachel at the November 1851 session. Taylor explained that the apprenticing of the children would "prevent them from strolling about in Poverty and Idolness [sic]."[31]

Local courts also appear to have used the same law that affected the Locus family to bind out the children of men who abandoned their families. On May 29, 1854, after the Alamance County court determined that Ephraim Haithcock, a free man of color, had "abandoned his family," the body sent William Haithcock, "a boy of color & son of said Ephraim Haithcock," to Jesse McDaniel "to live after the manner of an apprentice & servant."[32] In a similar situation, the Halifax County court bound out Harriet, John, and Melissa Hammonds, the children of Willie and Betsey Hammonds, free persons of color, after determining that Willie had abandoned his family. According to a report presented at the May 1848 session, the Hammonds family had struggled without Willie's support for seven years before the court decided to intervene.[33]

Discriminatory alterations to the apprenticeship laws opened the door to unprecedented exploitation of poor persons of color and challenged the idea that apprenticeship was purely an institution intended to manage and educate the poor. At the 1836–37 General Assembly session, legislators amended the apprenticeship regulations to no longer require the "master of a colored apprentice to teach him or her to read and write."[34] In 1858, when the Halifax County clerk drew up the agreement for the apprenticeship of Anna Mitchell, a "Free negro," he struck the preprinted words "to read and write" from the document.[35] In other counties, administrators had bonds printed specifically for free people of color that excluded the language requiring literacy education.[36]

The largely unregulated practice of granting apprentices freedom dues opened the door to inconsistences in apprentice agreements. In some of these agreements, masters and courts decided to privilege boys over girls. On February 6, 1841, James Calloway promised the Wilkes County court to pay freedom dues to each of the apprenticed children of Polly Grinton, a free woman of color. He agreed to give to Polly Grinton's daughters Mary and Ann $100 apiece upon their turning twenty-one years of age. Calloway, however, guaranteed James, William, and John Grinton an additional $40 on their twenty-first birthdays.[37] Other cases reveal that white children received dues above those of free children of color. At the December 1857 session of Stokes County court, Joseph Joyce promised five-year-old Caleb Sizemore, a white boy, $90 and "one good suite of clothing" at the end of his apprenticeship. During the same session, C. B. Christian agreed to give Caleb Franklin, a free boy of color, also five years old, "ten dollars & good clothes."[38] Yet, other examples exist in which free children of color received guarantees equal to or greater than those given to white children. At the November 1858 term of Guilford County court, masters promised two white boys, Rufus L. Allen and Charles Hall, and John Friend, "an orphan boy of color," $100 each at the end of their terms of service.[39] In 1849, Jacob Clodfetter of Davidson County consented to give Riley Clodfetter, a white orphan, $75 and a freedom suit worth $15 at the end of his apprenticeship while R. J. Cicil of the same county assured Thomas Cane, a free boy of color, $110.50 on his twenty-first birthday.[40] Maybe Cicil decided to provide Cane with a larger sum than Riley Clodfetter because the law did not obligate him to educate Cane while Jacob Clodfetter had to provide his apprentice with basic mathematical and literacy instruction. Whatever the situation may have been in the Davidson County instance, the cases from around the state, viewed as a collective, suggest that potential masters and court officials used a variety of inconsistent formulas in order to determine freedom dues for both children of color and white boys and girls.

Difficulties for poor free people of color extended beyond the problems associated with apprenticeship. Although indentured servitude largely disappeared from North Carolina after the colonial period, adults around the state continued to become entrapped in servitude throughout the national period. Some free people of color signed long-term work agreements with people willing to feed or clothe them. Lawmakers did not regulate these contracts, which led to inconsistency in agreement terms. On July 11, 1818,

Betsy Boon of Onslow County, a free person of color, signed her X to an agreement placing her in the service of Jonas Johnston "to live after the manner of a servant" until Johnston's death. Under the arrangement, Boon was to serve her master "faithfully" and "gladly obey and not absent herself from her master's service without leave." In exchange for Boon's services, Johnston promised to provide her with a "sufficient diet and apparel fitting for a servant and also all other things necessary in sickness and in health."[41] In 1831, Nicy Simpson, a free woman of color from Tyrrell County, agreed to apprentice her daughter Rindy to Sarah Mann for sixteen years until the girl reached twenty-one years old. As part of an agreement drawn up on the same day, Nicy Simpson also bound herself to Sarah Mann. This contract stated that Nicy Simpson would serve Sarah Mann and her heirs for "Ninety Nine Years" as an "apprentice and servant." Mann simply agreed to find Nicy Simpson "something to Eat & warm lodging" in exchange for a lifetime of service.[42]

The historical record does not reveal whether free people of color always understood the agreements they generally marked with an X, but surviving documents establish that at least some adults of color became dissatisfied with the situations imposed on them by their new masters. On January 31, 1804, G. Elliot of Cumberland County advertised a reward for "a Mulatto Man, named Henry Davis," who had run away. He explained that Davis had "bound himself to me as a servant for a term of years."[43] Davis may have bound himself, but he had no plans to remain under Elliot's control for the duration of the agreed period. In a May edition of the *Greensboro Patriot*, Thomas Carbry of the town advertised a reward for the return of "a certain free mulatto by the name of William I. Mitchell." Carbry complained that Mitchell "being of full age, entered into a voluntary contract with me, binding himself to serve a certain time, for the purpose of learning the Carriage Making business. As soon as he acquired a sufficient knowl[e]dge of the trade . . . he [t]hought proper to take himself off." The abandoned master further declared that Mitchell had no cause to run away, "except that of being too well used."[44] Carbry may have believed that Mitchell had no cause to flee, but Mitchell certainly disagreed.

During the national period, legislation passed by the General Assembly opened the door to forced labor for free people of color. These laws targeted poor and underprivileged free people of color who failed to find work to the satisfaction of county justices or were unable to pay court fines. An

1827 law allowed county justices of the peace to arrest and hire out "any free negro or mulatto . . . who is able to labor, shall be found spending his or her time in idleness and dissipation, or who has no regular or honest employment or occupation."[45] At an 1828 session of Edgecombe County court, jurors found Allen Morgan, a "free negro," guilty of "idleness and dissipation." As a result, the court ordered Morgan hired out, and someone paid the county to work Morgan for a year.[46]

Legislation passed at the 1831–32 General Assembly session permitted a county to hire out for up to five years a "free negro or free person of colour" convicted of a crime and "unable to pay the fine imposed."[47] These acts became the undergirding to a much grander convict labor system that spread across the nation after the Civil War. Evidence from the surviving county court records strongly suggests that many jurisdictions purposely charged convicted free people of color excessive fines to guarantee their hiring out. These excessive fines were particularly the problem of the poor and those with limited connections to moneyed individuals willing to pay their fines. In at least one case, Surry County officials took advantage of the 1830s hiring law. On several instances between 1848 and 1850, Surry County officials sought the arrest of Michael Warden, a "free man of colour," and Anna Sturdevant, "a white woman," for the crime of "fornication and adultery." Finally, in December 1850, Stokes County sheriff John G. Hill located the couple and threw Warden in the county jail. Stokes County officials had Warden extradited to neighboring Surry County the next spring. The Surry County court quickly brought Warden to trial, where the jury found him, alone, guilty of fornication and adultery. The court assessed an extravagant judgment of $100 against Warden. With normal fines for such a conviction as low as $5 in many counties, Surry County officials undoubtedly meant to charge a penalty too great for Warden to pay and to have him hired out as a result. Their plan succeeded, and the court ordered the sheriff to hire out Warden to someone willing to pay his fine. With Warden standing before the courthouse steps, all stood quiet when the call came for someone willing to pay $100 for the free man of color's services. The sheriff resorted to taking bids until the crowd agreed that Mr. Dolson, with a bid of $25, would carry Warden home.[48]

North Carolina law and elites' contempt for and willingness to exploit the underprivileged made the state a difficult environment for many free people of color who were women, poor, or underage. The examples in this section reveal how elites used the intertwining of categorization as a person of color along with gender, age, and wealth to target underprivileged free people of color. They expose the difficulty of parsing out how specific forms of categorization and classification related to life outcomes. Impoverishment, categorization as a free person of color, or being a child never existed in isolation.

The Privileged

A small yet diverse and important group of individuals made up the population of free people of color who could be described as well-to-do in national-era North Carolina. Although society placed them in the same sociopolitical category as underprivileged free people of color, their experiences largely contrasted with the lives of unfortunate apprentices, destitute mothers, out-of-work fathers, and poor convicts. Changes to North Carolina law during the nineteenth century exposed privileged free people of color to discrimination in the courthouse and removed them from the polling places after 1835. Nevertheless, money, power, and influence allowed these free people of color to maneuver through society in ways of which many poor people, both white and of color, could only dream.

The backgrounds of North Carolina's privileged free people of color varied as widely as their talents. John C. Stanly and Donum Montford of Craven County and Louis Sheridan of Bladen County entered the world as slaves. Before his arrival in Caswell County, Thomas Day was born in Virginia to free parents. His mother, Morning Stewart Day, was the daughter of a free man of color, Thomas Stewart, who was a doctor and slaveholder in Dinwiddie County, Virginia. Matthew N. Leary and Ephraim Hammonds of Fayetteville were also born free. James D. Sampson's status at birth is shrouded in family myth and mystery.[49]

The exact paths these men used to achieve success are largely lost, but the fact that almost all of them were skilled and fairly well-educated helped them maintain the privileges obtained during different points in their lives. John C. Stanly and Ephraim Hammonds were master barbers. Donum Montford was one of New Bern's most respected plasterers. Louis Sheridan worked as a merchant and managed an upscale inn in Elizabethtown. Thomas Day's Milton cabinetmaking business was highly reputed across parts of North Carolina and Virginia. James D. Sampson ran a large carpentry business in Wilmington. Matthew N. Leary operated a firm that crafted, sold, and repaired harnesses, saddles, bridles, martingales, whips, collars, and hardware. All of these men had associates working in their businesses who allowed them to rake in significant profits.[50]

Most of the privileged free men of color were major land holders in their communities, often owning town lots along with farms or plantations. John C. Stanly, the wealthiest free man of color at any time in North Carolina history, owned several town lots in New Bern and plantations in Craven County. In 1815, his holdings totaled 1,500 acres. Below Stanly were men like James D. Sampson, who owned an estimated $14,000 worth of real estate according to the 1850 census. In 1861, Sampson's estate included nine town lots in Wilmington.[51]

As important craftspeople or large farmers, privileged free men of color generally were members of the master class. They were slaveholders, hired the slaves of their neighbors, or kept apprentices. Many of these men maintained guardianship over some combination of these dependents within their households. John C. Stanly was one of the largest slaveholders in Craven County during his lifetime. An account written after his death suggested he owned between sixty and one hundred slaves. A Craven County tax list confirms that Stanly held twenty-one people in bondage in 1815. The Craven County court also apprenticed numerous boys and girls to Stanly. Thomas Day, James D. Sampson, Matthew N. Leary, and Louis Sheridan owned much smaller numbers of slaves and managed apprentice workforces. In addition to owning slaves, Sheridan hired additional slave labor.[52]

Further demonstrating their power within North Carolina's social hierarchy, free people of color did not limit themselves to owning human property but also sold their human chattel at leisure or when necessary. By trading in human property, privileged persons of color reaffirmed their authority as members of the master class and reinforced the important lineation between the free and the enslaved. On April 17, 1819, John C. Stanly placed an advertisement for the sale of "Roger, a Ship Carpenter, Peter Fagan, a Cooper & Stevedore, George, a Cooper, and Allen, a Sailor."[53] Sometime before his departure from North Carolina in the late 1830s, Louis Sheridan sold a man known as Larry or Larry Richardson to William Harris.[54] The sales of these enslaved people would have led to a forced refiguring of their daily lives. Some may have had to break or rearrange family ties while all had to readjust to the management styles of new masters.

Like many white enslavers, privileged free people of color were responsible for the management of their labor force, which included the discipline and recovery of runaway slaves. The language free men of color used in runaway advertisements strongly suggests that these men valued their authority over others more than any sense of comradery based in their common categorization as people of color with their underlings. On November 21, 1815, John C. Stanly issued an advertisement for the return of "a Negro boy slave, called BRISTER WARWICK." Stanly explained that Warwick "is supposed to have taken the road to Washington, North-Carolina, as he was seen 12 miles to the Southward of that place . . . and was a little distance behind a gang of sailors who were travelling northwardly."[55] Like other southern slaveholders, Stanly alluded to the idea that his bondsman absconded in order to make his way north to freedom. Matthew N. Leary's newspaper ad for the recovery of "a Negro man named LUKE" made a similar connection between absconding slaves and the North as a haven for such runaways. In his March 29, 1853, advertisement, Leary described Luke as "about five feet six or eight inches high, dark complected, has a scar on the side of one of his eyes . . . stout built, weighs about 175 or 180 pounds." He provided newspaper readers with two possible scenarios to explain what may have happened to Luke. In both, Leary implicated other free people of color as the agents most likely to help his runaway bondsman find freedom. He explained that Luke "has relatives in the County of Sampson, among them a half-brother named Sam Boon,—a free man of color,—and may possibly be lurking in that neighborhood, as I am informed he was seen about there a short time since." If Luke did not seek help from his brother, Leary believed that "possibly he may have obtained free papers, and is endeavoring to escape to a free State, as I understand some free persons of color removed from Sampson county last week to Indiana."[56] Leary's statements reinforced all of the common beliefs of radical southern slaveholders of his day which connected runaways with the physical presence of free people of color and the temptation of freedom in the North. His desire to restore his human property superseded any sympathy he may have had for the plight of other free people of color, especially those who might harbor runaway slaves.

Free men of color who kept other persons of color as apprentices also dealt with the recovery of their subordinates. These instances demonstrate that unequal power fueled tensions among free persons of color, and that the will of privileged free men of color could interfere with the personal objectives of the underprivileged. On October 26, 1814, Ephraim Hammonds placed an advertisement for the return of a "free man of color" bound to him to learn "the Barber[']s trade." Hammonds offered "Five Dollars Reward" and to "pay all expense for his delivery."[57] Donum Montford's April 1, 1826, advertisement for the return of an apprentice named Bill Spellman circulated in issues of the *Newbern Sentinel*. In his advertisement, Montford asserted, "All persons are forwarned [*sic*] from harbouring or impolying [*sic*] said Apprentice, under the penalty of the law" and he offered a five-cents reward for Spellman's recovery.[58] The ways by which Hammonds and Montford demanded the return of their apprentices were no different from those of their white counterparts. They were forceful in their attempts to restore the master-apprentice relationship, even when they shared a common social categorization with their trainees. In these relationships, the hierarchy of the workplace overrode the importance of common freedom status and racial categorization.

Following the paths set by many noted slave masters of their time, free persons of color who sold human beings and sought to extract labor from enslaved persons and apprentices also maintained the capacity to act as emancipators and supporters of greater civil liberties for people of color. They overcame the conflict between assisting their own family members, friends, and close associates out of bondage and, at the same time, trading in the flesh of others. John C. Stanly held the dual role of being a large slaveholder and one of North Carolina's most important emancipators. After gaining his own freedom, Stanly procured the funds to purchase and manumit his wife and children. In addition, he assisted in the emancipation of his brother-in-law and several other enslaved associates. Even Brister Warwick, who Stanly had advertised as a runaway, received his freedom through Stanly's efforts. In addition, Stanly along with Louis Sheridan were local agents of *Freedom's Journal*, which featured antislavery articles and was the first newspaper in the United States published by free persons of color. Stanly also assisted the Quakers in their plans to liberate slaves and send them to free territories.[59] These examples reveal that privileged free people of color dealt with a tension between operating successful economic enterprises, which in the South generally required enslaving other people, and opposing proslavery ideologies, which often suggested that all people of color were inferior to whites and inspired the curbing of free people of color's legal rights.

Until the conclusion of the Civil War, educational opportunities for most people of color were quite limited. Yet those with wealth overcame the common social and economic barriers that prohibited or severely restricted the formal educational attainment of the masses. Although the state excluded their sons and daughters from public education, privileged free people of color provided their children with basic and advanced education. John C. Stanly's son John S. Stanly was better educated than the majority of his contemporaries. Born around the turn of the century, John S. Stanly taught at a school for children of color in New Bern. John P. Green, a student of John S. Stanly, recalled, "As a reader, speller and penman, he was not surpassed; and in all the studies, pertaining to a thorough English education, he was the equal of the best." John S. Stanly passed on the legacy bestowed upon him and sent his daughter to college. In the 1850s, Sarah Stanly attended Oberlin College in Ohio. During the same decade, Ann Maria Hazle, a fellow New Bern native and daughter of Richard Hazle, a free man of color, artisan, and slaveholder, joined Sarah Stanly at the northern Ohio school.[60] Thomas Day's push for his children's education paralleled that of the New Bern elites. Day sent his daughter Mary Ann along with her brothers Thomas Jr. and Devereux to Wesleyan Academy in Wilbraham, Massachusetts, to further their educations. James D. Sampson's son John Patterson Sampson attended school in Cambridge, Massachusetts, before matriculating into and completing Comer's College in Boston. A younger son, Benjamin Kellogg Sampson, completed Oberlin College in the 1860s. Later in life, the Sampson brothers earned their doctorates.[61]

Throughout the pre–Civil War period, only the obituaries of the wealthy and highly respected or infamous appeared in local North Carolina newspapers. As a result, the obituary section of newspapers was generally the exclusive domain of white elites. On extremely rare occasions, notices about the deaths of privileged free people of color interrupted the usual pattern. Upon his death in 1841, New Bern's *Spectator* and at least one additional paper printed John C. Stanly's obituary. The papers exclaimed that Stanly "possessed an intellect of the first order, had a most retentive memory, and his mind was well stored with useful knowledge. He was a kind and affectionate husband, a tender and indulgent father, and his correct and gentlemanly deportment secured for him the affection and esteem of all his acquaintance."[62] Even during a period in which whites regularly debated the proper position of free people of color in North Carolina, the editors of some newspapers did not fret about how to discuss Stanly's position in society. Stanly's privilege in life allowed for the public memorialization of his death.

The examples in this section highlight many of the major contrasts between the lives of privileged free people of color and the existences of their poorer counterparts. Largely through their wealth and reputation, privileged free persons of color skirted around the limitations society imposed on most people of color. They avoided many impositions experienced by those free people of color with fewer privileges, such as the forced apprenticeship of their children, exclusion from higher education, and hiring out for failure to pay court fines.

The Yeomen and Artisans

Among free people of color, a small number of nonslaveholding small landowners and artisans existed between the underprivileged and affluent. Like their wealthier neighbors, small landowning free people of color discovered success through an assortment of avenues, and they traveled a variety of paths to achievement. These free people of color, like their colonial counterparts, maintained some sense of control over their own fortunes and those of their dependents. Yet unlike in the colonial period, they existed in much larger numbers and on rare occasions included women among their ranks. Their wealth kept them out of states of dependence and largely protected them from complete failure or seizure of their freedom because of court defeats. Their position, however, could be precarious during bad economic times or periods of major hardship at home or work. Their mastery over others was largely limited to their family members and the occasional apprenticed worker. Nevertheless, some of these people, through their personal successes and reputations, created a social network that supported them during times of trouble and protected them from the most egregious abuses generally experienced by the poor.

Through their exploits, these free people of color became owners of generally small yet sometimes significant landholdings. On the higher end of the spectrum were men like Isham Chavis of Cumberland County. When he died in the 1790s, Chavis owned five tracts of land totaling 770 acres. Further down the ladder were people like Ephraim Manuel. By 1804, Manuel had accumulated 198 acres in Sampson County. Claiborne Wiggins of

Franklin County was more typical of national-period landowners of color. During the 1850s, Wiggins controlled a small parcel containing 24.5 acres.[63] The ownership of real property separated these free people of color from their poorer counterparts. Landownership could potentially lead to a degree of economic independence and self-mastery that the poor, although free, lacked because of their dependency on wages or sustenance from their masters, or obligations to landlords.

In addition to acquiring real estate, free people of color accumulated an assortment of personal property. Those situated at both the bottom and higher ends of the economic spectrum kept livestock. Among Gabriel Locklear's many assets in 1848 were hogs and cattle along with more expensive animals including horses, oxen, and a mule. His Halifax County estate also consisted of tools and products found on the typical North Carolina farm such as a plough and weeding hoes, axes, corn, and fodder. Some people, seeking more than just practical possessions, owned luxury goods such as pleasure carriages and jewelry. In 1855, Asbury Reid of Gates County was the owner of a gold watch. The next year, Willis Boyt of the same county paid taxes on a pleasure carriage and a silver watch.[64] Personal property ownership was not unique to the artisans, small landholders, or their slaveholding counterparts, as most poor people maintained some assortment of personal possessions. The quality of their possessions or the types of possessions, however, would have symbolized economic differences, and in many circles, codified social dissimilarity to the poor. Creators of the North Carolina tax system believed that the ownership of luxury goods, such as carriages and watches, like land, placed people who possessed them in a unique economic category. People who owned luxury items, regardless of racial categorization, paid higher property taxes than their less-endowed neighbors.

While many successful free people of color invested their money in real estate and other forms of property, some used their savings to purchase family members out of bondage. Thomas Newton, a "master of the carpenter business" in Craven County during the early nineteenth century, purchased his wife, Sarah. In a petition for his wife's freedom, Newton promised that his professional acumen would continue to allow him to "maintain himself, wife & children."[65] At some point before 1838, Henry I. Patterson, a highly respected bricklayer and plasterer in Raleigh, saved enough money to purchase his wife, Emmaline. After buying his wife, Patterson and eighty-one of his white neighbors petitioned the General Assembly for her freedom.[66] Wealth provided Newton and Patterson the opportunity to free their wives from slavery and protect their descendants from the legal limitations imposed on enslaved people. Their financial security also helped to convince their supporters that both men could provide for their soon-to-be formerly enslaved family members and that those kinspeople would not become burdens on the local population.

The opportunity to loan money allowed free people of color with means to increase their holdings by collecting interest on debt and sometimes simply to help friends in need. At his death in the late 1840s, William Croker of Orange County held notes against several free people of color and white people. Hector Locklear, a Robeson County blacksmith, loaned money to an equally diverse group of men. By 1857, the debts owed to Locklear's estate totaled $2,382.19.[67] These men, as participants in the money-lending business, made themselves essential actors in their local economies. Their prosperity gave them financial and social power over their neighbors and provided them with potential means for additional income.

Secure enough to support themselves or searching for ways to expand their businesses, some middling free people of color could afford to take on apprentices and hired workers. At the November 1830 session of Gates County court, the justices ordered "Washington Smith a free boy of colour & son of Hulda Smith be bound an apprentice to John Saunders a free man of colour to learn the trade of a Millwright."[68] In 1854, the Beaufort County court apprenticed John Powers, a free boy of color, to the successful caulker Southy Keys. The next year, the same court bound Alston Wiggins and Harry Wiggins, free boys of color and sons of Sabry Wiggins, to Isaiah Keys and Shadrack Keys, adjoining landholders and free men of color. Isaiah Keys promised to teach Alston Wiggins farming while Shadrack Keys agreed to instruct Harry Wiggins in the cooper's trade.[69] Like their wealthier counterparts, these free men of color had the authority to shape the futures of young people of lower social and economic statuses. With only the local courts as their overlords, these men held tremendous power over how their apprentices lived. Similar to other masters, they determined their apprentices' work hours, schedules, and diets. Furthermore, they held the power to discipline their young charges.

Like other members of the master class, middling free people of color dealt with runaway apprentices who sought to break their contracts, ran from abusive masters, or needed a break from their arduous work. Free persons of color like John E. Patterson, a plasterer in Fayetteville, faced the difficult task of keeping their workforces in line. On January 16, 1846, Patterson distributed an advertisement for the return of his runaway apprentice Willis Stuart alias Willis Jones. Willis was "a bright Mulatto, of small stature" with "a full head of hair, of a dark brown color, and nearly straight." He had the opportunity to learn to read and write, "though rather imperfectly."[70] Regardless of the opportunities Patterson provided Willis, the master's demands conflicted with the young man's objectives. Although neither Patterson nor his apprentice were elites, small but important differences in power and affluence drew them apart.

By accumulating bits of wealth over their lifetimes, small property–holding free persons of color provided their descendants with legacies. In 1835, Nathaniel Newsom of Northampton County arranged for the distribution of his property among his descendants. He left his lands in North Carolina to his sons Nathaniel and Willis. His daughter Dorothy Archer received real estate located in Logan County, Ohio. The younger Nathaniel Newsom also inherited his father's brandy still. Sely Byrd, Charlotte Haithcock, and Edith Roberts collected $10 each upon their father's death. The elder Newsom gifted a bed and furniture to his daughter Elizabeth. At their mother's passing, Elizabeth Newsom along with her sister Telitha Hawley would collect the proceeds from the sale of their father's livestock, farming tools, and remaining furniture.[71] Before his death in the 1850s, Hardy Richardson of Halifax County devised a will distributing a wide range of property to his wife, children, and grandchildren. He left land to his wife, Darcas; sons, Edward, Abner, Alfred, and Mason; daughters, Louisa and Mary; and grandchildren. Richardson also passed on a "stock of horses, hogs, cows, and sheep," bonds, and cash to his wife and children.[72] Property divisions left the younger generations with less than their forebearers. Yet property inheritance provided heirs a step up over their poor neighbors and potentially gave some of the savviest among them the opportunity to build additional wealth from their inheritances. Free people of color could also translate property inheritances into educational opportunities for their children, the foundation for new homes, or the expansions of old farms. Robert C. Kenzer's study of postbellum North Carolina suggests that some of this transferred wealth and property continued to support free people of color and their descendants long after the Civil War.[73]

Like their colonial predecessors, widowed free women of color of the national period often faced hardships after the passing of their spouses because of the limited property rights and rights to children guaranteed by the law to women of their status. Widows of color sometimes had to petition their local courts in order to receive financial support from their husbands' estates. During February 1833, Keziah Overton sent a request to the Perquimans County court for "her year's provisions" from the estate of her husband, Benjamin.[74] Once the court accepted a widow's claim for support, the widow still had to depend on the court to provide her with adequate provisions. Other widows devised schemes to keep their children under the legal control of their family members. Failure to make such arrangements could potentially allow unscrupulous county justices to bind out the children of successful families of color to nonkin. Avoiding this situation after the death of her husband, Zachariah, Zilla Pierce Cordon of Beaufort County had the local court apprentice her underage sons Alexander and Humphrey F. Cordon to their brother, whose name was also Zachariah.[75] In a world in which they experienced limited rights to property and their children, some free women of color became astute negotiators within the social and political system. They attempted to secure their personal wishes as best as possible and avoid the hardships of less affluent women whose financial and familial situations nearly collapsed with the deaths of their husbands. These free women of color shared the experiences of white women in the same situations, who only through better social connections could avoid the possible troubles associated with the death of husbands.

The experiences of nonslaveholding artisans and landholders reinforce the importance of differing levels of wealth and power among free people of color. The most fortunate of this population enjoyed many of the same opportunities as their wealthier counterparts, including ownership of significant landholdings and mastery over apprentices. Even those free people of color at the lower ends of the propertied and artisan spectrum enjoyed a type of stability and security unavailable to their underprivileged neighbors. Of course, the experiences of women and men among this group could differ drastically. North Carolina law placed a burden on women, especially widows, which required them to be sometimes savvier than men of their same status in order to protect their personal interests and those of their immediate family members.

꙳ꙮ

In the United States' earliest years, radical proslavery ideologues, through their propaganda and legislative achievements, sought to blur the social and economic distinctions among free persons of color and between free people of color and slaves. The law permitting the binding of children from poor families of color, including those families with a male head of the household, sought to denigrate the status of poor free men of color and put them on par with poor women. Yet wealth, gender, educational attainment, and other forms of human organization continued to shape the diverse experiences of free people of color in North Carolina. Whether a free person of color was a man or a woman or rich or poor mattered to that individual and that individual's community. Poor free people of color struggled to maintain control over their daily lives. The struggle was particularly difficult for free women of color. Free persons of color with property, a group composed disproportionately of men, sought to wield whatever power they had over their dependents. Radicals may have portrayed free people of color as the equals of slaves but slaveholding free persons of color understood the situation differently and regularly sought to control their bondspeople and apprentices. Laws discriminating against free people of color burdened the wealthy free persons of color as well as the poor. The more well-to-do free people of color, however, could use their wealth and influence to overcome some of the burdens of bigotry. At the same time, even the power of wealth could overcome only some of the challenges of being a person of color and also a woman. Free women of color who lived beyond the bounds of poverty enjoyed benefits connected directly to their economic statuses but lacked access to important privileges, including rights to their children.

CHAPTER 7

Guilty or Innocent?

Free People of Color in the Courts

During the fall of 1822, Peter Harsting, Mack Crump, John P. Hodgens, and Miles Worsham, all white men, appeared in Rowan County Superior Court charged with riot, false imprisonment, and assault and battery. According to the *Western Carolinian*, Harsting contacted justices of the peace to obtain an order to flog a "free negro" for what the paper described as "some mischief he had done." The justices gave permission for the flogging to commence and cited an "old law" that allowed "Justices of the Peace to authorize the summary punishment of *slaves*" as justification for the beating of a free man. The paper explained that this was their "fatal error" and further clarified that David Valentine "was free, the law knew no distinction between him and a white man. He should have been indicted, and brought into Court for trial, in the same manner that free white cit[i]zens are."[1] The Superior Court jury followed the same rationale, found the four defendants guilty of the charges, and imposed hefty fines, including a $1,200 penalty against Harsting. After the criminal trial, Valentine brought the defendants back to court to face civil charges. Jurors for the civil case also sided with Valentine and awarded him $200 in damages.[2]

The case of David Valentine is just one of many instances in which a free person of color found justice in a legal system that prohibited persons of color from testifying against whites, permitted only white men to serve as jurors and judges, and allowed sometimes radically different punishments for whites and people of color convicted of the same crimes. The latter of these opened the door to abuse of the justice system. Yet, in most cases, maintaining order and promoting social stability were the primary interests of pre–Civil War courts. Focusing on these goals, judges and juries did not assume that all free people of color were inherently criminal or incompetent. Normally, the courts evaluated each free person of color as an individual with value to important community institutions.

The appearances of free persons of color as plaintiffs and defendants in the courts demonstrate that officials incorporated them into local political communities and saw them as within bounds of their society, not on its periphery or beyond its limits. Free people of color appeared in courts across the state as both plaintiffs and defendants in civil suits, with whites and sometimes free people of color on the other side. They more frequently appeared in the courts to face criminal charges as well as to support criminal cases against others. Determining a general set of statistical outcomes for these cases is impossible because of the varying conditions of court records across the state. The existing records, however, provide insight into the spectrum of situations free people of color faced within the justice system and the diversity of outcomes produced by judges and juries.

Although community leaders used the courts largely to maintain public order, sometimes discrimination within the law created opportunities for legally sanctioned law-breaking and corruption by white authorities. Discrimination within the law included the inability of people of color to testify against whites and differential punishment based on a defendant's racial categorization. Communities developed strategies to overcome the legal exclusion of testimony from people of color against whites. Laura F. Edwards argued that "judgments rested on the situated knowledge of observers in local communities, in which an individual's 'credit' (also known as character or reputation) was established through family and neighborly ties and continually assessed through gossip networks. Local officials and juries judged the reliability of testimony based on an individual's credit as well as on impersonal, prescriptive markers of status, such as gender, race, age, or class." Under such a system even free people of color could obtain "legal authority." Their viewpoints could travel through local gossip networks and help develop "the terms of legal matters before they even entered the system."[3] Nevertheless, unscrupulous debtors and criminals took advantage of the law and committed deeds against free people of color and the larger community, knowing that if the only witness to these acts was a free person of color or a slave, justice could be avoided. Laws allowing for differential punishment had an equally troubling impact on the execution of justice. The laws that allowed local courts to hire out convicted free people of color who failed to pay their fines led to the issuance of excessive monetary penalties, in violation of the federal Constitution. These steep fines guaranteed that the courts would have to hire out convicted persons. Legislators' failures to provide county officials with clear guidelines about the types of crimes that could be punished by hiring out and to prevent the exaction of excessive fines perverted the state's judiciary beyond the simple discriminatory language found in the law. A thorough evaluation of the court records suggests that this perversion was limited. Nonetheless, its utter existence challenged attempts to maintain order and, more importantly, disrupted the lives of real people, especially the poor, who might lose their physical liberty along with months and sometimes years of productivity.

Criminal Cases

During the national period, free people of color appeared as victims and defendants in a wide range of criminal cases concerning simple thefts, murders, and slave rebellions. The surviving court records from around North Carolina reveal numerous instances of all white juries finding free people of color not guilty of sometimes serious offenses. Furthermore, courts again and again convicted individuals, white and of color, of crimes against free people of color. These cases do not suggest that every case was decided by an impartial jury or prove that the courts never convicted some innocent people. Nonetheless, they demonstrate that in courts around the state, judges and jurors did not view all free people of color as inherently criminal. They saw free people of color through a multidimensional lens in which a person's character or reputation, economic position, value to the community, gender, and other forms of status could be evaluated along with local gossip and court testimony. As Edwards has aptly argued, for judges and jurors the point of litigation "was to restore order, not to protect individuals."[4] Additionally, a system of localized law opened the door to a wide array of punishments. For the same conviction, North Carolinians could expect varying punishments depending on the location, time, past record, and the specific individuals involved in the case.

The historical record suggests that free people of color charged with minor offenses could expect a variety of outcomes at their trials' conclusions including conviction, acquittal, and dropped charges. Most of the criminal cases with free people of color as defendants that appeared before the local courts concerned allegations related to minor infractions such as petit larceny, selling liquor without a license, carrying a gun without a license, fornication and adultery, simple assault, and fighting. The following examples demonstrate that the courts did not treat alleged petty criminals as inherently guilty but instead sought to restore the public order by convicting and punishing the guilty and releasing the acquitted.

The petit larceny cases of Nancy Whitaker and James Butler reveal that free people of color could expect some level of impartiality from the local courts. In August 1826, Orange County officials ordered Nancy Whitaker, "a woman of color," to appear before the Court of Pleas and Quarter Sessions to face such a charge. Jurors indicted Whitaker for stealing "a quantity of flour viz. one quart, of the value of six pence, the proper goods and chattel of one Thomas N. S. Hargis."[5] Approximately three years later, Gates County jurors ordered James Butler, "a free man of colour," to appear in court for the same crime. On April 1, 1829, Butler allegedly stole "one peck of corn of the value of six pence."[6] In these cases, the Orange County jury sided with Whitaker while Gates County residents found Butler guilty.[7] Allegations of petit larceny were too common for juries to simply convict all those whom grand juries indicted for the crime. Free people of color were too important to their communities to simply be haphazardly sent to trial and thoughtlessly convicted.

Those free people of color accused of selling liquor without a license could also expect that the courts would not automatically assume their guilt. At the beginning of the national period, free persons of color, like their white neighbors, could apply to the county court for a liquor license, and those dealers who failed to do so could face this charge. After the passage of the act prohibiting free people of color from distributing spirits in 1845, however, all free people of color engaged in liquor sales were breaking the law. At the spring 1853 term of Orange County Superior Court, jurors accused Adeline Mitchell, a "free woman of colour," of vending "spirituous liquor to one Anderson Brockwell by the small measure." Mitchell had allegedly broken the law by selling the liquor, which amounted to "less than a quart," without a license. Of course, by this point, North Carolina prohibited all free people of color from selling liquor and banned the county courts from issuing liquor licenses to free people of color. During the September court session, a jury found Mitchell guilty of illegally retailing, with Brockwell, the purchaser, as the main witness in the case. However, Mitchell was among the luckier people to come to court that session. After handing down a guilty verdict, the court allowed an arrest of judgment in her case. Wiley Revels, "a free man of color," from Henderson County found himself under suspicion of violating the ban. In the fall of 1857, jurors accused Revels of selling "spirituous liquor" to James M. Davis and Samuel Orr.[8] After Revels appeared in court several times, the state dropped the case against him.[9]

Even a rumor of armed free people of color and slaves roaming the country could ramp up the adrenalin of radical white men looking for conflict. Yet communities did not try free people of color accused of carrying unlicensed weapons with the automatic assumption of guilt. Following the passage of the 1841 state law requiring free people of color to register their weapons with county officials, free men of color began to appear before the courts, sometimes frequently, because of their alleged failure to register their guns and knives. George Robeson, Jerry Johnston, Theophilus George, William Cally, Jacob Sampson, and Richard Morris, all free persons of color, appeared at the October 1845 session of Craven County Superior Court charged with "keeping a musket" without licenses. The same jury found all of the men "not guilty."[10] At the July 1856 term of the Wilson County Court of Pleas and Quarter Sessions, jurors alleged that Willis Jones Jr., "a free person of color . . . did wear & carry about his person a pistol" without a license.[11] Three months later, jurors for the same court indicted Ivy Evans, "a free negro," for the same offense.[12] A jury for the October session of court found Evans guilty, and during the next session, another jury found against Jones on the same charge.[13]

The county justices brought free people of color into court for a variety of crimes related to the regulation of sex and intimate social relations. Most common among these was fornication and adultery, which North Carolina law treated as a singular crime. A significant percentage of the fornication and adultery cases involving free people of color relate to the alleged sexual relations or cohabitation between them and white people of the opposite sex. Since the colonial period, North Carolina lawmakers had tried to discourage such relationship through legislation, and many localities took advantage of their efforts by prosecuting and convicting unmarried couples. In September 1825, Pasquotank County jurors charged Jordan Edge, "of col[or]," and Lurana Hewitt, "a white woman," with "living together in an unlawful manner."[14] A jury for the spring 1826 term of Superior Court found the couple guilty.[15] Many other courts around the state convicted

unmarried couples in the same manner. Yet conviction was not the outcome for all couples rumored to be engaging in illicit intimate relations.
Slightly more than a decade after the Edge-Hewitt case, Thomas Flew Ellen,
a white man, and Priscilla Jones, "a free woman of colour," faced fornication and adultery charges in Nash County.[16] In this case, jurors for the May
1837 session of court cleared the couple of alleged criminal activity.[17] In a
similar case, Asa Etheridge, a white man, and Eliza Boon, "a free woman
of color," appeared before the Tyrrell County court.[18] There, in the fall of
1852, jurors found Etheridge and Boon not guilty.[19] North Carolina's financial penalty against, and later all-out ban on, marriage between persons of
color and whites placed most of these couples in serious social, legal, and
economic binds. North Carolina lawmakers may have intended to use the
law to solidify supposed divisions between the so-called "races," yet the
legal restrictions made criminals out of men and women who, had the law
allowed, likely would have married. Of these cases, a closer study would
probably reveal that the vast majority of cases prosecuted involved free men
of color and white women. Those cases not involving free people of color
and whites involved couples of free people of color who jurors believed had
failed to marry.

In their attempts to regulate the intimate lives of North Carolinians,
lawmakers also criminalized maintaining houses of prostitution and other
centers of illicit intercourse. Rumors brought many people both white and
of color into the county courts for "keeping a disorderly house." Yet allegations of keeping a house of ill-repute did not automatically lead to conviction. At the May 1850 court session, grand jurors presented their case
against Patsey Huckaby, "a free woman of color & spinster," and James
Huckaby, "a free person of color & laborer." Their indictment alleged that
the Huckabys "at Chapel Hill . . . did keep an illgoverned & disorderly
house of ill fame." Furthermore, the Huckabys supposedly allowed "lewd,
immoral & disorderly persons, both black & white & of both sexes to as-
semble & meet together, both in the day time & in the night time" at their
home and permitted those people "profanely to curse & swear & take the
Lord's name in vain & to tipple, get drunk, quarrel & fight & to carry on the
practice of illicit sexual intercourse & then & there to do & commit other
disorderly conduct."[20] When the Huckabys appeared in court, however, a
jury cleared them of the charges.[21]

Attacks on individuals, fights, and domestic violence were parts of regular life in many North Carolina localities. Free people of color were not exempt from these incidents and came before the courts charged with assault and battery or inciting an affray. As in cases of other common crimes tried by local jurisdictions, free people of color could expect a variety of outcomes, including some in their favor. In the spring of 1837, Caswell County jurors charged Philip Roberts, Julia Bowers, and Polly Bass, "free negroes," with fighting "with, to, and against each other . . . to the terror of all the good citizens then and there assembled."[22] Officials failed to locate Roberts and Bowers. Bass, however, appeared before the Superior Court, where a jury convicted her.[23] During the spring 1846 term of Robeson County Superior Court, a grand jury alleged that Andrew Lowrie, a free man of color, "did make an assault" upon John McLauchlin, a white man from the community.[24] Upon his appearance for trial, Lowrie pled guilty to the charges. Although Lowrie submitted to the charges, the court ultimately decided in his favor by suspending any judgment in the case.[25] Lowrie left the court a free man. In 1852, Yadkin County officials ordered the sheriff to bring Morgan Myers, "a free man of color," before the court to face charges for an assault and battery against Jonathan Shore, a white man.[26] At the December session of Superior Court, Yadkin County residents convicted Myers of assaulting Shore.[27] After learning of the accusations against Laney Potter, "a free negro girl," a grand jury for the August 1856 term of Randolph County's Court of Pleas and Quarter Sessions indicted her for assault against Margaret Hutson.[28] Facing trial for striking Hutson with a chair, Potter decided to forgo a trial and pled guilty to the charge.[29]

For many North Carolina lawmakers, part of maintaining the peace and order of the state was restricting the interactions between enslaved people and free persons who were not their masters, including free people of color. Politicians across the state ran for public office by promising that they supported the tough policing of slaves and their free compatriots. In many contests, the free person of color became the poster child of the individual most likely to corrupt enslaved people. In such campaigns, free people of color were the abolitionists trying to convince otherwise docile slaves to run to freedom in the North or the low-level criminals pressuring bondspeople to steal from their masters. Fulfilling their campaign promises, North Carolina lawmakers provided localities with a continuously growing list of crimes related to interactions with slaves. Although politics motivated many lawmakers to pass strong legislation to protect slavery, local officials could not make decisions driven purely by popular politics. They did not let a combination of political fervor and wild rumor take control of their local courtrooms, even when free people of color came before the courts for allegedly having illicit relations with slaves.

Of the numerous crimes involving slaves that grand juries brought against free people of color, unlawful cohabitation between them and enslaved people was among the most commonly pursued cases. Showing a willingness to not simply consider rumors but take evidence into consideration, juries absolved and convicted free people of color charged with this crime. At the spring 1851 session of Orange County Superior Court, jurors alleged Milly Walker, "a free negro, on the fifteenth day of March AD 1849 and on divers other days and times between that day and the day of the taking of this inquisition . . . unlawfully did cohabit and live together as man and wife with a certain male slave named Charles Liggins the property of one John Liggins."[30] On her appearance in court, a jury heard Walker's case and found her not guilty.[31] In September 1856, grand jurors for the Northampton County court presented a case against "Penny Wiggins a free person of color and Caesar a slave the property of Richard Parker" and claimed the couple "did unlawfully and adulterously bed and cohabit together, and did then and there unlawfully commit adultery and fornication."[32] At the December session of court, a jury relieved Caesar of the charges but found Wiggins guilty.[33] A grand jury indicted David Manly of Craven County, "a free negro," for the same crime in September of 1859. The jurors accused Manly of unlawfully intermarrying and cohabitating with "a certain female slave named Emeline the property of one Mary Sanders."[34] When Manly came before the Court of Pleas and Quarter Sessions three months later, a jury absolved him of the charges.[35]

In order to prevent enslaved people from trading their masters' goods with free persons, lawmakers passed a series of laws designed to protect slave masters' property from free people and enslaved middlemen who might trade their masters' property for their own benefit. Seeking to secure the public order, which always included protecting personal property, officials hauled free people of color into courts for illicit dealings with slaves including illegally trading with slaves, selling liquor to slaves, and gambling with slaves. Some of those free people of color who appeared in the courts for these crimes were convicted. Juries exonerated others. Occasionally, the courts decided that such cases were of minimal importance and dropped the charges against the indicted persons. At the spring 1851 term of the Granville County court, jurors believed Henry Parker, "a free negro," had broken the law when he purportedly purchased from a "slave named Elijah the property of one Thomas L. Williams . . . two bushels of wheat," and they charged Parker with "trading with a slave."[36] Over a year later, a jury for the September 1852 court session found Parker guilty of trading with Elijah.[37] The Northampton County court called Shepherd Mitchell, "a free person of color," to appear in court after grand jurors alleged that he "on the first day of May 1840" sold "one gill of spirituous liquor to a certain negro slave Edmund the property of William Buffalow."[38] In June 1841, the prosecutor for the case decided to discontinue pursuing the charges against Mitchell and the court dropped the case from the docket.[39] At the Spring 1851 session of Caswell County Superior Court, jurors charged Lewis Cozens, John Wilson the younger, and Freeman Howard, "free negroes," with playing "games of cards with a certain slave named Henry the property of one George W. Prendergast."[40] Three years after the presentment of the charges, Caswell County official finally brought Howard to trial, where a jury acquitted him.[41] During the fall 1856 session of Superior Court, Randolph County jurors indicted Alexander Scott, "a free man of color," for unlawfully playing "a game of cards with a slave named Clark the property of one Ezra Beckerdite." A year later, the solicitor decided to drop the case against him after the sheriff reported that Scott was "not to be found in my county."[42]

White community members' fluctuating suspicions of free people of color as leaders of slave rebellions sometimes landed free persons of color before the courts. Allegedly leading or supporting a slave rebellion was a serious charge that could lead to death. The seriousness of the charge appears to have pushed county officials to take special care that free people of color accused of such crimes received trials as fair as possible. As a result, the courts often absolved the few free persons of color charged with inciting rebellion. In September 1821, Jones County jurors brought charges against Henry Black, "a free person of colour," for "insurrection & rebellion." They suspected that Black had aided "a number of negro slaves, to the number of five and more," who ran away from their masters and "wickedly and feloniously did consult, advise, and conspire together, to rebel, and make insurrection against their lawful owners." Black allegedly aided the slaves in assaulting "Hardy Collins, with intent . . . to kill and murder." Upon Black's arraignment, his attorneys, John Stanly and William Gaston, requested that the court move their client's case to another jurisdiction, citing their belief that the "prejudice" in Jones County was such that "every one seems ready to pronounce him guilty." Recognizing that Jones County residents might fail to produce an impartial jury, the court conceded and sent Black's case to neighboring Craven County.[43] After two trials, a jury in April 1822 exonerated Black of the insurrection and rebellion charges.[44] In 1836, on the other side of the state, Ashe County justices of the peace issued a warrant for the arrest of William P. Waters "a collard man," who they believed was guilty of "trying to raise an insurrection with the negroes."[45] Upon Waters's appearance at the Ashe County Superior Court, a grand jury decided against pursuing the case, and the court discharged Waters.[46] George Washington Freeman of Robeson County was not quite so lucky. During the September 1845 term of Robeson County Superior Court, a grand jury indicted Freeman of being "in a conspiracy with Isaac a slave the property of Duncan McLellan" and providing Isaac and his enslaved associates with "arms and ammunition."[47] The grand jurors also alleged that Freeman "did habour and maintain Isaac." Upon learning of the charges against him, Freeman requested that officials move his trial out of Robeson County. He declared that his "prosecution was instituted by eight persons, who are indorsed on the bill as witnesses" and "that they are in fact & truth prosecutors, and are engaged in the management of this proceeding, and are very anxious to convict." Noting these men's popularity in the community and his own obscurity, Freeman contended that he could not have "a fair & impartial trial" in Robeson County. Court officials granted his request and sent Freeman to neighboring Richmond County for trial.[48] A year after his initial indictment, a Richmond County jury absolved Freeman of inciting insurrection.[49]

Alleged murder was another type of serious case that local officials had to police carefully in order to curb unjustified public executions. Free people of color across the state appeared in courts charged with murder. Yet juries generally did not assume the guilt of these accused people, and in many instances when juries believed free people of color had killed other people, they still acted with caution by convicting those alleged murderers of the lesser charge of manslaughter. The difference between a manslaughter conviction and murder conviction was life and death. In 1841, Anderson Mayo, a free man of color from Orange County, received the death penalty after conviction for the murder of his wife, Jesse.[50] Other free people of color charged with murder received more favorable judgments than Mayo. At the

September 1811 Chowan County Superior Court session, jurors alleged that Nancy Robbins, "a free person of colour of Indian Extraction," assaulted a "male negro slave named Allen, the property of one John Dickinson" and with a knife wounded Allen "upon the Left side, between the Ribs, and behind the left pass of the Breast." The attack left Allen with a mortal wound "three inches" wide and "six inches deep." After hearing testimony from an assortment of Chowan County residents, free and enslaved, a jury acquitted Robbins of murder but found her guilty of manslaughter.[51] McDowell County grand jurors for the spring 1846 term of Superior Court charged Rachel Shade, a "single woman" and "free person of color," with strangling to death and stoning her "female child." Furthermore, they claimed Shade left the child's body "beneath a stone, leaves and rubbish . . . so to conceal the death of the said female child." After her arrest, Shade appeared in court and requested a postponement, which would provide her with the time to gather witnesses who could testify on her behalf. The court granted her request.[52] Finally, Shade faced a jury during the fall court session. The prosecution failed to convince the jury that Shade was guilty of murder, and the body decided to convict Shade on a misdemeanor charge.[53]

Most legal actions like Rachel Shade's murder case were not tried as murder but as concealing the death of a child. Officials in many localities apparently understood that proving that a baby was born alive and that an infanticide took place was more difficult than simply demonstrating that a person concealed the death of a baby. In the nineteenth century, the death of a baby was a familiar occurrence, but the concealment of that death was not common and conflicted with the courts' mission of keeping the peace. Since officials generally prosecuted only women for concealment, free women of color were the free persons of color generally indicted on the charge. Unlike many kinds of allegations, those against a person for concealment appear to have almost always led to conviction. With a baby's body as the evidence commonly used to start a proceeding against a woman, the court already had strong proof against the accused. In March 1843, Orange County officials charged Sooky Bishop, "a free woman of color," with "concealing the death of a child." They suggested that Bishop "being big with a certain male child . . . did bring forth the said child of the body of her . . . alone and in secret." After the birth, the baby died under unknown circumstances, and the "as soon as the said male child was dead" Bishop allegedly "did throw, put, and place the said male child under and beneath a quantity of shucks." Upon discovery of the baby's body, Bishop had stated that her son's birth was "taken so suddenly," and she had left the baby planning to retrieve him after and bring him home "as soon as it got dark."[54] At Bishop's trial, a jury rejected her story and decided she was guilty of concealing her son's death.[55] Martha Bowser of Tyrrell County, "a free woman of color," faced a situation similar to Bishop's when grand jurors for the fall 1853 Superior Court charged her with concealment. They alleged that Bowser delivered a boy and a girl and attempted to "conceal" their deaths, but admitted "that it might not come to light" whether the children were "born alive or not."[56] Focusing solely on the question of whether Bowser concealed her babies' deaths, a jury returned a verdict against Bowser and found her guilty of concealment.[57] The convictions of Bishop, Bowser, and many other women suggest that women found defending themselves from charges of concealment nearly impossible. Even if their children were delivered dead, women did not possess the right to dispose of their offsprings' remains privately. Births and deaths, like women's sexuality, were within the realm of public interest, even when the women were free persons of color.

Although people considered burglary more serious than the related property crime of petit larceny, jurisdictions made equal efforts to learn the truths behind both types of alleged crime. Free people of color indicted for burglary, like their counterparts charged with less serious property crimes, could expect either favorable outcomes or convictions. During September 1821, a Craven County grand jury brought charges against Richard Morris, "a free man of color" and "labourer." The indictment stated that on October 10, 1820, Morris "about the hour of twelve in the night" entered the "dwelling house of Samuel and Joseph Oliver" of New Bern and "feloniously and burglariously" stole "one hogshead of molasses, of the value of fifty shillings."[58] At the April 1822 session of court, a jury found Morris not guilty of burglary but convicted him of grand larceny.[59] Grand jurors for the spring 1834 Gates County Superior Court charged Mills Reid, "a free man of colour," with burglary. They contended that Reid on March 1, 1834, at "about the hour of one in the night . . . feloniously and burglariously did break and enter" Jacob Powell's home and removed "ten pounds of bacon of the value of ten shillings, two gallons of brandy of the value of ten shillings, one bushel of meal of the value of ten shillings."[60] Upon hearing his case, a Gates County jury found Reid guilty of burglary.[61]

Beyond the previously mentioned charges, local officials indicted free persons of color for a variety of other, rather obscure offenses. As with many of the previous cases discussed in the section, free people of color could expect a diversity of outcomes. During December 1840, Northampton County grand jurors alleged that Clary Mabry, "a free person of color . . . did hawk & peddle candy & sugar" without "having obtained a legal license so to hawk, peddle & sell the said candy & sugar."[62] That same month, for reasons unknown, officials for the county court dismissed the case against Mabry.[63] Grand jurors for the spring 1854 Superior Court for Granville County alleged "Doctor Howell, a free negro . . . unlawfully and knowingly did mismark one hog and one pig the property of Thomas Thomason . . . with the intent then and there to defraud him the said Thomas Thomason."[64] At the following court session, twelve Granville County residents acquitted Howell of "mismarking."[65] At the March 1836 session of Superior Court, Orange County grand jurors indicted Henry Harris, a free person of color, for burning down the county's "public prison and common jail" in Hillsborough on October 6, 1835. After his arrest, Harris requested that the court allow his trial to be transferred to another jurisdiction. He explained in a statement that "he hath reason to believe & doth believe that his name hath been so associated with the said burning, in popular estimation in said county, as to produce a general bias in public opinion against this affiant."[66] Orange County officials granted Harris's request and sent him to trial in neighboring Caswell County. In Caswell County, a jury for the spring 1836 term found Harris guilty of the arson.[67] Keeping an unlawful fence was another of the minor charges free people of color faced in the county courts. During the September 1857 term of the Beaufort County Court of Pleas and Quarter Sessions, grand jurors indicted Moses Blango, "a free negro," for this crime. They charged that Blango, "being possessed of and having under cultivation a certain piece of cleared ground . . . then and there unlawfully did fail and neglect to keep his fence during crop time."[68] After Blango's arrest and appearance in court, a jury found him guilty.[69]

The variety of criminal case types and verdicts demonstrates that North Carolina officials generally acted under the assumption that the law entitled free people of color to a formal public hearing and that juries did not assume free people of color were inherently criminal or inevitably guilty when accused of disturbing the peace. Nevertheless, the punishments that courts handed down to some of the convicts in the earlier-mentioned cases reveal that jurisdictions sometimes allowed harsher sentences for certain free people of color than generally permitted. North Carolina law sanctioned the public sale of the services of convicted free people of color, while white convicts, no matter the crime committed, did not meet the same fate. Localities always had a choice as to whether they would sentence a free person of color to pay a high fine or be hired at public auction. Furthermore, the courts could decide whether to apply fines too excessive for convicted free people of color to pay.

After their convictions, Rachel Shade of McDowell County and Henry Parker of Granville County faced the possibility of public hiring out along with dozens and maybe hundreds of other free persons of color during the antebellum period. After her conviction for manslaughter, the court assessed a fine of $150 against Shade. Upon Parker's conviction for purchasing "two bushels of wheat," the court required him to pay a $100 fine. Shade and Parker appeared in front of their respective county courthouses for sale after failing to pay the excessive fines imposed on them by the courts. In both cases, the amounts of the fines suggest that the courts intended to hire out the convicted free people of color and assured that result through the excessive fines.

The historical record fails to explain the rationale for the selective hiring out of free people of color. The surviving records, however, indicate that the courts were willing to hire out free people of color for a variety of crimes. At the March 1855 term, a jury found Roland Lomack guilty of assault and battery and the Cumberland County court ordered the sheriff to hire out Lomack to anyone willing to pay his $15 fine. In 1859, after a conviction for drunkenness, the Craven County sheriff hired out Abby Lewis for failing to pay a $40 penalty.[70] Without our knowing anything about the reputations of Rachel Shade, Henry Parker, or convicted people involved in other cases, we can discern that the legal actions demonstrate that the state's failure to carefully regulate the application of high fines and potential hiring out sanctioned extreme inconsistencies in the application of punishment. The reality that someone convicted of manslaughter could receive the same punishment as a person found guilty of a minor disturbance such as drunkenness was an aberration within the law as a whole. In addition, this uneven application of punishment had real impact for convicted free people of color who thus failed to earn wages while hired out. Those who had families to care for likely struggled to support their former dependents. Others may have lost opportunities for personal economic advancement. In all cases in which courts hired out convicted persons, those free people of color lost the most basic ability to make many day-to-day decisions.

Although public sales were undeniably degrading punishments, being condemned to forced servitude for a set time was far from being enslaved. The state prevented the local courts from hiring out free people of color beyond terms of five years, and the courts attempted to protect those free people of color whose temporary masters sought to overextend their authority. The experience of Elizabeth Post, a free woman of color hired out by officials in Cumberland County, highlights the difference between a person hired out and an enslaved person. In 1857, Post appeared before a court in Wilmington claiming that her temporary master, James Bryant, had attempted to remove her from North Carolina to sell her as a slave. With no one to contest her claim, a judge set Post free.[71] In North Carolina, an enslaved person could not challenge sale out of the state in the courts, but Post was a free woman of color, and the fact that she was hired out could not override the basic rights she held as a free person.

As illustrated by the case described at the beginning of this chapter, the relationship between local criminal justice and free people of color was not limited to incidents involving free defendants of color. Officials across the state brought white people into court to face charges for alleged offenses against free people of color. Since the colonial period, North Carolina law had prohibited free people of color from testifying against white people, including those who committed offenses against them. This law sometimes created serious problems for free people of color and their attorneys who pursued legal action against alleged white offenders. Nevertheless, the efforts of savvy lawyers along with judges and jurors who placed restoring the public peace over outright hostility against free people of color prevented this law from completely corrupting the legal process.

For jurisdictions around the state, trying whites for assaulting free people of color was a significant part of their efforts to maintain and restore the public peace. Free people of color could not testify against the white individuals who purportedly assaulted them. Nevertheless, testimony from white witnesses, the presence of bruises, cuts, and other wounds, and sometimes even the cooperation of the alleged abuser could secure favorable outcomes for victims categorized as free people of color. At the fall 1849 term of Rockingham County Superior Court, jurors indicted James Holt and Hardin Turner, white "laborers," for an assault on Berryman Alexander, "a free man of color." The presentment against Holt and Turner alleged that the two men made an "assault" and "cut off" the ears of Alexander.[72] During the spring 1850 court session, both men pled guilty to maiming Alexander and agreed to serve time in prison.[73] On August 25, 1859, John W. Duggins filed a complaint regarding an alleged assault with Stokes County justice of the peace B. F. Wilson. According to Wilson, Duggins explained that "James M. Wells did on the 24th day of August in the night . . . assault and beat one Susan Box a free woman of color in her own house."[74] In reaction to the report, Wilson issued a warrant for Wells's arrest, and a grand jury indicted Wells for the alleged crime. Upon his appearance in the Stokes County Court of Pleas and Quarter Sessions, Wells submitted to the charges against him and agreed to pay a fine and court costs.[75]

On rare occasions, local courts sought to restore order in their communities by adjudicating cases of alleged murder of free people of color by whites. Although the victims of murder would not have been able to testify against their white assailants even if they had lived, communities still tried to uncover the facts of the deaths of free neighbors of color. Sometimes what they discovered or believed allowed alleged white murderers to walk free while in other cases juries decided to convict. During the fall 1836 session of Perquimans County Superior Court, jurors presented a murder case against Joseph G. Barclift, a white man, for the murder of John Hamilton, "a free boy of colour." They alleged that on July 3, 1836, Barclift used a "stick" to "strike" Hamilton "upon the back part of the head" and left the boy with a "mortal wound of the length of three inches and of the depth of one inch." Barclift also supposedly used a "whip" to inflict "several mortal strokes, wounds, and bruises in and upon the head, breast, back, belly and sides" of Hamilton.[76] At the same court session, a jury decided Barclift was not guilty of murder and moved against convicting him of a lesser charge.[77] At the fall 1856 session of Randolph County Superior Court, a grand jury initiated a case against Alexander Hooker, a white man, for the murder of John Chavis, a free person of color. The jurors alleged that Hooker "feloniously, willfully and of his malice aforethought" shot Chavis with a "rifle-gun" and gave him a "mortal wound." After spending time in the county jail waiting for the court to hear his case, Hooker appeared before a jury who found him guilty of the murder.[78]

In addition to assault and murder cases, the courts also had to adjudicate cases involving whites accused of stealing free people of color and attempting to sell them into bondage. Again, free people of color could not testify against their alleged captors. Nevertheless, sometimes the courts could find ways around this limitation. During the September 1821 court session, a Perquimans County grand jury charged John H. Edwards, William Moore, George Freeman, and Andrew Baker with crimes against Barney Turner, "a free man of mixed blood." The juror suspected that the four white men "by violence" had kidnapped Turner and transported him to neighboring Gates County with the "intention to appropriate" him "to their own use." In Gates County, the men allegedly planned to "sell and dispose" of Turner "as a slave." Baker's fate is unclear. Upon their appearances in court, Moore and Freeman submitted to the charges against them and agreed to pay fines. John H. Edwards, however, chose to place his fate with a jury. After deciding to face a trial, Edwards complained that he could not receive a fair trial in Perquimans County and requested that his case be moved to another jurisdiction. Accepting his request, Perquimans County officials sent his case east to Pasquotank County. There, a jury found Edwards guilty of the crimes against Turner.[79]

Beyond violent crimes, whites also faced charges of committing various property-related crimes against free people of color. Sometimes, the outcomes of these cases favored free people of color and in other instances, alleged white criminals won the juries' votes. At the spring 1860 Superior Court session in Orange County, jurors brought charges against two white men, Henry Parks and Columbus Nichols, for breaking into the home of Sophia Mitchell, "a free woman of color." They alleged that Parks and Nichols "did break open the door of the dwelling house of one Sophia Mitchell . . . and did then and there, unlawfully, violently, forcibly, imperiously and with a strong arm, enter the said dwelling house."[80] By March, a jury decided against Sophia Mitchell and exonerated Parks and Nichols.[81]

In cases in which they were defendants and alleged victims, free persons of color could expect a variety of results from the local courts. Surviving records demonstrate that regardless of their positions in cases, free people of color could find favorable outcomes. Of course, all free people of color were not so fortunate, and the courts found them guilty of crimes or ruled against their interests. As some of the cases discussed in this chapter reveal, a ruling against one free person of color could be a decision in favor of another. Without knowing exactly how juries came to their decisions in cases involving free people of color, the surviving records prevent further interrogation of the cases to determine the fairness of trials and the degree to which some jurors' prejudice against free people of color played a role in decisions. The historical record, however, does reveal that local justice systems around the state permitted some free people of color to receive discriminatory forms of punishment such as hiring out. At the same time, discriminatory punishment was not universal. Their inconsistent application suggests that although discriminatory sentencing was present in the local justice systems, the ways that courts handed out those punishments reflected local concerns and considerations about the reputation and status of individual free people of color. In many ways, the state sanctioned discrimination, but leaders in localities were the primary administrators of prejudicial outcomes, just as they were the ultimate decision makers in cases favoring free persons of color.

Civil Cases

The experiences of free people of color in the local judiciaries of North Carolina included their participation in civil cases in addition to their involvement in criminal actions. The appearances of free persons of color before the courts in civil actions demonstrate that officials incorporated them into local political communities and understood them as within the bounds of their society, not on its periphery or beyond its limits. Free persons of color appeared in the local courts as plaintiffs and defendants. Those individuals on the opposing side of free people of color were white persons and people of their same sociopolitical status. As in criminal cases, free people of color discovered both favorable and unfavorable outcomes in civil actions. Some of them received positive judgments in cases involving both other free people of color and white persons on the opposing side. Yet others discovered that the courts were unwilling to oblige them, sometimes because jurors believed they were in the wrong and in other instances because the state's prejudicial laws prevented the courts from fully pursuing their cases.

Free people of color appeared in the local courts as plaintiffs and defendants in a variety of lawsuits over debts. Across the state, free people of color were plaintiffs in cases involving white defendants. In 1812, Donum Montford, a free man of color, brought a suit against John Dewey, a white man, for an outstanding debt in the Craven County court. Before the case appeared in court, Dewey had commissioned Montford to complete plastering work on a house and fireplace along with coating windows. After the completion of the work, Dewey had paid part of the bill but still owed Montford thirty-seven pounds and four pence. Montford brought him to court to recover the remaining amount. Upon their appearance in court in June 1813, Dewey sought to avoid a trial and admitted that he was still indebted to Montford.[82] Almost two years later, John Wilson, "a man of color," sued John Street, a white merchant, for a debt. Before the filing of the lawsuit, both men had kept accounts against one another; Wilson's account for Street included charges for a variety of construction projects, and Street's account for Wilson was comprised of purchases of various goods such as cloth, whisky, silk, nails, and hats. Wilson worried that he might not recover the money owed to him by Street after learning that Street had left or was planning to leave town. Wilson decided to take legal action. When the case appeared before the Orange County Superior Court in September 1816, the jury sided with Wilson and issued a judgment against Street for forty-five pounds, six shillings, nine pence, and three farthings, the difference between Wilson's account and Street's account.[83]

In several jurisdictions, free people of color appeared on the other side of civil debt cases as defendants facing white plaintiffs. White plaintiffs never had to face the same handicaps that prevented some free people of color from proving their cases against whites. The lack of a legal handicap, however, did not guarantee them victory before the courts. In 1801, Peggy Hargrove, a white woman, sued James Chavis, a free man of color, in the Granville County Court of Pleas and Quarter Sessions for a debt. Hargrove claimed that Chavis had purchased a table from her and owed her back rent. The court received a note showing that Chavis had paid part of his debt but still owed money. After hearing the case, the court issued a judgment against Chavis for two pounds, eleven shillings, and eight pence plus court costs. In a late 1840s case, Lemuel R. Jernigan, a white man, as the administrator of William Jordan's estate, filed suit against Meredith Lee, a free man of color, for debts owed to Jordan's estate. At the May 1849 session of the Gates County Court of Pleas and Quarter Sessions, a jury found in favor of Lee. Jernigan decided to appeal the case to the county superior court. Lee won the appeal case, and the court issued a judgment against Jordan for the cost of the proceedings.[84]

Beyond using the courts to secure debts, free people of color brought their neighbors and relatives to court to settle disputes over the property of deceased family members. In 1816, Mariam Hathcock, a free woman of color, sued Sterling Hathcock, the administrator of her husband's estate, to recover widow's support. Following the filing of her complaint, the Northampton County court ordered Sterling Hathcock to provide her with one year's support, which included "six barrels of corn, 350 lbs. of pork, one barrel of herrings."[85] In 1832, Catherine Lowry, a free woman of color, pursued a case against her uncle Thomas Lowry in the Robeson County court to obtain a share of her father's estate. Thomas Lowry, the administrator of Catherine's father's estate, argued that Catherine was illegitimate and therefore had no title to his brother's property. Yet several witnesses attested that Catherine's parents, James Lowry and Nancy Sweat, were married.[86]

Free people of color pursued restitution for physical abuse by filing lawsuits in the local courts. During the summer of 1810, Mason Cuff, a free man of color, sued Kinchen Norfleet, a white man, for one hundred pounds damages in the Gates County court. Cuff alleged that Norfleet had committed an "assault and Battery" upon him.[87] At the April 1811 Superior Court term, jurors heard Cuff's case on appeal, found Norfleet at fault, and awarded Cuff six pounds, fifteen shillings, and six pence damages.[88] On February 5, 1848, Matthew Locklear, a free man of color, filed a suit against Alexander McPhail, Evander Bethea, and Peter Smith, all white men, in Robeson County Superior Court. He charged that the defendants "tied him and led him about two miles and then assaulted and beat" him "in a most outrageous manner with rods and clubs." Before the case against the men appeared in front of the court, Locklear swore an additional complaint against the defendant Peter Smith, "a man of wealth and influence," whom he accused of "circulating reports unfavorable to" his "character." He believed Smith was trying to manipulate the case by turning the public against him and prevent "a fair and impartial trial." Furthermore, Locklear contended that he was "extremely poor and has few or no friends and very little influence and has no means of counteracting the great weight of influence brought to operate against him."[89] Even with Locklear's concern about local impartiality, officials decided to continue the case in Robeson County. Locklear, however, soon learned that he had a few more allies than he believed originally. At the spring 1850 session of Superior Court, jurors found in favor of Locklear and provided him with $10 in damages against the defendants.[90]

In another abuse case, Elizabeth Patrick, a free woman of color, filed a complaint against Joseph Green, a white man who held her two children Betsey and Alexander as apprentices, in 1856. Patrick charged that Green abused her children and asked the court to rescind the bonds of apprenticeship on Betsey and Alexander. The Brunswick County court found that Green had "not kindly treated and properly provided for" Betsey and Alexander Patrick, and "rescinded and cancelled" the apprenticeships. The court restored custody of the Patrick children to their mother by apprenticing them directly to Elizabeth.[91] In this case, the court demonstrated that free people of color, even as servants, had certain rights and could not be freely abused by their masters. Whites who owned slaves had the right to abuse their bondspeople without public correction, but free people of color were not property, and as free persons had the right to challenge violations of their basic liberties.

When their intimate relationships fractured, free people of color came to the courts to lodge complaints against their spouses and file for divorces. During the fall 1844 session of Robeson County Superior Court, Edmund Kersey, "a free person of color," presented a petition for divorce against his wife, the former Milly Purnell. He charged that his wife had "openly abandoned herself to the most lewd and vicious course and entirely disregarded the pledge which she had made having frequently indulged in criminal conversation with one Henry Collcott and others." Edmund also claimed that his wife had deceived him by presenting herself as a person of "mixed blood" while in reality "being a white person."[92] Immediately following the divorce filing, Robeson County officials failed to locate Milly Kersey. The court did not conclude the case until 1847, when it dismissed the suit.[93] In 1846, Eliza Deal Jordan sued for divorce from her husband of six years, Theophilus Jordan, in Chowan County. Eliza claimed that she and Theophilus had lived together for about three years after their marriage. Later in the marriage, Theophilus abandoned her. After leaving Eliza, Theophilus engaged in an adulterous relationship with Mary Ann Banks of Hertford County. Eliza proclaimed that she was "unwilling longer to be the subject to an individual so fruitless to his marriage vows."[94] In 1860, Lawrence James filed for divorce from his wife Arilla James in Martin County Superior Court. Lawrence James alleged that Arilla James had taken up with "negro man Jim the property of Henry Rodgerson." When the Jameses' case appeared before court, the jurors found in favor of the husband.[95] The cases of the Kerseys, Jordans, and Jameses highlight the importance of the state in the domestic lives of all North Carolinians, including free people of color. Just like their white neighbors, free people of color sought out the local judiciary to remedy their domestic disputes when their own attempts failed. The courts served as tools for plaintiffs seeking to resolve their quarrels and uphold their own status within their communities. The individuals who filed suits against their spouses attempted to prove to their neighbors that although their spouses did not follow the rule of law, they were law-abiding, worthy members of their societies.

Resolving civil disputes involving free people of color were part of the local courts' missions to keep the peace and maintain the public order. These cases reveal that peace and order included requiring the payment of debts, protecting the assets of property owners and their heirs, preventing the physically abused from becoming potential charges of the state, and defending the institution of marriage. Because free people of color were part of their communities and not outsiders, local officials responded to potential disruptions involving them in order to fulfill their duties to the larger communities and more importantly reinforce the public order that kept them secure and in power.

Free people of color in national-period North Carolina found a variety of legal outcomes in the local courts, some toward their favor and some against. Favorable outcomes for free people of color suggest that at least some courts and juries did not automatically assume they were criminals. The significance of those cases in which free people of color came out on the losing side is more difficult to interpret. Without the opportunity to review the evidence presented against each person and the conduct of the people in the courtroom, it is impossible to surmise which of those persons who lost their cases received fair trials. Furthermore, no surviving records could provide certainty about the guilt or fault of one individual or another. After examining the penalties levied against certain free people of color, however, the historical record demonstrates that explicit bias against particular free people of color existed within courtrooms across the state. Courts' willingness to hire out free people of color convicted of certain crimes, a penalty that could not be enforced against any other category of persons, shows that radical proslavery legislation had an important influence on crime and punishment within the state. Yet a glance over the surviving court records also reveals that free people of color were more likely to face punishments other than hiring out after a court found them guilty. Whatever can be said about the outcomes of cases involving free persons of color, the performances of these cases illuminate the importance local communities placed on maintaining public order and peace. Even as radical legislators crafted the law to be increasingly discriminatory against free people of color, local officials did not view all free people of color as pariahs within their society and provided them with opportunities to confirm their inclusion in their communities in county courtrooms.

✛

CHAPTER 8

The Fight for Liberty

Civil War and Reconstruction

On November 17, 1861, a subscriber to Raleigh's *Semi-Weekly Standard* from Wilkesboro wrote to inform the editor, William Holden, of the story of Ann Grinton, "a free colored woman." The Wilkes County observer explained, "I am sure that you will esteem worthy of notice in the columns of your valuable paper, the generosity of a free colored woman, Ann Grinton, living in the family of Dr. Calloway, towards the soldiers of this county." The source continued that Grinton "is repeatedly sending articles of apparel and food, which the soldier must appreciate-and seldom an opportunity passes that she does not largely contribute." The writer went on to give Holden a comprehensive list of twenty-seven different items that Grinton purportedly delivered to the rebel army.[1] The communication about Grinton leaves many unanswered questions, most important among them: Why would Ann Grinton, a free woman of color, support an army fighting for a nation whose vice-president declared it was created "upon the great truth that the negro is not equal to the white man"?[2]

Viewing Grinton's actions as reflections of her sentiments as the *Semi-Weekly* subscriber suggested would possibly be a misreading of her intentions and oversimplify her situation as a free person of color in Civil War North Carolina. Most free people of color like Ann Grinton sought to maintain their free status and survive during the tumultuous war years. As a diverse population with various opinions about slavery, secession, and simply how to survive, free people of color responded in a variety of ways to the major changes in their society. Some worked with their rebel neighbors and therefore cast away airs of suspicion about their loyalty. Other free people of color quietly supported the U.S. government or tried to remain neutral. Both were fairly easy choices since North Carolina law banned them from membership in the state regiments. The majority proceeded with their prewar daily activities and continued to interact regularly with their white neighbors who backed the rebellion. A few free people of color, many whose appearances could not distinguish them from white men, illegally joined the rebel army. Most of North Carolina's free men of color who served during the war, however, fought for the United States. They battled those who challenged their basic civil liberties and attempted to place them on an equal footing with slaves. Prorebel forces had become the common enemy of most free people of color and slaves alike, therefore setting some of them on the course to develop a political alliance in the years to come.

Although the political interests of free people of color and enslaved people united as the Civil War progressed, the diversity of ways that free people of color reacted to and participated in the Civil War demonstrates how different their position continued to be in comparison to that of enslaved people. Though some whites sought to intrude in their lives through the introduction of additional legal restrictions during the war, free people of color ultimately continued to maintain a status closer to white freedom than to enslavement. When free people of color made decisions during the war years, they took the maintenance of the freedoms that they already possessed into consideration, while slaves sought a freedom that they did not have but wanted to realize by generally supporting the rebellion's suppression.

The historiography on free people of color in the South, with a few exceptions, is silent on the Civil War's influence in their lives.[3] Yet the Civil War era was the most important point of change for free people of color in North Carolina. The most significant debates over their social and political position took place during this time. At the onset of the war, state lawmakers stripped the right to bear arms from free people of color, prevented them from employing slaves, and began to impress them into the service of the rebels as laborers. For the first time, North Carolina imposed forced labor on significant numbers of free people of color. Before this period, jurists only sporadically used the laws prescribing forced labor for free people of color found guilty of crimes. During the war, however, they imposed forced labor even on law-abiding persons of color. These actions led free people of color to understand that North Carolina law would no longer protect their rights to life, liberty, and property.

Suppression of the rebellion eventually settled this dilemma, and the policy decisions that accompanied it destroyed the legal supports and economic apparatus of slavery in the South. North Carolinians, however, were unsure what their state would look like without human bondage. Facing an uncertain future, individuals formerly categorized as free people of color staked claims to citizenship and sought a voice in discussions of the state's future. They pursued remedies for the wrongs of the past and access to political and economic power. During North Carolina's long Reconstruction period, they won many victories: at the ballot box, in the form of social programs, and as the voice of constituencies of color. Conservatives, who looked to the past for a model of the appropriate social order, however, fought to slow the progress of persons of color in society.

Life in a Rebel State

Building on their argument that the liberties of free people of color jeopardized the maintenance of slavery, radical proslavery ideologues continued to attack the position of free people of color and called for increased limitations on their basic civil rights during the 1860s. Calmer persons held off full assaults on free people of color, including demands for their enslavement, but some free people of color found the actions of proslavery radicals too grave to ignore. In the coming years free people of color generally proceeded silently but did not overlook their neighbors' hostilities. Some free people of color, for their own profit or more likely for their own survival, continued to work side by side with their white neighbors who supported the rebellion. Others hoped for U.S. victory and the end of the radical proslavery regime.

Obsessed with protecting slavery and preventing collusion between slaves and free people of color, radical proslavery ideologues pushed through the General Assembly two acts explicitly limiting the civil rights of free people of color. Five months before secession, the state legislature passed laws preventing them from keeping weapons and severely limiting their control of and interaction with slaves. The weapons law prohibited free people of color from keeping on their person or in their homes shotguns, muskets, pistols, swords, sword canes, daggers, Bowie knives, powder, or shot. Keeping a weapon was only a misdemeanor; however, the law explicitly stated that if found guilty, a free person of color would be fined no less than $50, a hefty penalty, which for most would mean hiring out at public auction. The law reducing free people of color's control of slaves offered a similar fate and levied a $100 fine for each offense. This act prohibited free people of color from buying or hiring slaves and prevented slaves from working as apprentices to free people of color. Those free people of color who had slaves before the passage of the act could continue to own those slaves, but additional purchases were banned.[4]

These legislative acts reminded free people of color and maybe even some concerned whites of radical proslavery ideologues' willingness to compromise the liberties of the free to preserve and expand slavery. The new legislation challenged the civil rights of free people of color, limited their access to certain types of private property, and denied them the right to bear arms even in the defense of their own homes. These laws charted the course of life for most free people of color under the rebel regime. Free people of color remained unbound to slave masters in law, but in practice the state had the right to impose itself in the daily lives of free people of color. Under the guise of war effort, proslavery radicals now mandated significant restrictions on and power over the activities of free persons of color. However, the degree to which North Carolinians more generally supported these actions or to what extent local officials enforced the new laws is unclear.

Although the political and social position of free people of color was at its lowest point just prior to and during the Civil War, the enemies of free people of color still could not suppress their liberties fully. At the same session in which free people of color lost their right to bear arms and purchase or hire slaves, several arguably more radical bills failed to pass. Lotte W. Humphrey, an Onslow County Democrat, again attempted to push through a bill to enslave free people of color. His bill died in committee. A similar bill proposed by Democrat Charles T. Davis of Bladen County met the same fate. A "bill to bind out certain free persons of color" proposed by N. H. Street, a Craven County Democrat, floundered with Humphrey's bill in the senate. During a discussion about tax reform, J. R. Stubbs, a Whig who represented Washington County and Martin County, offered an amendment that would have levied a capitation tax on "free colored inhabitants of the state," but he later rescinded the amendment.[5] Even a petition from Currituck County, which cited the Dred Scott decision, described "free negro population" as "not citizens under the constitution" and called for "the removal of the negroes from the State," could not motivate the General Assembly to accept the radicals' most extreme positions.[6]

The response to Democratic senator Thomas J. Pitchford's bill to allow certain free people of color to become slaves highlights the failure of radicals to subjugate free persons of color fully during the 1860–61 session. After presenting his proposal, the senate sent Pitchford's bill to the Senate Judiciary Committee for consideration. Upon reaching the committee, Pitchford failed to gain enough support from his colleagues. W. W. Avery, a fellow Democrat and chairman of the committee, explained that "according to the decisions of our Supreme Court, the constitution recognizes free persons of color as citizens of this State, and being citizens, the law must protect them in the enjoyment of life, liberty and property, except when they have forfeited the same for crime." He continued, "Under our constitution, therefore, as interpreted by our courts, no free person, either colored or white, can be enslaved by legislative enactment, even by their own consent." Avery concluded, "While the decisions of the courts stand unreversed, the object contemplated by this bill can only be obtained by an amendment of the Constitution. The committee recommended that the bill do not pass."[7] The rejection of Pitchford's bill reveals the limited reach of the sentiments expressed by Justice Roger B. Taney in the Dred Scott decision. Although Justice Taney contended that people of color had no rights, North Carolina lawmakers did not agree. The majority of Avery's committee gave more credence to the state court than to the federal judiciary. North Carolina lawmakers were not alone in their unwillingness to use the Dred Scott precedent against free people of color in their state. In Maryland, the state court of appeals also rejected Justice Taney's attack on the status of free people of color.[8]

Even in the midst of war, several bills restricting the rights of free people of color failed in the state legislature. In 1863, the House Judicial Committee considered a bill to "prevent slaves and free persons of color from having and owning dogs," which died in the legislature.[9] The state assembly also debated a bill to enslave all of the state's free people of color convicted of crimes. A more rigid piece of legislation requiring the removal or enslavement of all free people of color passed in Arkansas, but all mass enslavement attempts failed in North Carolina.[10]

When discriminatory legislation passed in the General Assembly, radical proslavery ideologues still encountered challenges from their more moderate constituents. After the passage of legislation limiting the rights of free people of color in early 1861, fifteen white justices of the county court of Hertford County, most of whom were wealthy and heavily involved in local politics, petitioned the legislature in protest of the weapons ban. They requested a "modification" of the ban that would allow county courts to decide who among the free persons of color should or should not be allowed to carry weapons. The petitioners argued that "a just discrimination among applicants and the grant of such favor to deserving persons is itself a strong incentive to persons of this class to maintain a good character and deport themselves properly."[11] These men recognized that stripping additional rights from free people of color only made them more likely to rebel against the political system. As free people of color began to feel increasingly powerless and grew to understand that the law treated them not only as second-class, but as pseudo-citizens, they became less likely to support other objectives of that law, including the protection of slavery.

Although the most radical proslavery advocates despised them, some officials understood that free people of color could play an important role in the rebel war effort. With North Carolina's secession from the Union in the middle of 1861, county officials enlisted the aid of free people of color to help the secessionist cause. State law prohibited free people of color from enlisting in the military service as soldiers. Nevertheless, free people of color served both willingly and through coercion in other capacities. Throughout the war, county and rebel officials called free people of color to work on a variety of military-related projects.

At the beginning of the war, neither the state nor the rebel government had concluded that laborers needed to be obtained through conscription, and white North Carolinians recruited free people of color to work for pay as laborers and cooks. In April 1861, before North Carolina formally left the union, officials in Gates County offered, "all the free negroes who shall volunteer to cook or do other service shall be paid and if their families want any meat and bread they shall be furnished."[12] The following September, Pasquotank County leaders "ordered that the county commissary furnish with provisions the families of such free negroes as have been sent to work on the forts, the amounts furnished to be deducted from their wages."[13] Offers like this one enticed at least a few free people of color, desperate for work, to labor for the rebels.

North Carolina's secession and changes in the state's commercial alliances pulled free people of color into the rebel economy. Some free people of color, who owned their own businesses or farms, had to participate in that economy, but did not necessarily have to work overtly under the direction of the rebel forces. Matthew N. Leary Jr., a Fayetteville saddler, sold the rebels numerous leather goods. On May 16, 1861, he wholesaled one hundred canteen straps to the Sampson County Rangers. A rebel commander ordered equipment for one hundred soldiers from him on June 19, 1861. Leary promised to supply each man with a cartridge box, cap box, bayonet scabbard, and belt. On November 6, 1861, he sold two artillery harnesses to the state for $450. The next year, Leary sold twelve pounds of sole leather to a rebel artillery company.[14] As in the antebellum period, skilled free people of color remained essential to the North Carolina economy during the Civil War. Increased demand for military wares during the war only raised the importance of artisans like Leary. As a wise businessman with a family to support, Leary simply took advantage of the growing market.

Wilmington was a major site of market participation by free people of color because of its position as North Carolina's main economic hub during the war. The city, which remained under rebel control until the last months of the war, was an important port for business coming in and out of the rebel-held territory. In such a place, free people of color found multiple opportunities to make incomes from government spending. Some people earned money completing menial tasks, such as Bennett Boon, whom the government paid for digging a well at the rebel stable yard on July 16, 1862. Elvin Artis profited from the rebel war effort by performing more skilled tasks. During December 1862, the rebel government paid Artis, an experienced carpenter, for helping to construct a wharf on the Cape Fear River. In the same month, Artis also received pay for the construction of two coffins for deceased soldiers. On February 19 of the next year, Artis sold the rebels twenty pounds of rope for $10.[15]

Those with few financial opportunities also found themselves pushed into the rebel economy. During September 1861, the Pasquotank County court agreed to parole Aaron Spellman from jail and send him to work on the fort at Roanoke Island under the stipulation that they would deduct jailing fees from his pay. In the same month, two crews of free men of color from Orange County, totaling sixteen men, received pay from the state for working on Beacon Island. The following month saw Gates County officials remove E. P. Reid, John Reid, and Fletcher Smith from their apprenticeships to work on Roanoke Island's fortifications. During July 1862, Thomas, Peter, and George Clark all filed claims for work done under the commissary at

Garysburg. The men received only $10 per month for their labor, but for some, this pay undoubtedly was better than no allowance.[16]

Volunteer laborers at the beginning of the war completed a variety of tasks essential to the development of North Carolina's wartime defense system. By April 1861, free men of color across the state had started to gather at Fort Macon to improve the rebel defenses. Crews composed mostly of laborers traveled from counties such as Craven, Jones, Greene, Wayne, Edgecombe, and Lenoir to the far coast. On arrival at the fort, the laborers joined in the construction of transportation infrastructure such as rail lines and bridges. They set up and mounded guns around the fort. Their work also included digging earthworks, moving sand around the fort's premises, and constructing breastworks. While at work, many of the men became ill or infirm. Some returned to the construction projects after recovering while commanders simply discharged others.[17]

By 1862, some officials were no longer willing to let free people of color decide whether they wanted to apply their labor to the rebel effort. In April 1862, the *Fayetteville Observer* reported that "it is difficult to procure free colored men as servants, cooks & c." The paper's source for the story suggested that "the Convention give us authority to impress them into that service with responsable [sic] pay."[18] In several parts of the state, officials began the mass conscription of free men of color into the government's service. During December 1862, Cumberland County officials, with instructions from the rebel commander in Wilmington, ordered "all free negroes between the ages of sixteen and fifty years inclusive except . . . Blacksmiths, Pilots on boats running between Fayetteville and Wilmington, one Barber for each shop . . . shoemakers & harness makers" to work the fortifications at Wilmington.[19] Ten months later, Cumberland County officials issued a comparable order requiring free men of color to work on Cumberland County's fortifications. Similar impressments took place in other parts of the state. Solomon Oxendine of Robeson County recalled that rebel officials arrested him and sent him to help construct the breastworks at Fort Fisher. Other free men of color from Robeson County also labored at this fort.[20]

The conscription of free people of color into the rebel service strengthened the state's manpower for the war, but the removal of able-bodied men from the home front created serious problems for people simply trying to survive. In August 1861, this potentially was the case of Jeremiah Day, a free man of color from Orange County. With the support of four white men, Day complained to the governor that Captain Miller, commander of a rebel volunteer unit, wanted to impress Day's two nephews, Sterling and Leonidas Day. He explained that the rebel army had already taken five of his sons, and at seventy years of age, he and his wife would become destitute and dependent on the county if Captain Miller took the two boys.[21] The impressments of free people of color also threatened the livelihoods of white families who depended on free laborers of color. On May 5, 1864, Delia Wilder of Wake County, a white woman, petitioned rebel Secretary of War James A. Seddon to protect Bryant Morgan, a free man of color, from possible impressment. With her husband in the army, her eldest son dead, and left with an elderly mother, a "very infirm" enslaved woman, and eight small children, Wilder employed Morgan as a field laborer on her farm. Wilder's representative explained that if Morgan "is taken from her by the Government that it will be with great difficulty for her to carry on her farm & support herself & family."[22] Even during the divisive times of the Civil War, the lives of free people of color and their white neighbors continued to be indelibly intertwined. As before the war, free people of color were essential participants in local economies. Now that the rebel government had removed thousands of white men from their communities to the battlefields, the importance of free laborers of color at home only increased.[23]

As the war dragged on, officials not only became more insistent that free men of color work for the rebel cause but also decided that expanding their role in the war effort called for a reduction in the benefits free people of color could receive for their service. In Chowan County, local officials rescinded their offer to provide for the families of free men of color serving the rebels. In February 1862, the officials ordered that "hereafter no orders for provisions be given to families of free negroes in the service of the State."[24] This order would have allowed officials to divert increasingly limited provisions to the families of white rebel troops.

The lack of volunteer participation early in the war suggests that most free people of color were unwilling to support the rebellion directly. When white rebels finally attempted to force free men of color from their homes, many resisted or attempted to escape. The October 16, 1861, issue of the *Raleigh Register* reported that in Wilkes County a "free negro," only referred to as "Fletcher," fled from a group of men who sought to impress him as a servant in the army. Fletcher ran from the men, but was "pursued and caught." Cornered, Fletcher pulled a pistol and killed one of the men. After the killing, the surviving men captured Fletcher and hauled him to the jail in Wilkesboro. In Wilkesboro, an "excited crowd" gathered around the jail, removed Fletcher, and proceeded to hang him.[25]

Direct resistance often was dangerous, so some free people of color simply sought to evade impressments. Isaac Griffin of Pasquotank County avoided forced labor by staying away from home any time the rebels were near, and he recalled years later that he "had to leave home several times to keep from being carried off by the rebels."[26] George, James, and Richard Gray, all free men of color from Haywood County, attempted to evade impressments by arguing that someone else owned their services. In September 1864, each man responded to their recruitments by claiming they had deeded their labor to James R. Love for ninety-nine years and could not be taken from his service.[27]

On some occasions, the support of local white neighbors helped free people of color gain official exemption from impressment. In 1864, Wilson Williams, with the support of his white Montgomery County neighbors, gained a release from service. The men who investigated the petition for Williams's exemption noted that Williams "is 43 years old, that his wife (a white woman) is 27 years old and has 6 children the oldest a girl is 14 years, and the two next are twin boys twelve years old, next a boy 7 years old and the youngest 2 years old." They continued, "he cultivates one acre of land and makes shoes and hires himself to labor for others frequently—and supports his family" and concluded "that the family cannot get along without him . . . that he would be of more service, at home, by supporting his family than in the army." Upon receiving the report, Lieutenant Thomas H. Haughton determined that Williams's "family could not support itself in his absence though his wife (a white woman) did marry a free negro yet I do not think her large family of little children should suffer on that account."[28]

White supporters often gained approval for the exemption of free people of color from army labor by explaining how they personally might benefit from the labor of those persons of color. On July 24, 1864, an army conscription officer granted Lettie J. Rush's request to exempt Madison Chavis of Randolph County from service. In his report, the officer stated that the "Pet[ione]r is the wife of a soldier who has been in the army already a year or two. [The] Pet[ione]r has two small children. [The] free negro has two small children also. She has no one to work for her except said free

negro." He determined, "This is meritorious case. I therefore approve it."
William Ridge, also of Randolph County, convinced an officer to give John
Oxendine a similar work release. Captain Pearson, after learning of Ridge's
claim resolved "it is believed right & fair" for Ridge "to retain" Oxendine.
According to the case report, Ridge had "six sons in [the] service" and was
"not able to support himself and wife."[29] In these cases, conscription officers linked white families' sacrifice for the rebellion to merit. That merit in
turn could be used by those families to gain extra support denied to their
neighbors who had not made equal sacrifices. In these cases, the extra support came in the form of labor performed by free men of color.

Some free people of color avoided impressments but still had to deal
with trouble from rebels at home. During the war, the rebels twice confis-
cated property from John A. Chavers, a fairly well-to-do free man of color
from Wilkes County. Chavers claimed that in 1863 the rebels took several
hundred pounds of bacon and corn without providing payment. Near the
close of the war in 1865, rebel forces again visited Chavers, and they took
away his clothing, watch, money, and bed linens. Isaiah Simmons, a free
man of color from Fayetteville, faced harassment from members of the local
rebel home guard. In 1863, the home guard arrested Simmons and detained
him for a day for allegedly providing "information" to rebel deserters. Toward the end of the war, rebel soldiers picked up Simmons for being a
"damned union rascal." They attempted to hold Simmons, but he escaped
during the middle of the night.[30]

In Robeson County, rebel actions against free persons of color went far
beyond harassment. A series of murders in 1864 and 1865 initiated a conflict
between the county's free people of color and rebel sympathizers that lasted
well past the end of the war. On November 4, 1864, local officials found the
bodies of Allen Lowry Jr. and Wesley Lowry about a mile and half from
the house of James Brantley Harris, a rebel. An inquest into the murders
concluded that Harris had shot each "in the face and head," leaving them
with their "brains running out."[31] Months after the murders, rebels laid
siege to the home of Allen Lowry, a kinsman of Allen Lowry Jr. and Wesley
Lowry. Calvin Lowry recalled that "a company of about seventy-five men
surrounded his father's house" on March 3, 1865. The band of ruffians proceeded to arrest Calvin Lowry, his parents, brothers, and sisters and lock
them up in a house. The gang of brutes removed Allen Lowry and William Lowry, Calvin's father and brother, from the house and charged them

with harboring escaped prisoners. According to Calvin Lowry, the crowd taunted his father and brother by claiming that "if they had reported the Yankees [to the rebels] they would have received cretid [credit] for it." Following this taunt, the gang of tyrants murdered Allen and William Lowry. Next, they bound Calvin's mother, Mary Lowry, to a tree. Someone from the crowd aimed toward her but shot just above her head, frightening Mary but leaving her physically unharmed.[32]

Although most were less-than-willing supporters of the rebellion, a minority of free people of color placed their stakes with the rebels. Their cooperation with the rebels demonstrates the diversity of opinions among free people of color about survival strategy, secession, political loyalties, and rebel social policy.[33] An undeterminable number of free people of color from Robeson County supported the rebellion by both offering money and provisions and volunteering for the army. In 1862, Washington Lowery and Joseph Locklear donated one pair of socks each, Ollen Hammons contributed $3, and Ferebe Chavis gave three pairs of socks to Col. T. J. Morisey's North Carolina unit. Rebel officials listed Henry Revels, Stephen Hammons, and B. J. Chavis, all free men of color, among a roster of volunteers from Robeson County in 1861. Whether they saw battle is unclear. The law disqualified persons of color from serving as soldiers in the rebel forces, and since these men volunteered for local units, the commanders of their outfits likely knew that they could not legally employ these men as soldiers. Some free people of color discovered ways to get around the law and join the rebel forces. Solomon Oxendine, a free man of color from Robeson County, explained that some of his cousins joined the rebel army by crossing into South Carolina to enlist.[34] In South Carolina, officials likely did not know these men's history, which gave them better chances of fighting without being detected.

For those free men of color in other parts of North Carolina who desired to join the rebel forces, officials in charge of enlistments appear to have allowed certain men honorary white status. These free men of color joined regiments from their home counties, and probably those who enlisted them knew they were considered persons of color. In September 1861, Samuel Chavers, a free man of color from Orange County, volunteered for the rebel army, and fought with a rebel regiment at several battles until found to be "partly of negro descent." Discharged from the army at the end of 1862 for this reason, Chavers later reenlisted in the same regiment and continued to fight for the rebels until he met his death in May 1864 at Jericho Ford, Virginia. Several members of the Goins family, a free family of color from Moore County, also fought for the rebels. Henry, Andrew, Richard, and John W. Goins all served with the 35th North Carolina Troops. In July 1862, Andrew Goins died during a battle outside of Richmond, Virginia, leaving a wife and children back in Moore County. Rachel Goins, Andrew's wife, successfully collected her husband's back pay. Although the Goinses were not generally classified as "white" at home, army and local government officials treated them as though they were any other military family.[35]

The historical record provides little insight concerning the motives of North Carolina's free people of color who aided the rebel cause. Maybe their reasoning was similar to the rationale of the free people of color of New Orleans who offered their services to the secessionists. These men claimed that they submitted themselves to the rebel government in hopes that their allegiance would convince the rebels to treat them as equals to whites.[36] Some free people of color may have been motivated by individual allegiances to white friends and family members who served with the rebels. Others may have viewed publicly supporting the rebellion as a means of gaining favor from rebel whites and removing suspicion that they might be secretly supporting Union victory. In some of the rarest cases, free people of color may have agreed with the radical proslavery and secessionists' propaganda, which labeled the North as the oppressor of the South. Maybe they, like so many of their white neighbors, believed that the federal government was trying to impose its will and interfere with the South's peculiarities.[37] Regardless of their motives, the free people of color who supported the rebellion attempted to distinguish themselves from the majority of people of their status, who did not support secession. Nevertheless, their actions should not negate the intertwined interests of white supremacy, radical proslavery thought and proslavery dollars as the major causes, goals, and assumptions behind the rebellion.[38]

The state's participation in the rebellion interfered in the lives of all North Carolinians at one point or another, but many free people of color found ways to continue experiencing a semblance of their antebellum lives during the war years. As in the antebellum period, free people of color still played critical roles in agricultural production and helped to shape social life. Free people of color across the state continued to operate farms and do other kinds of work to support their livelihoods. Living in Harnett County during the war, Raleigh Seaberry moved his family back and forth between Averysboro and Smith's Ferry to farm rented land at the best price that he could get. Seaberry also worked as a cooper during this time. Exempt from service on account of rheumatism, William H. Haithcock cultivated twenty acres of rented land in 1864. Free children of color continued to work apprenticeship assignments. Counties still supported their poor people, even when the poor were free persons of color. Jason Bass, a free man of color who began collecting provisions from the Person County wardens of the poor in the 1850s, continued to receive a subsidy through at least 1862. As late as February 1865, the wardens of the poor in Edgecombe County distributed support to free people of color including Angelina Jones, Ballard Archer, and Caty Hagans. Free people of color also attended church with whites through the war. In June 1864, white members of the Meherrin Baptist Church in Hertford County approved the establishment of a Sabbath school for the children of free congregants of color.[39]

Free people of color found a variety of ways to survive the tumultuous years of war behind the rebel lines. Continuing with their daily lives was the primary strategy for most of them. Some people of color, however, responded to pressure from the rebels with active resistance, while others conformed to local officials' demands. Through further legal restrictions, forced labor, and discriminatory pay for work, rebel officials generally demonstrated to free people of color that the state needed them as a means to its goal of independence and had no intention of placing them and whites on equal footing. Nevertheless, in a few cases, rebel officials broke ranks with the general opinion and allowed free people of color to participate in the war against the U.S. government side by side with whites as their peers. Most North Carolina officials agreed that the war with the federal government was a battle for Southern independence and an endeavor for the protection of slavery, but whites never came to a clear consensus about what role free people of color should play in their struggle.

The U.S. Effort

As the war progressed, several small victories allowed U.S. forces to capture parts of eastern North Carolina and southern Virginia. These developments along with Abraham Lincoln's Emancipation Proclamation opened the doors for antirebel forces in North Carolina, including free people of

color, to work toward ending the insurrection in the South. Lincoln's proclamation, issued at the beginning of 1863, reintroduced slave emancipation
as a war tactic to weaken the rebel war effort and economy.[40] Yet more
importantly for free people of color, the proclamation offered them the
opportunity to serve in the U.S. Army and Navy. Free people of color, tired
of cooperating with the rebels simply to survive, now had an opportunity
to redirect their efforts. The Emancipation Proclamation, applying primarily to territories held by the rebels, liberated few slaves, but it gave free
people of color a chance to resist further collaboration with the rebels. As
free people of color began to enlist in the U.S. Army after the issuance of
the Emancipation Proclamation, they joined bands of runaway slaves and
recently emancipated people to serve the U.S. government. Their fight to
suppress the rebellion was the first significant collaborative effort between
free people of color, many of whose families had been free for generations,
and men and women whose newfound freedom could be retained only
with the defeat of the Slave Power.

Lincoln's call for the enlistment of colored troops at the beginning of
1863 opened the doors for free people of color in the eastern part of North
Carolina to join the federal war effort. With the piedmont and western
North Carolina in rebel hands during most of the war, free men of color
in these areas typically could not risk running away from their obligations
at home to fight for their country. However, their eastern brethren took
advantage of the new situation. Free men of color from eastern counties,
especially those with significant free populations of color such as Hertford,
Pasquotank, and Craven, trickled into the federal ranks between 1863 and
1865. Fighting for the United States gave free men of color the opportunity
to earn steady incomes, escape the vigilance of rebel officials, learn new
skills, and work to preserve and expand their civil liberties.

At the first chance after the Emancipation Proclamation, free men of
color from northeastern North Carolina who could evade rebel troops and
home guards rushed to federal strongholds in coastal North Carolina and
tidewater Virginia to enlist in the U.S. Army. By July 1863, Washington
County residents including George Boston, Friley James, and Charles Pierce
made their way to Plymouth and New Bern to enlist with the 36th U.S. Colored Infantry. Brothers Parker D. Robbins and Augustus Robbins, who lived
in Bertie County at the beginning of the war, crossed over the state border
to sign up with the 2nd U.S. Colored Cavalry on January 1, 1864.[41]

The federal movement into Hertford County along with the new policy of enrolling colored troops in the U.S. Army shifted the circumstances of impressed free men of color by 1864. Advancing federal troops removed the men from rebel service at Pitch Landing, carried them from Hertford County to Roanoke Island, and then relocated them to New Bern. James Turner, who worked at Pitch Landing, remembered that upon their arrival in New Bern, U.S. officials mustered the free men of color into service. These free men of color, along with recently emancipated slaves, served in the 14th U.S. Colored Heavy Artillery stationed on the North Carolina coast. Other free men of color arrived to join the federal forces in a similar fashion.[42] The U.S. Army offered free men of color a refuge from rebel authority and an opportunity to earn wages.

Life for free men of color in the 14th U.S. Colored Heavy Artillery and many other units exposed them to a world they had never seen before. The majority of the men from Hertford County had worked as farm hands before their arrival in the east and had never lived away from home. Most of them resided in tight circles of kin and close friends and rarely had intimate interaction with enslaved people. Many of these men continued these practices in the army, sharing tents with men from home, who were often brothers or childhood friends. However, some branched out and made acquaintance with men recently emancipated from slavery. King Outlaw of Bertie County was one of the ex-slaves with whom Hertford County free men of color became friendly during the war. After the war, Outlaw married the stepdaughter of one of his Hertford County comrades, Enoch Luton, a free man of color, and eventually settled in his wife's home county.[43]

Along with new people, free men of color came into contact with a host of new diseases. Smallpox, dysentery, typhoid fever, and tuberculosis debilitated and often killed troops by the thousands.[44] In 1864, while serving with the 38th U.S. Colored Infantry, Raynor Lilly of Perquimans County contracted smallpox. Lilly entered the smallpox hospital in Norfolk, Virginia, where he lingered with the painful disease for weeks before succumbing. Within four months of his enlistment in 1863, George Boston of Washington County, a member of the 36th U.S. Colored Infantry, passed away under the same circumstances while stationed in Portsmouth, Virginia.[45]

The fight against rebel oppression also entailed many costs on the battlefield for free men of color. One mishap in battle could lead to serious injury and even death. During an engagement at Deep Bottom, Virginia, in 1864, a shell exploded and injured the eye of Washington Flood of Northampton County, who fought with the 37th U.S. Colored Infantry. At the same battle, Levi Collins of Hertford County suffered a wound to his hip while fighting with the 38th U.S. Colored Infantry. The wound eventually led to Collins's death a year after the war. As a participant in a Union charge in 1864, Isaac Overton of Pasquotank County died on the battlefield while serving with the 36th U.S. Colored Infantry at New Market Heights, Virginia.[46]

Although away from their communities, some free men of color attempted to reconstruct some semblance of home by bringing family along with them or finding a wife while stationed with the army. Martin Rooks, originally from Gates County, carried his son Henry with him during the war. The time Henry spent with his father would be the last moments that the two would spend together. On their return home, Martin Rooks succumbed to smallpox. Martha Newsome of Hertford County recalled going to New Bern with her first cousin Boone Nickens, who was a soldier in the 14th U.S. Colored Heavy Artillery, and the rest of the Nickens family. She stayed in New Bern with her relatives until her cousin's discharge.[47]

The opportunity to send money home served as an important motivating force for free men of color in the U.S. Army. John Godett of Craven County was one of countless men who recognized military service as a means to provide for their families. After the death of their parents, George and Elizabeth, Godett and his brother had taken charge of their younger siblings. Following the enactment of the Emancipation Proclamation, Godett joined the U.S. Army, through which he secured regular wages. Isaac Carter, Godett's bunk mate and neighbor, remembered that Godett put money "in a letter at Morehead City, N. C. and sent it to his brother Jesse P. Godett for the support of his two sisters & brother."[48]

Military service was an opportunity for illiterate people of color, both free and recently emancipated, to learn to read and write. Teachers in the army camps helped soldiers study reading and writing in their spare time. While stationed at Jacksonville and Beaufort, Frances Beecher taught troops in the 35th U.S. Colored Infantry, commanded by her husband Colonel James Beecher, to read and write. She recalled that some soldiers found the lessons difficult, "while others learned at once." Beecher further remembered that "whenever they had a spare moment, out would come a spelling-book or a primer or Testament, and you would often see a group of heads around one book."[49] Julius Mackey of Hyde County, who served with the regiment taught by Beecher, recalled "I learned how to write after I enlisted and toward the last of my service, I signed the muster roll."[50] The literacy training that Mackey and other soldiers received during their stint in the army provided them with a critical life skills advantage, which served them long after the war's end.

Naval service offered free men of color who had familiarity with water navigation the optimal opportunity to use their expertise. Joshua Nickens of Hertford County, who had been a boatman before the war, joined the U.S. Navy after the announcement of the Emancipation Proclamation. Nickens's younger cousins Thomas P. and Lawrence E. Weaver became first-class boys on the U.S.S. Miami, which sailed in the same fleet with Nickens's ship, the U.S.S. Whitehead. The crews of both ships engaged in several battles against the rebels on the waters of North Carolina and Virginia.[51]

Aiding their country was a costly effort for free people of color who lost limbs, lives, and treasure in the process. The cost of war, however, ultimately brought an end to the rebellion and the collapse of an oppressive regime. When President Lincoln issued the Emancipation Proclamation, he not only ushered thousands of former slaves into the federal ranks but also offered free people of color the opportunity to assert themselves against a political system that had slowly stripped away their civil liberties for generations. When North Carolina's political leaders joined the rebellion, they forced supporters of the legitimate government, persons of color and white alike, into silence. Their closed lips were a tactic for survival, but when the U.S. government provided the opportunity, silent free men of color quickly turned into war-ready troops. These soldiers may have fought against their state government's political goals, but ultimately, they still stood for the fundamental protection of their homes.

Victory at Home

Serving in the armed forces was not the full extent of free people of color's participation in the effort to put down the rebellion. Free people of color still at home aided recently escaped federal runaways from rebel camps. Several households sacrificed precious foodstuffs to passing U.S. regiments on the march without rations. Many families surrendered their valuable property to U.S. troops in need of horses, wagons, boats, and other modes of transportation. The sacrifices of free people of color often were very costly for families barely scraping by in a disastrous southern economy. However, their contributions were invaluable to the suppressing of the insurrection and the ending of rebel injustices against free people of color.

While traveling through rebel-held territory attempting to reach the federal lines, U.S. troops who had recently escaped from enemy prisons depended on free people of color to provide them with shelter and provisions. William Jacobs of Richmond County recalled helping a soldier who had escaped from a rebel prison in South Carolina. About a year before the end of the war, the soldier stayed with Jacobs for more than a week. After the soldier had recovered some of his strength, Jacobs sent him under the cover of darkness by wagon to his cousins Edmond and William Chavers in Fayetteville. Once the soldier arrived in Fayetteville, the Chaverses gave the soldier a map and sent him across the Cape Fear River. From there, the soldier continued toward the federal line.[52]

On numerous occasions, U.S. Army officials asked free persons of color to forfeit their necessities and provide U.S. soldiers on the move with provisions. Free people of color gave freely to the army. However, sometimes overly aggressive federal troops left their gracious hosts without many of their most precious assets. Confiscations of property largely affected the most successful free people of color, those with their own farms. Sometime during July 1864, a Pennsylvania cavalry unit passing through Gates County via Suffolk, Virginia, stopped at the house of Asbury Reid and requested provisions. Reid recalled that the soldiers took corn, fodder, and the vegetables growing in his garden. Once the troops seized the provisions, the troops commenced to cook in Reid's house and yard. In 1865, U.S. troops visited Bryant Simmons's home in Wayne County. Simmons remembered that the troops took corn, lard, bacon, peas, and fodder from his residence. The confiscation took place without Simmons's permission.[53] These U.S. actions at the homes of Reid and Simmons certainly set back their families financially. Crops had to be replanted and provisions replaced during the most difficult times of the war.

The cost of supporting the federal government also included the loss of transportation. U.S. officials fulfilled their needs by confiscating boats, horses, carts, and other modes of transport from locals near their encampments. These confiscations often left free people of color without horses to plow their fields, carts to move their goods, and boats to navigate the rivers. Soon after the capture of New Bern, U.S. Army officials seized the *Susan* and the *Water Witch*, both partially owned by William Martin, a farmer in Craven County who had used the boats to transport lumber and rosin from his farm to New Bern. Federal troops depleted the William and Dizzy Snellings family farm in Wake County of its most valuable assets. Over a period of three or four days in April 1865, U.S. troops seized from the Snellings place two horses, two carts, harnesses, and saddles in addition to corn, syrup, cattle, sheep, chickens, and goats. Dizzy Snellings remembered that "nearly everything we had was taken from us except our beds—everything in the house and outside was taken."[54]

For free persons of color, problems with the U.S. Army went beyond simple seizure of property. During the Battle of Plymouth in April 1864, U.S. troops seized Harriet Toodle's Washington County home, along with the houses of at least five of her neighbors. These homes became key positions for the Union troops during the battle. Outside of Toodle's home, the U.S. forces constructed trenches. After the days-long battle, Union troops surrendered to a much smaller rebel force, leaving what remained of Toodle's home under rebel control.[55]

For free people of color, the cost of defeating the rebellion sometimes included dealing with general unruliness from federal troops. Some federal soldiers preyed upon North Carolinians regardless of which side they supported during the war. At the war's end, the Scott family, who lived on the outskirts of Raleigh during the war, had a run-in with troops. William Scott, who was a boy at the time, recalled U.S. troops came to his family's house and took their rations. Scott's father, angered by the abusive troops, sought out their commander and reported the incident. The Scotts were lucky; the U.S. officers responded kindly to the report by sending them replacement rations. Scott's mother returned the officers' kindness by cooking for them.[56]

Free people of color on the home front were critical participants in the U.S. military's triumph in North Carolina. They sacrificed their time, safety, and most precious possessions to U.S. troops. Some free people of color happily gave to the cause of preserving their nation, while others found the extent to which federal troops were willing to take from them extremely frustrating. Whether they gave freely or by force, their contribution helped the success of the federal campaign in North Carolina. For some free people of color, the death of slavery and the defeat of the radical proslavery regime must have been well worth the short-term costs.

Reconstruction

On August 1, 1867, Republicans from Hertford, Bertie, Northampton, and Gates Counties, along with their peers from Southampton County, Virginia, gathered in Murfreesboro for a celebration of freedom. They commemorated the death of slavery in the British West Indies and its gradual collapse in much of the old Spanish empire. Their celebration's most important commemoration, however, was the fall of chattel bondage in the United States. School children and adults alike sang patriotic tunes. Everyone came dressed in their best garments. Many former slaves were part of the crowd that day. Yet those people of color who were free before the Civil War played a leading role in this grand celebration of liberty. Reverend William Reid, a freeborn man, served as president of the event. James Henry Harris, who was also born free, gave a powerful speech about Republican principles and entitlements and responsibilities of people of color in the new era. This gathering of 2,500 to 3,000 in Murfreesboro was just one example of the changing times after the Civil War.[57]

The outcome of the Civil War shattered the segmented social order of North Carolina, which had divided the enslaved from the free. Lincoln's Emancipation Proclamation led slavery to its legal death, and the Constitution's Thirteenth Amendment, ratified at the end of 1865, became the final nail in the coffin of human bondage in the United States. The latter half of the 1860s ushered in a contest for power among the various elements of society. Free people of color and the newly emancipated people sought seats at the victors' table, a voice in the political dialogue, and a guarantee of long-denied civil rights. Pro-Union whites and those whites who became dissatisfied with the old rebel regime pursued the chance to take power after years of bending to the demands of radical proslavery ideologues. The Fourteenth Amendment to the U.S. Constitution finally clarified that all people born in the United States, including people of color, were citizens of the country. The Fifteenth Amendment permanently overrode de facto race-based voting restrictions. The defeated, but not destroyed, proslavery and white supremacist conservative element hunted for a strategy to take back control and prevent persons of color from gaining political advantage.

In a political situation so contested, how would prewar free people of color fare? Soon after the rebel defeat, free people of color in several localities dealt with backlash from supporters of the old regime. They generally had been against that regime, and many had taken up arms in its defeat. People of color, both long free and recently emancipated, became the targets of infuriated whites seeking revenge against the victors. Conservative whites assaulted them, destroyed their property, and created a variety of other schemes meant to derail their progress in society. Yet in the face of these obstacles, people of color sought power and gained political influence. With the ascension of the Republicans in the South, individuals formerly categorized as free people of color entered state and local politics. They also found a place in less formal political activity as preachers, teachers, and community organizers. Prewar free people of color, who were often propertied and educated because of the liberties they had enjoyed during the era of slavery, had an advantage in North Carolina's new social order.[58]

After the war's end, antebellum free people of color met numerous challenges from former rebels who hoped to maintain power even after their defeat. Returning to Hertford County after their service with the 14th U.S. Colored Heavy Artillery, John Bizzell, John Collins, Andrew Reynolds, James Manly, Richard Weaver, Miles Weaver, and Bryant Manly encountered Colonel Joshua Garrett's militia unit. Garrett's men "formed in a line of Battle" and halted the discharged troops. Claiming he had orders from the Department of War, Garrett demanded that the men of color surrender their arms. The discharged troops later found out that Garrett seized their guns because they "had bin [been] in the U S Servis [Service]." They recognized that Garrett had taken guns from no one else. After John Bizzell reached home, he met another challenge. A gang of four or five armed men led by Jesse Sewell, a white man, demanded to search his house. Under threat, Bizzell granted the invaders permission to search. They "plundered" the home and stole the ammunition for Bizzell's recently seized gun.[59]

Following the end of the rebellion, rebel sympathizers continued to control many county governments and used their position to challenge the newly won rights of people of color. On February 1, 1866, William Reid, Moses Boon, Orrell Green, William Rooks, and several freedmen complained to officials at the Freedmen's Bureau about abuses by prorebel officials. They asked for protection from "unloyal white men" who took away their children and hired them out to "the white man." These men of color also asked for the removal of Dr. O. B. Savage, the acting Freedmen's Bureau official in Gates County, whom they claimed "confused both black and white." Their request for correction of abuses and the removal of a prorebel official was a defensive act but also had proactive implications. The Gates County people of color explained that action on the part of the Freedmen's Bureau would allow them to "take care" of their wives and children and "do all public Dutys [sic]."[60]

Conservative whites also sought to prevent the empowerment of people of color through a string of discriminatory regulations titled "An Act Concerning Negroes and Persons of Color or of Mixed Blood," which the General Assembly passed in 1866. Many of these regulations were reminiscent of the antebellum laws that had targeted poor free persons of color and in some cases were actually revised versions of those acts. The new law's second section declared: "That all persons of color, who are now inhabitants of this State, shall be entitled to the same privileges and subject to the same burthen and disabilities as by the laws of the State were conferred on, and attached to, free persons of color, prior to the ordinance of emancipation, except as the same may be changed by law." Under the new code, people of color still could not testify in courts against whites. Intermarriage between people of color and whites continued to be prohibited. The law also required the presence of a "white person who can read and write" when a person of color entered into a contract to sell or purchase livestock. When before a court, a person of color was supposed to receive a warning directly from the court "to declare the truth." A person of color convicted by a court "of an assault with an intent to commit rape upon the body of a white female" would suffer the death penalty.[61]

Although prorebel whites attempted to block their social advancement, people of color continued striving for political inclusion and increased social privilege. At the local level, those formerly classified as free persons of color worked for the improvement of people of color and their home communities by serving as educators, establishing social organizations, seeking official positions, and fighting for the rights of the underprivileged. Through advantages obtained during the prewar years such as wealth, literacy, and social connections, they provided North Carolina with crucial leadership during an era of social instability. Steven Hahn suggested that antebellum free persons of color "had come to see their destinies as inextricably linked" to the interests of the masses of people of color, "some because they saw no real possibility for a meaningful separate peace with any group of southern whites, and most because the process of mobilization had increasingly acquainted them with the political sensibilities and styles of the freedpeople."[62] Alliances between those long free and those who obtained their freedom through war were relationships of convenience, not necessarily manifestations of selfless political unity based on common racial categorization.

Not content with the attempts of white conservatives to maintain control over the state, people of color came together to demand political power and civil rights. A group composed of former slaves and free people of color converged on Raleigh for the first Freedmen's Convention on September 29, 1865. Over one hundred men, including James Henry Harris, John P. Sampson, and Isham Sweat, all antebellum free persons of color, came together to consider the future of the state's people of color. They joined with leaders who were former slaves such as Abraham H. Galloway and Stewart Ellison, to advocate for equal rights, allegiance to the federal government, and U.S. recognition of Liberia and Haiti.[63] In October 1866, 117 delegates, some free during the antebellum period and others recently emancipated, gathered for the second Freedmen's Convention in Raleigh. Led by James Henry Harris of Wake County, the convention set out to organize and demand the vote for people of color in the state. The North Carolina State Equal Rights League was born of this convention. The constitution of the league, developed during the convention, declared that the goal of the league was "to secure, by political and moral means, as far as may be, the repeal of all laws and parts of laws, State and National that make distinctions on account of color."[64] In July 1867, a delegation under Harris, acting president of the State Equal Rights League, arrived in Washington, D.C., to request the dissolution of North Carolina's state government.[65]

Several antebellum free men of color began their political work at home before rising to statewide prominence. On June 5, 1867, John T. Reynolds of Northampton County wrote Captain Alexander Moore of the Second Military district requesting an appointment as a register of voters. As he was a key figure in the Baptist movement for people of color, Reynolds's presence at the upcoming local election would assure people of color the right to vote without intimidation. Reynolds would later enter state politics as a repre-

sentative from Northampton and Halifax Counties.[66] Parker D. Robbins of
Bertie County, a U.S. cavalry veteran and skilled mechanic, worked for the
protection of people in his home community before entering state office.
On May 28, 1868, Robbins wrote to the commanding officers at Goldsboro
on behalf of Mustapha Holley, a man of color. He complained that Amos
Peel, "a white rebble [sic]," attacked Holley with a stick and "[k]nocked him
down."[67] Incapacitated and possibly illiterate, Holley would have been in no
position to present a grievance to federal officials, but Robbins's assistance
made this injustice public.

Across the state, antebellum free men of color help to lead the expansion
of the Republican Party at the local and state levels. In 1868, James S. Leary of
Cumberland County represented the state party at the National Convention
in Chicago. James Oxendine of Robeson County and James Henry Harris of
Wake County served on the party's State Executive Committee in the same
year. Others helped to run the local party organizations. In Gates County,
the entire Republican committee, composed of Asbury Reid, Lemuel Washington Boon, and Orrill Green, were born free before the Civil War. Halifax County's organization included the freeborn John H. Lynch of Brink-
leyville. Franklin County organizers counted Hilliard Dunston, a bricklayer,
plasterer, and antebellum free man of color, among their number.[68]

Supporting the Republican Party allowed antebellum free people of color
to organize a collective challenge to Conservative power and white supremacy in North Carolina. Sinclair Lowry, James Oxendine, and Cary Wilkins
joined other Republicans to face down Robeson County Conservatives who
threatened "that the 'niggers,' 'radicals,' 'scalawags,' 'carpet-baggers' and
'native low white trash' could never hold another Fourth of July celebration
in Robeson." In a snub to local Conservatives, the county's Republicans led
a Fourth of July celebration at Back Swamp Church that attracted more
than three thousand people in 1868. Wilkins offered a prayer and spoke.
"Enterprising colored citizens" sold "lemonade, cakes, candies, ice cream and
cider." The celebration concluded with the crowd endorsing Ulysses Grant
for president in the upcoming election.[69]

From the time the U.S. forces retook North Carolina during the Civil
War into the twentieth century, antebellum-era free people of color were
instrumental in the development of local education. Henry Sampson and
Matthew Locklear, both born free, were among the first teachers at Freedmen's schools in Robeson County. In the postwar years, John P. and Su-

san W. Sampson, children of the wealthy free man of color James D. Sampson, served the people of Wilmington as teachers. In addition to teaching, John P. Sampson worked as clerk to the superintendent of schools for the Freedmen's Bureau in Wilmington.[70] These trailblazers in the postwar education of people of color overcame obstacles of student poverty and limited funding to help elevate those long denied formal education. Their participation in the mass education of people of color was a political act that challenged the social order of the past, which failed to support and often denied people of color basic literacy.

The work of people of color and other supporters of the federal government ultimately led to the convening of a Constitutional Convention at the beginning of 1868. Freeborn delegates from the Freedmen's Convention James Henry Harris and Cuffee Mayo of Granville County, along with men such as Parker D. Robbins of Bertie County and Henry C. Cherry of Edgecombe, both free before the war, participated in the Constitutional Convention and helped craft the state's new supreme law. They joined with white Republicans and former slaves, including notable men like Abraham Galloway, to draft new legislation for North Carolina.[71]

With many of the obstacles preventing people of color from voting and serving in public office removed, several men of color who were free before the war ran for and won positions as senators and representatives in the North Carolina General Assembly. From 1868 to 1899, all four freeborn participants in the Constitutional Convention represented their localities in Raleigh. These men came from the eastern and northern piedmont counties of the state, where people of color made up significant portions of and sometimes the majority of the population.[72] Craven County, a county with one of the largest free populations of color before the war, sent several men of that background to Raleigh, including Israel B. Abbott, John R. Good, Edward H. Hill, and Willis D. Pettipher.[73]

While certain men of color aspired to higher office, many men who were free before the war made local politics their top priority. Several localities had men of this stripe running their community affairs by the end of the 1860s. Bladen County citizens elected John Spaulding as county commissioner. Matthew N. Leary held the same position in Cumberland County. William D. Newsome and William Reid were county commissioners in Hertford County. In Washington County, Theophilus Ash served as the coroner. William Kellogg received an appointment from Governor William W. Holden to serve as an alderman for Wilmington in 1868. Norfleet Dunston and Albert Farrar, as representatives of the Western Ward and Middle Ward, respectively, joined Raleigh's board of commissioners in 1869. During the same year, Alfred Howe became a member of Wilmington's Board of Assessors.[74]

Following the passage of the 1868 Constitution, people of color continued to face challenges from supporters of the old regime who sought to reinstitute white supremacy at the local and state levels. Antebellum free people of color and their allies responded to the threat through collective organizing. A group of Republican electors from Bogue Township in Columbus County, including members of antebellum free families of color such as the Blanks, Mitchell, Moore, Spaulding, Jacobs, Freeman, and Webb families, asked Governor Holden to support their attempt to remove a justice of the peace from power. They contended that the county commissioners had appointed the justice of the peace, J. W. Hall, without acting "in accordance with the Laws of our state." In their 1869 petition, the Republican electors informed Holden that they sought local law enforcement composed of "men that Constitutionally qualified at least."[75] The next year, a group of petitioners from Robeson County, which included several antebellum free people of color from the Oxendine, Lowry, Revels, Wilkins, and Locklear families, begged Governor Holden to protect them from white men who sought the "wholesale massacre of the colored people of this county." They were concerned that if Holden declared martial law in order to quell the violence that had spread over Scuffletown and other parts of the county since the end of the war, white supremacists in the area would seize the opportunity "to destroy us."[76]

The murders of several members of the Lowry family in 1864 and 1865 had motivated many free people of color and their allies to commence a war against white supremacists and rebel sympathizers in Robeson County. Through the second half of the 1860s into the 1870s, Henry Berry Lowry, a son of Allen Lowry, whom rebels murdered in 1865, led a struggle against rebel sympathizers in his community. During the years in which the Lowry band was active, officials charged members with murders, robberies, burglaries, and other crimes. Henry Berry Lowry's brothers Sinclair and Purdie chose to fight against white supremacy through formal political channels. But Henry Berry Lowry had less faith in a system backed by unscrupulous politicians and officials allegedly converted from an adherence to treason and white supremacy. Lowry was ultimately proven correct. Pressured by white conservatives, Governor Holden, a Republican, issued a proclamation offering the hefty sum of $500 for Henry Berry Lowry's arrest. The governor also issued a bounty of $200 on each member of Lowry's posse.[77]

People of color, including those free before the war, played a crucial role in the development of postslavery society, but their influence never reached its full potential. In 1872, Conservatives took control of state government with the help of the Ku Klux Klan.[78] People of color continued to participate in both formal and informal politics after this temporary but significant switch in state political power. They, however, never procured any significant additional gains in power after this point. Their inability to secure more power at the state level restricted most of their political influence to the local level and within segregated institutions such as schools and churches. Yet their work at the local level and within segregated institutions allowed people of color to continue with personal development through education and small business ownership long after the war's end.

The Civil War ushered in social and political changes that significantly altered the position of free people of color in North Carolina. During the years 1861 through 1865, the radical proslavery political machine in North Carolina took its most oppositional stance against free people of color. They lost their right to defend themselves with weapons, and masses of free men of color temporarily lost the privilege to determine the use of their own labor. The most pivotal change brought on by the Civil War, however, came with its aftermath. The conclusion of the war and the death of slavery officially ended the legal distinctions between people of color. Free people of color were no longer categorized within a distinct sociopolitical category.

In some sense, the radical proslavery politicians and pundits of the antebellum period had been correct in their assertion that free people of color were a threat to slavery. At the moment free people of color stood against the proslavery regime, slavery indeed met its death. When federal troops advanced into North Carolina, they persuaded free men of color to take up arms against the rebellion, and by default, fight for the defeat of one of the most extreme proslavery movements the world had ever seen. Since the beginning of the century, proslavery radicals had engaged in a political offensive against free people of color, stripping them of many of their civil liberties. The majority of free people of color, primarily focused on day-to-day survival and surrounded by traitors to the national government, waited to see what would happen to the few precious freedoms they still retained by 1861. Their inaction did not imply consent to what was going on around them. Many of them realized that slavery was a constant threat to their freedom. When slavery's demise became the military and political objective of the federal government, free people of color then felt safe to take a stand.

The end of the Civil War and the ratification of the Thirteenth Amendment to the Constitution marked the end of the legal distinction between free people of color and the formerly enslaved. During the second half of the 1860s, North Carolina officially recognized two distinct sociopolitical groups, white people and colored people, with the Cherokees in the western mountains as the exception. In many cases, the results of this political transformation created significant changes on the ground. Those formerly categorized as free people of color and the freedmen joined together in politics and social organization. During Reconstruction, they united with moderate and liberal whites to support Republican political control. Both those long free and those recently liberated struggled to secure civil rights. Their shared fight against the rebellion, their mutual goal of equality with whites, as well as a group of common enemies—white supremacists—pushed those formerly categorized as free people of color and recently freed people into a political coalition. This coalition produced North Carolina's first elected representatives of color, numerous organizations, and educational institutions.

Epilogue
Remaking Race

A lthough common cause brought together many of those formerly categorized as free persons of color with recently emancipated people,
the ancestral, historical, and social differences that had divided so many of
them before the Civil War did not completely dissipate. In many parts of
North Carolina, whites and antebellum free people of color sought to continue and sometimes reinforce old social divisions. In some communities,
individuals formerly categorized as free people of color used endogamous
marriage and separate social institutions, such as churches and schools, to
hold onto or create social distinctiveness. Localities often treated these people as socially and even racially distinct from the freedmen. Those people
of color who understood themselves to be different from other persons of
color sought to reshape the racial order to their own liking. Some individuals and their descendants once categorized as "free people of color" or "free
negroes" assumed new public faces as "Indians" and even in some cases as
"whites."

Long after the Civil War, individuals once categorized as "free people of
color" and their descendants in communities across the state continued to
view themselves as distinct from the freedmen. In most areas, these people
failed to acquire an officially recognized racial category separate from the
freedmen. Instead, community members used the phrase "Old Free Issue"
to refer to persons of color who had been free before the Civil War and
"New Free Issue" for those who gained their liberty after the rebel defeat.[1]
These unofficial categories provided individuals formerly categorized as free
people of color with a way to distinguish themselves without providing
them with tangible privileges over freedmen. Such a social arrangement
existed around Kittrell in Vance County (formerly Granville County). In
1886, O. W. Blacknall recalled, "My neighborhood contains an 'Ol' Isshy'

town. . . . It stands about five miles from the railroad station, and consists of some half a dozen families, scantily provided with fathers, crowded into as many little huts scattered here and there on a 'slipe' of very poor, rocky ridge." He described the people in the Old Issue neighborhood as "intensely clannish and loyal to each other, timid and suspicious of the outside world." Although the people of the Old Issue town fell into the same racial category as the freedmen, Blacknall observed that the Old Issue had "an abiding dislike of the 'New Isshy,' especially if he is black." The Old Issue drew a strict line between themselves and freedmen, which had harsh consequences if broken. Blacknall explained, "A marriage, even a *liaison*, with one [of the New Issue] would be instantly fatal to the reputation of any female among them [the Old Issue]."[2]

Some descendants of free people of color attempted to impose this informal racial divide on institutions as well as on sexual relations and close social interactions. While conducting research on people of color in Hertford County during the early twentieth century, E. Franklin Frazier learned from a local minister about a plan to separate "mulattoes" and "blacks" within a community school. Frazier's informant, who ran the school, explained, "The feeling was such between mulattoes and blacks that they wanted me to place the mulattoes on the second floor and the blacks on the third floor of the school dormitory."[3] A similar situation existed in neighboring Gates County. Before the Civil War, the people in Gates County established New Hope Baptist Church for free people of color in the area. According to Isaac Harrell, freedmen could not participate in church services long after the war ended. He wrote that "the church was built in 1859 and no slaves were admitted; even after the war it would not for a long time admit any negro who had been a slave, the line always being drawn between those 'born free and those shot free.'"[4] Legal distinctions between free and slave ended with emancipation. Yet that change did not necessarily correlate with social practices. Postwar North Carolina was legally divided through racial categories, but these legal divisions did not create racial community among people classified as "colored."

By the late nineteenth century, informal social distinctions became racialized in parts of southeastern North Carolina. With the support of neighboring whites, some individuals formerly categorized as "free people of color" pushed for and won recognition from their localities and the state as falling under a distinct "Indian" racial category. In 1885, the state created a new "Croatan Indian" racial category, a recognition that allowed some individuals once classified as "free people of color" in counties such as Robeson, Richmond, and Sampson to create their own institutions, most particularly public schools.[5]

This move from "colored" to "Indian" was most notable in Robeson County, where hundreds of families long classified as "colored," "mulatto," or "negro" took on a new official designation. The family of Hugh Oxendine provides a glimpse into the larger phenomenon. In the 1860 census, the enumerator classified Hugh Oxendine, his wife Eliza, and all of their children as "mulatto."[6] Census enumerators continued to categorize the Oxendine family as "mulatto" in subsequent censuses up to 1880.[7] When a federal official visited Robeson County to discuss Oxendine's claim against the government for property taken during the late war, he asked him whether he had taken the rebel loyalty oath. Hugh Oxendine offered the standard response given by people of color: "That oath was not taken in this county by col'd [colored] people."[8] This statement suggests that Oxendine understood himself to be "colored," that his neighbors recognized him as such, and most importantly, that the legal limitations forced on people of color applied to him. Oxendine's acknowledgment that he was a "colored" person, however, does not say anything about his heritage other than that people in his community believed that Oxendine had some non-European ancestry. Indeed, by 1900, Oxendine's racial categorization had changed. The enumerator of the 1900 census classified Hugh Oxendine and his family as "Indian," and upon Oxendine's death, the local registrar also categorized him as "Indian."[9]

Post–Civil War social reorganization did not limit racial recategorization for people once classified as people of color to the new "Indian" categorization. Recategorization as "white" had always been an option for those free people of color whose physical appearances signified whiteness to most observers. Individuals who could be viewed as "white" because of their appearances but who were known in their communities as persons of color could escape second-class racial status by leaving their homes and re-settling where local people were unfamiliar with their family histories. This process proceeded into the postwar era and continues into the present. Local knowledge was an important part of determining racial categorization in rural communities. Community members denied "white" racial status to some people whose physical features met accepted criteria of whiteness because they belonged to families generally known to be "colored." By moving to areas where that local knowledge did not exist, however, people once labeled "colored" immediately became "white." This transformation happened to the son of Hugh Oxendine. In 1860, the census enumerator listed Hugh's son John Wesley Oxendine, like the rest of his family, as "mulatto."[10] Yet sometime before his death in 1927, John Wesley Oxendine left Robeson County and moved to Henderson County, in the western part of the state. In Henderson County, the people categorized John Wesley Oxendine as "white."[11] This racial transformation could not have happened in Robeson County because locals knew the history of the Oxendine family and understood that all Oxendines in the county, regardless of their appearance, were "people of color" or "Indian."

In an unknown number of instances, communities occasionally recategorized individuals once labeled people of color as white, allowed them to stay in their communities as such, and even permitted these individuals once categorized as people of color to marry legally among whites in their localities.[12] Rebel service may have placed some free people of color onto the path to being reclassified as white by their communities.[13] Two men with connections to the rebel cause, Sheridan F. Nickens and Bilson B. Barber, both saw a shift in their racial categorization. In the 1850 census for Duplin County, Nickens along with other relatives are listed as "mulatto."[14] Yet in 1863 Nickens joined the rebel army, which prohibited people of color from enlisting.[15] Rebel enlistment agents categorized Nickens as white because they either did not know Nickens's background or ignored any signs or information suggesting that some people classified Nickens as a person of color. Nickens's categorization as "white" stuck after the Civil War. Nickens and his mother, Margaret, both designated as "mulatto" in 1850, appeared as "white" in the 1870 Duplin County census.[16] In 1880, the census enumerator again counted Nickens and his family as "white."[17] Death records for Nickens's children show that the registrar categorized all of them as "white."[18] With the help of local officials, the Duplin County Nickens family became classified as "white." The same shift occurred for Bilson B. Barber, who served with the Yadkin County Home Guard during the Civil War.[19] The home guard, like the rebel army, was an institution officially limited to whites. In 1850 and 1860, census enumerators in Surry and Yadkin Counties described Barber and his relatives as "mulatto."[20] During the 1870 census enumeration, however, the census taker categorized Barber, his wife, and children as "white."[21] From this point on, the Barber family appears as "white" in the records. Whatever memory of the Barbers' former categorization as people of color remained in the Yadkin County community, it failed to alter the new consensus that the Barbers were "white."

Decades after the Civil War, other communities gave those individuals once categorized as "free people of color" the opportunity to become "white." This new categorization allowed them to avoid Jim Crow restrictions placed on "colored" people. Sometime between 1880 and 1900, the Jacobs family of Richmond County made the transition from "colored" to "white." Before the Civil War, census records for the family of William Jacobs list members as "mulatto."[22] In 1870 and 1880, the census enumerators continued to categorize the Jacobs family as "mulatto."[23] William Jacobs seemed to understand that people in his neighborhood considered him a "colored" person. In 1874, when interviewed by federal officials about his Civil War experience, Jacobs claimed he was "on the Union side as much as I could being a col'd [colored] man I had no vote or influence."[24] Nevertheless, by the 1900 census, the Jacobses who remained in Richmond County were no longer "colored." The enumerator of that census counted all of William Jacobs's descendants as "white."[25] Locals continued to view the Jacobs family members who remained in the county after 1900 as "white" and local registrars listed the Jacobses as "white" on vital records.[26]

Divisions among those designated by their communities as "colored" along with occurrences of racial recategorization demonstrate the limitations of studying racial categories as reflective of stable social divisions. People constantly make and reshape racial categories and their defining attributes for various social purposes.[27] Those individuals who lived as "free people of color" lived in a society where racial categorization was not a self-identification used to reflect heritage. Racial categories were constantly changing concepts. Communities and politicians sometimes changed the rules of racial categorization to reshape the social hierarchy or enhance the status of someone by removing them from a less-privileged racial category. Some people once categorized as "colored" exploited fissures in racial rationale, which depended so much on physical appearance or local historical knowledge, to be reclassified as "white." As social and political needs changed, the people restructured the racial order to meet those demands.[28]

Acknowledgments

Many people played an imperative role in the completion of this book. First, I would like to thank those involved at the early stages, particularly Kathleen DuVal and Malinda Maynor Lowery, who provided invaluable guidance and criticism. I am especially grateful to Kathleen DuVal for her editorial assistance. Her comments and suggestions have made me a better writer and a more careful thinker. Numerous conversations with Malinda Maynor Lowery allowed me to test ideas and develop my project. Theda Perdue supported my work from the point of my initial acceptance into the UNC history program and shared her wisdom throughout my tenure. Zaragosa Vargas introduced me to a wide span of historiography, which greatly improved my perspective on the topic of race in both U.S. and world contexts. Watson Jennison acted as a dedicated teacher and offered cogent remarks. I owe an enormous debt to Holly Brewer, Phyllis Hunter, and Colleen Kriger for their encouragement and guidance. My editor, Rand Dotson, and the staff at LSU Press made the publishing process as smooth as possible. Jo Ann Kiser and an anonymous reader for LSU Press provided thoughtful comments and edits that greatly improved this book. Special thanks to Mishio Yamanaka for making the map for this book and providing feedback on the manuscript. Several other people have shared information, offered important critiques, and provided invaluable support, including Angenita Boone, Forest Hazel, Paul Quigley, Brett Shadle, Kirt von Daacke, Peter Wallenstein, Merilyn Weaver, LaDale Winling, Julie Winch, Audra Wolf, Eva Sheppard Wolf, and members of the Triangle Early American History Seminar.

I would like to acknowledge the numerous institutions that supported my research. The history departments at the University of North Carolina at Chapel Hill, University of North Carolina at Greensboro, University of

South Carolina, and Virginia Tech, the Center for the Study of the American South, North Caroliniana Society, and the Royster Society all aided in the completion of this book. Both present and former staff members at the State Archives of North Carolina, many of whom I consider good friends, provided countless hours of assistance in making copies, retrieving archival materials, and helping me locate sources. I also received valuable assistance from the staffs of the National Archives, Library of Virginia, Southern Historical Collection, North Carolina Collection, Joyner Library at East Carolina University, Library of Congress, Oberlin College Archives, Guilford College's Quaker Archives, and the Ohio History Center.

Finally, I would like to express my deepest gratitude to my family and friends, who believed in me even when others did not. My parents and grandparents have stood beside me since day one, and I am forever grateful. My siblings have always been there when I needed them most. I also want to acknowledge the dedication of several aunts, uncles, cousins, and friends. To anyone I may have forgot, you know who you are, and I greatly appreciate you.

Notes

Abbreviations Used in Notes

ECUJL   East Carolina University Joyner Library, Greenville, NC
LVA   Library of Virginia, Richmond, VA
NARA   National Archives and Records Administration, Washington, DC
SANC   State Archives of North Carolina, Raleigh, NC
SHC   Southern Historical Collection, Chapel Hill, NC

Introduction

1. Charles W. Chesnutt, "The Free Colored People of North Carolina," *Southern Workman*, 31, no. 3 (1902): 136–41.

2. For more about the sources used for this book, see "A Note on Primary Sources" in the Bibliography section.

3. Orlando Patterson, *Slavery and Social Death: A Comparative Study* (Cambridge, MA: Harvard University Press, 1982), 1–14.

4. My contentions about the status of free people of color in North Carolina generally agree with the findings of Judith Kelleher Schafer. In her study of New Orleans, Schafer argued that "although city ordinances and state law conspired to deprive free and freed people of color from social, political, and economic equality, being able to function as an autonomous individual and keep one's own wages represented tremendous advantages over being a slave." See Judith Kelleher Schafer, *Becoming Free, Remaining Free: Manumission and Enslavement in New Orleans, 1846–1862* (Baton Rouge: Louisiana State University Press, 2003), xiv.

5. *Dred Scott v. John F. A. Sandford*, 60 U.S. 393 (1857); *Journal of the Senate of the General Assembly of the State of North-Carolina at Its Session of 1860-'61*, 209, 274.

6. Seth Rockman, *Scraping By: Wage Labor, Slavery, and Survival in Early Baltimore* (Baltimore: Johns Hopkins University Press, 2009), 3.

7. For more on radicals using free people of color as scapegoats, see William W. Freehling, *The Road to Disunion*, Volume II: *Secessionists Triumphant, 1854–1861* (New York: Oxford University Press, 2007), 185–201.

8. William S. Powell, *North Carolina through Four Centuries* (Chapel Hill: University of North Carolina Press, 1989), 245–50.

9. *Heads of Families at the First Census of the United States Taken in the Year 1790 North Carolina* (Washington: Government Printing Office, 1908), 8; *Return of the Whole Number of Persons within the Several Districts of the United States, According to "An act providing for the Second Census or Enumeration of the Inhabitants of the United States"* (1801), 2J; *Census for 1820* (Washington: Gales and Seaton, 1821), 114; *Abstract of the Returns of the Fifth Census, Showing the Number of Free People, the Number of Slaves, the Federal or Representative Number, and the Aggregate of Each County of Each State of the United States* (Washington: Duff Green, 1832), 19–20; *Compendium of the Enumeration of the Inhabitants and Statistics of the United States, As Obtained at the Department of State, from the Returns of the Sixth Census* (Washington: Thomas Allen, 1841), 40–42, 366–75; *The Seventh Census of the United States: 1850* (Washington: Robert Armstrong, 1853), 297–331; *Population of the United States in 1860* (Washington: Government Printing Office, 1864), 348–61.

10. See tables for population figures.

11. *Return of the Whole Number of Persons within the Several Districts of the United States, According to "An act providing for the Second Census or Enumeration of the Inhabitants of the United States"* (1801), 2J; *The Seventh Census of the United States: 1850* (Washington: Robert Armstrong, 1853), 297–331; *Population of the United States in 1860*, by Joseph C. G. Kennedy, Superintendent of Census (Washington: Government Printing Office, 1864), 348–61.

12. See Karen Blu, *The Lumbee Problem: The Making of an American Indian People* (Cambridge: Cambridge University Press, 1980); Gerald Sider, *Living Indian Histories: Lumbee and Tuscarora People in North Carolina with a New Preface* (Chapel Hill: University of North Carolina Press, 2003); Malinda Maynor Lowery, *Lumbee Indians in the Jim Crow South: Race, Identity, and the Making of a Nation* (Chapel Hill: University of North Carolina Press, 2010); Marvin Richardson, "Racial Choices: The Emergence of the Haliwa-Saponi Indian Tribe, 1835–1971" (Ph.D. diss., University of North Carolina at Chapel Hill, 2016).

13. Ruby Lee Thigpen Whitehurst also found a similar rejection of the term "black" during her oral history research on the "Piney Woods" community. See Ruby Lee Thigpen Whitehurst, *Pine Needles: Authentic Stories As Told by Piney Woods/Free Union, Conetoe, and Currituck Relatives* (Ruby Lee Thigpen Whitehurst, 2011), 24, 93; For examples of use of the term "free blacks," see "Speech of Mr. Venable," *Weekly Standard* (Raleigh), October 23, 1850; "Our Free Blacks—What Should Be Done!," *Raleigh Register*, November 5, 1851; "Condition of the Free Blacks at the North" *Tri-Weekly Commercial* (Wilmington), October 11,1855; "Free Blacks in the United States—Probable Reenactment of the Slavery Laws in the Northern States," *Weekly Standard* (Raleigh), August 10, 1859.

14. James H. Merrell, *The Indians' New World: Catawbas and the Neighbors from European Contact through the Era of Removal* (Chapel Hill: University of North Carolina Press, 1989), 108–9; Helen C. Rountree and Thomas E. Davidson, *Eastern Shore Indians of Virginia and Maryland* (Charlottesville: University of Virginia Press, 1997); Ruth Wallis Herndon and Ella Wilcox Sekatu, "The Right to a Name: The Narragansett People and Rhode Island Officials in the Revolutionary Era," in *After King Philip's War: Presence and Persistence in Indian New England*, ed. Colin G. Calloway (Hanover: University Press of New England, 1997), 114–143; Ruth Wallis Herndon and Ella Wilcox Sekatu, "Colonizing the Children: Indian Youngsters in Servitude in Early Rhode Island," in *Reinterpreting New England Indians and the Colonial Experience*, ed. Colin G. Calloway and Neal Salisbury (Boston: Colonial Society of Massachusetts, 2003); Daniel R. Mandell, *Tribe, Race, History: Native Americans in Southern New England, 1780–1880* (Baltimore: Johns Hopkins University Press, 2008); Jean M. O'Brien, *Firsting and Lasting: Writing Indians Out of Existence in New England* (Minneapolis: University of Minnesota Press, 2010); Nancy Shoemaker, *Native American Whale-*

men and the World: Indigenous Encounters and the Contingency of Race (Chapel Hill: University of North Carolina Press, 2015).

15. Herndon and Sekatu, "The Right to a Name," 118.

16. Jack D. Forbes, *Black African and Native Americans: Color, Race and Caste in the Evolution of Red-Black Peoples* (New York: Basil Blackwell, 1988).

17. Rogers Brubaker, Mara Loveman, and Peter Stamatov, "Ethnicity as Cognition," *Theory and Society* 33, no. 1 (2004): 45. Others have made similar arguments, see Barbara Jeanne Fields, "Slavery, Race and Ideology in the United States of America," *New Left Review* (May–June 1990): 110; Sarah Daynes and Orville Lee, *Desire for Race* (New York: Cambridge University Press, 2008), 1.

18. Frank Tannenbaum was one of the first scholars to argue for significant differences between the way racial categories operated in Latin America and the way they did in the United States. See Frank Tannenbaum, *Slave and Citizen: The Negro in the Americas* (New York: Knopf, 1947). The works of other scholars helped to popularize Tannenbaum's thesis. See Carl N. Degler, *Neither Black nor White: Slavery and Race Relations in Brazil and the United States* (New York: Macmillan, 1971); Herbert S. Klein, *Slavery in the Americas: A Comparative Study of Virginia and Cuba* (Chicago: University of Chicago Press, 1967).

19. Anne McClintock, *Imperial Leather: Race, Gender and Sexuality in the Colonial Contest* (New York: Routledge, 1995), 9; Richard B. Allen, "Free Women of Colour and Socio-Economic Marginality in Mauritius, 1767–1830," *Slavery and Abolition* 26 (August 2005): 181–97; Andrew B. Fisher and Matthew D. O'Hara, eds., *Imperial Subjects: Race and Identity in Colonial Latin America* (Durham, NC: Duke University Press, 2009); Richard B. Allen, "Marie Rozette and Her World: Class, Ethnicity, Gender, and Race in Late Eighteenth- and Early Nineteenth-Century Mauritius," *Journal of Social History* 45 (2011): 345–65; Joanne Rappaport, *The Disappearing Mestizo: Configuring Difference in the Colonial New Kingdom of Granada* (Durham: Duke University Press, 2014), 236.

20. Kimberlé Crenshaw, "Mapping the Margins: Intersectionality, Identity Politics, and Violence against Women of Color," *Stanford Law Review* (July 1991): 1242.

21. Loren Schweninger, "Property Owning Free African-American Women in the South, 1800–1870," *Journal of Women's History* 1 (Winter 1990): 13–44; Adele Logan Alexander, *Ambiguous Lives: Free Women of Color in Rural Georgia, 1789–1879* (Fayetteville: University of Arkansas Press, 1991); Whittington B. Johnson, "Free African-American Women in Savannah, 1800–1860: Affluence and Autonomy Amid Adversity," *Georgia Historical Quarterly* 76 (Summer 1992): 260–83; Kimberly S. Hanger, "'Desiring Total Tranquility' and Not Getting It: Conflict Involving Free Black Women in Spanish New Orleans," *The Americas* 54 (April 1998): 541–56; Wilma King, *The Essence of Liberty: Free Black Women during the Slave Era* (Columbia: University of Missouri Press, 2006); Janice L. Sumler-Edmond, *The Secret Trust of Aspasia Cruvellier Mirault: The Life and Trials of a Free Woman of Color in Antebellum Georgia* (Fayetteville: University of Arkansas Press, 2008); Amrita Chakrabarti Myers, *Forging Freedom: Black Women and the Pursuit of Liberty in Antebellum Charleston* (Chapel Hill: University of North Carolina Press, 2011); Emily Clark, *The Strange History of the American Quadroon: Free Women of Color in the Revolutionary Atlantic World* (Chapel Hill: University of North Carolina Press, 2013); Leslie M. Harris and Daina Ramey Berry, eds., *Slavery and Freedom in Savanah* (Athens: University of Georgia Press, 2014); Warren E. Milteer, Jr., "The Strategies of Forbidden Love: Family across Racial Boundaries in Nineteenth-Century North Carolina," *Journal of Social History* 47 (Spring 2014): 612–26; Jessica Millward, *Finding Charity's Folks: Enslaved and Free Black Women in Maryland* (Athens: University of Georgia Press, 2015);

Joyce Linda Broussard, *Stepping Lively in Place: The Not-Married Women of Civil-War-Era Natchez, Mississippi* (Athens: University of Georgia Press, 2016); Elizabeth C. Neidenbach, "'Refugee from St. Domingue Living in This City': The Geography of Social Networks in Testaments of Refugee Free Women of Color in New Orleans," *Journal of Urban History* 42 (2016): 841–62.

22. John Henderson Russell, *The Free Negro in Virginia 1619–1865* (Baltimore: Johns Hopkins Press, 1913), 124.

23. James M. Wright, *The Free Negro in Maryland 1634–1860* (New York: Columbia University Selling Agents, 1921), 16–17.

24. John Hope Franklin, *The Free Negro in North Carolina 1790–1860* (Chapel Hill: University of North Carolina Press, 1943), 223–24.

25. Ira Berlin, *Slaves without Masters: The Free Negro in the Antebellum South* (New York: New Press, 1974), xiii.

26. Gary B. Mills, *The Forgotten People: Cane River's Creoles of Color* (Baton Rouge: Louisiana State University Press, 1977); Michael P. Johnson and James L. Roark, *Black Masters: A Free Family of Color in the Old South* (New York: W. W. Norton, 1984); Michael P. Johnson and James L. Roark, *No Chariot Let Down: Charleston's Free People of Color on the Eve of the Civil War* (Chapel Hill: University of North Carolina Press, 1984); Alexander, *Ambiguous Lives*; Thomas E. Buckley, S. J., "Unfixing Race: Class, Power, and Identity in an Interracial Family," *Virginia Magazine of History and Biography* 102 (July 1994): 346–80; Julie Winch, *The Clamorgans: One Family's History of Race in America* (New York: Hill & Wang, 2011); Eva Sheppard Wolf, *Almost Free: A Story about Family and Race in Antebellum Virginia* (Athens: University of Georgia Press, 2012); Turk McCleskey, *The Road to Black Ned's Forge: A Story of Race, Sex, and Trade on the Colonial American Frontier* (Charlottesville: University of Virginia Press, 2014).

27. Melvin Patrick Ely, *Israel on the Appomattox: A Southern Experiment in Black Freedom from the 1790s through the Civil War* (New York: Knopf, 2004), x.

28. For examples, see Kirt von Daacke, *Freedom Has a Face: Race, Identity and Community in Jefferson's Virginia* (Charlottesville: University of Virginia Press, 2012); Richard C. Rohrs, "The Free Black Experience in Antebellum Wilmington, North Carolina: Refining Generalizations about Race Relations," *Journal of Southern History* 78 (August 2012): 613–38; David W. Dangerfield, "Turning the Earth: Free Black Yeomanry in the Antebellum South Carolina Lowcountry," *Agricultural History* 89 (Spring 2015): 200–224.

29. Berlin's "slaves without masters" model continues to be influential. In her work on marriage, Tera W. Hunter concluded, "Free Blacks were literally and figuratively akin to slaves. They were often related to slaves by blood and marriage, which tied them in perpetual knots of abjection." See Tera W. Hunter, *Bound in Wedlock: Slave and Free Black Marriage in the Nineteenth Century* (Cambridge, MA: Harvard University Press, 2017), 119.

1. Making Race, Remembering Freedom: Constructing Racialized Liberty

1. George Bennett's Certificate, Norfolk County Free Negro and Slave Records, LVA; Joseph Bennett's Certificate, Norfolk County Free Negro and Slave Records, LVA.

2. Answer of Sarah Robbins et al., Gates County Land Divisions, Box 1, Petition for Division of Land 1820, SANC; Gates County Court Minutes, Volume 1, 55, SANC.

3. Gates County Record of Deeds, Volume 2, 272–75, SANC.

4. 1810 U.S. Federal Census, Gates County, North Carolina.

5. See Sarah Daynes and Orville Lee, *Desire for Race* (New York: Cambridge University Press, 2008).

6. In her work about colonial North Carolina, Kirsten Fischer argued that by the late eighteenth century "European Americans generally believed that race was inherent to the body and visible in physical traits that in turn revealed the moral and intellectual capacities of an individual." Fischer's argument about the belief in biological race is well-supported. Yet her argument does not negate the differences between the ways people conceptualized biological race and the actual ways people determined racial classification based on a variety of evaluation techniques that were unscientific and subjective. See Kirsten Fischer, *Suspect Relations: Sex, Race, and Resistance in Colonial North Carolina* (Ithaca, NY: Cornell University Press, 2002), 1–2.

7. Joanne Rappaport discovered a similar understanding of race as connected to "blood" in Spanish colonial New Kingdom of Granada. See Rappaport, *The Disappearing Mestizo*, 30.

8. Brubaker, Loveman, and Stamatov, "Ethnicity as Cognition," 41.

9. *State v. William Chavers* (1857), 7249 State v William Chavers 50 NC 11 (Dec. 1857), Supreme Court Cases, SANC.

10. William D. Valentine Diary, Volume 12, 164–65, SHC.

11. David Dodge, "The Free Negro of North Carolina," *Atlantic Monthly*, January 1886, 29–30. David Dodge was the pen name of Oscar William Blacknall.

12. "Twenty Dollars Reward," *Western Carolinian* (Salisbury), September 26, 1831.

13. "5 Cents Reward," *Carolina Federal Republican* (New Bern), December 7, 1816.

14. "Stolen," *Encyclopedian Instructor* (Edenton), December 11, 1792.

15. "$10 Reward," *Daily Progress* (Raleigh), June 17, 1863.

16. *State v. William P. Watters* (1843), 3540 State vs. Watters 1843, Supreme Court Cases, SANC.

17. *Park and Company v. Chavis*, Edenton District Records of the Superior Court, Box 27, 1773, SANC.

18. *John v. Johnston*, Edenton District Records of the Superior Court, Box 42, 1795, SANC.

19. For a full discussion of dictionary definitions of racial terms, see Forbes, *Black Africans and Native Americans*.

20. For further discussion of "Indian" as a social construction, see Alexandra Harmon, *Indians in the Making: Ethnic Relations and Indian Identities around Puget Sound* (Berkeley: University of California Press, 1998).

21. For other studies discussing the reclassification of specific indigenous population from Indians to racial others, see Rountree and Davidson, *Eastern Shore Indians of Virginia and Maryland*; Mandell, *Tribe, Race, History*; Warren E. Milteer, Jr., "From Indians to Colored People: The Problem of Racial Categories and the Persistence of the Chowans in North Carolina," *North Carolina Historical Review* 93 (January 2016): 28–57.

22. Gates County Record of Deeds, Volume A2, 33, SANC.

23. 1790 U.S. Federal Census, Gates County, North Carolina.

24. 1800 U.S. Federal Census, Gates County, North Carolina.

25. Patrick H. Garrow, *The Mattamuskeet Documents: A Study in Social History* (Raleigh, NC: Division of Archives and History, 1995).

26. Benjan. Case Certificate, Perquimans County Slave Papers, Box 2, Certificates of Free Negroes, SANC.

27. Logan County Register of Free Negroes, Ohio History Center.

28. "State Convention," *Newbern Spectator*, November 20, 1835.

29. Deposition Sarah Bennett, Wayne County Records of Slaves and Free Persons of Color, Box 4, Deposition of Sarah Bennett re: Isaac Edins, free born son of Ann Edins 1799, SANC.

30. Onslow County Court Minutes, Volume 14, 37, SANC.

31. Longtom Apprentice Order, Hyde County Apprentice Bonds and Records, Box 1, 1771–1811, SANC.

32. Petition of Jenny Ash, Bertie County Slave Records, Box 6, Slave Papers 1781–1786, SANC.

33. Milteer, "From Indians to Colored People," 28–57; Garrow, *The Mattamuskeet Documents*.

34. Craven County Court Minutes, Volume 12, 54, 58, SANC.

35. Craven County Slaves and Free Negroes, Box 10, Petition for freedom in the General Court, Maryland, William Dowrey vs. Francis Thomas 1793, SANC.

36. Michael H. Fisher, *Counterflows to Colonialism: Indian Travellers and Settlers in Britain 1600–1857* (Delhi: Permanent Black, 2004), 20–102, and Shompa Lahiri, and Shinder Thandi, *A South-Asian History of Britain: Four Centuries of Peoples from the Indian Sub-Continent* (Oxford: Greenwood World Publishing, 2007), 1–21.

37. Folarin Shyllon, *Black People in Britain 1555–1833* (London: Oxford University Press, 1977), 122–24; Roxann Wheeler, *The Complexion of Race: Categories of Difference in Eighteenth-Century British Culture* (Philadelphia: University of Pennsylvania Press, 2000), 160–61; Kathy Chater, "Black People in England, 1660–1807," *Parliamentary History* 26 (2007): 66–83. In his studies of French and British colonial Mauritius, Richard B. Allen found that the category "free people of color" also included individuals with ties to India. See Allen, "Marie Rozette and Her World," 345–65.

38. Walter Clark, ed., *The State Records of North Carolina*, vol. 23 (Goldsboro: Nash Brothers, 1904), 62–66, and *The State Records of North Carolina*, vol. 24 (Goldsboro: Nash Brothers, 1906), 14–15.

39. Petition of Augustus Cabarrus, Chowan County Miscellaneous Slave Records, Box 33, Petition for Emancipation, SANC.

40. Petition of Hannah Pritchet, Chowan County Miscellaneous Slave Records, Box 33, Petition for Emancipation 1828, SANC. See Harriet Jacobs, *Incidents in the Life of a Slave Girl*, for a more detailed account of the arrangement between Horniblow and Pritchet.

41. Bertie County Court Minutes, Volume 5, 22–23, SANC.

42. Pasquotank County Court Minutes, Volume 10, 203, SANC; Petition of Thomas Sylvester, Pasquotank County Records of Slaves and Free Persons of Color, Box 9, Bonds and petitions to free slaves 1778, 1792?, 1793–1800, SANC.

43. Petition of Ann G. Daly & Others, Craven County Slaves and Free Negroes, Box 10, Petitions to emancipate slaves, petitions for freedom and bonds for emancipated slaves 1795–1799, SANC.

44. Petition of Samuel Street, Craven County Slaves and Free Negroes, Box 10, Petitions to emancipate slaves, petitions for freedom and bonds for emancipated slaves 1822–1829, SANC.

45. Petition of James Sumner et al, Perquimans County Slave Records, Box 2, Slave Papers-Petitions for Emancipation 1776–1825, SANC.

46. John Hogg Petition for Emancipation of Frank, Orange County Slave Records, Box 8, Slave Records 1801–824, SANC; John Hogg Petition Decree, Orange County Slave Records, Box 8, Slave Records 1801–824, SANC.

47. Orange County Court Minutes, Volume 9, 349, SANC.

48. Brunswick County Court Minutes, Volume 2, 13, SANC.

49. Africa Petition, Orange County Slave Records, Box 8, Slave Records 1783–1799, SANC; Africa Order for Liberation, Orange County Slave Records, Box 8, Slave Records 1783–1799, SANC.

50. Thomas Jordan to the Court, Pasquotank County Records of Slaves and Free Persons of Color, Box 9, Bonds and petitions to free slaves 1778, 1792?, 1793–1800, SANC.

51. Edgecombe County Court Minutes, Volume 5, front cover, February 1783, SANC; Petition of Samuel Jasper, General Assembly Session Records, November 1792-January 1793, Box 3, Petitions (Emancipation), SANC; Petition of George Merrick, General Assembly Session Records, December 1791-January 1792, Box 3, Petitions (Miscellaneous), SANC.

52. Thos Newby Petition 1787, Perquimans County Slave Records, Box 2, Slave Papers-Petitions for Emancipation-1776–1825, SANC.

53. Saml Jackson Pet. For Ichabud, Pasquotank County Records of Slaves and Free Persons of Color, Box 9, Bonds and petitions to free slaves 1778, 1792?, 1793–1800, SANC.

54. Petition of Stephen L. Ferrand, Craven County Slaves and Free Negroes, Box 10, Petitions to emancipate slaves, petitions for freedom and bonds for emancipated slaves 1822–1829, SANC.

2. Colonial Liberties, Colonial Constraints: Defining Freedom in Early North Carolina

1. Granville County Record of Wills, Volume 1, 164, 176–179, SANC; Chavis Bond to Keep Ordinary, Granville County Ordinary Bonds, Box 1, Ordinary Bonds 1748, SANC; Granville County Court Minutes, Volume 1, 57, SANC; *King v. Chevous*, Granville County Criminal Action Papers, Box 1, 1747, SANC; *Smith v. Chavis*, Granville County Civil Action Papers, Box 4, 1751, SANC; *Chavis v. Parker*, Granville County Civil Action Papers, Box 5, 1752, SANC; *Chavers v. Ridley*, Granville County Civil Action Papers, Box 10, 1757, SANC; O. W. Blacknall, "Negro Slave Holders and Slave Owners," *News and Observer*, October 31, 1895, 2.

2. Kathleen Wilson, *A New Imperial History: Culture, Identity and Modernity in Britain and the Empire, 1660–1840* (Cambridge: Cambridge University Press, 2004), 6.

3. Anne McClintock, *Imperial Leather: Race, Gender and Sexuality in the Colonial Contest* (New York: Routledge, 1995), 9. Joanne Rappaport made a similar argument about the "mestizo" category's relationship with "various forms of social distinction" such as "gender, occupation, religion, geographic origin, or noble status" in Spanish colonial New Kingdom of Granada. See Joanne Rappaport, *The Disappearing Mestizo: Configuring Difference in the Colonial New Kingdom of Granada* (Durham, NC: Duke University Press, 2014), 226.

4. In his study of race in Georgia, Watson W. Jennison found that colonial Georgians recognized distinctions among free people of color based on class. He argued, "Georgia's authorities envisioned a legal structure that recognized distinctions among free people of color, which reflected the authorities' beliefs about race as well as class. Elite whites in both colonies understood that free people of African descent were not all equal. . . . Factors such as birth and wealth stratified people into different social categories." See Watson W. Jennison, *Cultivating Race: The Expansion of Slavery in Georgia, 1750–1860* (Lexington: University Press of Kentucky, 2012), 74–75. There is growing literature examining the relationship between racial categorization and gender in British colonial America. This recent scholarship has argued that "race" in colonial America cannot be fully understood without close attention to the importance of gender and

the regulation of sexuality in shaping how people conceived and regulated "race" in the colonial context. See Kathleen M. Brown, *Good Wives, Nasty Wenches, and Anxious Patriarchs: Gender, Race, and Power in Colonial Virginia* (Chapel Hill: University of North Carolina Press, 1996); Fischer, *Suspect Relations*; Jennifer L. Morgan, *Laboring Women: Reproduction and Gender in New World Slavery* (Philadelphia: University of Pennsylvania Press, 2004); Jennifer M. Spear, *Race, Sex, and Social Order in Early New Orleans* (Baltimore: Johns Hopkins University Press, 2009).

5. For further discussion of racial categorization and law in other colonies, see Edmund S. Morgan, *American Slavery, American Freedom: The Ordeal of Colonial Virginia* (New York: W. W. Norton, 1975); A. Leon Higginbotham, Jr., *In the Matter of Color: Race and the American Legal Process: The Colonial Period* (New York: Oxford University Press, 1978).

6. Walter Clark, ed., *The State Records of North Carolina*, vol. 23 (Goldsboro: Nash Brothers, 1904), 62–66.

7. June Purcell Guild, *Black Laws of Virginia* (Richmond: Whittet & Shepperson, 1936), 126, 130–31; Thomas Bacon, *Laws of Maryland at large, with proper indexes: Now first collected into one compleat body, and published from the original acts and records, remaining in the Secretary's-office of the said province: Together with notes and other matters, relative to the constitution thereof, extracted from the provincial records: To which is prefixed, the charter, with an English translation* (Annapolis: Jonas Green, 1765), 360.

8. Clark, *The State Records of North Carolina*, vol. 23, 106.

9. Clark, *The State Records of North Carolina*, vol. 23, 106–7.

10. For more on conditions in colonial North Carolina, see Alan D. Watson, *Society in Colonial North Carolina* (Raleigh: North Carolina Office of Archives and History, 1996).

11. Clark, *The State Records of North Carolina*, vol. 23, 345.

12. The General Assembly passed a reworded iteration of this law in 1760. Walter Clark, ed., *The State Records of North Carolina*, vol. 25 (Goldsboro: Nash Brothers, 1906), 283, 445.

13. For discussion of the creative approaches taken by local people to overcome the law's effects, see Laura F. Edwards, *The People and Their Peace: Legal Culture and the Transformation of Inequality in the Post-Revolutionary South* (Chapel Hill: University of North Carolina Press, 2009), 7–8.

14. Clark, *The State Records of North Carolina*, vol. 25, 418–19.

15. Kimberlé Crenshaw has observed similar trends beyond the colonial period. See Crenshaw, "Mapping the Margins," 1241–1300.

16. Brown, *Good Wives, Nasty Wenches, and Anxious Patriarchs*, 192–93.

17. Delany Mallato's Indenture, Pasquotank County Apprentice Bonds and Records, Box 1, Apprentice Bonds and Records B, SANC.

18. Chowan County Miscellaneous Records, Volume 1, 86, SANC.

19. Chowan County Court Minutes, Volume 6, January 1767, SANC; Chowan County Miscellaneous Records, Volume 14, 88, 129–130, SANC; Chowan County Miscellaneous Records, Volume 15, 7, 86, SANC; Chowan County Miscellaneous Records, Volume 16, 39–40, SANC.

20. Karin L. Zipf, *Labor of Innocents: Forced Apprenticeship in North Carolina, 1715–1919* (Baton Rouge: Louisiana State University Press, 2005), 7.

21. For further discussion of the multigenerational influence of the servitude system, see Fischer, *Suspect Relations*, 128–29. For further discussion of changes in the apprenticeship system after the American Revolution, see Holly Brewer, "Apprenticeship Policy in Virginia: From Patriarchal to Republican Policies of Social Welfare," in *Children Bound to Labor: The Pauper Ap-*

prentice System in Early America ed. Ruth Wallis Herndon and John E. Murray (Ithaca, NY: Cornell University Press, 2009), 183–97.

22. Edmund Chancey 1753 Will, Secretary of State Records of Probate: Wills, Box 5, 718–721, SANC.

23. Edgecombe County Inventories, Accounts, and Sales of Estates, Volume 1, 23–24, SANC.

24. Amiah Sanderlin Indenture, Bertie County Apprentice Indentures, Box 7, 1750–1759, SANC.

25. Pen Pugh Indenture, Bertie County Apprentice Indentures, Box 7, 1760–1770, SANC

26. Chowan County Court Minutes, Volume 5, 131, SANC.

27. Chowan County Court Minutes, Volume 6, January 1767, SANC.

28. Historians have found contrasting situations in other colonies. John Wood Sweet argued that "town officials typically failed to provide free people of color the same protections they routinely granted to even the poorest whites." See John Wood Sweet, *Bodies Politic: Negotiating Race in the American North, 1730–1830* (Baltimore: Johns Hopkins University Press, 2003), 66.

29. Pasquotank County Court Minutes, Volume 1, October 1745, January 1745, SANC; Chaney Mallattoes Bonds, Pasquotank County Apprentice Bonds and Records, Box 1, Apprentice Bonds and Records B, SANC.

30. Petition of Bob Boe, Pasquotank County Apprentice Bonds and Records, Box 1 Apprentice Bonds and Records B, SANC.

31. Pasquotank County Court Minutes, Volume 2, October 1760, SANC.

32. Craven County Court Minutes, Volume 5, 247, SANC.

33. Beaufort County Court Minutes, Volume 2, 37, SANC.

34. Onslow County Court Minutes, Volume 5, 63, SANC.

35. Craven County Court Minutes, Volume 6, 65, SANC.

36. T. H. Breen and Stephen Innes, *"Myne Owne Ground": Race and Freedom on Virginia's Eastern Shore, 1640–1676* (New York: Oxford University Press, 1980), 22.

37. Bertie County Record of Deeds, Volume B, 289–90, SANC; Halifax County Record of Deeds, Volume 5, 452–453, SANC; Granville County Record of Deeds, Volume A, 66–67, 82–83, SANC; Granville County Record of Deeds, Volume B, 47–48, 408–10, SANC; Granville County Record of Deeds, Volume C, 73–74, SANC; Granville County Record of Deeds, Volume D, 25–27, SANC; Granville County Record of Deeds, Volume E, 322–25, SANC; Granville County Record of Deeds, Volume H, 235–37, SANC; List of Taxables, Granville County Taxables, Box 20, 1758, SANC; List of Taxables, Granville County Taxables, Box 20, 1760–1761, SANC.

38. In his study of colonial Mexico City, R. Douglas Cope argued that when one person of color could own another, "property rights prevailed over racial order." See R. Douglas Cope, *The Limits of Racial Domination: Plebeian Society in Colonial Mexico City, 1660–1720* (Madison: University of Wisconsin Press, 1994), 162.

39. Inventory of the Estate of Peter George, Craven County Estates Records, Box 54, George, Peter 1763, SANC; Craven County Record of Deeds, Volume 8, 221, SANC.

40. Bertie County Tax List for 1751, Colonial Court Records Taxes and Accounts, Box 190, Tax Lists-Bertie-1751, 1753, 1754 Estate Tax-Beaufort Pet., n.d., SANC.

41. *Manley v. Goodwin*, Bertie County Civil Action Papers, Box 5, 1758-1, 1759-1, SANC; *Manley v. Goodwin*, Bertie County Civil Action Papers, Box 6, 1760, SANC; Order for a Road from Cotton's Landing, Bertie County Road, Bridge, and Ferry Records, Box 1, Road Papers 1751–1755, SANC.

42. Negro Toney's Petition, Pasquotank County Civil Action Papers, Box 3, 1748, SANC.

43. Negro Toney's Petition, Pasquotank County Civil Action Papers, Box 3, 1748, SANC.

44. Pasquotank County Court Minutes, Volume 1, July 1748, SANC.

45. For examples of white women dealing with similar issues, see Zipf, *Labor of Innocents*, 20–22.

46. Granville County Record of Wills, Volume 1, 164, 176–79, SANC.

47. Bertie County Estates Records, Box 35, Joseph Hall, SANC.

48. Beaufort County Court Minutes, Volume 1, 46, SANC.

49. Petn of Sundry Inhabitants of Northampton, Edgecombe & Granville Counties, General Assembly Session Records, Box 2, Nov–Dec 1762 Lower House Papers, Certificates of election, petition not acted on Estimate of pay and allowances, SANC.

50. North Carolina was not the only colonial society to impose discriminatory taxes on free persons of color. For other examples, see David W. Cohen and Jack P. Greene, eds., *Neither Slave nor Free: The Freedmen of African Descent in the Slave Societies of the New World* (Baltimore: Johns Hopkins University Press, 1972), 38, 153.

51. Petition from the Inhabitants of Granville County, General Assembly Session Records, November–December 1771, Box 5, Nov–Dec 1771 Lower House Papers Petitions rejected or not acted on, SANC.

52. *Dom. Rex v. Joseph Bass*, Colonial Court Papers Criminal Papers-General Court 1735–1737 Criminal Papers-General and Assize Courts 1738–1739, Box 176, General Court and Assize Criminal-1739, SANC; Colonial Court Records Miscellaneous Dockets-General Court 1739, Volume 119, October 1739, SANC.

53. *Manley v. Goodwin*, Bertie County Civil Action Papers, Box 5, 1758-1, 1759-1, SANC; Manley v. Goodwin, Bertie County Civil Action Papers, Box 6, 1760, SANC.

54. Laura Edwards defined "keeping the peace" as "keeping everyone—from the lowest to the highest—in their appropriate places, as defined in specific local contexts." She argued that local courts in post-Revolutionary North Carolina sought to maintain the peace even by providing subordinate people with "direct access to localized law." Although her arguments focus on the post-Revolutionary South, colonial period court cases suggest that her contentions about the peace could easily be extended to colonial North Carolina. See Laura F. Edwards, *The People and Their Peace: Legal Culture and the Transformation of Inequality in the Post-Revolutionary South* (Chapel Hill: University of North Carolina Press, 2009), 7.

55. William S. Powell, *North Carolina through Four Centuries* (Chapel Hill: University of North Carolina Press, 1989), 116.

56. Ira Berlin, *Many Thousands Gone: The First Two Centuries of Slavery in North America* (Cambridge: Belknap Press, 1998), 123.

57. Application of Benjamin Reed, File S41976, *Revolutionary War Pension and Bounty-Land Warrant Application Files*, National Archives Microfilm Publication; Application of William Lomack, File S41783, *Revolutionary War Pension and Bounty-Land Warrant Application Files*, National Archives Microfilm Publication; Application of Benjamin Richardson, File W4061, *Revolutionary War Pension and Bounty-Land Warrant Application Files*, National Archives Microfilm Publication; Application of William Taburn, File W18115, *Revolutionary War Pension and Bounty-Land Warrant Application Files*, National Archives Microfilm Publication.

* * *

3. Debating Freedom: The Radical War against Free People of Color

1. "Important Bills," *North Carolina Standard* (Raleigh), November 23, 1858.

2. James A. Patton to J. S. T. Baird, General Assembly Session Records, November 1858–February 1859, Box 9, House Committee Reports, SANC.

3. Haywood Day Civil War Pension, NARA.

4. Report of Com on Judiciary, General Assembly Session Records, November 1858–February 1859, Box 9, Senate Committee Reports, SANC.

5. Franklin, *Free Negro in North Carolina*, 211–25; Berlin, *Slaves without Masters*, 343–80.

6. Michael F. Holt, *The Fate of Their Country: Politicians, Slavery Extension, and the Coming of the Civil War* (New York: Hill & Wang, 2004).

7. Watson Jennison found this to be the approach of Georgia proslavery ideologue Joseph Lumpkin. See Watson Jennison, "Rewriting the Free Negro Past: Joseph Lumpkin, Proslavery Ideology, and Citizenship in Antebellum Georgia," in *Creating Citizenship in the Nineteenth-Century South*, ed. William A. Link, David Brown, Brian Ward, and Martyn Bone (Gainesville: University Press of Florida, 2013), 41–63.

8. Bill Cecil-Fronsman, *Common Whites: Class and Culture in Antebellum North Carolina* (Lexington: University of Kentucky Press, 1992), 82.

9. Francois Xavier Martin, ed. *The Public Acts of the General Assembly of North-Carolina, Volume I* (Newbern: Martin & Ogden, 1804), 191–93.

10. Martin, *Public Acts*, 266.

11. Martin, *Public Acts*, 431–32.

12. *Laws of North-Carolina* (Edenton: Hodge & Wills, 1796), 10–11.

13. *Journal of the Senate of North-Carolina At a General Assembly begun and held at the City of Raleigh, on Monday the nineteenth Day of November, in the Year of our Lord One Thousand Eight Hundred and Four, and in the Twenty Ninth Year of the Independence of the United States of America: It being the first Session of this General Assembly* (Raleigh: Gales, 1805).

14. *Journal of the House of Commons of the State of North-Carolina At a General Assembly, begun and held at the City of Raleigh, on Monday the twentieth Day of November, in the Year of our Lord One Thousand Eight Hundred and Nine, and in the Thirty-Fourth Year of the Independence of the United States of America: It being the first Session of this General Assembly* (Raleigh: Gales and Seaton, 1809), 49; *Journal of the Senate of North-Carolina At a General Assembly, begun and held at the City of Raleigh, on Monday the twentieth Day of November, in the Year of our Lord One Thousand Eight Hundred and Nine, and in the Thirty-Fourth Year of the Independence of the United States of America: It being the first Session of this General Assembly* (Raleigh: Gales & Seaton, 1809), 48.

15. Martin, *Public Acts*, 178–79.

16. Report of the Committee of Prop. & Grievances On the Petition of Cato Sabo, General Assembly Session Records, November–December 1807, Box 2, Joint Committee Reports (Propositions and Grievances), SANC.

17. Petition of the Free Colored Inhabitants of the Town of Fayetteville for the benefit of the Book Debt Law, General Assembly Session Records, November 1821–January 1822, Box 4, Petitions (Miscellaneous), SANC.

18. *Muster Rolls of the Soldiers of the War of 1812: Detached from the Militia of North Carolina in 1812 and 1814* (Raleigh: Ch. C. Raboteau, 1851), 7–8, 18–19, 30–31, 36–37.

19. *The Laws of the State of North Carolina, Enacted in the Year 1812* (Raleigh: Thomas Henderson, 1813), 1.

20. *Journal of the Senate at a General Assembly begun and held at the City of Raleigh, on Monday the twenty-first day of November, in the year of our Lord one thousand eight hundred and fourteen, and in the thirty-ninth year of the Independence of the United States of America, it being the first Session of this Assembly,* 5; *The Laws of the State of North-Carolina, Enacted in the Year 1814* (Raleigh: Thomas Henderson, 1815), 3.

21. Walter Clark, ed., *The State Records of North Carolina,* vol. 25 (Goldsboro: Nash Brothers, 1906), 445.

22. *The Laws of North-Carolina, Enacted in the Year 1821* (Raleigh: Thomas Henderson, 1822), 41–42.

23. Petition of Sundry Persons of Colour of Hertford County, General Assembly Session Records, November–December 1822, Box 4, Petitions (Miscellaneous), SANC.

24. Guild, *Black Laws of Virginia,* 95; Marina Wikramanayake, *A World in Shadow: The Free Black in Antebellum South Carolina* (Columbia: University of South Carolina Press, 1973), 161. Melvin Patrick Ely found that Virginia's registration law was only sporadically enforced in Prince Edward County. See Ely, *Israel on the Appomattox,* 251–53.

25. "Foreign and Domestic Gleanings," *Wilmington and Delaware Advertiser,* January 12, 1826; "State Legislature," *Raleigh Register,* February 9, 1827; "North Carolina," *Newbern Sentinel,* March 10, 1827.

26. "North Carolina," *Newbern Sentinel,* March 10, 1827.

27. Resolution for Judiciary Committee—In Senate Nov. 28th 1829, General Assembly Session Records, November 1829–January 1830, Box 6, Senate Committee Reports (Judiciary-Miscellaneous), SANC.

28. Report of Judiciary Committee—In Senate December 12th 1829, General Assembly Session Records, November 1829–January 1830, Box 6, Senate Committee Reports (Judiciary-Miscellaneous), SANC.

29. In 1832, Virginia passed a law allowing localities to try "free negroes" charged with felonies by tribunal instead of a jury. See Guild, *Black Laws of Virginia,* 106–8.

30. William W. Freehling, *The Road to Disunion: Secessionists at Bay, 1776–1854* (New York: Oxford University Press, 1990), 292.

31. *Acts Passed by the General Assembly of the State of North Carolina, at the Session of 1830–31* (Raleigh: Lawrence & Lemay, 1831), 9–10.

32. *Journals of the Senate and House of Commons of the General Assembly of the State of North Carolina, at the Session of 1830–1831* (Raleigh: Lawrence & Lemay, 1831), 156–63.

33. See David Walker, *Walker's Appeal, In Four Articles; Together with a Preamble, To the Coloured Citizens of the World, But in Particular, and Very Expressly, to Those of the United States of America* (Boston: David Walker, 1830).

34. *Acts Passed by the General Assembly of the State of North Carolina, at the Session of 1830–31,* 11.

35. *Acts Passed by the General Assembly of the State of North Carolina, at the Session of 1830–31,* 14–15.

36. *Acts Passed by the General Assembly of the State of North Carolina, at the Session of 1830–31,* 16.

37. *Acts Passed by the General Assembly of the State of North Carolina, at the Session of 1830–31,* 29–30.

38. Freehling, *The Road to Disunion: Secessionists at Bay, 1776–1854,* 292, 302.

39. *Acts Passed by the General Assembly of the State of North Carolina, at the Session of 1830–31,* 12–14.

40. Guild, *Black Laws of Virginia,* 72.

41. *Journals of the Senate and House of Commons of the General Assembly of the State of North-Carolina at the Session of 1828–29* (Raleigh: Lawrence & Lemay, 1829), 131, 159.

42. Memorial of the Inhabitants of the Town of Milton, General Assembly Session Records, November 1830–January 1831, Box 2, House Bills (Dec. 23), SANC; *Acts Passed by the General Assembly of the State of North Carolina, at the Session of 1830–31*, 79.

43. Memorial of the Inhabitants of the Town of Milton, General Assembly Session Records, November 1830–January 1831, Box 2, House Bills (Dec. 23), SANC.

44. "Incendiary Publications," *Newbern Spectator*, October 7, 1831; "Incendiary Publications," *Raleigh Register*, September 22, 1831.

45. *Acts Passed by the General Assembly of the State of North Carolina, at the Session of 1831–32* (Raleigh: Lawrence & Lemay, 1832), 28–29.

46. *Acts Passed by the General Assembly of the State of North Carolina, at the Session of 1831–32*, 7.

47. *Acts Passed by the General Assembly of the State of North Carolina, at the Session of 1831–32*, 10–11.

48. *Journals of the Senate and House of Commons of the General Assembly of the State of North Carolina at the Session of 1831–32* (Raleigh: Lawrence & Lemay, 1832), 197, 236.

49. Memorial of Sundry Citizens of the Town of Newbern, General Assembly Session Records, November 1831–January 1832, Box 6, Petitions (Miscellaneous), SANC.

50. Petition of the Subscribers Citizens of Wilmington, General Assembly Session Records, November 1831–January 1832, Box 5, Senate Committee Reports, SANC.

51. Memorial and Petition of the Religious Society of Friends, convened at New Garden, in Guilford County, North-Carolina, in the Eleventh month, 1834, General Assembly Session Records, November 1834–January 1835, Box 5, Petitions (Miscellaneous), SANC.

52. For further discussion of the debate over suffrage for free people of color, see John Hope Franklin, *The Free Negro in North Carolina 1790–1860* (Chapel Hill: University of North Carolina Press, 1943), 107–20; Lacy K. Ford, *Deliver Us from Evil: The Slavery Question in the Old South* (New York: Oxford University Press, 2009), 418–45.

53. *Proceedings and Debates of the Convention of North-Carolina, Called to Amend the Constitution of the State; Which Assembled at Raleigh, June 4, 1835* (Raleigh: Joseph Gales & Son, 1836), 67.

54. Nicholas Wood discovered similar motivations for disfranchisement of free men of color in Pennsylvania. He argued that "disfranchisement reduced the disparity between black slavery and black freedom while preempting the possibility that blacks could become an antislavery voting bloc in Pennsylvania." See Nicholas Wood, "'A Sacrifice on the Altar of Slavery': Dough-face Politics and Black Disfranchisement in Pennsylvania, 1837–1838," *Journal of the Early Republic* 32 (Spring 2011): 75–106.

55. *Proceedings and Debates*, 69.

56. *Proceedings and Debates*, 71.

57. *Journals of the Senate and House of Commons of the General Assembly of the State of North Carolina, at its Session in 1825* (Raleigh: Bell & Lawrence, 1826), 75.

58. *Journals of the Senate and House of Commons of the General Assembly of the State of North-Carolina, at the Session of 1826–27* (Raleigh: Lawrence & Lemay, 1827), 15.

59. "The Hon. Jesse Speight," *Greensboro Patriot*, November 11, 1835.

60. *Proceedings and Debates*, 61.

61. *Rules of Order for the Government of the General Assembly of North Carolina: To Which are Prefixed the Constitutions of North Carolina and of the United States* (Raleigh: Philo White, 1836), 15.

62. "Convention Question," *Raleigh Register-Weekly*, April 21, 1835.

63. "The Convention," *Fayetteville Observer*, June 16, 1835.

64. Lacy Ford also suggests that the results of the convention "determined once and for all that political participation was the exclusive domain, not of all freemen, but of free white males." Ford, *Deliver Us from Evil*, 443.

65. *Laws of the State of North Carolina Passed by the General Assembly at the Session of 1840–41* (Raleigh: W. R. Gales, 1841), 61–62.

66. Petition of Citizens and Inhabitants of the County of Craven, General Assembly Session Records, November–December 1835, Box 6, Petitions, SANC.

67. Petition of Subscribers of the County of Halifax, General Assembly Session Records, November 1840–January 1841, Box 5, Petitions, SANC.

68. See Wright, *The Free Negro in Maryland*, 106–7; Ely, *Israel on the Appomattox*, 278. Although Maryland and Virginia prohibited firearm ownership by free people of color, both Wright and Ely found that free people of color did overcome these bans. In Maryland, the weapons ban only lasted from 1824 to 1831, and later the state legislature replaced the ban with a licensing program similar to North Carolina's weapons law. Ely found that free people of color in Prince Edward County continued to own firearms after Virginia prohibited free people of color from owning guns following the Nat Turner rebellion in 1831.

69. Memorial of Sundry Citizens of Robeson County, General Assembly Session Records, November 1840–January 1841, Box 4, Senate Committee Reports, SANC.

70. *Laws of the State of North Carolina Passed by the General Assembly at the Session of 1844–45* (Raleigh: Thomas J. Lemay, 1845), 123–24.

71. 1850 U.S. Federal Census, Robeson County, North Carolina, the Upper Division, 321.

72. *Public Laws of the State of North Carolina Passed by the General Assembly at Its Session of 1858–59* (Raleigh: Holden & Wilson, 1859), 71.

73. Memorial from the Citizens of Plymouth, General Assembly Session Records, November 1850–January 1851, Box 8, Petitions, SANC.

74. Petition of Hertford County Citizens, General Assembly Session Records, October–December 1852, Box 8, Petitions (Liquor), SANC.

75. *Population of the United States in 1860*, by Joseph C. G. Kennedy, Superintendent of Census (Washington: Government Printing Office, 1864), 358.

76. *Journals of the Senate and House of Commons, of the General Assembly of the State of North Carolina, at its Session of 1850-'51* (Raleigh: Seaton Gales, 1851), 534, 571; "Members of the Legislature," *Weekly Standard*, November 20, 1850.

77. Memorial of the Citizens of Onslow Relating to Free Negroes, General Assembly Session Records, November 1858–February 1859, Box 10, Petitions, SANC.

78. Petition of Citizens of the County of Northampton, General Assembly Session Records, November 1856–February 1857, Box 10, Petitions, SANC.

79. Grand Jury Presentments, Gates County Criminal Action Papers, Box 12, 1842, SANC; 1850 U.S. Federal Census, Gates County, North Carolina; Gates County Criminal Action Papers, SANC. Some records from 1844 are mixed in with the records from 1842.

80. See Caswell County Criminal Action Papers, Box 22, 1844, SANC; Caswell County Criminal Action Papers, Box 23, 1844–1845, SANC.

81. *State v. Charles Oxendine* (1837), 2585 State v. Oxendine 1837, Supreme Court Cases, SANC.

82. *State v. William Manuel* (1838), 2597 State vs Manuel 1838, Supreme Court Cases, SANC.

83. *State v. Elijah Newsom* (1844), 3408 State vs Newsom 1844, Supreme Court Cases, SANC.

84. See *State v. Harris Melton and Ann Byrd* (1852), 6431 State v Harris Melton and Ann Byrd 44 N.C. 49 (Dec. 1852), Supreme Court Cases, SANC.

85. See *State v. Whitmel Dempsey* (1849), 4723 State vs Dempsey June 1849, Supreme Court Cases, SANC; E. Franklin Frazier, *The Negro Family in the United States* (Chicago: University of Chicago Press, 1939), 254.

86. *State v. William Chavers* (1857), 7249 State v William Chavers 50 NC 11 (Dec. 1857), Supreme Court Cases, SANC.

87. *State v. Lawrence Davis* (1859), 7705 State v. Lawrence Davis 52 N.C. 52 (Dec. 1859), Supreme Court Cases, SANC.

88. In *State v. Jowers*, Pearson argued that white men had the right to use extrajudicial means to "correct" the insolence of "free negroes." He also suggested that "it is unfortunate" that "free negroes" "exist in our society." Pearson saw a distinction between Lawrence Davis's attempt to defend himself and what he characterized as insolence. See *State v. Atlas Jowers* (1850), 6717, *State v. Atlas Jowers*, 33 N.C. 555 (Dec. 1850), Supreme Court Cases, SANC.

89. *Dred Scott v. John F. A. Sandford*, 60 U.S. 393 (1857).

4. Community and Conflict: Free People of Color in Society

1. William D. Valentine Diary, Volume 14, 110, SHC.

2. Oath of Allegiance, Bertie County Miscellaneous Records, Box 12, Revolutionary War Papers (oaths of allegiance, 1778; and land warrants, 1821), SANC; Walter Clark, ed., *The State Records of North Carolina*, vol. 22 (Goldsboro: Nash Brothers, 1907), 168–79.

3. *Muster Rolls of the Soldiers of the War of 1812: Detached from the Militia of North Carolina, In 1812 and 1814* (Raleigh: C. Raboteau, 1851), 18–19, 36–37.

4. Gates County Court Minutes, Volume 8, 121, SANC; Robeson County Court Minutes, Volume 5, 224, SANC.

5. Ben Persons' Overseer of Road, Northampton County Road Records, Box 1, 1816, SANC.

6. Robeson County Court Minutes, Volume 5, 268, SANC.

7. Election begun and held at Powell's place in Gates County, Gates County Election Records, Box 2, 1819, SANC; Election began and held at G. B. Lee's Store, Orange County Election Records, Box 4, 1835, SANC; *Proceedings and Debates of the Convention of North-Carolina, Called to Amend the Constitution of the State; Which Assembled at Raleigh, June 4, 1835* (Raleigh: Joseph Gales & Son, 1836), 70. Voters in the Orange County election included members of the Jeffries, Corn, Guy, Stewart, Wadkins, Jones, and Whitmore families.

8. Petition from Sundry People to Court to Counteract a Petition for working on the Waccamaw Lake, Thomas Smith McDowell Papers, Box 2, Subseries 1.2, #23, SHC.

9. "Simultaneous Meeting," *Fayetteville Observer*, March 11, 1834.

10. "Sixty Dollars Reward," *Wilmington Gazette*, May 5, 1803.

11. "110 Dollars Reward," *Hillsborough Recorder*, December 19, 1821.

12. Nathan Bass Estate, Granville County Estates Records, Box 8, Nathan Bass 1837, SANC; Henry Bow Estate, Pasquotank County Estates Records, Box 11, Bow, Henry 1845, SANC.

13. See Jon F. Sensbach, *A Separate Canaan: The Making of an Afro-Moravian World in North Carolina, 1763–1840* (Chapel Hill: University of North Carolina Press, 1998); Christ Church, New Bern Parish Register, Volume 1, SANC; Cool Springs Baptist Church (Eure) Minutes, SANC;

Meherrin Baptist Church Minutes, SANC; Milton Presbyterian Church Session Minutes and Register, Volume 1, SANC; Mt. Tabor Baptist Church Minutes and Various Records, SANC; Oxford Presbyterian Church Session Minutes, SANC; Sacred Heart Cathedral Catholic Diocese of Raleigh, Baptisms, Marriages, Deaths, Originals, Volume 1, SANC; St. John's Episcopal Church (Fayetteville) Parish Register, Volume 2, SANC.

14. Christ Church, New Bern Parish Register, Volume 1, 11, SANC.

15. Sacred Heart Cathedral Catholic Diocese of Raleigh, Baptisms, Marriages, Deaths, Originals, Volume 1, 6, SANC.

16. Oxford Presbyterian Church Session Minutes, 92, SANC.

17. Cushing Biggs Hassell Diary, Volume 4, 289, Cushing Biggs Hassell Papers, Box 1, Folder 6, SHC.

18. Cushing Biggs Hassell Diary, Volume 5, 371–372, Cushing Biggs Hassell Papers, Box 1, Folder 7, SHC.

19. "Religious Intelligence," *General Assembly's Missionary Magazine*, September 1805.

20. Petition for William B. Hammons to Preach, General Assembly Session Records, November 1840–January 1841, Box 4, House Committee Reports, SANC.

21. "Education," *Raleigh Register, and North-Carolina Weekly Advertiser*, August 25, 1808.

22. Harriet Peck to Isaac Peck, March 1, 1839, Peck Family Papers, Friends Historical Collection, Guilford College Library.

23. John Vann Papers, Box 3, Estate Cotton, Christian 1816, SANC; Receipts from Isabella Hinton Harris, James Boon Papers, Correspondence and Accounts, Box 1, Correspondence, etc., 1839–1851, n.d., SANC. For more about the education of free people of color in other parts of the United States, see E. Franklin Frazier, *The Free Negro Family* (Nashville, TN: Fisk University Press, 1932), 14–16.

24. Report of the Wardens of the Poor, Granville County Wardens of the Poor, Box 4, Wardens of the poor accounts 1828–1830, SANC.

25. Sneeds Certificate, Granville County Wardens of the Poor, Box 4, Wardens of the poor accounts 1836–1839, SANC.

26. Orange County Minutes of the Wardens of the Poor, Volume 2, 158, 232, SANC.

27. John H. Cook and A. A. McKethan to Governor Reid, Governors Papers, Box 135, Correspondence, Petitions, etc. April 1, 1854-April 30, 1854, SANC.

28. Bryan W. Herring to Thomas Bragg, Governors Papers, Box 138, Correspondence, Petitions, etc. April 1, 1855–April 30, 1855, SANC.

29. John Pettiford Civil War Pension Records, NARA.

30. Leroy P. Graf and Ralph W. Haskins, ed., *The Papers of Andrew Johnson Volume 4, 1860–1861* (Knoxville: University of Tennessee Press, 1976), 537–38.

31. Statement of Sarah Jackson, Perquimans County Slave Papers, Box 2, Certificates of Free Negroes, No Date, 1733–1861, SANC.

32. Statement of Nancy Wilson, Perquimans County Slave Papers, Box 2, Certificates of Free Negroes, No Date, 1733–1861, SANC.

33. Statement of William Gregory, Perquimans County Slave Papers, Box 2, Certificates of Free Negroes, No Date, 1733–1861, SANC.

34. *Acts of the General Assembly Relative to the Town of Fayetteville, and the Ordinances of the Magistrate of Police and Commissioners of Fayetteville* (Fayetteville: Edward J. Hale, 1846); *Ordinances for the Government of the Town of Hillsborough* (Hillsborough: Dennis Heartt, 1858).

35. "Reported for the Sentinel, Office of Police, August 7th, 8th, & 9ᵗʰ," *North Carolina Sentinel* (New Bern), August 18, 1827.

36. Harriet A. Jacobs, *Incidents in the Life of a Slave Girl: Written By Herself* (Boston, 1861), 63–67.

37. Solon Borland to Roscius C. Borland, Governors Papers, Volume 62, SANC.

38. *The African Repository and Colonial Journal, Volume VII* (Washington, DC: James C. Dunn, 1832), 245.

39. H. G. Burton to John Branch, Governors Papers, Volume 48, SANC.

40. J. G. De Roulhac Hamilton, ed., *The Papers of Thomas Ruffin, Volume II* (Raleigh, N.C.: Edwards & Broughton Printing Company, 1918), 205–6.

41. "A Mob," *Raleigh Microcosm*, October 22, 1842.

42. "Disgraceful Outrage," *Raleigh Register*, October 18, 1842.

43. For more on the concept of the "peace," see Edwards, *The People and Their Peace.*

44. John P. Green, *Fact Stranger than Fiction: Seventy-Five Years of a Busy Life with Reminiscences of Many Great and Good Men and Women* (Cleveland: Riehl Printing Company, 1920), 45–47.

45. "Washington Mechanic Association," *North State Whig* (Washington), July 31, 1850.

46. For more on the colonization movement in North Carolina, see Claude A. Clegg III, *The Price of Liberty: African Americans and the Making of Liberia* (Chapel Hill: University of North Carolina Press, 2004).

47. For an in-depth discussion of free people of color and kidnapping, see Carol Wilson, *Freedom at Risk: The Kidnapping of Free Blacks in America, 1780–1865* (Lexington: University Press of Kentucky, 1994).

48. George W. Crawford to Governor Graham, February 25, 1848, William Alexander Graham Papers, Box 3, Corresp. 1848, SANC.

49. "Girl of Colour," *Raleigh Register*, December 15, 1801.

50. "Notice," *Hillsborough Recorder*, March 15, 1820; "Notice," *Hillsborough Recorder*, March 22, 1820; "Notice," *Hillsborough Recorder*, March 29, 1820.

51. Carol Wilson suggested that "what made the practice of kidnapping possible was the strong and deeply rooted belief in white superiority." Yet as the North Carolina examples show, the kidnapping of free people of color was not so much a product of white superiority as it was the result of individuals' criminality and greed. White North Carolinians and other white Americans could easily have believed that they were superior to people of color and still stood against kidnapping. At least some whites saw kidnapping as a crime against their communities and a threat to their preferred social order. See Wilson, *Freedom at Risk*, 1.

52. Green, *Fact Stranger than Fiction*, 43–44.

53. William D. Valentine Diary, Volume 15, 72–73, SHC; Isaac S. Harrell, "Gates County to 1860," in *Historical Papers of the Trinity College Historical Society* (Durham, NC: Seeman Printer, 1916), 66; *Minutes of the Chowan Baptist Association* (Raleigh, NC: Biblical Recorder Office, 1852), 8–9; *Minutes of the Fifty Fourth Annual Session of the Chowan Baptist Association Held with the Church at Edenton, NC* (1860), 12–13.

54. G. A. Johnson to Samuel Tredwell, October 27, 1825, Charles E. Johnson Collection, Samuel Tredwell Papers, Folder 11, SANC.

55. James Roberts to Willis Roberts, 1830, Roberts Family Papers, Library of Congress.

56. Willard B. Gatewood, Jr., "'To Be Truly Free': Louis Sheridan and the Colonization of Liberia," *Civil War History* 29 (December 1983): 332–48; 1850 U.S. Federal Census, Cambridge, Wayne County, Indiana, 26; Autobiography of Hiram Revels, 2–3, Carter G. Woodson Papers,

Container 11, Additional Manuscripts- Revels, Hiram R. Autobiography, Library of Congress; William E. Bigglestone, *They Stopped in Oberlin: Black Residents and Visitors of the Nineteenth Century* (Oberlin: Oberlin College, 2002), 50–52, 163–65; "Lewis S. Leary," *The North-Carolinian* (Fayetteville), November 12, 1859.

57. Luther P. Jackson concluded that the contribution of "free Negroes" to the Virginia economy caused "all the schemes to deport the entire group" to meet "dismal failure." See Luther Porter Jackson, *Free Negro Labor and Property Holding in Virginia, 1830–1860* (New York: D. Appleton-Century Company, 1942), 229. H. E. Sterkx similarly concluded that the importance of free people of color to the Louisiana economy "goes a long way toward explaining why schemes to deport free colored persons as a group met with such dismal failure." See H. E. Sterkx, *The Free Negro in Ante-Bellum Louisiana* (Rutherford, NJ: Fairleigh Dickinson University Press, 1972), 239. Barbara Jeanne Fields found a similar situation in Maryland. She concluded that "the perennial movement to colonize free black people in Africa failed for a number of reasons . . . but the most important reason was that, whatever white Marylanders might say or think about the danger or mischief of the free black population, the economy of the state could not dispense with them." See Barbara Jeanne Fields, *Slavery and Freedom on the Middle Ground: Maryland during the Nineteenth Century* (New Haven, CT: Yale University Press, 1985), 71.

58. Thos Sheridan's Agreement, Thomas Smith McDowell Papers, Box 3, Subseries 1.3, #39, SHC.

59. Milton Presbyterian Church Session Minutes and Register, Volume 1, 250–51, SANC; Patricia Phillips Marshall and Jo Ramsay Leimenstoll, *Thomas Day: Master Craftsman and Free Man of Color* (Chapel Hill: University of North Carolina Press, 2010).

60. R. H. Mosley to Jesse Faulcon, James Boon Papers, Box 1, Correspondence, etc., 1839–1851, n.d., SANC.

61. James Boon Papers, Box 1, Correspondence, etc., 1839–1851, n.d., SANC.

62. "New Barber Shop," *Fayetteville Observer*, July 15, 1824.

63. "New Establishment," *Fayetteville Observer*, October 29, 1833.

64. "E. B. Revels, Barber, Hair Dresser and Perfumer," *Carolina Watchman* (Salisbury), February 4, 1837.

65. Wardens of Perqs Co. to Penny Norfleet, Perquimans County Poor House Records, Box 2, Feb 1845, SANC; The Wardens of Perquimans Co. to Clarisa Overton, Perquimans County Poor House Records, Box 2, Feb 1845, SANC; Wardens of the Poor of Perqs County to Willis H. Bagley, Perquimans County Poor House Records, Box 2, Nov 1843, SANC.

66. The Wardens of Perquimans County to Jacob Parker, Perquimans County Poor House Records, Box 2, Feb 1845, SANC.

67. Wardens of Craven County to James Y. Green, Craven County Wardens of the Poor, Box 2, Wardens of the Poor 1841–1842, SANC.

68. Poor House to Richard Hazel, Craven County Wardens of the Poor, Box 2, Wardens of the Poor 1844, SANC; The Wardens of the Poor to R. Hazle, Craven County Wardens of the Poor, Box 2, Wardens of the Poor 1844, SANC.

69. State of North Carolina for Repairs Gov' House 1837, Governors Papers, Box 88.1, Governor's Mansion Expenses, receipts, 1837–1839 Legislative Chambers Remodeling expenses, 1838–1839, SANC; "Comptroller's Report," *Raleigh Register*, December 5, 1845; "Report of the Comptroller of Public Accounts," *Raleigh Register*, December 1, 1849.

70. Chowan County Court Minutes, Volume 19, 509, SANC.

71. Wake County Court Minutes, Volume 19, 30, SANC; "Comptroller's Report," *Raleigh Register*, November 28, 1845. William Chavis of Wake County is a different person from William Chavis of Granville County.

72. Person County Court Minutes, Volume 13, 248, SANC.

73. Certificate of Freedom for Cicero Richardson, Cumberland County Apprentice Bonds and Records, Box 1, 1832, SANC.

74. Gates County Court Minutes, Volume 11, November 1846, SANC.

75. 1860 U.S. Federal Census, Gatesville District, Gates County, North Carolina, 44; 1850 U.S. Federal Census, Wilmington, New Hanover County, North Carolina, 889.

76. "New Establishment," *Raleigh Register*, August 7, 1847; "New Establishment," *Raleigh Register*, August 14, 1847; "New Establishment," *Raleigh Register*, August 18, 1847; 1850 U.S. Federal Census, Raleigh, Wake County, North Carolina, 262.

77. 1860 U.S. Federal Census, Wadesboro, Anson County, North Carolina, 79, 85.

78. 1860 U.S. Federal Census, Salisbury, Rowan County, North Carolina, 1; 1860 U.S. Federal Census, Warrenton, Warren County, North Carolina, 12; 1860 U.S. Federal Census, Western District, Halifax County, North Carolina, 9.

79. List of Persons Composing the Crew of the Schooner Sally Ann, Manumission Society Papers, Series 1, 1826 June #3, SHC.

80. Lemuel Sawyer, Esq., "On the Fisheries of North Carolina," *Plough, the Loom and the Anvil*, March 1859.

81. Account Book, John Vann Papers, Box 2, Fishery Accounts (Mount Gallant), SANC.

82. William D. Valentine Diary, Volume 7, 91, SHC.

83. J. A. Anderson to Chesson and Armstead, John B. Chesson Papers, Box 1, Chesson Papers Miscellaneous, SANC.

84. For more on people of color in North Carolina's maritime industries and a description of the "fishing courts," see David S. Cecelski, *The Waterman's Song: Slavery and Freedom in Maritime North Carolina* (Chapel Hill: University of North Carolina Press, 2001), 90–91.

85. Percival Perry, "The Naval-Stores Industry in the Old South, 1790–1860," *Journal of Southern History* 34 (November 1968): 509–26; 1860 U.S. Federal Census, Columbus County, North Carolina, 59–60; 1860 U.S. Federal Census, Bladen County, North Carolina, 83, 85–86; Gates County Registration of Slaves to Work in the Great Dismal Swamp, Volume 1, 71, 255, SANC.

86. Petition of Joseph Rowland Free Man Granville Cty, Governor Edward P. Dudley Papers, Box 89, Correspondence, Petitions, etc. May 1, 1839–May 30, 1839, SANC.

87. "Fatal Accident," *Weekly Commercial* (Wilmington), July 20, 1849.

88. 1850 U.S. Federal Census, McDowell County, North Carolina; 1850 U.S. Federal Census, Montgomery County, North Carolina; William S. Powell, *North Carolina through Four Centuries* (Chapel Hill: University of North Carolina Press, 1989), 311–15.

89. "Well-Digging," *Milton Chronicle* (Milton), January 8, 1858.

90. Robert A. Jones Account Book, 34, 329–32, SHC.

91. 1860 U.S. Federal Census, Bertie County, North Carolina, 22; 1860 U.S. Federal Census Agricultural Schedule, Bertie County, North Carolina, 7–8, Francis T. Hawks Papers, SHC; 1860 U.S. Federal Census Agricultural Schedule, Alamance County, North Carolina, 17–20, Francis T. Hawks Papers, SHC.

92. *State v. Evan Perkins*, Edenton District Records of the Superior Court, Box 44, 1797, SANC; Examination of Evan Perkins, Edenton District Records of the Superior Court, Box 44, 1797,

SANC; Evidence of David Hall & Willoughby Sammons, Edenton District Records of the Superior Court, Box 44, 1797, SANC.

93. "A shocking accident," *Raleigh Register*, November 30, 1821; Thomas O'Dwyer Diary, Samuel Jordan Wheeler Diaries, Volume 1, SHC; Hertford County Record of Wills, Volume A, 61–63, SANC.

94. Application of B. Davison for detail of Gabe Thompson, Thomas Ruffin Papers, Box 30, Folder 463, SHC.

95. 1860 U.S. Federal Census, Raleigh, Wake County, North Carolina, 71–72.

96. Thomas O'Dwyer Diary, Samuel Jordan Wheeler Diaries, Volume 1, SHC.

97. Dr. Newsome J. Pittman Medical Account Book, 45, 123, 167, 300, Nash County Historical Society Papers, SHC.

98. Barnes and Bardin Ledger, Volume 1, 37, SANC; Barnes and Bardin Ledger, Volume 2, 249, SANC; Barnes and Bardin Ledger, Volume 3, 26, 233, SANC.

99. John N. Benners Journal, 72–73, 106, SANC.

100. See Franklin, *The Free Negro in North Carolina*; Clegg, *The Price of Liberty*.

5. Freedom and Family: Relations with the Free and Enslaved

1. Raynor Lilly alias Reynold Lilly Pension File, NARA.

2. Gary B. Mills made a similar argument about the social organization of free people of color in Louisiana. See Mills, *The Forgotten People*.

3. Walter Clark, ed., *The State Records of North Carolina*, vol. 23 (Goldsboro: Nash Brothers, 1904), 65, 160; *Acts Passed by the General Assembly of the State of North Carolina at the Session of 1830–1831* (Raleigh: Lawrence & Lemay, 1831), 9–10.

4. Bertie County Tax List for 1751, Colonial Court Records Taxes and Accounts, Box 190, Tax Lists-Bertie-1751, 1753, 1754 Estate Tax-Beaufort Pet., n.d., SANC; List of Taxables, Granville County Taxables, Box 20, 1758, SANC; List of Taxables, Granville County Taxables, Box 20, 1760–1761, SANC. Herbert G. Gutman surmised that free people of color, unlike the slaves in his study, may have practiced endogamous marriage for economic purposes, but his study did not explore the subject further. The evidence from North Carolina suggests that Gutman may have been at least partially correct. See Herbert G. Gutman, *The Black Family in Slavery and Freedom, 1750–1925* (New York: Vintage Books, 1976), 90. Gary Mills's findings in the Cane River settlement of Louisiana also support this assertion. See Mills, *The Forgotten People*, 210.

5. Robert C. Kenzer, *Kinship and Neighborhood in a Southern Community: Orange County, North Carolina, 1849–1881* (Knoxville: University of Tennessee Press, 1987), 6–17.

6. See Granville County Taxables, Box 20, SANC, for records showing presence of free families of color in early Granville County; Will of Lewis Anderson, Granville County Wills, Box 2, Lewis Anderson 1785, SANC; Lewis Anderson Estate Papers, Granville County Estates Records, Box 5, Lewis Anderson 1805, SANC; Will of Lewis Anderson, Granville County Wills, Box 2, Lewis Anderson 1805, SANC; Will of Edward Bass, Granville County Wills, Box 3, Edward Bass 1800, SANC; Mecklenburg County Free Negro Register, LVA. For further discussion of the Granville County kinship networks, see Victoria Bynum, *Unruly Women: The Politics of Social and Sexual Control in the Old South* (Chapel Hill: University of North Carolina Press, 1992), 77–82.

7. See Marriage Bonds for Wake and Warren Counties, SANC. Examples also appear in the

Mecklenburg County Free Negro Register located in the Mecklenburg County Courthouse in Boydton, Virginia.

8. See Will of Edward Nickin, Lancaster County Wills, 1719–1749, LVA; Norfolk County Tithable Lists, 1732–1752, LVA; Norfolk County Tithable Lists, 1752–1783, LVA; Princess Anne County Deed Book 23, 226, LVA; Bertie County Tax List for 1751, Colonial Court Records Taxes and Accounts, Box 190, Tax Lists-Bertie-1751, 1753, 1754 Estate Tax-Beaufort Pet., n.d., SANC. For further discussion of these families, see Warren Eugene Milteer, Jr., *Hertford County, North Carolina's Free People of Color and Their Descendants* (Burlington: Milteer Publishing, 2016).

9. See Marriage Bonds for Robeson, Alamance, Orange and Caswell Counties, SANC; For further discussion of the kinship networks in Robeson and Orange Counties, see Lowery, *Lumbee Indians in the Jim Crow South*; Forest Hazel, "Occaneechi-Saponi Descendants in the North Carolina Piedmont: The Texas Community," *Southern Indian Studies* 40 (1991): 3–30. Adele Logan Alexander found similar networks among free people of color in antebellum Georgia. See Alexander, *Ambiguous Lives*, 103–6.

10. See Marriage Bonds for Halifax and Orange Counties, SANC.

11. E. Horace Fitchett found evidence of economically driven endogamy among free people of color in Charleston, South Carolina. See E. Horace Fitchett, "The Traditions of the Free Negro in Charleston, South Carolina," *Journal of Negro History* 25 (April 1940): 139–52.

12. Application of George Hilliard, File 34532, *Eastern Cherokee Applications of the U.S. Court of Claims, 1906–1909*, National Archives Microfilm Publication.

13. "Memories of Uncle Jackson," *A Folk History of Slavery in the United States from Interviews with Former Slaves, 1936–1938*, vol. 11, 3, Federal Writers' Project of the Works Progress Administration.

14. *Acts Passed by the General Assembly of the State of North Carolina at the Session of 1830–1831*, 9–10.

15. Pasquotank County Apprentice Bonds and Records, Box 2, Apprentice Bonds and Records O, SANC.

16. Petition of Lemuel Overton, General Assembly Session Records, SANC.

17. Petition of Charles Johnson, General Assembly Session Records, November–December 1795, Box 2, Senate Bills (Dec. 1), SANC.

18. Chowan County Wills, Volume B, 270–274, SANC; Chowan County Wills, Volume C, 237, SANC. For an examination of a similar situation, see Johnson and Roark, *Black Masters*.

19. Petition of Gustavus Adolphus Johnson, Chowan County Miscellaneous Slave Records, Box 33, Petition for Emancipation 1822, SANC.

20. "Interview with Emma Stone," *A Folk History of Slavery in the United States from Interviews with Former Slaves, 1936–1938*, vol. 11, 325, Federal Writers' Project of the Works Progress Administration.

21. Scholars have found similar conditions in other parts of the antebellum South. See Gary B. Mills, "Miscegenation and the Free Negro in Antebellum 'Anglo' Alabama: A Reexamination of Southern Race Relations," *Journal of American History* 68 (June 1981): 16–34; Thomas E. Buckley, S. J., "Unfixing Race: Class, Power, and Identity in an Interracial Family," *Virginia Magazine of History and Biography* 102 (July 1994): 346–80; Martha Hodes, *White Women, Black Men: Illicit Sex in the Nineteenth-Century South* (New Haven, CT: Yale University Press, 1997); Joshua D. Rothman, *Notorious in the Neighborhood: Sex and Families across the Color Line in Virginia, 1787–1861* (Chapel Hill: University of North Carolina Press, 2003); von Daacke, *Freedom Has a Face*.

22. William D. Valentine Diary, Volume 13, 85, SHC; Hertford County Court Minutes, Volume 3, March 1854, SANC; Warren E. Milteer, Jr., "The Strategies of Forbidden Love: Family across Racial Boundaries in Nineteenth-Century North Carolina," *Journal of Social History* 47 (Spring 2014): 612–26.

23. John Vann Papers, Box 4, Will Noah Cotton 1815, SANC; John Vann Papers, Box 3, Estate Cotten, Christian 1816, SANC.

24. In early nineteenth century North Carolina, there could be a very strict line between the freedom enjoyed by some free people of color and the burden of slavery held by many in slaved persons. Free people of color could and in the case of the Cottons did benefit from slave labor. In this case, the intellectual development of the Cotton children was funded by the work of a class of people who were prohibited from enjoying any sort of formal education. John Vann Papers, Box 3, Estate Cotten, Christian 1816-Estate Cotten, Noah 1815, SANC.

25. A Bill to alter the names of Wiley Wiggins Ricks Wiggins Micajah Wiggins and John Wiggins and to legitimate them, General Assembly Session Records, November 1825–January 1826, Box 3, Senate Bills (Dec. 24), SANC.

26. The death certificates for Sarah Reynolds and John C. Jones confirm that Jacob Ing was the father of Esther Jones's children. See Sarah Reynolds Death Certificate and John C. Jones Death Certificate, Ohio Death Certificates, Ohio History Center. William C. Jones Apprentice Bond, Nash County Apprentice Bonds, Box 2, J, SANC; William Reynolds and Sally Jones Marriage Bond, Nash County Marriage Bonds, SANC; Benjamin Reynolds and Mary Jones Marriage Bond, Nash County Marriage Bonds, SANC; James White and Celia Jones Marriage Bond, Nash County Marriage Bonds, SANC; Adam Artist and Lousinda Jones Marriage Bond, Nash County Marriage Bonds, SANC; Marriage Jacob Ing to Clerk of the County Court, Nash County Miscellaneous Records, Box 1, Correspondence to clerk of Superior court concerning eligibility of Jesse Boon and Elizabeth Jones, free persons of color, to marry, 1844, SANC.

27. Certificate of Freedom, Elizabeth Boon, Ozette Pittman Bell Collection, PC 1622, SANC.

28. Edgecombe County Wills, Volume G, 344, SANC.

29. Claim of Ann Revels 55190, Southern Claims Commission Records, NARA; 1850 U.S. Federal Census, Fayetteville District, Cumberland County, North Carolina, 3a-3b, 4b.

30. Cumberland County Record of Deeds, Volume 41, 398, SANC; Cumberland County Wills, Volume I, 326, SANC. By 1860, Ann and Waddle openly lived in the same house with their children Mary and Dallas. See 1860 U.S. Federal Census, Fayetteville, Cumberland County, North Carolina, 87.

31. Hertford County Court Minutes, Volume 2, 126, 156, SANC.

32. Perquimans County Wills, Volume F, 375, SANC.

33. Scholars have uncovered numerous examples of free women of color who had relationships with white men obtaining significant financial benefit because of those relationships. See Myers, *Forging Freedom*, 135–138; Clark, *The Strange History of the American Quadroon*, 97–131. However, discussion of the possible benefits free men of color could provide white women is absent from the literature.

34. Affidavit of John Blackman and James Lane, Montgomery County Miscellaneous Records, Box 3, Statement Concerning Turner and Hussey families whose ancestor was a mulatto, 1860, SANC.

35. David Strickland Bastardy Bond, Robeson County Bastardy Bonds and Records, Box 1, 1854, SANC; 1850 U.S. Federal Census, Southern Division, Robeson County, North Carolina,

356b–357a; 1850 U.S. Federal Census, Northern District, Alamance County, North Carolina, 69a; 1860 U.S. Federal Census, Alamance County, North Carolina, 81 (Kitty Paul is listed as white in this census enumeration); James McCray Bastardy Bond, Orange County Bastardy Bonds and Records, Box 6, 1845, SANC; Death Certificate for Jennie Dickey, Alamance County, North Carolina, SANC.

36. Petition of Jane Mulder, Davie County Miscellaneous Records, Box 8, Slaves and Free Negroes, Petition regarding mistreatment of free Negro bound as apprentice, 1837, SANC; Pasquotank County Apprentice Bonds and Records, Box 1, Apprentice Bonds and Records H, SANC; 1850 U.S. Federal Census, Pasquotank County, North Carolina, 320b.

6. Liberty Intersected: Race, Gender, and Wealth

1. *Jane Milton v. Elisha Milton*, Guilford County Divorces, Box 4, Milton, Elisha and Jane, SANC.

2. 1860 U.S. Federal Census, South Division, Guilford County, North Carolina, 28–29.

3. Zipf, *Labor of Innocents*, 22–24. For more on women's rights in divorce proceedings, see Bynum, *Unruly Women*, 63–64, 68–69, 72–77; Edwards, *The People and Their Peace*, 159–160, 176–179, 212–214.

4. See Franklin, *Free Negro in North Carolina*, 122–30; Zipf, *Labor of Innocents*; Richard C. Rohrs, "Training in an 'art, trade, mystery and employment': Opportunity or Exploitation of Free Black Apprentices in New Hanover County, North Carolina, 1820–1859?" *North Carolina Historical Review* 90 (April 2013): 127–48.

5. Bynum, *Unruly Women*, 99–100; Zipf, *Labor of Innocents*, 15, 21–22.

6. J. Wiggins to B. Raby, Bertie County Apprentice Indentures, Box 8, 1796–1797, SANC; T. Wiggins to B. Raby, Bertie County Apprentice Indentures, Box 8, 1796–1797, SANC.

7. Sampson County Court Minutes, Volume 1, 105.

8. Apprentice Indenture Charles Chance, Onslow County Apprentice Bonds and Records, Box 1, 1810–1819, SANC; Apprentice Indenture Ezekiel Chance, Onslow County Apprentice Bonds and Records, Box 1, 1810–1819, SANC; Apprentice Indenture Nancy Chance, Onslow County Apprentice Bonds and Records, Box 1, 1810–1819, SANC.

9. Rockingham County Court Minutes, Volume 1, 19–20, SANC.

10. Indenture M. Evans & V. Evans to James O'Kelly, Chatham County Apprentice Bonds and Records, Box 1, 1817, SANC.

11. Karin L. Zipf argued that apprentice assignments included a degree of racial discrimination for boys. She found that "Black male apprentices" were usually bound as farmers compared to "white males" who were more likely to have access to a wider range of training. See Zipf, *Labor of Innocents*, 37.

12. Currituck County Court Minutes, Volume 3, 93, SANC.

13. Beaufort County Court Minutes, Volume 4, 515–16, 518, 525, 527–30, SANC.

14. Wake County Court Minutes, Volume 1, 187, SANC.

15. Wake County Court Minutes, Volume 3, 299, 318, SANC.

16. Carteret Justices vs. George Gillikin, Notice to Defendt & Suba to witnesses, Carteret County Miscellaneous Records, Box 4, Apprentice Records 1816, SANC.

17. Moore County Court Minutes, Volume 4, 48, SANC.

18. Orange County Court Minutes, Volume 9, 607, SANC.

19. "Forty Shillings Reward," *North-Carolina Gazette* (New Bern), August 2, 1794.

20. Ruth Tillett vs Zachariah Jordan Petition, Pasquotank County Records of Slaves and Free Persons of Color, Box 10, Court Actions Involving Slaves 1734–1860 (broken series), SANC.

21. Martin, *Public Acts*, 178–79.

22. Petition of Temperance Chavers, Brunswick County Apprentice Bonds and Records, Box 1, 1810–1819, SANC.

23. Timothy Hunter Papers, Correspondence and Financial Papers, 1826–1842, ECUJL.

24. Zil. Hagans Petition, Wayne County Apprentice Bonds and Records, Box 4, 1824, SANC.

25. *State v. Ann Burke*, Chowan County Criminal Action Papers, Box 7, 1817, SANC. The "free negroes and mulattoes" named as defendants in this case include Ben James, Polly James, Betty James, Nancy James, Cloe Reuben, Deborah Mustapha, Samuel Overton, Rachel Overton, Peggy Demsey, Polly Mack, Ann Burke, Sarah Gaskins, Polly Vickery, Milley Vickery, Tempey Vickery, Valentine Vickery, William Vickery, Sally James, Dorcas James, Phillis James, Lettice Pea alias Banks, Sally Pea, Polly Pea, Elizabeth Pea, Anna Pea, Jack Pea, Betty Reuben, Polly Reuben, George Reuben, and Fanny Reuben.

26. "Three Dollar Reward," *North-Carolinian* (Fayetteville), April 5, 1845.

27. "$5 Reward," *Greensboro Patriot*, January 16, 1857.

28. Petition of Oma White, Onslow County Apprentice Bonds and Records, Box 1, 1860–1869, SANC.

29. Lydia Pettiford and Reuben Bass against Lewis Pettiford, Ridley Jones, and Charles Kinnon, Wake County Apprentice Bonds and Records, Box 1, Apprentice bonds—Bass, Thomas and Ned, SANC.

30. *Acts Passed by the General Assembly of the State of North Carolina at Its Session Commencing on the 25th of December, 1826* (Raleigh: Lawrence & Lemay, 1827), 13–16.

31. Notice to Willy Locus, Nash County Apprentice Bonds, Box 2, L, SANC.

32. Alamance County Court Minutes, Volume 1, 357, SANC.

33. Halifax County Court Minutes, Volume 7, May 1848, SANC.

34. *The Revised Statutes of the State of North Carolina Passed by the General Assembly at the Session of 1836-7* (Raleigh: Turner & Hughes, 1837), 68.

35. Anna Mitchell Indenture, Halifax County Miscellaneous Records, Box 3, Apprentice bonds and records 1858, SANC.

36. For examples, see Danl Turner's Bond for Benjn Overton, Pasquotank County Apprentice Bonds and Records, Box 2, O, SANC; Perquimans County Apprentice Bonds, Volume 2, SANC.

37. Indentures of Mary Grinton & others, Wilkes County Apprentice Bonds and Records, Box 3, 1840–1858, SANC.

38. Stokes County Court Minutes, Volume 18, December 1857, SANC.

39. Guilford County Court Minutes, Volume 16, 34, SANC.

40. Riley Clodfetter to Jacob Clodfetter Indentures, Davidson County Apprentice Bonds and Records, Box 3, Cane-Crouch, SANC; Thomas Cane to R. J. Cicil Indentures, Davidson County Apprentice Bonds and Records, Box 3, Cane-Crouch, SANC.

41. Betsy Boon to Jonas Johnston, Onslow County Apprentice Bonds and Records, Box 1, 1810–1819, SANC.

42. Nicy Simpson Indentures to Sarah Mann, Tyrrell County Apprentice Bonds and Records,

Box 2, 1830–1833, SANC; Nicy Simpson's indentures for her daughter Rindy, Tyrrell County Apprentice Bonds and Records, Box 2, 1830–1833, SANC; M & N Simpson to Esther Tarkinton Indenture, Tyrrell County Apprentice Bonds and Records, Box 2, 1810–1812, SANC.

43. "Ten Dollar Reward," *Raleigh Minerva*, February 27, 1804.

44. "Five Cents Reward," *Greensboro Patriot*, May 19, 1830.

45. *Acts Passed by the General Assembly of the State of North Carolina at Its Session Commencing on the 25th of December, 1826* (Raleigh: Lawrence & Lemay, 1827), 13–16.

46. "Law," *North-Carolina Free Press* (Halifax), September 5, 1828.

47. *Acts Passed by the General Assembly of the State of North Carolina, at the Session of 1831–32* (Raleigh: Lawrence & Lemay, 1832), 12–13.

48. *State v. Michael Warden*, Surry County Criminal Action Papers, Box 8, 1851, SANC.

49. Alexr Stewart & Lydia Stewart to John alias Jno Stanly deed of Emancipation, Slave Collection, Box 1, Slave Papers Deed of Emancipation 1795, SANC; Gautier Petition, General Assembly Session Records, November–December 1799, Box 3, Petitions (Emancipation), SANC; Patricia Phillips Marshall and Jo Ramsay Leimenstoll, *Thomas Day: Master Craftsman and Free Man of Color* (Chapel Hill: University of North Carolina Press, 2010), 10; Application of Isaac Hammonds, File W7654, *Revolutionary War Pension and Bounty-Land Warrant Application Files*, National Archives Microfilm Publication; "One Hundred Dollars Reward," *Weekly Raleigh Register*, November 30, 1802; "James D. Sampson," *Negro History Bulletin* 3 (January 1940): 56. The narrative presented in this document, written over a hundred years after Sampson's birth, suggests he was born a slave. In the region in which Sampson lived, however, there were many free people of color who carried the Sampson surname but have no documented connection with prior enslavement.

50. Loren Schweninger, "John Carruthers Stanly and the Anomaly of Black Slaveholding," *North Carolina Historical Review* 67 (April 1990): 159–92; Application of Isaac Hammonds, File W7654, *Revolutionary War Pension and Bounty-Land Warrant Application Files*, National Archives Microfilm Publication; *Donum Montford v. John Dewey*, Craven County Civil Action Papers, Box 9, 1813 (4), SANC; "Look Here," *People's Press and Wilmington Advertiser*, November 6, 1835; "Thomas Day, Cabinetmaker," *Milton Gazette and Roanoke Advertiser*, March 1, 1827; Marshall and Leimenstoll, *Thomas Day*, 19–43; "Saddles, Bridles, Harness, & c.," *Fayetteville Observer*, October 4, 1837; "Self-adjusting Pad Tree," *Fayetteville Observer*, February 5, 1850.

51. Schweninger, "John Carruthers Stanly and the Anomaly of Black Slaveholding," 159–92; List of taxable property in the town of Newbern A.D. 1815, Treasurer's and Comptroller's Papers, Box 3, Tax List Craven 1815, SANC; 1850 U.S. Federal Census, Wilmington, New Hanover County, North Carolina, 444b; Inventory of the Estate of James Sampson decd 1861, New Hanover County Estates Records, Box 95, Sampson, James 1861, SANC.

52. "Bits of the History of New Berne," *Daily Journal* (New Bern), August 27, 1882; "Reminiscences," *Morning Star* (Raleigh), December 5, 1897; List of taxable property in the town of Newbern A.D. 1815, Treasurer's and Comptroller's Papers, Box 3, Tax List Craven 1815, SANC; Craven County Court Minutes, Volume 26, 241, SANC; Craven County Court Minutes, Volume 27, 296, 346–47, 551, SANC; Thomas Day's Bond for the Safe Keeping of Archibald Clark an Indented Servant, Caswell County Apprentice Bonds and Records, Box 1, Apprentice Records C, SANC; Apprentice Bond M N Leary for William Thigpen, Cumberland County Apprentice Bonds and Records, Box 2, 1843, SANC; Indenture of Henry Conner, New Hanover County Apprentice Bonds and Records, Box 3, 1835–1839, SANC; Indenture of Haskel M Conner, New Hanover

County Apprentice Bonds and Records, Box 3, 1835–1839, SANC; Indenture of Nathl Conner, New Hanover County Apprentice Bonds and Records, Box 3, 1835–1839, SANC; James Sampson to State Indenture & Bond For William Henry, New Hanover County Apprentice Bonds and Records, Box 3, 1843–1845, SANC; J Sampson to State Bond & Indenture For Robt Sweat, New Hanover County Apprentice Bonds and Records, Box 3, 1843–1845, SANC.

53. "Four Negro Men for Sale," *Newbern Sentinel*, May 8, 1819.

54. "Ten Dollars Reward," *Wilmington Chronicle*, March 23, 1842.

55. "20 Dollar Reward," *Norfolk Gazette and Publick Ledger*, December 7, 1815.

56. "Fifty Dollars Reward," *Fayetteville Semi-Weekly Observer*, April 4, 1853.

57. "Deserted," *The Star* (Raleigh), October 28, 1814.

58. "Five Cents Reward," *Newbern Sentinel*, April 8, 1826.

59. Jno C Stanly's bond for the emancipation of Kitty his wife & two children, Box 10, Petitions to emancipate slaves, petitions for freedom and bonds for emancipated slaves 1800–1809, SANC; Pet. Of J. C. Stanly praying emancipation of Jack the property of said J. C. Stanly, Craven County Slaves and Free Negroes, Box 10, Petitions to emancipate slaves, petitions for freedom and bonds for emancipated slaves 1800–1809, SANC; Pet of Jno C Stanly, Craven County Slaves and Free Negroes, Box 10, 1810–1819, SANC; Jno C Stanly's Petition, Craven County Slaves and Free Negroes, Box 10, 1810–1819, SANC; John C. Stanly Petition for Emancipation, Craven County Slaves and Free Negroes, Box 10, Petitions to emancipate slaves, petitions for freedom and bonds for emancipated slaves 1822–1829, SANC; "Authorized Agents," *Freedom's Journal* (New York), January 18, 1828.

60. John P. Green, *Fact Stranger than Fiction: Seventy-Five Years of a Busy Life with Reminiscences of Many Great and Good Men and Women* (Cleveland: Riehl Printing Company, 1920), 42–44; *Quinquennial Catalogue of Oberlin College* (Oberlin: News Printing Company, 1900), 76.

61. Marshall and Leimenstoll, *Thomas Day*, 48–51; "Obituary," *New York Age*, July 23, 1927; *Annual Catalogue of the Officers and Students of Oberlin College for the College Year 1858–59* (Oberlin: Evangelist Office, 1858), 8; *Quinquennial Catalogue of Oberlin College*, 83.

62. "Died," *North State Whig* (Washington, NC), November 17, 1841.

63. Inventory of the property of Isham Chavis, Cumberland County Estates Records, Box 13, Chavis, Isham 1795, SANC; A true inventory of the Estate of Ephraim Manuel, Sampson County Estates Records, Box 093, Manuel, Ephraim 1804, SANC; Survey Plot and Report of the jury of the land belonging to the estate of Claiborne Wiggins decd, Franklin County Estates Records, Box 79, Wiggins, Claiborn 1857, SANC.

64. Halifax County Record of Estates, Volume 4, 516; Gates County List of Taxables, Volume 5, 211–12, 299–300, SANC

65. Thos Newton a man of colour petition for the freedom of his wife, Craven County Slaves and Free Negroes, Box 10, Petitions to eman. Slaves No Date, SANC.

66. Petition of Henry Patterson, General Assembly Session Records, November 1838–January 1839, Box 4, Petitions, SANC.

67. Wiley Alford Administrator of Hector Locklier decd in account with said Estate, Robeson County Estates Records, Box 37, Locklear, Hector 1857, SANC; 1850 U.S. Federal Census, Upper Division, Robeson County, North Carolina, 320.

68. Gates County Court Minutes, Volume 9, 167, SANC.

69. Beaufort County Court Minutes, Volume 9, 18 Sept 1854, 4 June 1855, 5 June 1855, SANC; 1860 U.S. Federal Census, Long Acre, Beaufort County, North Carolina, 138.

70. "Five Dollars Reward," *Wilmington Chronicle*, February 4, 1846.

71. Nathaniel Newsom's Will, Northampton County Wills, Box 32, Newsom, Nathaniel 1835, SANC.

72. Halifax County Record of Wills, Volume 5, 7–8, SANC.

73. Robert C. Kenzer, *Enterprising Southerners: Black Economic Success in North Carolina, 1865–1915* (Charlottesville: University Press of Virginia, 1997), xiii–xiv.

74. Keziah Overton Dower & Provisions, Perquimans County Estate Records, Box 80, Overton, Benjamin, SANC.

75. Beaufort County Court Minutes, Volume 9, March 18, 1851, SANC.

7. Guilty or Innocent? Free People of Color in the Courts

1. "The Superior Court," *Newbern Sentinel*, November 9, 1822.

2. Rowan County Superior Court Minutes, Volume 2, September 1822–March 1823, SANC.

3. Edwards, *The People and Their Peace*, 7–8. Kimberly M. Welch found a similar legal environment for people of color in the Natchez district. See Kimberly M. Welch, *Black Litigants in the Antebellum American South* (Chapel Hill: University of North Carolina Press, 2018).

4. Edwards, *The People and Their Peace*, 102–3.

5. *State v. Nancy Whitaker*, Orange County Criminal Action Papers, Box 26, 1826, SANC.

6. *State v. James Butler*, Gates County Criminal Action Papers, Box 7, 1829, SANC.

7. Orange County Court Minutes, Volume 19, August 1826, SANC; Gates County Superior Court Minutes, Volume 2, October 1827, SANC.

8. *State v. Wiley Revels*, Henderson County Criminal Action Papers, Box 16, 1857, SANC.

9. Henderson County Superior Court Minutes, Volume 2, Spring 1858, SANC.

10. Craven County Superior Court Minutes, Volume 4, October 1845, SANC.

11. *State v. Willis Jones*, Wilson County Criminal Action Papers, Box 1, 1856, SANC.

12. *State v. Ivy Evans*, Wilson County Criminal Action Papers, Box 1, 1856, SANC.

13. Wilson County Court Minutes, Volume 1, 86, 97, SANC.

14. *State v. Jordan Edge and Lurana Hewitt*, Pasquotank County Criminal Action Papers, Box 6, 1825, SANC.

15. Pasquotank County Superior Court Minutes, Volume 1, Spring 1826, SANC.

16. *State v. Thomas Flew Ellen*, Nash County Criminal Actions Concerning Fornication and Adultery, Box 27, 1837, SANC.

17. Nash County Court Minutes, Volume 10, May 1837, SANC.

18. *State v. Asa Etheridge and Eliza Boon*, Tyrrell County Records of Slaves and Free Persons of Color, Box 3, Criminal actions concerning slaves and free persons of color 1851–1854, SANC.

19. Tyrrell County Superior Court Minutes, Volume 3, September 1852, SANC.

20. *State v. Patsey Huckaby and James Huckaby*, Orange County Criminal Action Papers, Box 49, 1850, SANC.

21. Orange County Court Minutes, Volume 26, August 1850, SANC.

22. *State v. Philip Roberts, Julia Bowers, and Polly Bass*, Caswell County Criminal Action Papers, Box 18, 1838, SANC.

23. Caswell County Superior Court Minutes, Volume 2, Fall 1837, SANC.

24. *State v. Andrew Lowrie*, Robeson County Criminal Action Papers, Box 14, 1846, SANC.

25. Robeson County Superior Court Minutes, Volume 1, Fall 1846, SANC.

26. *State v. Morgan Myers*, Yadkin County Criminal Action Papers, Box 1, 1852, SANC.

27. Yadkin County Superior Court Minutes, Volume 1, December 1852, SANC.

28. *State v. Laney Potter*, Randolph County Records of Slaves and Free Persons of Color, Box 2, Criminal actions concerning slaves and free persons of color, SANC.

29. Randolph County Court Minutes, Volume 13, February 1857, SANC.

30. *State v. Milly Walker*, Orange County Criminal Action Papers, Box 50, 1851, SANC.

31. Orange County Superior Court Minutes, Volume 4, September 1851, SANC.

32. *State v. Penny Wiggins and Caesar (a slave)*, Northampton County Criminal Action Papers, Box 20, 1856, SANC.

33. Northampton County Court Minutes, Volume 11, December 1856, SANC.

34. *State v. David Manly*, Craven County Criminal Actions Concerning Slaves and Free Persons of Color, Box 9, 1859, SANC.

35. Craven County Court Minutes, Volume 38, 397, SANC.

36. *State v. Henry Parker*, Granville County Criminal Action Papers, Box 36, 1851, SANC.

37. Granville County Superior Court Minutes, Volume 6, September 1852, SANC.

38. *State v. Shepherd Mitchell*, Northampton County Criminal Action Papers, Box 18, 1840, SANC.

39. Northampton County Court Minutes, Volume 8, June 1841, SANC.

40. *State v. Lewis Cozens, John Wilson Junior, and Freeman Howard*, Caswell County Criminal Action Papers, Box 28, 1853, SANC.

41. Caswell County Superior Court Minutes, Volume 3, 13, SANC. The minutes describing the outcomes of Wilson's and Cozens's cases have not survived or are missing.

42. *State v. Alexander Scott*, Randolph County Criminal Action Papers, Box 44, 1856, SANC; Randolph County Superior Court Minutes, Volume 2, Fall 1857, SANC.

43. *State v. Harry Black*, Craven County Criminal Action Papers, Box 5, 1822, SANC.

44. Craven County State Docket Minutes, Volume 1, April 1822, SANC.

45. *State v. William P. Waters*, Ashe County Criminal Action Papers, Box 1, 1836–1837, SANC.

46. Ashe County Superior Court Minutes, Volume 2, September 1836, SANC.

47. *State v. George Freeman*, Robeson County Records Concerning Slaves and Free Persons of Color, Box 3, Slave & free persons of color 1845, SANC.

48. *State v. George Freeman*, Robeson County Records Concerning Slaves and Free Persons of Color, Box 3, Slave & free persons of color 1846, SANC.

49. Richmond County Superior Court Minutes, Volume 3, 17, SANC; *State v. George W. Freeman*, Richmond County Criminal Action Papers, Box 18, 1846, SANC.

50. Orange County Superior Court Minutes, Volume 3, September 1841.

51. *State v. Nancy Robbins*, Chowan County Criminal Action Papers, Box 6, 1811, SANC; Chowan County Superior Court Minutes, Volume 2, October 1811, SANC.

52. *State v. Rachel Shade*, McDowell County Records of Slaves and Free Persons of Color, Box 1, State vs. Rachel Shade 1846, SANC.

53. McDowell County Superior Court Minutes, Volume 1, 14, 15, 27, 29, 31, SANC.

54. *State v. Sooky Bishop*, Orange County Criminal Action Papers, Box 44, 1843, SANC.

55. Orange County Superior Court Minutes, Volume 3, March 1843, SANC.

56. *State v. Martha Bowser*, Tyrrell County Records of Slaves and Free Persons of Color, Box 3, Criminal actions concerning slaves and free persons of color 1851–1854, SANC.

57. Tyrrell County Superior Court Minutes, Volume 3, September 1853, SANC.

58. *State v. Richard Morris*, Craven County Criminal Action Papers, Box 5, 1821, SANC.

59. Craven County State Docket Minutes, Volume 1, April 1822, SANC.

60. *State v. Mills Reid*, Gates County Criminal Action Papers, Box 8, 1834, SANC.

61. Gates County Superior Court Minutes, Volume 3, April 1834, SANC.

62. *State v. Clary Mabry*, Northampton County Criminal Action Papers, Box 18, 1840, SANC.

63. Northampton County Court Minutes, Volume 8, December 1840, SANC.

64. *State v. Doctor Howell*, Granville County Criminal Action Papers, Box 38, 1854, SANC.

65. Granville County Superior Court Minutes, Volume 6, September 1854, SANC.

66. *State v. Henry Harris*, Orange County Criminal Action Papers, Box 37, 1836, SANC.

67. Caswell County Superior Court Minutes, Volume 2, Spring 1836, SANC.

68. *State v. Moses Blango*, Beaufort County Criminal Action Papers, Box CRX 114, 1857, SANC.

69. Beaufort County State Docket County Court Minutes, Volume 2, December 1857, SANC.

70. Cumberland County Court Minutes, Volume 34, March 1855, SANC; Craven County Court Minutes, Volume 38, 278, 308, SANC.

71. "Habeas Corpus Case," *Weekly Raleigh Register*, December 9, 1857.

72. *State v. James Holt and Hardin Turner*, Rockingham County Records of Slaves and Free Persons of Color, Box 3, Criminal actions re. free persons of color—State vs. Holt and Turner 1850, SANC.

73. Rockingham County Superior Court Minutes, Volume 3, Spring 1850, SANC.

74. *State v. James M. Wells*, Stokes County Criminal Action Papers, Box 13, 1859, SANC.

75. Stokes County Court Minutes, Volume 18, December 1859, SANC.

76. *State v. Joseph G. Barclift*, Perquimans County Criminal Action Papers, Box 9, 1836, SANC.

77. Perquimans County Superior Court Minutes, Volume 1, Fall 1836, SANC.

78. *State v. Alexander Hooker*, Randolph County Criminal Action Papers, Box 7, 1856, SANC. After his conviction, Hooker's neighbors petitioned the governor for a pardon. On October 1, 1856, Governor Thomas Bragg pardoned Alexander Hooker.

79. *State v. John H. Edwards, William Moore, George Freeman, and Andrew Baker*, Perquimans County Criminal Action Papers, Box 6, 1821, SANC; Perquimans County Superior Court Minutes, Volume 1, October 1821, SANC; Pasquotank County Superior Court Minutes, Volume 1, Spring 1822, SANC.

80. *State v. Henry Parks and Columbus Nichols*, Orange County Criminal Action Papers, Box 65, 1860, SANC.

81. Orange County Superior Court Minutes, Volume 4, March 1860, SANC.

82. *Donum Montford v. John Dewey*, Craven County Civil Action Papers, Box 9, 1813 (4), SANC; Craven County Court Minutes, Volume 23, 406, SANC.

83. *John Wilson v. John Street*, Orange County Civil Action Papers, Box 51, 1816, SANC; Orange County Superior Court Minutes, Volume 1, September 1816, SANC.

84. *Peggy Hargrove v. James Chavis*, Granville County Civil Action Papers, Box 46, 1800, SANC; Gates County Estates Records, Box 66, Jordan, William 1848, SANC; Gates County Court Minutes, Volume 11, May 1849, SANC; Gates County Superior Court Minutes, Volume 3, March 1849, SANC.

85. Northampton County Estates Records, Box 104, Hathcock, Reuben 1815, SANC.

86. Robeson County Estates Records, Box 38, Lowrey, James 1832, SANC.

87. *Mason Cuff v. Kinchen Norfleet*, Gates County Civil Action Papers, Box 5, 1811, SANC.

88. Gates County Superior Court Minutes, Volume 1, 30, SANC.

89. *Matthew Locklear v. Alexander McPhail, Evander Bethea, and Peter Smith*, Robeson County Civil Action Papers, Box 7, 1849, SANC.

90. Robeson County Superior Court Minutes, Volume 1, Spring 1850, SANC.

91. *Betsey Patrick v. Joseph Green*, Brunswick County Apprentice Bonds and Records, Box 1, 1850–1859, SANC.

92. *Edmund Kersey v. Milly Kersey*, Robeson County Divorce Records, Box 3, Kersey, Edmund vs. Milly 1847, SANC.

93. Robeson County Superior Court Minutes, Volume 1, Fall 1847, SANC.

94. *Eliza Jordan v. Theophilus Jordan*, Chowan County Divorce Records, Box 2, Divorce- Eliza Jordan vs. Theophilus Jordan, SANC.

95. Martin County Superior Court Minutes, Volume 2, Fall 1860, Fall 1861, SANC.

8. The Fight for Liberty: Civil War and Reconstruction

1. "Wilkesboro, N.C., Nov. 17, 1861," *Semi-Weekly Standard* (Raleigh), November 30, 1861.

2. Alexander Stephens, "Corner Stone" (Savannah, Georgia, March 21, 1861).

3. Partial exceptions include Johnson and Roark, *Black Masters*; Ely, *Israel on the Appomattox*; Gary B. Mills, "Patriotism Frustrated: The Native Guards of Confederate Natchitoches," *Louisiana History* 18 (Autumn 1977): 437–51; Edna Greene Medford, "'I Was Always a Union Man': The Dilemma of Free Blacks in Confederate Virginia," *Slavery and Abolition* 15 (December 1994): 1–16. John Hope Franklin's study of free people of color in North Carolina ends in 1860. Richard Reid's work on North Carolina's U.S. Colored Troops mentions some free people of color by name but does not examine how the war specifically affected free people of color and instead offers analysis of the war's effect on "blacks" as a whole. See Richard M. Reid, *Freedom for Themselves: North Carolina's Black Soldiers in the Civil War Era* (Chapel Hill: University of North Carolina Press, 2008).

4. *Public Laws of the State of North Carolina Passed by the General Assembly at Its Session of 1860–61* (Raleigh: John Spelman, 1861), 68–69.

5. *Journal of the Senate of the General Assembly of the State of North-Carolina at Its Session of 1860-'61* (Raleigh: John Spelman, 1861), 45, 77, 145–46, 402; Edward Cantwell, ed., *Journal of the House of Commons of North-Carolina, Session of 1860-'61* (Raleigh: John Spelman, 1861), 3, 485, 501; "The National Executive Committee of the Democratic Party," *Daily Exchange* (Baltimore), June 25, 1860; "The Onslow Cavalry-Candidates in Onslow," *National Democrat* (Raleigh), September 15, 1860; "Democratic Meeting in Bladen," *Weekly Courier* (Fayetteville), June 9, 1860; "Legislature of N.C. 1860-'61," *Times* (Greensboro), August 25, 1860.

6. Currituck County Memorial, General Assembly Session Records, November 1860–February 1861, Box 8, Petitions, SANC.

7. "Election Returns," *Standard* (Raleigh), August 11, 1858; *Journal of the Senate of the General Assembly of the State of North-Carolina at Its Session of 1860-'61*, 209, 274; "Democratic State Convention," *Semi-Weekly Standard* (Raleigh), March 10, 1860.

8. *Dred Scott v. John F. A. Sandford*, 60 U.S. 393 (1857); Martha S. Jones, *Birthright Citizens: A History of Race and Rights in Antebellum America* (New York: Cambridge University Press, 2018), 138–43.

9. Resolution, Headen of Chatham, General Assembly Session Records, January–February 1863, Box 2, House Resolutions (250–390 and unnumbered), SANC.

10. Bernard H. Nelson, "Legislative Control of the Southern Free Negro, 1861–1865," *Catholic Historical Review* 32 (April 1946): 28–46. William W. Freehling noted that after the passage of the enslavement law in Arkansas and the exodus of most of the state's free people of color, the next legislature allowed the remaining free people of color to stay in the state with their freedom intact. See Freehling, *The Road to Disunion, Volume II*, 200.

11. Petition of Justices of the County Court of Hertford, General Assembly Session Records, August–September 1861, Box 4, Petitions (Aug.–Sept. 1861), SANC.

12. Gates County Court Minutes, Volume 13, 108, SANC.

13. Pasquotank County Court Minutes, Volume 18, 149, SANC.

14. M. N. Leary, Confederate Papers Relating to Citizens or Business Firms, 1861–65, NARA.

15. Bennett Boon, Confederate Papers Relating to Citizens or Business Firms, 1861–65, NARA; Elvin Artis, Confederate Papers Relating to Citizens or Business Firms, 1861–65, NARA.

16. Gates County Court Minutes, Volume 13, 136, SANC; Pasquotank County Court Minutes, Volume 18, 148, SANC; List of Claims, General Assembly Session Records, August–September 1861, Box 4, Miscellaneous Reports, SANC; List of Claims, General Assembly Session Records, January–February 1863, Box 2, Jan.–Feb. 1863 Misc. Reports, SANC.

17. Alexander Justice Papers, Folder 13, Volume 2, 1–33, SHC.

18. "Camp Servants," *Fayetteville Observer*, April 7, 1862.

19. Cumberland County Court Minutes, Volume 40, 327, SANC.

20. Claim of Solomon Oxendine 21329, Southern Claims Commission Approved Claims, NARA.

21. Application to Discharge Jerry Day a free person of color, Governor's Papers, Governor Henry T. Clark, G. P. 154 Correspondence September 1861, G. P. 155 Correspondence October 1861, Correspondence: August 21–31, 1861, SANC.

22. Mrs. Ashley Wilder to James A. Seddon, Alonzo T. and Millard Mial Papers, Correspondence 1862–1871, Box 3, Folder 1, SANC. The literature on the relations between white women and people of color on the home front has focused exclusively on interactions between white women and enslaved people.

23. Local stands against the conscription of free people of color were not limited to North Carolina. Ervin L. Jordan Jr. found similar reaction to the impressments of free people of color in some areas of Virginia. See Ervin L. Jordan Jr., *Black Confederates and Afro-Yankees in Civil War Virginia* (Charlottesville: University of Virginia Press, 1995), 203.

24. Chowan County Court Minutes, Volume 21, February 1862, SANC.

25. "A White Man Murdered by a Free Negro—The Murderer Hung," *Raleigh Register*, October 16, 1861.

26. Claim of Isaac Griffin 20625, Southern Claims Commission Approved Claims, NARA.

27. Habeus Corpus Petitions for George Casey, James Casey, and Richard Gray, Haywood County Miscellaneous Records, Box 6, Habeas corpus petitions to be exempted from military service for James L. Edwards, Griffin Henson, Whipple C. Hill, and Jesse R. Palmer, 1863; George Casey, James Casey, and Richard Gray, "free negroes," 1864, SANC.

28. Wilson Williams Free Negro Petition to remain at home & support his family, Confederate States of American Bureau of Conscription 7th North Carolina Congressional District Records, Box 2, Folder 21, SHC; Board of Inr. to Lt. T. H. Haughton, Confederate States of

American Bureau of Conscription 7th North Carolina Congressional District Records, Box 2, Folder 21, SHC.

29. Letter Book, Confederate States of American Bureau of Conscription 7th North Carolina Congressional District Records, Box 2, Folder 34, SHC.

30. Claim of Isaiah Simmons 10953, Southern Claims Commission Approved Claims, NARA.

31. State vs. J. B. Harris for Murdering the Lowries 1864, Robeson County Coroner's Inquests, Box 1, 1864, SANC; "For the Observer," *Fayetteville Observer*, October 21, 1863.

32. Calvin Lowry Sworn Statement, Records of the Field Offices for the State of North Carolina, Bureau of Refugees, Freedmen, and Abandoned Lands, 1865–1872, Roll 69, NARA. For more on the postwar conflict in Robeson County, see William McKee Evans, *To Die Game: The Story of the Lowry Band, Indian Guerillas of Reconstruction* (Syracuse, NY: Syracuse University Press, 1995).

33. Studies on free people of color in Louisiana suggest that such a diversity of opinions existed among this population. See Mary F. Berry, "Negro Troops in Blue and Gray: The Louisiana Native Guards, 1861–1863," *Louisiana History* 8 (Spring 1967): 165–90; Mills, "Patriotism Frustrated," 437–51.

34. "Contributions from Col. T. J. Morisey's 58th N. C. M. (Robeson)," *Fayetteville Observer*, 29 December 1862; Robeson County Court Minutes, Volume 10, 250–253, SANC; Claim of Solomon Oxendine 21329, Southern Claims Commission Approved Claims, NARA.

35. Samuel Chavers Service Record, Compiled Service Records of Confederate Soldiers Who Served in Organizations from the State of North Carolina, NARA; Henry Goins Service Record, Compiled Service Records of Confederate Soldiers Who Served in Organizations from the State of North Carolina, NARA; Andrew Goins Service Record, Compiled Service Records of Confederate Soldiers Who Served in Organizations from the State of North Carolina, NARA; Richard Goins Service Record, Compiled Service Records of Confederate Soldiers Who Served in Organizations from the State of North Carolina, NARA; John W. Goins Service Record, Compiled Service Records of Confederate Soldiers Who Served in Organizations from the State of North Carolina, NARA.

36. James M. McPherson, *The Negro's Civil War: How American Negroes Felt and Acted during the War for the Union* (New York: Pantheon Books, 1965), 23–24.

37. Barbara Jeanne Fields noted that "when propagandists for secession before the Civil War emphasized the danger that the Northerners might encroach upon Southerners' right of self-determination, they emphasized a theme that resonated as well with the world of non-slaveholders as with that of planters, even though the two worlds differed as night from day." This type of propaganda may have resonated with some free people of color and may have produced an equal result. A free person of color did not have to be an ardent defender of slavery to find the proslavery ideologues' propaganda appealing. See Barbara Jeanne Fields, "Slavery, Race and Ideology in the United States of America," *New Left Review* (May–June 1990): 111.

38. Since the end of the war, several prorebel interests have attempted to argue that because some free people of color fought for or supported in some other capacity the rebellion, Southern secession was not about the racial order or about slavery. However, this book and many other works have demonstrated that the legislative battles before secession and secession itself are indelibly linked to the radical proslavery movement. White supremacists' ideology and the political targeting of free people of color were essential parts of the radical proslavery methodology.

39. Claim of Raleigh Seaberry 10453, Southern Claims Commission Approved Claims, NARA; Claim of William H. Haithcock 20604, Southern Claims Commission Approved Claims, NARA; Person County Court of Wardens of the Poor Minutes, Volume 2, April 1858, January 1859, April 1862, SANC; Edgecombe County Wardens of the Poor Minutes, Volume 1, 78–79, SANC; Meherrin Baptist Church Minutes, 228, SANC.

40. James Oakes argued that from the beginning of the war the Republicans viewed emancipation as a key objective and important war tactic. See James Oakes, *Freedom National: The Destruction of Slavery in the United States, 1861–1865* (New York: W. W. Norton, 2013).

41. George Boston Service Record, Compiled Military Service Records of Volunteer Union Soldiers Who Served with the United States Colored Troops: Infantry Organizations, 36th through 40th, NARA; Friley James Service Record, Compiled Military Service Records of Volunteer Union Soldiers Who Served with the United States Colored Troops: Infantry Organizations, 36th through 40th, NARA; Charles Pierce Service Record, Compiled Military Service Records of Volunteer Union Soldiers Who Served with the United States Colored Troops: Infantry Organizations, 36th through 40th, NARA; Parker D. Robbins Service Record, Compiled Military Service Records of Volunteer Union Soldiers Who Served with the United States Colored Troops: 1st through 5th United States Colored Cavalry, 5th Massachusetts Cavalry (Colored), 6th United States Colored Cavalry, NARA; Augustus Robbins Service Record, Compiled Military Service Records of Volunteer Union Soldiers Who Served with the United States Colored Troops: 1st through 5th United States Colored Cavalry, 5th Massachusetts Cavalry (Colored), 6th United States Colored Cavalry, NARA.

42. John Cumbo Pension File, NARA; Thomas Reynolds Pension File, NARA.

43. King Outlaw Pension File, NARA.

44. Drew Gilpin Faust, *This Republic of Suffering: Death and the American Civil War* (New York: Alfred A. Knopf, 2008), 4.

45. Reynold Lilly Service Record, Compiled Military Service Records of Volunteer Union Soldiers Who Served with the United States Colored Troops: Infantry Organizations, 36th through 40th, NARA; George Boston Service Record, Compiled Military Service Records of Volunteer Union Soldiers Who Served with the United States Colored Troops: Infantry Organizations, 36th through 40th, NARA.

46. Washington Flood Pension File, NARA; Levi Collins Pension File, NARA; Isaac Overton Service Record, Compiled Military Service Records of Volunteer Union Soldiers Who Served with the United States Colored Troops: Infantry Organizations, 36th through 40th, NARA.

47. Martin Rooks Pension File, NARA; Boone Nickens Pension File, NARA.

48. John Godett Pension File, NARA.

49. McPherson, *The Negro's Civil War*, 211.

50. Julius Mackey Pension File, NARA.

51. Joshua Nickens Pension File, NARA; Lawrence E. Weaver Pension File, NARA.

52. Claim of William Jacobs 301, Southern Claims Commission Approved Claims, NARA.

53. Claim of Asbury Reid 4303, Southern Claims Commission Approved Claims, NARA; Claim of Bryant Simmons 12254, Southern Claims Commission Approved Claims, NARA.

54. Claim of William Martin 20239, Southern Claims Commission Approved Claims, NARA; Claim of William Snellings Estate 13204, Southern Claims Commission Approved Claims, NARA.

55. "The Fight at Plymouth," *Fayetteville Semi-Weekly Observer*, May 5, 1864.

56. "William Scott," *A Folk History of Slavery in the United States from Interviews with Former Slaves, 1936–1938*, vol. 11, 261–62, Federal Writers' Project of the Works Progress Administration.

57. "Republican Celebration of the First of August in Murfreesborough," *Weekly Standard* (Raleigh), August 14, 1867.

58. For more on violence against people of color during Reconstruction, see Eric Foner, *Reconstruction: America's Unfinished Revolution, 1863–1877* (New York: Harper & Row, 1988). Other historians have found free people of color played a major role in Reconstruction politics and often held disproportionate influence in Reconstruction politics. See Thomas Holt, *Black over White: Negro Political Leadership in South Carolina during Reconstruction* (Urbana: University of Illinois Press, 1977); Edmund L. Drago, *Black Politicians and Reconstruction in Georgia: A Splendid Failure* (Athens: University of Georgia Press, 1992).

59. John Bizzell et al. Complaint, Records of the Field Offices for the State of North Carolina, Bureau of Refugees, Freedmen, and Abandoned Lands, 1865–1872, Roll 35, NARA.

60. James Gillem & Others Complaint, Records of the Field Offices for the State of North Carolina, Bureau of Refugees, Freedmen, and Abandoned Lands, 1865–1872, Roll 36, NARA.

61. *Public Laws of the State of North-Carolina, Passed by the General Assembly at the Session of 1865-'66, and 1861-'62-'63 and 1864, Together with Important Ordinances Passed by the Convention of 1866* (Raleigh: Robert W. Best, 1866), 101–5.

62. Steven Hahn, *A Nation under Our Feet: Black Political Struggles in the Rural South from Slavery to the Great Migration* (Cambridge: Belknap Press, 2003), 210.

63. "The Freedmen's Convention Official Proceedings," *Journal of Freedom* (Raleigh), October 7, 1865; Deborah Beckel, *Radical Reform: Interracial Politics in Post-Emancipation North Carolina* (Charlottesville: University of Virginia Press, 2011), 44–46.

64. *Minutes of the Freedmen's Convention, Held in the City of Raleigh, on the 2nd, 3rd, 4th and 5th of October 1866* (Raleigh: Standard Book and Job Office, 1866), 3–7, 26–27; Eric Foner, *Freedom's Lawmakers: A Directory of Black Officeholders during Reconstruction, Revised Edition* (Baton Rouge: Louisiana State University Press, 1996), 96–97.

65. "Negro Delegation from North Carolina," *Raleigh Register*, July 19, 1867.

66. John T. Reynolds to Capt. Alexander Moore, Records of the Field Offices for the State of North Carolina, Bureau of Refugees, Freedmen, and Abandoned Lands, 1865–1872, Roll 32, NARA; Jeffrey J. Crow, Paul D. Escott, and Flora J. Hatley, *A History of African Americans in North Carolina Revised Edition* (Raleigh: North Carolina Office of Archives and History, 2002), 235.

67. Parker D. Robbins to Commanding Officer of the Post, Records of the Field Offices for the State of North Carolina, Bureau of Refugees, Freedmen, and Abandoned Lands, 1865–1872, Roll 49, NARA.

68. "Republican Platform," *Daily Standard* (Raleigh), May 14, 1868.

69. "Fourth of July in Robeson," *Weekly Standard* (Raleigh), July 15, 1868.

70. Monthly Report of Sub-Assistant Commissioner (or Agent) February 1868, Records of the Field Offices for the State of North Carolina, Bureau of Refugees, Freedmen, and Abandoned Lands, 1865–1872, Roll 77, NARA; 1870 U.S. Federal Census, City of Wilmington, New Hanover County, North Carolina, 41; "James D. Sampson," *Negro History Bulletin* 3 (January 1940): 56; Foner, *Freedom's Lawmakers*, 188.

71. Foner, *Freedom's Lawmakers*, 44, 97, 144, 184. For more on Galloway, see David S. Cecelski, *The Fire of Freedom: Abraham Galloway and the Slaves' Civil War* (Chapel Hill: University of North Carolina Press, 2012).

72. For further discussion of the roles of areas with majorities of people of color in North Carolina politics, see Eric Anderson, *Race and Politics in North Carolina, 1872–1901: The Black Second* (Baton Rouge: Louisiana State University Press, 1981).

73. Crow, Escott, and Hatley, *A History of African Americans in North Carolina*, 235.

74. "Official," *Daily Standard* (Raleigh), May 21, 1868; "Municipal Affairs," *Wilmington Post*, July 30, 1868; "Proceedings of the Commissioners of Raleigh," *Daily Standard* (Raleigh), January 11, 1869; "The New Board of Alderman—The First Session," *Daily Journal* (Wilmington), January 12, 1869.

75. Petition, General Assembly Session Records, November 1869–March 1870, Box 5, Petitions, SANC.

76. Petition of Citizens of Burnt Swamp Township and Vicinity, Governors Papers, Box 225, Correspondence: Undated [1870], SANC.

77. Estate of Allen Lowrey, Robeson County Estates Records, Box 38, Lowrey, Allen 1866, SANC; Proclamation of Outlawry, Robeson County Criminal Action Papers Concerning Henry Berry Lowery, Box 183, Proclamation of "Lowrey Gang" as Outlaws, 1869, SANC; "State of North Carolina. $300 Reward," *Daily Journal* (Wilmington), December 14, 1866; "The Republicans of Robeson," *Weekly Standard* (Raleigh), March 18, 1868; Petition of Citizens of Burnt Swamp Township and Vicinity, Governors Papers, Box 225, Correspondence: Undated [1870], SANC; "A Proclamation," *Daily Standard* (Raleigh), November 11, 1870.

78. Crow, Escott, and Hatley, *A History of African Americans in North Carolina*, 88–93.

Epilogue: Remaking Race

1. E. Franklin Frazier, *The Negro Family in the United States* (Chicago: University of Chicago Press, 1939), 237.

2. David Dodge, "The Free Negro of North Carolina," *Atlantic Monthly* (January 1886): 30.

3. Frazier, *The Negro Family in the United States*, 136–37.

4. Isaac S. Harrell, "Gates County to 1860," in *Historical Papers of the Trinity College Historical Society* (Durham, NC: Seeman Printer, 1916), 66.

5. Karen I. Blu, *The Lumbee Problem: The Making of an American Indian People* (Cambridge: Cambridge University Press, 1980), 62–65; George E. Butler, *The Croatan Indians of Sampson County, North Carolina: Their Origin and Racial Status; a Plea for Separate Schools* (Durham, NC: Seeman Printery, 1916), 28–45. For the original texts of 1885 law, see *Laws and Resolutions of the State of North Carolina, Passed by the General Assembly at Its Session of 1885* (Raleigh: P. M. Hale, 1885), 92–94.

6. 1860 U.S. Federal Census, North Division, Robeson County, North Carolina, 78.

7. 1870 U.S. Federal Census, Burnt Swamp Township, Robeson County, North Carolina, 11; 1880 U.S. Federal Census, Burnt Swamp Township, Robeson County, North Carolina, Supervisor's District No. 3, Enumeration District No. 178, 25.

8. Claim of Hugh Oxendine 21330, Southern Claims Commission Approved Claims, NARA.

9. Hugh Oxendine Death Certificate, SANC.

10. 1860 U.S. Federal Census, North Division, Robeson County, North Carolina, 78.

11. John W. Oxendine Death Certificate, SANC.

12. For further discussion of free people of color and their descendants "passing" for white, see Virginia R. Domínguez, *White by Definition: Social Classification in Creole Louisiana* (New Bruns-

wick, NJ: Rutgers University Press, 1986); Daniel J. Sharfstein, *The Invisible Line: Three American Families and the Secret Journey from Black to White* (New York: Penguin Press, 2011).

13. In his study of Edgefield, South Carolina, Orville Vernon Burton discussed an example of this practice. See Orville Vernon Burton, *In My Father's House Are Many Mansions: Family and Community in Edgefield, South Carolina* (Chapel Hill: University of North Carolina Press, 1985), 222–23.

14. 1850 U.S. Federal Census, North Division, Duplin County, North Carolina, 45b.

15. Sheridan F. Nickens Service Record, Complied Service Records of Confederate Soldiers Who Served in Organizations from the State of North Carolina, NARA.

16. 1870 U.S. Federal Census, Kenansville Township, Duplin County, North Carolina, 29.

17. 1880 U.S. Federal Census, Magnolia Township, Duplin County, North Carolina, Supervisor's District No. 3, Enumeration District No. 78, 19.

18. Joe Edward Nickens Death Certificate, SANC; Alice Willis Death Certificate, SANC; Ida Nickens Bland Death Certificate, SANC.

19. Claim of Bilson B. Barber 4090, Southern Claims Commission Approved Claims, NARA.

20. 1850 U.S. Federal Census, The Southern Division, Surry County, North Carolina, 176b; 1860 U.S. Federal Census, Yadkin County, North Carolina, 112.

21. 1870 U.S. Federal Census, Buck Shoal Township, Yadkin County, North Carolina, 7.

22. 1850 U.S. Federal Census, Wolf Pit District, Richmond County, North Carolina, 280a; 1860 U.S. Federal Census, Rockingham District, Richmond County, North Carolina, 66.

23. 1870 U.S. Federal Census, Wolf Pit Township, Richmond County, North Carolina, 31; 1880 U.S. Federal Census, Wolf Pit Township, Richmond County, North Carolina, Supervisor's District No. 3, Enumeration District No, 170, 33.

24. Claim of William Jacobs 301, Southern Claims Commission Approved Claims, NARA.

25. 1900 U.S. Federal Census, Marks Creek Township, Richmond County, North Carolina, Supervisor's District No. 4, Enumeration District No. 86, 17.

26. Anderson Jacobs Death Certificate, SANC.

27. Ariela J. Gross, *What Blood Won't Tell: A History of Race on Trial in America* (Cambridge, MA: Harvard University Press, 2008), 8.

28. For further discussion of the importance of local beliefs and knowledge in determining racial categorization, see Gross, *What Blood Won't Tell.*

Bibliography

A NOTE ON PRIMARY SOURCES

This study uses a variety of sources to explore the category "free people of color" and the individuals who fell under it. In this book, court records, censuses, vital records, church minutes, wills, deeds, newspapers, pensions, and oral histories come together to reveal the life stories of individuals whose existence has long been buried in the archives. Each source provides a powerful and important insight into the past. Yet it is necessary to note their limitations. The destruction of significant portions of North Carolina's local court records, wills, and deeds has placed limits on this study. Localities across the state have lost records due to fires, floods, war, and simple carelessness. Many of the counties with the largest populations of free people of color have experienced significant record losses, including Halifax, Hertford, Robeson, and Wake. The predicament of the colonial-period records is particularly pitiful. The colonial records for most of the counties with significant populations of free people of color are either no longer in existence or partial. These limitations in the surviving records leave many questions about the lives and experiences of North Carolina's earliest free people of color. The links between free persons of color and North Carolina's indigenous people are obscured by the destruction of records in counties with significant colonial-period indigenous populations.

The surviving records from both the colonial and the national periods often only tell fragmented stories. Most counties, especially after the 1790s or so, have surviving court minute books that document the occurrences of court cases, recordings of deeds and apprentice agreement, and other local court matters. These records, however, are limited in their historical impact because the corresponding loose papers that relate to entries are often missing. Commonly, court clerks recorded court cases in minute books without providing information about the charge, the names of alleged victims, or the racial categorizations of the parties involved in the legal actions. This information is available only in the case papers, which are missing or incomplete for several counties. In most cases, quantitative analysis of court cases is severely limited by the clerks' bland or fickle notetaking. Furthermore, those case papers that survived tend to be not as rich as the local court records of other states. North Carolina's local courts rarely recorded oral testimony as part of the permanent record. The court minutes for counties such as Camden, Gates, Halifax, Perquimans, Tyrrell, Wake, and Warren note the issuance of freedom papers, which documented the free status of person of color. Yet North Carolina counties, unlike those in neighboring Virginia, had no formal system for recording the papers issued in registries.

Jurisdiction inconsistencies make North Carolina's records incredibly difficult to use for county-to-county comparative work or to determine statewide trends. During the national period, county governments as well as the General Assembly could grant freedom to enslaved people through manumission, and the various jurisdictions involved in changing the status of individuals from enslaved to free recorded their activities in a myriad of places. County-level manumissions appear in minute books, deed books, and wills, as well as in collections of loose papers. As mentioned earlier, county record collections frequently are fragmented. Therefore, county-level manumission records are scattered among record groups and are incomplete. At the state level, manumission records are better organized, but likely represent only a small fragment of the manumissions that took place in North Carolina. The state's court records have limitations similar to those of the manumission records. Most of North Carolina's court cases took place at the local level. Yet the process of dividing cases among the levels of local courts was inconsistent across counties. The counties lower courts, the Courts of Pleas and Quarter Sessions, heard most of their communities' less-consequential cases, while the District Courts and, later, county Superior Courts dealt with cases of higher severity along with appeals from the lower courts. Localities defined which cases belonged in each type of court differently. In one county, the Court of Pleas and Quarter Sessions would hear a particular type of crime while that same crime might be heard in a higher court in the neighboring county. Furthermore, the types of cases delved out to each court in a particular county could change over time.

Sources beyond those produced by the local courts have both similar and different types of limitations. Scholars have long recognized that federal census records have shortcomings. Census takers commonly miscounted populations by failing to register individuals or by overcounting. Federal guidelines also asked enumerators to categorize individuals into racial or color categories and identify whether those people were free or enslaved. Inconsistent racial or color categorization over the enumeration years is a common feature of the federal censuses. Depositions from pension records and other forms of oral testimony suffer from another set of limits including inconsistences, false testimony, and misremembering. Scholars continue to debate the use of oral sources, and those who use them must devise strategies to identify problems.

ARCHIVAL SOURCES

East Carolina University Joyner Library, Greenville, NC
    Timothy Hunter Papers

Library of Congress, Washington, DC
    Roberts Family Papers

Library of Virginia, Richmond, VA
    Lancaster County
        Wills
    Mecklenburg County
        Free Negro Register
    Norfolk County
        Free Negro and Slave Records; Tithable Lists
    Princess Anne County
        Deeds

National Archives and Records Administration, Washington, DC
    Civil War Pension Files
    Compiled Military Service Records of Volunteer Union Soldiers Who Served
        with the United States Colored Troops
    Compiled Service Records of Confederate Soldiers Who Served in Organiza-
        tions from the State of North Carolina
    Confederate Papers Relating to Citizens or Business Firms
    Records of the Field Offices for the State of North Carolina, Bureau of Refu-
        gees, Freedmen, and Abandoned Lands
    Revolutionary War Pension and Bounty-Land Warrant Application Files South-
        ern Claims Commission Approved Claims

Ohio History Center, Columbus, OH
    Logan County Register of Free Negroes

Southern Historical Collection, Chapel Hill, NC
    Cushing Biggs Hassell Papers
    Robert A. Jones Account Book
    Alexander Justice Papers
    Manumission Society Papers
    Thomas Smith McDowell Papers
    Nash County Historical Society Papers

William D. Valentine Diary
Samuel Jordan Wheeler Diaries

State Archives of North Carolina, Raleigh, NC
  Alamance County
      Court Minutes
  Barnes and Bardin Ledgers
  Beaufort County
      Court Minutes
  Ozette Pittman Bell Collection
  John N. Benners Journal
  Bertie County
      Apprentice Indentures; Civil Action Papers; Court Minutes; Estates Re-
         cords; Miscellaneous Records; Road, Bridge, and Ferry Records; Slave
         Records
  James Boon Papers
  Brunswick County
      Apprentice Bonds and Records
  Camden County
      Miscellaneous Records
  Carteret County
      Court Minutes; Miscellaneous Records
  Caswell County
      Apprentice Bonds and Records; Criminal Action Papers; Superior Court
         Minutes
  Chatham County
      Apprentice Bonds and Records
  John B. Chesson Papers
  Chowan County
      Court Minutes; Divorce Records; Miscellaneous Records; Miscellaneous
         Slave Records
  Christ Church, New Bern Parish Register
  Cleveland County
      Records of Slaves and Free Persons of Color
  Colonial Court Papers
      Criminal Papers
      Colonial Court Records
      Taxes and Accounts
  Craven County
      Court Minutes; Estates Records; Record of Deeds; Slaves and Free Negroes
         Records; Superior Court Minutes

Cumberland County
    Court Minutes; Record of Wills
Currituck County
    Court Minutes
Davidson County
    Apprentice Bonds and Records
Edenton District
    Records of the Superior Court
Edgecombe County
    Court Minutes; Wardens of the Poor Minutes; Wills
Franklin County
    Estates Records; Miscellaneous Records
Gates County
    Court Minutes; Criminal Action Papers; Election Records; Superior Court
        Minutes
General Assembly Session Records
Governors Papers
William Alexander Graham Papers
Granville County
    Criminal Action Papers; Estates Records; Record of Wills; Taxables; War-
        dens of the Poor
Halifax County
    Court Minutes
Haywood County
    Miscellaneous Records
Henderson County
    Criminal Action Papers; Superior Court Minutes
Hertford County
    Court Minutes
Hyde County
    Apprentice Bonds and Records; Court Minutes; Record of Deeds
Lincoln County
    Miscellaneous Records
Martin County
    Superior Court Minutes
McDowell County
    Records of Slaves and Free Persons of Color; Superior Court Minutes
Meherrin Baptist Church Minutes
Alonzo T. and Millard Mial Papers
Milton Presbyterian Church Session Minutes and Register
Montgomery County

Apprentice Bonds; Miscellaneous Records
Mount Tabor Baptist Church Minutes and Various Records
Nash County
    Apprentice Bonds; Court Minutes; Marriage Bonds; Miscellaneous
        Records
New Hanover County
    Apprentice Bonds and Records; Estates Records
Onslow County
    Apprentice Bonds and Records; Court Minutes
Orange County
    Civil Action Papers; Court Minutes; Election Records; Minutes of the
        Wardens of the Poor; Superior Court Minutes
Oxford Presbyterian Church Session Minutes
Pasquotank County
    Apprentice Bonds and Records; Civil Action Papers; County Court Min-
        utes; Estates Records; Superior Court Minutes
Perquimans County
    Criminal Action Papers; Poor House Records; Slave Papers; Superior Court
        Minutes
Person County
    Court of the Wardens of the Poor Minutes; Record of Wills
Robeson County
    Bastardy Bonds and Records; Civil Action Papers; Court Minutes; Crim-
        inal Action Papers; Divorce Records; Estates Records; Records Con-
        cerning Slaves and Free Persons of Color; Superior Court Minutes
Rockingham County
    Court Minutes; Records of Slaves and Free Persons of Color; Superior
        Court Minutes
Sacred Heart Cathedral Catholic Diocese of Raleigh, Baptisms, Marriages,
    Deaths, Originals
Saint John's Episcopal Church (Fayetteville) Parish Register
Sampson County
    Court Minutes; Estates Records; Miscellaneous Records
Slave Collection
Stokes County
    Court Minutes
Supreme Court Cases
Surry County
    Criminal Action Papers
John Vann Papers
Tyrrell County

Apprentice Bonds and Records; Records of Slaves and Free Persons of
Color; Superior Court Minutes
Wake County
Court Minutes
Wayne County
Apprentice Bonds and Records; Records of Slaves and Free Persons of Color
Wilkes County
Apprentice Bonds and Records

NEWSPAPERS

Carolina Federal Republican (New Bern)
Carolina Watchman (Salisbury)
Daily Journal (New Bern)
Daily Journal (Wilmington)
Daily Standard (Raleigh)
Encyclopedian Instructor (Edenton)
Fayetteville Observer (Fayetteville)
Freedom's Journal (New York)
General Assembly's Missionary Magazine (Philadelphia)
Greensboro Patriot (Greensboro)
Hillsborough Recorder (Hillsborough)
Journal of Freedom (Raleigh)
Morning Star (Raleigh)
National Democrat (Raleigh)
Newbern Sentinel (New Bern)
New York Age (New York)
News and Observer (Raleigh)
Norfolk Gazette and Publick Ledger (Norfolk)
North-Carolina Gazette (New Bern)
North Carolina Sentinel (New Bern)
North State Whig (Washington)
Raleigh Microcosm (Raleigh)
Raleigh Minerva (Raleigh)
Raleigh Register (Raleigh)
Weekly Standard (Raleigh)
Wilmington Chronicle (Wilmington)
Wilmington Gazette (Wilmington)
Wilmington Post (Wilmington)

PUBLISHED PRIMARY SOURCES

Abstract of the Returns of the Fifth Census, Showing the Number of Free People, the Number of Slaves, the Federal or Representative Number, and the Aggregate of Each County of Each State of the United States. Washington, DC: Duff Green, 1832.

Acts Passed by the General Assembly of the State of North Carolina, at the Session of 1830–31. Raleigh: Lawrence & Lemay, 1831.

Acts Passed by the General Assembly of the State of North Carolina, at the Session of 1831–32. Raleigh: Lawrence & Lemay, 1832.

A Folk History of Slavery in the United States from Interviews with Former Slaves, 1936–1938, Federal Writers' Project of the Works Progress Administration.

Annual Catalogue of the Officers and Students of Oberlin College for the College Year 1858–59. Oberlin: Evangelist Office, 1858.

Census for 1820. Washington: Gales & Seaton, 1821.

Clark, Walter, ed. *The State Records of North Carolina,* vol. 23. Goldsboro: Nash Brothers, 1904.

——. *The State Records of North Carolina,* vol. 24. Goldsboro: Nash Brothers, 1906.

——. *The State Records of North Carolina,* vol. 25. Goldsboro: Nash Brothers, 1906.

——. *The State Records of North Carolina,* vol. 22. Goldsboro: Nash Brothers, 1907.

Compendium of the Enumeration of the Inhabitants and Statistics of the United States, As Obtained at the Department of State, from the Returns of the Sixth Census. Washington, DC: Thomas Allen, 1841.

Green, John P. *Fact Stranger than Fiction: Seventy-Five Years of a Busy Life with Reminiscences of Many Great and Good Men and Women.* Cleveland: Riehl Printing Company, 1920.

Guild, June Purcell. *Black Laws of Virginia.* Richmond: Whittet & Shepperson, 1936.

Heads of Families at the First Census of the United States Taken in the Year 1790 North Carolina. Washington, DC: Government Printing Office, 1908.

Journal of the House of Commons of the State of North-Carolina At a General Assembly, begun and held at the City of Raleigh, on Monday the twentieth Day of November, in the Year of our Lord One Thousand Eight Hundred and Nine, and in the Thirty-Fourth Year of the Independence of the United States of America: It being the first Session of this General Assembly. Raleigh: Gales & Seaton, 1809.

Journal of the Senate of the General Assembly of the State of North-Carolina at Its Session of 1860-'61. Raleigh: John Spelman, 1861.

Journals of the Senate and House of Commons of the General Assembly of the State of North Carolina, at its Session in 1825. Raleigh: Bell & Lawrence, 1826.

Journals of the Senate and House of Commons of the General Assembly of the State of North-Carolina, at the Session of 1826–27. Raleigh: Lawrence & Lemay, 1827.

Journals of the Senate and House of Commons of the General Assembly of the State of North-Carolina, at the Session of 1828–29. Raleigh: Lawrence & Lemay, 1829.

Journals of the Senate and House of Commons of the General Assembly of the State of North Carolina, at the Session of 1830–1831. Raleigh: Lawrence & Lemay, 1831.

Journals of the Senate and House of Commons of the General Assembly of the State of North Carolina at the Session of 1831–32. Raleigh: Lawrence & Lemay, 1832.

Journal of the Senate of North-Carolina At a General Assembly begun and held at the City of Raleigh, on Monday the nineteenth Day of November, in the Year of our Lord One Thousand Eight Hundred and Four, and in the Twenty Ninth Year of the Independence of the United States of America: It being the first Session of this General Assembly. Raleigh: Gales, 1805.

Journal of the Senate of North-Carolina At a General Assembly, begun and held at the City of Raleigh, on Monday the twentieth Day of November, in the Year of our Lord One Thousand Eight Hundred and Nine, and in the Thirty-Fourth Year of the Independence of the United States of America: It being the first Session of this General Assembly. Raleigh: Gales & Seaton, 1809.

The Laws of North-Carolina, Enacted in the Year 1821. Raleigh: Thomas Henderson, 1822.

Laws and Resolutions of the State of North Carolina, Passed by the General Assembly at Its Session of 1885. Raleigh: P. M. Hale, 1885.

Laws of the State of North Carolina Passed by the General Assembly at the Session of 1840–41. Raleigh: W. R. Gales, 1841.

Laws of the State of North Carolina Passed by the General Assembly at the Session of 1844–45. Raleigh: Thomas J. Lemay, 1845.

Laws of the State of North Carolina Revised, Under the Authority of the General Assembly. Raleigh: J. Gales, 1821.

Martin, Francois Xavier, ed. *The Public Acts of the General Assembly of North-Carolina, Volume I.* Newbern: Martin & Ogden, 1804.

Minutes of the Freedmen's Convention, Held in the City of Raleigh, on the 2nd, 3rd, 4th and 5th of October 1866. Raleigh: Standard Book and Job Office, 1866.

Muster Rolls of the Soldiers of the War of 1812: Detached from the Militia of North Carolina, in 1812 and 1814. Raleigh: C. Raboteau, 1851.

Population of the United States in 1860. Washington, DC: Government Printing Office, 1864.

Proceedings and Debates of the Convention of North-Carolina, Called to Amend the Constitution of the State; Which Assembled at Raleigh, June 4, 1835. Raleigh: Joseph Gales & Son, 1836.

Public Laws of the State of North Carolina Passed by the General Assembly at Its Session of 1858–59. Raleigh: Holden & Wilson, 1859.

Public Laws of the State of North Carolina Passed by the General Assembly at Its Session of 1860–61. Raleigh: John Spelman, 1861.

Public Laws of the State of North-Carolina, Passed by the General Assembly at the Session of 1865–'66, and 1861–'62, –'63 and 1864, Together with Important Ordinances Passed by the Convention of 1866. Raleigh: Robert W. Best, 1866.

Quinquennial Catalogue of Oberlin College. Oberlin, OH: News Printing Company, 1900.

Return of the Whole Number of Persons within the Several Districts of the United States, According to "An act providing for the Second Census or Enumeration of the Inhabitants of the United States." 1801.

Revised Code of North Carolina Enacted by the General Assembly at the Session of 1854. Prepared under the Acts of the General Assembly. Boston: Little, Brown & Company, 1855.

The Revised Statutes of the State of North Carolina Passed by the General Assembly at the Session of 1836–7. Raleigh: Turner & Hughes, 1837.

Rules of Order for the Government of the General Assembly of North Carolina: To Which Are Prefixed the Constitutions of North Carolina and of the United States. Raleigh: Philo White, 1836.

The Seventh Census of the United States: 1850. By J. D. B. DeBow, Superintendent of the United States Census. Washington, DC: Robert Armstrong, Public Printer, 1853.

Walker, David. *Walker's Appeal, in Four Articles; Together with a Preamble, To the Coloured Citizens of the World, But in Particular, and Very Expressly, to Those of the United States of America.* Boston: David Walker, 1830.

SECONDARY SOURCES

Alexander, Adele Logan. *Free Women of Color in Rural Georgia, 1789–1879.* Fayetteville: University of Arkansas Press, 1991.

Allen, Richard B. *Slaves, Freedmen, and Indentured Laborers in Colonial Mauritius.* New York: Cambridge University Press, 1999.

———. "Free Women of Colour and Socio-Economic Marginality in Mauritius, 1767–1830." *Slavery and Abolition* 26 (August 2005): 181–97.

———. "Marie Rozette and Her World: Class, Ethnicity, Gender, and Race in Late Eighteenth-and Early Nineteenth-Century Mauritius." *Journal of Social History* 45 (2011): 245–65.

Anderson, Benedict. *Imagined Communities: Reflections on the Origin and Spread of Nationalism.* Rev. ed. New York: Verso, 1991.

Anderson, Eric. *Race and Politics in North Carolina, 1872–1901: The Black Second.* Baton Rouge: Louisiana State University Press, 1981.

Aslakson, Kenneth R. *Making Race in the Courtroom: The Legal Construction of Three Races in Early New Orleans.* New York: New York University Press, 2014.

Barfield, Rodney D., and Patricia M. Marshall. *Thomas Day: African American Furniture Maker.* Raleigh: North Carolina Office of Archives and History, 2005.

Barnes, L. Diane. *Artisan Workers in the Upper South: Petersburg, Virginia, 1820–1865.* Baton Rouge: Louisiana State University Press, 2008.

Beckel, Deborah. *Radical Reform: Interracial Politics in Post-Emancipation North Carolina.* Charlottesville: University of Virginia Press, 2011.

Berkhofer, Robert F., Jr. *The White Man's Indian: Images of the American Indian from Columbus to the Present.* New York: Alfred A. Knopf, 1978.

Berlin, Ira. *Slaves without Masters: The Free Negro in the Antebellum South.* New York: New Press, 1974.

———. *Many Thousands Gone: The First Two Centuries of Slavery in North America.* Cambridge: Belknap Press, 1998.

Berry, Brewton. *Almost White.* New York: Macmillan Company, 1963.

Berry, Mary F. "Negro Troops in Blue and Gray: The Louisiana Native Guards, 1861–1863." *Louisiana History* 8 (Spring 1967): 165–90.

Bishir, Catherine W. *Crafting Lives: African American Artisans in New Bern, North Carolina, 1770–1900.* Chapel Hill: University of North Carolina Press, 2013.

Blu, Karen I. *The Lumbee Problem: The Making of an American Indian People.* Cambridge: Cambridge University Press, 1980.

Bogger, Tommy L. *Free Blacks in Norfolk, Virginia, 1790–1860: The Darker Side of Freedom.* Charlottesville: University Press of Virginia, 1997.

Breen, T. H., and Stephen Innes. *"Myne Owne Ground": Race and Freedom on Virginia's Eastern Shore, 1640–1676.* New York: Oxford University Press, 1980.

Brooks, James F., ed. *Confounding the Color Line: The Indian-Black Experience in North America.* Lincoln: University of Nebraska Press, 2002.

Brophy, Alfred L. "The Nat Turner Trials." *North Carolina Law Review* 91 (2013): 1817–1880.

Broussard, Joyce Linda. *Stepping Lively in Place: The Not-Married Women of Civil-War-Era Natchez, Mississippi.* Athens: University of Georgia Press, 2016.

Brown, Kathleen M. *Good Wives, Nasty Wenches, and Anxious Patriarchs: Gender, Race, and Power in Colonial Virginia.* Chapel Hill: University of North Carolina Press, 1996.

Brown, Letitia Woods. *Free Negroes in the District of Columbia 1790–1846.* New York: Oxford University Press, 1972.

Brubaker, Rogers. *Ethnicity without Groups.* Cambridge, MA: Harvard University Press, 2004.

———. *Grounds for Difference.* Cambridge, MA: Harvard University Press, 2015.

———. *Trans: Gender and Race in an Age of Unsettled Identities.* Princeton, NJ: Princeton University Press, 2016.

Brubaker, Rogers, Mara Loveman, and Peter Stamatov. "Ethnicity as Cognition." *Theory and Society* 33 (2004): 31–64.

Brubaker, Rogers, Margit Feischmidt, Jon Fox, and Liana Grancea. *Nationalist Politics and Everyday Ethnicity in a Transylvanian Town.* Princeton, NJ: Princeton University Press, 2006.

Buchanan, Thomas C. *Black Life on the Mississippi: Slaves, Free Blacks, and the Western Steamboat World.* Chapel Hill: University of North Carolina Press, 2004.

Buckley, Thomas E., S. J. "Unfixing Race: Class, Power, and Identity in an Interracial Family." *Virginia Magazine of History and Biography* 102 (July 1994): 346–80.

Burton, Orville Vernon. *In My Father's House Are Many Mansions: Family and Community in Edgefield, South Carolina.* Chapel Hill: University of North Carolina Press, 1985.

Bynum, Victoria E. *Unruly Women: The Politics of Social and Sexual Control in the Old South.* Chapel Hill: University of North Carolina Press, 1992.

———. *The Free State of Jones: Mississippi's Longest Civil War.* Chapel Hill: University of North Carolina Press, 2001.

Byrd, William L., III. *In Full Force and Virtue: North Carolina Emancipation Records, 1713–1860.* Westminster: Heritage Books, 1999.

———. *Against the Peace and Dignity of the State: North Carolina Laws Regarding Slaves, Free Persons of Color, and Indians.* Westminster: Heritage Books, 2007.

Calloway, Colin G., ed. *After King Philip's War: Presence and Persistence in Indian New England.* Hanover: University Press of New England, 1997.

Calloway, Colin G., and Neal Salisbury, eds. *Reinterpreting New England Indians and the Colonial Experience.* Boston: Colonial Society of Massachusetts, 2003.

Candlin, Kit, and Cassandra Pybus. *Enterprising Women: Gender, Race, and Power in the Revolutionary Atlantic.* Athens: University of Georgia Press, 2015.

Cecelski, David S. *The Waterman's Song: Slavery and Freedom in Maritime North Carolina.* Chapel Hill: University of North Carolina Press, 2001.

———. *The Fire of Freedom: Abraham Galloway and the Slaves' Civil War.* Chapel Hill: University of North Carolina Press, 2012.

Cecil-Fronsman, Bill. *Common Whites: Class and Culture in Antebellum North Carolina.* Lexington: University of Kentucky Press, 1992.

Censer, Jane Turner. *North Carolina Planters and Their Children, 1800–1860.* Baton Rouge: Louisiana State University Press, 1984.

Chater, Kathy. "Black People in England, 1660–1807." *Parliamentary History* 26 (2007): 66–83.

Chestnutt, Charles W. "The Free Colored People of North Carolina." *Southern Workman* 31 (1902): 136–41.

Clark, Emily. *The Strange History of the American Quadroon: Free Women of Color in the Revolutionary Atlantic World.* Chapel Hill: University of North Carolina Press, 2013.

Clegg, Claude A., III. *The Price of Liberty: African Americans and the Making of Liberia.* Chapel Hill: University of North Carolina Press, 2004.

Cohen, David W., and Jack P. Greene, eds. *Neither Slave Nor Free: The Freedmen of African Descent in the Slave Societies of the New World.* Baltimore: Johns Hopkins University Press, 1972.

Coleman, Arica L. *That the Blood Stay Pure: African Americans, Native Americans, and the Predicament of Race and Identity in Virginia.* Bloomington: Indiana University Press, 2013.

Cope, R. Douglas. *The Limits of Racial Domination: Plebeian Society in Colonial Mexico City, 1660–1720.* Madison: University of Wisconsin Press, 1994.

Cott, Nancy F. *Public Vows: A History of Marriage and the Nation.* Cambridge, MA: Harvard University Press, 2000.

Crenshaw, Kimberlé. "Mapping the Margins: Intersectionality, Identity Politics, and Violence against Women of Color." *Stanford Law Review* 43 (July 1991): 1241–1300.

Dangerfield, David W. "Turning the Earth: Free Black Yeomanry in the Antebellum South Carolina Lowcountry." *Agricultural History* 89 (Spring 2015): 200–224.

Daynes, Sarah, and Orville Lee. *Desire for Race.* New York: Cambridge University Press, 2008.

Deal, J. Douglas. *Race and Class in Colonial Virginia: Indians, Englishmen, and Africans on the Eastern Shore during the Seventeenth Century.* New York: Garland Publishing, 1993.

Degler, Carl N. *Neither Black nor White: Slavery and Race Relations in Brazil and the United States.* New York: Macmillan Publishing, 1971.

Delaney, Ted, and Phillip Wayne Rhodes. *Free Blacks of Lynchburg, Virginia, 1805–1865.* Lynchburg: Warwick House Publishing, 2001.

Dodge, David. "The Free Negro of North Carolina." *Atlantic Monthly* (January 1886): 20–30.

Dominguez, Virginia R. *White by Definition: Social Classification in Creole Louisiana.* New Brunswick, NJ: Rutgers University Press, 1986.

Dorsey, Jennifer Hull. *Hirelings: African American Workers and Free Labor in Early Maryland.* Ithaca, NY: Cornell University Press, 2011.

Drago, Edmund L. *Black Politicians and Reconstruction in Georgia: A Splendid Failure.* Baton Rouge: Louisiana State University Press, 1982.

DuBois, Laurent. *Avengers of the New World: The Story of the Haitian Revolution.* Cambridge, MA: Belknap Press, 2004.

Edwards, Laura F. *Scarlett Doesn't Live Here Anymore: Southern Women in the Civil War Era.* Urbana: University of Illinois Press, 2000.

——. *The People and Their Peace: Legal Culture and the Transformation of Inequality in the Post-Revolutionary South.* Chapel Hill: University of North Carolina Press, 2009.

Ely, Melvin Patrick. *Israel on the Appomattox: A Southern Experiment in Black Freedom from the 1790s through the Civil War.* New York: Alfred A. Knopf, 2004.

Escott, Paul D., ed. *North Carolinians in the Era of the Civil War and Reconstruction.* Chapel Hill: University of North Carolina Press, 2008.

Evans, William McKee. *To Die Game: The Story of the Lowry Band, Indian Guerrillas of Reconstruction.* Baton Rouge: Louisiana State University Press, 1971.

Faust, Drew Gilpin. *This Republic of Suffering: Death and the American Civil War.* New York: Alfred A. Knopf, 2008.

Fields, Barbara Jeanne. *Slavery and Freedom on the Middle Ground: Maryland during the Nineteenth Century.* New Haven, CT: Yale University Press, 1985.

——. "Slavery, Race and Ideology in the United States of America." *New Left Review* (May–June 1990): 95–118.

——. "'Origins of the New South' and the Negro Question." *Journal of Southern History* 67 (2001): 811–26.

Fischer, Kirsten. *Suspect Relations: Sex, Race, and Resistance in Colonial North Carolina.* Ithaca, NY: Cornell University Press, 2002.

Fisher, Andrew B., and Matthew D. O'Hara, eds. *Imperial Subjects: Race and Identity in Colonial Latin America.* Durham, NC: Duke University Press, 2009.

Foner, Eric. *Reconstruction: America's Unfinished Revolution, 1863–1877.* New York: Harper & Row, 1988.

———. *Freedom's Lawmakers: A Directory of Black Officeholders during Reconstruction Revised Edition.* Baton Rouge: Louisiana State University Press, 1996.

Forbes, Jack D. *Black Africans and Native Americans: Color, Race and Caste in the Evolution of Red-Black Peoples.* New York: Basil Blackwell, 1988.

Ford, Lacy K. *Deliver Us from Evil: The Slavery Question in the Old South.* New York: Oxford University Press, 2009.

Ford, Lisa. *Settler Sovereignty: Jurisdiction and Indigenous People in America and Australia,1788–1836.* Cambridge, MA: Harvard University Press, 2010.

Franklin, John Hope. *The Free Negro in North Carolina 1790–1860.* Chapel Hill: University of North Carolina Press, 1943.

Franklin, John Hope, and Loren Schweninger. *In Search of the Promised Land: A Slave Family in the Old South.* New York: Oxford University Press, 2006.

Frazier, E. Franklin. *The Free Negro Family: A Study of Family Origins before the Civil War.* Nashville: Fisk University Press, 1932.

———. *The Negro Family in the United States.* Chicago: University of Chicago Press, 1939.

Freehling, William W. *The Road to Disunion: Secessionists at Bay, 1776–1854.* New York: Oxford University Press, 1990.

———. *The Road to Disunion: Secessionists Triumphant, 1854–1861.* New York: Oxford University Press, 2007.

French, Jan Hoffman. *Legalizing Identities: Becoming Black or Indian in Brazil's Northeast.* Chapel Hill: University of North Carolina Press, 2009.

Garrow, Patrick H. *The Mattamuskeet Documents: A Study in Social History.* Raleigh: Division of Archives and History, 1995.

Gatewood, Willard B., Jr. "'To Be Truly Free': Louis Sheridan and the Colonization of Liberia." *Civil War History* 29 (December 1983): 332–48.

Gross, Ariela J. *What Blood Won't Tell: A History of Race on Trial in America.* Cambridge, MA: Harvard University Press, 2008.

Gutman, Herbert G. *The Black Family in Slavery and Freedom, 1750–1925.* New York: Vintage Books, 1976.

Hahn, Steven. *A Nation under Our Feet: Black Political Struggles in the Rural South from Slavery to the Great Migration.* Cambridge, MA: Belknap Press, 2003.

Hanger, Kimberly S. "'Desiring Total Tranquility' and Not Getting It: Conflict Involving Free Black Women in Spanish New Orleans." *Americas* 54 (April 1998): 541–56.

Harmon, Alexandra. *Indians in the Making: Ethnic Relations and Indian Identities around Puget Sound.* Berkeley: University of California Press, 1998.

Heinegg, Paul. *Free African Americans of Virginia, North Carolina, South Carolina, Maryland and Delaware.* http://www.freeafricanamericans.com.

Herndon, Ruth Wallis, and John E. Murray, eds. *Children Bound to Labor: The Pauper Apprentice System in Early America.* Ithaca, NY: Cornell University Press, 2009.

Higginbotham, A. Leon, Jr. *In the Matter of Color: Race and the American Legal Process: The Colonial Period.* New York: Oxford University Press, 1978.

Hodes, Martha. *White Women, Black Men: Illicit Sex in the Nineteenth-Century South.* New Haven, CT: Yale University Press, 1997.

Holt, Michael F. *The Fate of Their County: Politicians, Slavery Extension, and the Coming of the Civil War.* New York: Hill & Wang, 2004.

Holt, Thomas C. *Black over White: Negro Political Leadership in South Carolina during Reconstruction.* Urbana: University of Illinois Press, 1977.

Horton, James Oliver. *Free People of Color: Inside the African American Community.* Washington, DC: Smithsonian Institution Press, 1993.

Horton, James Oliver, and Lois E. Horton. *In Hope of Liberty: Culture, Community, and Protest among Northern Free Blacks, 1700–1860.* New York: Oxford University Press, 1997.

Hunter, Tera W. *Bound in Wedlock: Slave and Free Black Marriage in the Nineteenth Century.* Cambridge, MA: Belknap Press, 2017.

Hyde, Samuel C., Jr., ed. *Plain Folk of the South Revisited.* Baton Rouge: Louisiana State University Press, 1997.

Jackson, Luther Porter. *Free Negro Labor and Property Holding in Virginia, 1830–1860.* New York: D. Appleton-Century Company, 1942.

Jacobs, Margaret D. *White Mother to a Dark Race: Settler Colonialism, Maternalism, and the Removal of Indigenous Children in the American West and Australia, 1880–1940.* Lincoln: University of Nebraska Press, 2009.

Jeffrey, Thomas E. *State Parties and National Politics: North Carolina, 1815–1861.* Athens: University of Georgia Press, 1989.

Jennison, Watson W. *Cultivating Race: The Expansion of Slavery in Georgia, 1750–1860.* Lexington: University Press of Kentucky, 2012.

Johnson, Guion Griffis. *Ante-bellum North Carolina: Social History.* Chapel Hill: University of North Carolina, 1937.

Johnson, Michael P., and James L. Roark. *Black Masters: A Free Family of Color in the Old South.* New York: W. W. Norton and Company, 1984a.

———. *No Chariot Let Down: Charleston's Free People of Color on the Eve of the Civil War.* Chapel Hill: University of North Carolina Press, 1984b.

Johnson, Whittington B. "Free African-American Women in Savannah, 1800–1860: Affluence and Autonomy amid Adversity." *Georgia Historical Quarterly* 76 (Summer 1992): 260-83.

Johnston, James Hugo. *Race Relations in Virginia and Miscegenation in the South, 1776–1860.* Amherst: University of Massachusetts Press, 1970.

Jones, Martha S. *Birthright Citizens: A History of Race and Rights in Antebellum America.* New York: Cambridge University Press, 2018.

Jordan, Winthrop D. *White over Black: American Attitudes toward the Negro 1550–1812.* Chapel Hill: University of North Carolina Press, 1968.

Katzew, Ilona, and Susan Deans-Smith, eds. *Race and Classification: The Case of Mexican America.* Stanford, CA: Stanford University Press, 2009.

Kein, Sybil, ed. *Creole: The History and Legacy of Louisiana's Free People of Color.* Baton Rouge: Louisiana State University Press, 2000.

Kennedy, N. Brent, and Robyn Vaughan Kennedy. *The Melungeons: The Resurrection of a Proud People.* Rev. ed. Macon, GA: Mercer University Press, 1997.

Kenzer, Robert C. *Kinship and Neighborhood in a Southern Community: Orange County, North Carolina, 1849–1881.* Knoxville: University of Tennessee Press, 1987.

———. *Enterprising Southerners: Black Economic Success in North Carolina, 1865–1915.* Charlottesville: University Press of Virginia, 1997.

King, Wilma. *The Essence of Liberty: Free Black Women during the Slave Era.* Columbia: University of Missouri Press, 2006.

Kirby, Jack Temple. *Poquosin: A Study of Rural Landscape and Society.* Chapel Hill: University of North Carolina Press, 1995.

Klein, Herbert S. *Slavery in the Americas: A Comparative Study of Virginia and Cuba.* Chicago: University of Chicago Press, 1967.

Koger, Larry. *Black Slaveowners: Free Black Slave Masters in South Carolina, 1790–1860.* Columbia: University of South Carolina Press, 1985.

LaRoche, Cheryl Janifer. *Free Black Communities and the Underground Railroad: The Geography of Resistance.* Urbana: University of Illinois Press, 2014.

La Vere, David. *The Tuscarora War: Indians, Settlers, and the Fight for the Carolina Colonies.* Chapel Hill: University of North Carolina, 2013.

Lee, Susanna Michele. *Claiming the Union: Citizenship in the Post–Civil War South.* New York: Cambridge University Press, 2014.

Link, William A., David Brown, Brian Ward, and Martyn Bone. *Creating Citizenship in the Nineteenth-Century South.* Gainesville: University Press of Florida, 2013.

Litwack, Leon F. *North of Slavery: The Negro in the Free States, 1790–1860.* Chicago: University of Chicago Press, 1961.

Loveman, Mara. "Is 'Race' Essential?" *American Sociological Review* 64 (December 1999): 891–98.

———. *National Colors: Racial Classification and the State in Latin America.* New York: Oxford University Press, 2014.

Lowery, Malinda Maynor. *Lumbee Indians in the Jim Crow South: Race, Identity, and the Making of a Nation.* Chapel Hill: University of North Carolina Press, 2010.

———. *The Lumbee Indians: An American Struggle.* Chapel Hill: University of North Carolina Press, 2018.

Lubet, Steven. *The "Colored Hero" of Harper's Ferry: John Anthony Copeland and the War against Slavery.* New York: Cambridge University Press, 2015.

Mandell, Daniel R. *Tribe, Race, History: Native Americans in Southern New England, 1780-1880.* Baltimore: Johns Hopkins University Press, 2008.

Maris-Wolf, Ted. *Family Bonds: Free Blacks and Re-enslavement Law in Antebellum Virginia.* Chapel Hill: University of North Carolina Press, 2015.

Marshall, Patricia Phillips, and Jo Ramsay Leimenstoll. *Thomas Day: Master Craftsman and Free Man of Color.* Chapel Hill: University of North Carolina Press, 2010.

McCleskey, Turk. *The Road to Black Ned's Forge: A Story of Race, Sex, and Trade on the Colonial American Frontier.* Charlottesville: University of Virginia Press, 2014.

McClintock, Anne. *Imperial Leather: Race, Gender and Sexuality in the Colonial Contest.* New York: Routledge, 1995.

McPherson, James M. *The Negro's Civil War: How American Negroes Felt and Acted during the War for the Union.* New York: Pantheon Books, 1965.

———. *Battle Cry of Freedom: The Civil War Era.* New York: Oxford University Press, 1988.

Medford, Edna Greene. "'I Was Always a Union Man': The Dilemma of Free Blacks in Confederate Virginia." *Slavery and Abolition* 15 (December 1994): 1–16.

Merrell, James H. *The Indians' New World: Catawbas and Their Neighbors from European Contact through the Era of Removal.* Chapel Hill: University of North Carolina Press, 1989.

Mills, Gary B. *The Forgotten People: Cane River's Creoles of Color.* Baton Rouge: Louisiana State University Press, 1977.

———. "Patriotism Frustrated: The Native Guards of Confederate Natchitoches." *Louisiana History* 18 (Autumn 1977): 437–51.

———. "Miscegenation and the Free Negro in Antebellum 'Anglo' Alabama: A Reexamination of Southern Race Relations," *Journal of American History* 68 (June 1981): 16–34.

Millward, Jessica. *Finding Charity's Folks: Enslaved and Free Black Women in Maryland.* Athens: University of Georgia Press, 2015.

Milteer, Warren E., Jr. "The Strategies of Forbidden Love: Family across Racial Boundaries in Nineteenth-Century North Carolina." *Journal of Social History* 47 (Spring 2014): 612–26.

———. "Life in a Great Dismal Swamp Community: Free People of Color in Pre–Civil War Gates County, North Carolina." *North Carolina Historical Review* 91 (April 2014): 144–70.

———. "From Indians to Colored People: The Problem of Racial Categories and the Persistence of the Chowans in North Carolina." *North Carolina Historical Review* 93 (January 2016): 28–57.

Morgan, Edmund S. *American Slavery, American Freedom: The Ordeal of Colonial Virginia.* New York: W. W. Norton and Company, 1975.

Myers, Amrita Chakrabarti. *Forging Freedom: Black Women and the Pursuit of Liberty in Antebellum Charleston.* Chapel Hill: University of North Carolina Press, 2011.

Neidenbach, Elizabeth C. "'Refugee from St. Domingue Living in This City': The Geography of Social Networks in Testaments of Refugee Free Women of Color in New Orleans." *Journal of Urban History* 42 (2016): 841–62.

Oakes, James. *Freedom National: The Destruction of Slavery in the United States, 1861–1865.* New York: W. W. Norton and Company, 2013.

O'Brien, Jean. *Dispossession by Degrees: Indian Land and Identity in Natick, Massachusetts, 1650–1790.* New York: Cambridge University Press, 1997.

———. *Firsting and Lasting: Writing Indians Out of Existence in New England.* Minneapolis: University of Minnesota Press, 2010.

Painter, Nell Irvin. *Southern History across the Color Line.* Chapel Hill: University of North Carolina Press, 2002.

Patterson, Orlando. *Slavery and Social Death: A Comparative Study.* Cambridge, MA: Harvard University Press, 1982.

Perdue, Theda. *"Mixed Blood" Indians: Racial Construction in the Early South.* Athens: University of Georgia Press, 2003.

Powell, William S. *North Carolina through Four Centuries.* Chapel Hill: University of North Carolina Press, 1989.

Raboteau, Albert J. *Canaan Land: A Religious History of African Americans.* New York: Oxford University Press, 2001.

Race and Slavery Petitions Project, https://library.uncg.edu/slavery/petitions/

Rappaport, Joanne. *The Disappearing Mestizo: Configuring Difference in the Colonial New Kingdom of Granada.* Durham, NC: Duke University Press, 2014.

Richardson, Marvin. "Racial Choices: The Emergence of the Haliwa-Saponi Indian Tribe, 1835-1971." Ph.D. diss., University of North Carolina at Chapel Hill, 2016.

Roberts, Dorothy. *Fatal Invention: How Science, Politics, and Big Business Re-Create Race in the Twenty-First Century.* New York: New Press, 2011.

Roediger, David R. *The Wages of Whiteness: Race and the Making of the American Working Class.* Rev. ed. London: Verso, 1999.

Rohrs, Richard C. "The Free Black Experience in Antebellum Wilmington, North Carolina: Refining Generalizations about Race Relations." *Journal of Southern History* 78 (August 2012): 613–38.

———. "Training in an 'art, trade, mystery and employment': Opportunity or Exploitation of Free Black Apprentices in New Hanover County, North Carolina, 1820–1859?" *North Carolina Historical Review* 90 (April 2013): 127–48.

Rothman, Joshua D. *Notorious in the Neighborhood: Sex and Families across the Color Line in Virginia, 1781–1861.* Chapel Hill: University of North Carolina Press, 2003.

Rountree, Helen C. *Pocahontas's People: The Powhatan Indians of Virginia through Four Centuries.* Norman: University of Oklahoma, 1990.

Rountree, Helen C., and Thomas E. Davidson. *Eastern Shore Indians of Virginia and Maryland.* Charlottesville: University of Virginia, 1997.

Russell, John H. *The Free Negro in Virginia 1619–1865*. Baltimore: John Hopkins University Press, 1913.

Saunt, Claudio. *Black, White, and Indian: Race and the Unmaking of an American Family.* Oxford: Oxford University Press, 2005.

Schafer, Judith Kelleher. *Becoming Free, Remaining Free: Manumission and Enslavement in New Orleans, 1846–1862.* Baton Rouge: Louisiana State University Press, 2003.

Schultz, Mark. *The Rural Face of White Supremacy: Beyond Jim Crow.* Urbana: University of Illinois Press, 2005.

Schweninger, Loren. *Black Property Owners in the South, 1790–1915.* Urbana: University of Illinois Press, 1990.

———. "John Carruthers Stanly and the Anomaly of Black Slaveholding." *North Carolina Historical Review* 67 (April 1990): 159–92.

———. "Property Owning Free African-American Women in the South, 1800–1870." *Journal of Women's History* 1 (Winter 1990): 13–44.

Sensbach, Jon F. *A Separate Canaan: The Making of an Afro-Moravian World in North Carolina, 1763–1840.* Chapel Hill: University of North Carolina Press, 1998.

Sharfstein, Daniel J. *The Invisible Line: Three American Families and the Secret Journey from Black to White.* New York: Penguin Press, 2011.

Shoemaker, Nancy. *Native American Whalemen and the World: Indigenous Encounters and the Contingency of Race.* Chapel Hill: University of North Carolina Press, 2015.

Shyllon, Folarin. *Black People in Britain 1555–1833.* London: Oxford University Press, 1977.

Spear, Jennifer M. *Race, Sex, and Social Order in Early New Orleans.* Baltimore: Johns Hopkins University Press, 2009.

Spickard, Paul R. *Mixed Blood: Intermarriage and Ethnic Identity in Twentieth-Century America.* Madison: University of Wisconsin Press, 1989.

Sterkx, H. E. *The Free Negro in Ante-Bellum Louisiana.* Rutherford: Fairleigh Dickinson University Press, 1972.

Stevenson, Brenda E. *Life in Black and White: Family and Community in the Slave South.* New York: Oxford University Press, 1996.

Stoler, Ann Laura. *Carnal Knowledge and Imperial Power: Race and the Intimate in Colonial Rule.* Rev. ed. Berkeley: University of California Press, 2010.

Sumler-Edmond, Janice L. *The Secret Trust of Aspasia Cruvellier Mirault: The Life and Trials of a Free Woman of Color in Antebellum Georgia.* Fayetteville: University of Arkansas Press, 2008.

Sweet, John Wood. *Bodies Politic: Negotiating Race in the American North, 1730–1830.* Baltimore: Johns Hopkins University Press, 2003.

Tannenbaum, Frank. *Slave and Citizen: The Negro in the Americas.* New York: Alfred A. Knopf, 1947.

Taylor, Alan. *American Colonies.* New York: Viking Penguin, 2001.

Twinam, Ann. *Purchasing Whiteness: Pardos, Mulattos, and the Quest for Social Mobility in the Spanish Indies*. Stanford, CA: Stanford University Press, 2015.

Van Deusen, Nancy E. *Global Indios: The Indigenous Struggle for Justice in Sixteenth-Century Spain*. Durham, NC: Duke University Press, 2015.

Vincent, Stephen A. *Southern Seed, Northern Soil: African-American Farm Communities in the Midwest, 1765–1900*. Bloomington: Indiana University Press, 1999.

Von Daacke, Kirt. *Freedom Has a Face: Race, Identity, and Community in Jefferson's Virginia*. Charlottesville: University of Virginia Press, 2012.

Wallenstein, Peter. *Tell the Court I Love My Wife: Race, Marriage, and Law—an American History*. New York: Palgrave Macmillan, 2002.

Watson, Alan D. *Society in Colonial North Carolina*. Raleigh: North Carolina Office of Archives and History, 1996.

Welch, Kimberly M. *Black Litigants in the Antebellum American South*. Chapel Hill: University of North Carolina Press, 2018.

West, Emily. *Family or Freedom: People of Color in the Antebellum South*. Lexington: University Press of Kentucky, 2012.

Wheeler, Roxann. *The Complexion of Race: Categories of Difference in Eighteenth-Century British Culture*. Philadelphia: University of Pennsylvania Press, 2000.

Whitehurst, Ruby Lee Thigpen. *Pine Needles: Authentic Stories as Told by Piney Woods/Free Union, Conetoe, and Currituck Relatives*. Ruby Lee Thigpen Whitehurst, 2011.

Williamson, Joel. *New People: Miscegenation and Mulattoes in the United States*. New York: Free Press, 1980.

Wilson, Carol. *Freedom at Risk: The Kidnapping of Free Blacks in America, 1780–1865*. Lexington: University Press of Kentucky, 1994.

Wilson, Kathleen. *The Island Race: Englishness, Empire and Gender in the Eighteenth Century*. London: Routledge, 2003.

———, ed. *A New Imperial History: Culture, Identity and Modernity in Britain and the Empire, 1660–1840*. Cambridge: Cambridge University Press, 2004.

Winch, Julie. *The Clamorgans: One Family's History of Race in America*. New York: Hill & Wang, 2011.

———. *Between Slavery and Freedom: Free People of Color in America from Settlement to the Civil War*. Lanham, MD: Rowman & Littlefield, 2014.

Wolf, Eva Sheppard. *Race and Liberty in the New Nation: Emancipation in Virginia from the Revolution to Nat Turner's Rebellion*. Baton Rouge: Louisiana State University Press, 2006.

———. *Almost Free: A Story about Family and Race in Antebellum Virginia*. Athens: University of Georgia Press, 2012.

Wood, Nicholas. "A Sacrifice on the Altar of Slavery": Doughface Politics and Black Disfranchisement in Pennsylvania, 1837–1838." *Journal of the Early Republic* 32 (Spring 2011): 75–106.

Wright, James M. *The Free Negro in Maryland, 1634–1860.* New York: Columbia University Press, 1921.

Yellin, Jean Fagan. *Harriet Jacobs, A Life: The Remarkable Adventures of the Woman Who Wrote "Incidents in the Life of a Slave Girl."* New York: Basic Civitas Books, 2004.

Zipf, Karin L. *Labor of Innocents: Forced Apprenticeship in North Carolina, 1715–1919.* Baton Rouge: Louisiana State University Press, 2005.

Index

Calloway, James, 157
Cally, William, 175
Cambridge (Chowan County), 46
Cane, Thomas, 157
Carbry, Thomas, 158
Carteret County, NC, 41
Case, Benjamin, 22
Case, Sally, 22
Caswell County, NC, 66, 78, 106, 110, 130, 160, 177, 179, 183. *See also* Milton, NC
Chance, Charles. 149
Chance, Ezekiel, 149
Chance, Nancy, 149
Chancey, Edmund, 39
Chancey, Rachel, 39
Charles, Peter, 23
Chavers, Billy, 152
Chavers, Edmond, 212
Chavers, Elick, 152
Chavers, John A., 204
Chavers, Molly, 150
Chavers, Samuel, 205–6
Chavers, Temperance, 152
Chavers, William, 17, 82–84, 212
Chavis, Allen, 94
Chavis, B. J., 205
Chavis, Ferebe, 205
Chavis, Frances, 44
Chavis, Henry, 109
Chavis, Isham, 165
Chavis, James, 189
Chavis, John, 90, 92–93, 186
Chavis, Madison, 203
Chavis, Meredith, 91
Chavis, Philip, 19
Chavis, William, 31–32, 42–44, 90, 107
Chavis family, 129–30
Cherokees, 23, 222
Cherry, Henry C., 219
Chesnutt, Andrew Jackson, 139–40
Chesnutt, Ann, 139
Chesnutt, Charles Waddell, 1, 115
Chesnutt, George Washington, 139
Chesson and Armstead, 109
Chowan Baptist Association, 102
Chowan County, NC, 107, 134, 181, 191, 202
Chowans, 15–16, 20–21
Christian, C. B., 157
churches, 91–92, 102–6, 207, 218, 221, 223–24
Cicil, R. J., 157
Civil War, 194–215, 226–27

Clark (Randolph County), 179
Clark, Fanny, 149
Clark, George, 200
Clark, Lindy, 149
Clark, Matt, 149
Clark, Peter, 200
Clark, Sal, 149
Clark, Thomas, 200
Cleeves, James, 43–44
Clodfetter, Jacob, 157
Clodfetter, Riley, 157
Cochran, Edward, 108
Coff, Barny, 151
Collins, Hardy, 179
Collins, John, 215
Collins, Levi, 210
colonization movement, 76, 86, 100–101, 103–4
Columbus County, NC, 110, 220
Conner, Churchill, 150
Conrad, Delany, 108
Conrad, Sarah, 108
Cook, John H., 94
Cooper, Mary Ann, 144
Copeland, Anthony, 77
Copeland, James, 138
Copeland, John Anthony, 104, 116
Cordon, Alexander, 169
Cordon, Humphrey F., 169
Cordon, Zachariah, 169
Cordon, Zilla Pierce, 169
Corn, Dixon, 94, 111
Corn, E. G., 111
Corn, Ned, 111
Corn, Richardson, 111
Corn family, 111, 130
Cotanch, Dicey, 92
Cotton, Alexander, 43
Cotton, Christian, 137
Cotton, John, 138
Cotton, Lucinda, 138
Cotton, Micajah, 138
Cotton, Noah, 137–38
Cotton, Ricks, 138
Cotton, Wiley, 138
Cox, William, 149
Cozens, Lewis, 179
Craven County, NC, 7, 23–24, 26, 28, 40–41, 43, 73, 83, 101–2, 107, 113, 160–61, 166, 175, 178, 180, 182, 184, 189, 197, 210, 213, 219. *See also* New Bern, NC
Crawford, George W., 101

McLellan, Duncan, 180
McPhail, Alexander, 190
Mead, Timothy, 151
Mecklenburg County, VA, 129
Mendenhall, George C., 146
Merrick, George, 28
military: colored troops, 125, 208–11, 215; rebel
    army, 194–95, 202–3, 205–6; U.S. Army, 27,
    88, 125, 211–14; U.S. Navy, 208, 211
Mills, Rebecca, 108
Milton, Elisha, 146–47
Milton, Jane, 146–48
Milton, NC, 66, 105–6, 117, 160. *See also* Caswell
    County, NC
Minerva (Brunswick County), 27
Mitchell, Adeline, 174
Mitchell, Anna, 156
Mitchell, Jesse, 114
Mitchell, Polly, 135
Mitchell, Shepherd, 179
Mitchell, Sophia, 187
Mitchell, Tom, 18
Mitchell, W. H., 110
Mitchell, William I., 158
Mitchell, Zachariah, 88
Mitchell family, 129, 220
Montford, Donum, 160, 163, 188–89
Montgomery County, NC, 110, 142, 203
Moore, Alexander, 217
Moore, Anthony, 150
Moore, Benjamin, 150
Moore, Bett, 44
Moore, Dicey, 101–2
Moore, Keziah, 44
Moore, Lucy, 150
Moore, Lydia, 101–2
Moore, Mary, 44
Moore, Owen, 110
Moore, Stephen, 150
Moore, William, 187
Moore County, NC, 151, 206
Moore family, 220
Morgan, Allen, 159
Morgan, Bryant, 202
Morisey, T. J., 205
Morris, Richard, 175, 182
Mosley, Richard H., 106
mulatto, 8–9, 16–17, 19–29, 32–43, 45–46, 54, 57,
    58, 60–61, 64, 72–73, 83, 90–91, 98–99, 101,
    109, 111–12, 131, 144, 149–51, 153–56, 158–59,
    168, 224–27
Mulder, Jane, 144

Mullen, John, 133–34
Mustapha family, 153
Mustee, 8, 16, 19, 29, 32, 34–36, 83
Myers, Morgan, 177

Nacy (Perquimans County), 28
Nash, Frederick, 81
Nash, Solomon, 90
Nash County, NC, 6–7, 138–39, 156, 176
Nathan (New Hanover County), 28
Native Americans. *See* Cherokees; Chowans;
    Mattamuskeets
Nead, John, 41
Nelson, Hannah, 101
Nelson, John, 101
New Bern, NC, 68, 91, 97, 100, 102, 107–8, 118,
    151, 160–61, 164, 182, 208–10, 213. *See also* Cra-
    ven County, NC
Newby, Thomas, 28
New Hanover County, NC, 28. *See also* Wilming-
    ton, NC
Newsom, Elijah, 80–81
Newsom, Elizabeth, 168
Newsom, Nathaniel, 168
Newsom, Willis, 168
Newsome, Martha, 210
Newsome, William D., 219
Nichols, Columbus, 187
Nickens, Boone, 210
Nickens, James, 43
Nickens, Joshua, 211
Nickens, Sheridan F., 226
Nickens family, 126, 129–30
Norfleet, Kinchen, 190
Norfleet, Penny, 107
Norfolk, VA, 109, 209. *See also* Norfolk County,
    VA
Norfolk County, VA, 15, 130. *See also* Norfolk,
    VA
Northampton County, NC, 6–7, 22, 45, 77–78,
    89, 98, 103–4, 140, 168, 178–79, 183, 190, 210,
    214, 217–18
North Carolina General Assembly, 28, 33–36,
    45–46, 49–77, 100, 125, 134, 138, 156, 158–59,
    167, 196–99, 216, 219
North Carolina State Equal Right League, 217
North Carolina Supreme Court, 17, 79–84

Oberlin, OH, 104
Oberlin College, 122, 164
O'Dwyer, Thomas, 112–13
Oliver, Joseph, 182